CONSPIRACY IN CAMELOT

Conspiracy in Camelot
The Complete History of the Assassination of John Fitzgerald Kennedy

Jerry Kroth

Algora Publishing
New York

© 2003 by Algora Publishing.
All Rights Reserved
www.algora.com

No portion of this book (beyond what is permitted by
Sections 107 or 108 of the United States Copyright Act of 1976)
may be reproduced by any process, stored in a retrieval system,
or transmitted in any form, or by any means, without the
express written permission of the publisher.
ISBN: 0-87586-196-2 (ebook)

Library of Congress Cataloging-in-Publication Data

Kroth, Jerome A.
 Conspiracy in Camelot : the complete history of the assassination of John Fitzgerald Kennedy / by Jerry Kroth.
   p. cm.
Includes bibliographical references and index.
  ISBN 0-87586-247-0 (alk. paper) — ISBN 0-87586-246-2 (pbk. : alk. paper)
 1. Kennedy, John F. (John Fitzgerald), 1917-1963 — Assassination. I. Title.
E842.9.K76 2003
364.15'24'097309046—dc22
                               2003015447

Printed in the United States

For
Matthew, James, and Margaret Kroth

Acknowledgments

I would like to thank Trudy Burrows for her inspiration and my wife Anya, Bill Burton, and Jo Ann Vasquez who were there during the darker hours, Frank Cichowicz for his support, and Maya Kroth for editorial assistance. In addition, it is necessary to mention Norman O. Brown whose text, Love's Body, often forms the deep structure which organizes these thoughts, along with the insights of Jacqueline Kennedy Onassis for a remark which appears as the display quote for Chapter 7. It served as an important beacon in directing this work to its inevitable conclusions.

Tables, Lists and Figures

Tables and Lists

1.1	Kennedy-Lincoln Correspondence	20
3.1	Autopsy evidence impugned by the following witnesses present at Kennedy's admission to Parkland Hospital in Dallas	40
3.2	Deaths associated with Kennedy assassination	49
3.3	Suspicious deaths of HSCA and Senate Intelligence Committee witnesses	67
3.4	Significant individuals named in the literature as withholding information or engaged in disinformation about the assassination.	69
4.1	Individuals mentioned in conspiracy texts with respect to a Mafia aspect of the assassination	106
4.2	Jack Ruby's underworld connections and contacts	115
4.3	Important figures in the CIA assassination model	121
4.4	Eight 'soft' lines of evidence connecting Oswald to the CIA and military intelligence.	156
4.5	CIA efforts to dissociate itself from Oswald.	158
4.6	Deceptions and/or inaccuracies of Marina Oswald	172
4.7	The CIA-Mafia link	186
4.8	Summary of names in published conspiracy theories	190
6.1	Mob connections with the Kennedys	245
6.2	Chronology of events versus Bobby Kennedy's awareness	259
6.3	Kennedy's mistresses during his Presidency	263
6.4	Marilyn Monroe's lovers	269
6.5	Individuals alleged in the literature to have covered up or withheld information concerning Marilyn Monroe's death	270
6.6	Mental health status of major conspiracy school characters	302
6.7	Mental health status of more minor conspiracy school characters	302

FIGURES

1.1	Articles written about Kennedy vs. Elvis Presley five years after their respective deaths	17
1.2	Schools, hospitals and colleges named after Kennedy, Lincoln, Jefferson, and Nixon	17
3.1	Cause of death in Kennedy sample compared to national mortality norms	58
4.1	Jack Ruby's toll calls in 1963	117
5.1	Distribution of cover-up sources (including Mafia murders)	194
5.2	Possible assassins in Dealey Plaza, Nov. 22, 1963	195
5.3	Metropolitan Dallas on Nov. 22, 1963	201
5.4	Eugene Hale Brading as a case study in guilt by association	203
5.5	Metropolitan Dallas on Nov. 21, 1963, the eve of the assassination	205
6.1	A recently released, but redacted, document about Oswald from 1959	293
7.1	Feelings of confidence versus a sense of alienation since 1960	324
7.2	Violent crimes in the United States since 1963	325

TABLE OF CONTENTS

CHAPTER 1. JOHN FITZGERALD KENNEDY: INTRODUCTION TO THE DREAM	1
OSWALD	2
LUCIEN SARTI	2
CARLOS MARCELLO	3
THE CIA MONGOOSE TEAM	3
CHARLES HARRELSON	4
THE ELUSIVE PARTICLE	5
NUMINOSITY AND ARCHETYPE	7
THE KENNEDY WIT	10
A NEW IDEALISM	12
KENNEDY AND LINCOLN	18
CHAPTER 2. CASE CLOSED	23
EVIDENCE AGAINST OSWALD	24
Physical Evidence	24
Circumstantial Evidence	26
DR. PEPPER OR COCA-COLA: THE OBSESSION BEGINS	29
CHAPTER 3. REASONABLE DOUBT	33
EVIDENCE FAVORING OSWALD	34
EYEWITNESSES FAVORING OSWALD	36
BEST EVIDENCE FOR A CONSPIRACY	39
(1) A Fourth Shot	39
Exit Wound in the Back of the Head	40
Ballistics Inconsistencies	42
Ballistics/Autopsy Inconsistencies	43
Acoustic Evidence of a Fourth Shot	43
Further Evidence of a Fourth Shot: The Zapruder Film	44
Revisionism	45

(2) Deaths of Witnesses	48
Mary Pinchot Meyer	50
Rose Cheramie	51
Jerry Wald	52
Dorothy Kilgallen	52
David Ferrie and E. del Valle	53
State Department Officer	54
Other Deaths	54
Statistical Analysis	57
Unusual Accidents	60
(3.) Death of Witnesses Prior to Government Hearings	62
George deMohrenschildt	62
Carlos Prio	63
Charles Nicoletti	63
Sam Giancana	64
Leo Moceri	64
Regis Kennedy	65
William Sullivan	65
William Pawley and John Paisley	65
John Martino	66
(4.) The Cover Up	68
How to Look at this Data	79
The Hard Evidence of a Cover-Up	80
SUMMARY	86
Physical Evidence Favoring Oswald	86
A Fourth Shot	86
Pattern of Suspicious Deaths	87
Deaths Associated with Congressional Witnesses	87
Cover-up Actions as a Predictor of Conspiracy	87
CONCLUSION	88
CHAPTER 4. CONSPIRACY	93
1. THE JOHNSON THEORY	93
Essential Ideas	94
Strongest Points	100
Weakest Points	102
2. THE MOB THEORY	103
Essential Points	103
Hoover Wiretaps	105
Marcello	109
Who Killed the President?	110
Weaker Points	118

Table of Contents

3. THE CIA THORY	120
Essential Points	129
The Odio Incident and Loran Hall	135
Mexico City	139
The Vietnam Connection	141
Who Killed Kennedy?	142
Clues From Oswald Himself	147
Oswald's Dyslexia	147
Library Books	148
Oswald and Ferrie	150
"Better For You Not to Know!"	154
Strong Points in the CIA Conspiracy Model	156
Weak Elements	158
4. THE COMMUNIST CONSPIRACY	162
Oswald's Soviet Diary	167
Marina Nikolaevna Prusakova: Suspicions Increase	169
The Yuri Nosenko Affair	173
Soviet Motives	175
Inconsistencies in Soviet Behavior	177
5. THE CUBAN COMMUNIST CONSPIRACY	179
Strong Points	183
Weak Points	183
White Hand And Black Hand: The CIA and the Mob	185
SUMMARY	190
APPENDIX	191
CHAPTER 5. PARADOX	193
INTERPRETING THE FACTS	193
The Cover Up	194
Dealey Plaza	195
Jim Braden aka Eugene Hale Brading: A Leading Suspect?	199
H.L. Hunt	204
Richard Nixon	207
Clint Murchison	208
YET-TO-BE-DEVELOPED CONSPIRACY SCENARIOS	210
Suzy Chang and Maria Novotny	210
Mary Pinchot Meyer and the CIA	211
Modern-Day Conspiracy: James E. Files	215

Three Interviews with Inmate N-14006	215
Eugene Hale Brading	216
Richard Cain	216
Nofio Pecora	216
Dutz Murret	217
Joseph Campisi	217
Strong Points of the Files Version	222
Weaker Points	222
The Brothers Karamazov	223
CHAPTER 6. SHADOWS AND SECRETS	**227**
CAMELOT VS. CONSPIRACY SCHOOLS	227
J. EDGAR HOOVER'S HOMOSEXUALITY AND PARANOIA	232
KENNEDY SILENCE AND SECRETS	237
SHADOWS OF THE FATHER	238
SEX: THE SINS OF THE FATHER PASS TO THE SON	240
SECRECY BETWEEN THE BROTHERS?	242
JUNE 1963	249
ROBERT KENNEDY'S PERSONALITY	251
REVELATIONS FROM A COLLEAGUE	255
EVEN MORE RECENT REVELATIONS	257
EVEN DEEPER SECRETS: THE SHADOW OF JOHN FITZGERALD KENNEDY	260
The Adventures of J.J.	260
MORE SEXUALLY DYSFUNCTIONAL PLAYERS: MARILYN MONROE	268
The Monroe Cover Up	270
Events Leading To Her Death	271
A Curious Clue	273
JACKIE KENNEDY: WIDOW, BONE-CRUSHER, ENIGMA	276
Images of Jackie	279
LEE HARVEY OSWALD: PATSY, SPY, COUNTERSPY	284
Oedipal Elements and Jealousy	286
An Unconscious Hatred Of Kennedy?	287
Oswald the Mystery	289
Oswald, on the Right	290
Oswald, the Psycho	293
Oswald, the Mafia Patsy	296
Oswald, Not Guilty	297
'To Kill That Sonofabitch Kennedy!'	300
MENTAL STATUS OF THE MAIN CHARACTERS	301
CONCLUSION	303

APPENDIX:	304
Confusion of Theory and Fact	307
The First Bullet	308
CHAPTER 7. CAMELOT AND CAROUSELS	313
COLLECTIVE DENIAL	313
SYMBOLIC DISCERNMENT	316
The Carousel	316
Dream Interpretation	317
SYMBOLS IN THE MYTH	318
Camelot	318
Passion versus the Dream	319
Abraham Lincoln	320
THE COLLECTIVE SCAPEGOAT	321
THE KENNEDY TRAGEDY AS THE FORESHADOW OF AMERICAN TRAGEDY	323
THE SIGNIFICANCE OF THE NUMBER THREE	327
CONCLUSION	328
APPENDIX: A CHRONOLOGY OF OSWALD'S LIFE	329
SELECTED BIBLIOGRAPHY	333
PHOTO CREDITS	337
INDEX	339

CHAPTER 1. JOHN FITZGERALD KENNEDY: INTRODUCTION TO THE DREAM

He needed that job like a hole in the head.
— Jack Ruby [1]

Over 600 books have been written about the three-year presidency of John Fitzgerald Kennedy. It is one of the most imposing stories of the American twentieth century. With the recent release of thousands of pages of classified assassination documents, the American fascination — or perhaps we should say obsession — with the Kennedy assassination knows no bounds.

In high-energy physics there is a theory known as "super symmetry," in which two sub-atomic particles are predicted to appear in high-energy collisions. At the Fermilab, which houses one of the most expensive colliders, scientists were unable to find them. Rather than change the theory or abandon the search altogether, physicists argue they need an even bigger and more expensive machine to generate the 127 billion electron volts needed to finally see these two particles. As the machines get bigger, the particles get smaller, and the seemingly endless search marches forward relentlessly.

Super symmetry is somewhat a metaphor for the American fixation on the Kennedys and particularly the assassination. There is a sense that more books need to be written, more interviews held, more documents examined — and surely, then, this enormous massing of data will ultimately deliver the elusive

---

1. Talking about Kennedy, to the psychiatrist on his defense team. Quoted in Kantor, Seth. *The Ruby Cover-Up*. New York: Kensington Publishing, 1978, p. 93.

particle, the true story of the murder of the President, the final "ah ha" that brings the tragedy to a close.

In the meantime, the search for our elusive particle goes on. Here are a few of the loose ends and tantalizing theories that keep the searchers going:

OSWALD

Jim Moore, a minority voice among Kennedy assassination aficionados, claims that the Warren Commission was actually correct, and Lee Harvey Oswald was the sole conspirator. Moore says he has spent more time in Dallas than any other author and has traced and retraced Oswald's movements countless times. His most convincing argument is that Oswald left the Texas School Book Depository (where he was employed) and took a cab to his home. Instead of getting out where he should have, he had the cabbie drive him past his rented room by a few blocks and then walked back. Would an innocent man behave in this manner?

LUCIEN SARTI

Steve Rivele researched the CIA's Executive Action program. It led him to a Frenchman called Christian David, a 58-year-old serving time in Leavenworth, Kansas. David was a member of the Corsican network in South America and a drug trafficker. He was awaiting extradition to France in connection with a murder of a Moroccan politician.

Mr. David told Rivele he had information on the Kennedy assassination. He wanted to avoid extradition to France and was willing to deal with the U.S. government and reveal the true Mafia-connected killers of the President.[2]

According to David, Antoine Guerini, the Corsican Mafia boss in Marseille, accepted a contract to kill the President. Corsican drug trafficker and sharpshooter Lucien Sarti took the contract, instead. Sarti and two assassins flew from Marseille to Mexico City in the fall of 1963, crossing into Texas. Three gunmen were in position, and Sarti was the grassy knoll gunman. As the story goes, four shots were fired. The murderers lay low in Dallas for two weeks and were flown out of the country to Montreal.

Lucien Sarti was killed by Mexican police in 1972. The identity of his two accomplices is unknown. Despite his attempts to talk his way out of extradition, Christian David was sent to France, and the story seems to have gone nowhere since then

---

2. Summers, Anthony. *Conspiracy*. New York: McGraw-Hill, 1989.

Chapter 1. John Fitzgerald Kennedy: Introduction to the Dream

despite the fact that a Brazilian associate of Sarti corroborated the story in all of its essential details.

CARLOS MARCELLO

Marcello was a New Orleans mobster. Frustrated with organized crime, Robert Kennedy ordered him deported to Guatemala. Marcello surreptitiously returned to the U.S. in defiance of RFK. J. Edgar Hoover wiretapped Marcello and obtained evidence that Marcello had ordered a hit on President Kennedy. Hoover did not pass this information on to either the President or the Secret Service, however, and author Mark North alleges that Hoover knowingly permitted the contract to take place. Hoover's antipathy for the Kennedys, particularly Robert Kennedy, was well known.

In this paradigm, the origin of the assassination begins with the angry, resentful, harassed Mafia kingpin, Carlos Marcello. J. Edgar Hoover, instead of informing the Secret Service, acts as a silent co-conspirator and accomplice. North's book, *Act of Treason*, points the finger directly at Hoover for failing to prevent JFK's assassination.[3]

THE CIA MONGOOSE TEAM

Much has been written about the roles played by disaffected CIA personnel, the Bay of Pigs, and Kennedy's desire to "break the CIA into a thousand pieces." Kennedy intended to withdraw troops from Vietnam and close down covert anti-Castro operations, especially after his confrontation with Khrushchev during the 1962 Cuban missile crisis. The result was that anti-Castro CIA-inspired mechanics who were angry and felt betrayed by Kennedy took down the President. Mark Lane provides evidence in *Rush to Judgment* that the killer of John Fitzgerald Kennedy belonged to this group.

Robert Groden, another conspiracist, gives the following account:

> Marita Lorenz, former undercover operative for the CIA and FBI, told the News that her companions on the car trip from Miami to Dallas were Oswald, CIA contract agent Frank Sturgis, Cuban exile leaders Orlando Bosch and Pedro Diaz Lanz, and two Cuban brothers whose names she does not know. She said they were all members of Operation 40, a secret guerrilla group originally formed by the CIA in 1960 in preparation for the Bay of Pigs invasion. Ms. Lorenz

---

3. North, Mark. *Act of Treason.* New York: Carroll & Graf, 1991, p. 342

described Operation 40 as an "assassination squad" consisting of about 30 anti-Castro Cubans and their American advisers. She claimed the group conspired to kill Cuban Premier Fidel Castro and President Kennedy, whom it blamed for the Bay of Pigs fiasco... She said Oswald later visited an Operation 40 training camp in the Florida Everglades. The next time she saw him, Ms. Lorenz said, was at midnight in the Miami home of Orlando Bosch, who is now in a Venezuelan prison on murder charges... Ms. Lorenz claimed that Sturgis, Oswald, Bosch, and Diaz Lanz, former Chief of the Cuban Air Force, attended this meeting. She said the men spread Dallas street maps on a table and studied them... She said they left for Dallas in two cars soon after the meeting. They took turns driving, and the 1,300-mile trip took about two days. She added that they carried weapons — rifles and scopes in the cars.... A few days after this story came out, Sturgis was arrested in Lorenz' apartment, where he had gone to discuss matters with her. Then she testified before the Assassinations Committee... Ms. Lorenz, in her testimony... adds that Sturgis had also fired at the President. [4]

CHARLES HARRELSON

The father of actor Woody Harrelson experienced a psychotic episode in September 1980. He held a pistol to his head, but then reluctantly surrendered to authorities. In his dazed ramblings, he confessed to the ambush of Judge John Wood in San Antonio, Texas *and* the murder of John Kennedy.

Harrelson was an associate of Carlos Marcello's brother and was indicted with him for the murder of Judge Woods. His story of murdering Judge Woods was anything but the ramblings of a coke addict. He provided information substantial enough to result in an indictment and a conviction.

He also had connections to Jack Ruby. Some say Harrelson was one of the "tramps" picked up near the grassy knoll on the day of the assassination. A forensic anthropologist held that photos of the tramps matched a photo of Harrelson with a 90% likelihood of accuracy. Career criminal Chauncey Holt said that he was with Harrelson in Dealey Plaza on the day of the assassination. [5]

Harrelson later said that he was on cocaine and out of his mind when he made the confession, and despite this interesting aggregation of evidence, his Kennedy admissions were considered maniacal ravings and were dismissed. But authorities were less nonchalant when it came to the Judge Woods murder. For that, Harrelson is currently serving a life sentence.

---

4. Groden, Robert J., with Livingstone, Harrison E. *High Treason.* Baltimore: Conservatory Press, pp. 347-349.

5. Weberman, Alan J. and Canfield, Michael. *Coup D'Etat in America: The CIA and the Assassination of John F. Kennedy.* San Francisco, CA: Quick American Archives, 1992. pp. 345-346).

Chapter 1. John Fitzgerald Kennedy: Introduction to the Dream

THE ELUSIVE PARTICLE

Let us assume, with some tongue-in-cheek silliness, that a rifle belonging to a known-CIA operative named Larry Hintz was found in an attic by his children. Pretend for a moment that Mr. Hintz passed away in 1982. Let us further assume that Hintz left a note hidden in his personal safe confessing that he was the grassy knoll gunman and that he killed President Kennedy. Hintz's son turns the rifle over to the FBI for examination. In his posthumous confession, he names his superior, another former military man, and a former CIA contract agent. Corroborating evidence is given that this superior did exist, that Mr. Hintz worked for the CIA, that he was in Dallas at the time, and that his confession along with all other supportive information is so strong that the media itself begins believe that a second gunman has finally been found. The fourth shot heard on the motorcycle tape dictabelts by the House Select Assassination Committee is now explained once and for all. [6]

This hypothetical scenario represents the ultimate discovery of the elusive particle, the smoking gun, the end of the mystery, the final solution to the greatest murder mystery of the twentieth century. We have physical evidence, circumstantial evidence, witnesses, and corroborating witnesses. Is the case finally closed?

The problem in this completely made-up example is that, in a very short time, those who felt the Mafia was involved, from Marcello to Trafficante to Roselli and Hoffa, would be printing new texts suggesting that Hintz could not possibly have been the second gunman. Evidence would be presented, as it already has, that not only four shots but as many as six were fired; witnesses would be cited who heard that many. Wiretaps of Mafia figures ordering a contract hit on the President and further

---

6. This example was created arbitrarily and with an intent to be ludicrous. However, in the research for this book, an almost identical example was unearthed. Ricky Don White, of Medville, Texas claimed that his father, Roscoe White, was one of three CIA operatives ordered to kill Kennedy. His claims came from his father's diary, which has now allegedly disappeared. White claimed that his father was a CIA operative with a partner known as Saul. A similar claim was made almost 20 years ago by Hugh McDonald, Chief of Detectives of the Los Angeles County Sheriff's Department, who claimed that he had met and spoken with "Saul." McDonald claimed he learned that Saul, operating independent of any organization, was hired by certain private American citizens to execute Kennedy in Dallas. The only major difference between White's and McDonald's claims is that Chief McDonald was allegedly told by Saul that the contract on Kennedy was a private "hit" paid for by people who wanted Johnson to be President, while White believed that his father and Saul participated in Kennedy's murder as possible CIA agents. The killer was allegedly contacted in May of 1963 for a meeting in Haiti to discuss a privately arranged hit of President Kennedy. (Saul has never been found, but his photograph is included in the Warren Commission Report as Exhibit 237. According to McDonald, the Warren Commission acted as if it did not realize the significance of the exhibit. Zirbel, Craig. *The Texas Connection.* New York: Warner Books, 1991, pp. 66-67.

testimonials might resurrect Lucien Sarti as the sharpshooter imported by Marcello. The FBI would cite new evidence showing further collusion. Controversy again would erupt.

60 Minutes would produce a witness who claims Mr. Hintz could not have been the second gunman, because Hintz was in Seattle with a cousin at the time of the killing. Files would be re-opened, new theories and conspiracies put forward. Experts would appear to convincingly show that Oswald never met Hintz, so how could they both be shooting within the same 7.9 seconds in the same location, neither knowing anything about the other?

Gerald Ford would restate, as he predictably has done, that Oswald was the lone gunman and that the Warren Commission report was the only authentic and truthful rendering of the event.

The point of this hypothetical discussion is that, in the vast energy expended to locate the truth and to find the elusive particle, we may have made a very large mistake. That blunder was originally described by Heisenberg, the physicist, who alerted us to the fact that *the object observed is determined by the instrument used to observe it*. We pay little attention to the instrument, and are so preoccupied with the object we forget about the assumptions inherent in the instrument we are using in the first place.

The nature of this text is not to simply look at the assassination as an object, but also to examine the instrument used to process the information. The instrument in this case is the American psyche. Not only will this book look at the Kennedy assassination at an unprecedented level of detail and depth, but it will also consider some of the elements of mass psychology and myth, which obtain to this four-decade old collective American obsession.

The mysterious Mister X in Oliver Stone's movie *JFK* was actually L. Fletcher Prouty, a career intelligence officer who himself has written a book on the subject. In referring to all the books written about Kennedy, he remarks,

> In them you can find a myriad of obscure trivia dug up by these tireless researchers. But to no avail. That is not the path to the answer to the main question, "Why was Kennedy killed?" No one will ever know who killed the President. In that business, the "mechanics" are faceless and have chameleon identities that are skillfully shielded by the system.[7]

Like Prouty, some may believe the answer will never be known. Others, like Gerald Posner, already think the case is closed and nothing more needs to be written. The intent of this text is to review all the evidence, to do so meticulously, and yet not to

---

7. Prouty, Fletcher. *JFK: The CIA, Vietnam, and the Plot to Assassinate John F. Kennedy*. New Jersey: Carol Communications, 1992, p. 335.

lose sight of the instrument we are using to observe this data. When we understand the Kennedy assassination not only as an historic event but also as a myth that is deeply embedded in American psychology, perhaps we shall construct a fuller picture.

NUMINOSITY AND ARCHETYPE

John Fitzgerald Kennedy represented something far more unconscious than conscious to the American psyche. Kennedy was in office for a thousand days; his popularity at the polls for the upcoming election in 1964 was rising, but never overwhelming. He led his opponent by fewer than ten percentage points. The American "affair" with John F. Kennedy was only beginning. Kennedy's charisma was meagerly felt at the conscious level, while he was alive, compared to the virtual deification that happened after his death.

Americans now rate John F. Kennedy one of the best presidents in history. A poll of more than 70 noted historians, however, reveals that three-quarters consider him the most "overrated."[8] A conspicuous discrepancy exists between the unconscious, charismatic aura and a more objective appraisal of his actual record.

Kennedy's speeches, his rhetoric, possessed not only "vision" but also carried an element of the prophetic. They unleashed a wave of idealism and hope for the future. He asked for change, for a new beginning, for a new generation of Americans to come fully forth into the twentieth century:

---

8. A *Newsweek* poll published results showing Kennedy to have been the country's most popular president. 75% rated his presidency as good to great and 30% wished he were still president. However, American Heritage published a poll of 75 prominent historians and journalists, who ranked him the most overrated public figure in American history. (Reeves, Thomas C. *A Question of Character: The Life of John F. Kennedy*. Rocklin CA: Prima Publishing, 199, pp. 10-11). A more recent poll corroborates these findings: JFK ranked second among the last eleven presidents, in a nationwide poll of over 1,012 respondents. Roosevelt was the only one to outscore him. (*New York Post*, June 8 1997, p. 27.)

> For time and the world do not stand still. Change is the law of life. And those who look only to the past or the present are certain to miss the future.[9]

There were always one or two catch phrases that were not only inspirational, they seemed gauged to be memorized by the listeners — as if his speech writers wanted Kennedyisms carved in granite across the doorways of a dozen public buildings.

> It is the fate of this generation ... to live with a struggle we did not start, in a world we did not make.[10]

Yet he also elicited a sense of danger, of risk, of bringing a deeper consciousness to the public about the nature of the twentieth century and the problems of nuclear confrontation:

> For beneath today's surface glass of peace and prosperity are increasingly dangerous, unsolved, long postponed problems that will inevitably explode to the surface.[11]

Kennedy's Peace Corps challenged Americans to dream and to bring a new meaning to their lives by rolling up their own sleeves and putting into practice their deepest sentiments. His words were literate, his rhetoric alive, and the mission gloriously idealistic:

> George Bernard Shaw, speaking as an Irishman, summed up his approach to life: Other people, he said "see things and say: Why?... But I dream things that never were and I say: 'Why not?'"[12]

Idealism was always syncopated with foreboding and tempered with danger. There was always a need to see the new world order with care, caution, and above all, intelligence. His words amazed, frightened, stimulated, mesmerized. A generation fell into a state of almost perpetual trance:

> Every man, woman and child lives under a nuclear sword of Damocles, hanging by the slenderest of threads, capable of being cut at any moment by accident or miscalculation or madness.[13]

---

9. Sorenson, Theodore C. *Kennedy.* New York: Harper & Row, 1965, p. 324.
10. *Ibid.,* p. 231.
11. *Ibid.* p. 19.
12. *Ibid.,* p. 387.
13. *Ibid.,* p. 378.

> We have the power to make this the best generation of mankind in the history of the world — or to make it the last.[14]

Presidents did not speak like this. Presidents did not look like this, either. There was a certain pacifism in his words, as if with his election came a zeitgeist of peace, rationality, problem-solving, compromise, eschewing arrogance and bellicosity. It was a new world he intended to steward quite different from the patina of the ugly American:

> Those self-appointed generals and admirals who want to send someone else's son to war ought to be kept at home by the voters and replaced in Washington by someone who understands what the twentieth century is all about.[15]

Kennedy's words were not only a new voice and vision, but his charm, ease, and encyclopedic fluency with facts were spellbinding. Americans remembered Truman's proletarian clarity, Eisenhower's mumbling unintelligibility, and Nixon's humorless monotone. Kennedy sparkled by comparison, and his command of the facts was seemingly boundless:

> In 1953 the dictator of Peru was given a medal by the United States. In 1954 the dictator of Venezuela was awarded the Legion of Merit by our ambassador. In 1955 our Secretary of the Navy went to Argentina and made an eloquent address comparing dictator Peron to Lincoln — to Peron's advantage. In 1956 the dictator of Paraguay received his medal from America. We have warmly embraced Trujillo, the brutal despot of the Dominican Republic. . .We have dumped more than $500 million worth of arms and ammunition into Latin America over the past eight years, much of which has been used to strengthen the hand of dictatorships. And even now, despite the hard lessons of the past, our Air Force is planning to invite the co-dictator of Nicaragua to Washington as a guest of honor. . . Although the Cold War will not be won in Latin America, it may very well be lost there.[16]

---

14. *Ibid..*, p. 304.
15. *Ibid.*, p. 399.
16. *Ibid.*, p. 111.

THE KENNEDY WIT

If Kennedy's rhetoric did not satisfy all of those unconscious American cravings, his wit seemed to fill up whatever vacuum remained. JFK brought theater and entertainment to the White House in a way completely unknown before:

> Q. Mr. President, back on the subject of Presidential advisers, Congressman Baring of Nevada, a Democrat, said you would do much better if you got rid of some of yours — and he named Bowles, Ball, Bell, Bunche, and Sylvester.
>
> The President: Yes, he has a fondness for alliteration and for the "B's." And I would not add Congressman Baring to that list as I have a high regard for him and for the gentlemen that he named. But congressmen are always advising presidents to get rid of presidential advisers. That is one of the most constant threads that runs through American history, and presidents ordinarily do not pay attention, nor do they in this case. [17]

Campaigning in Ohio in 1962, he said:

> There is no city in the United States in which I get a warmer welcome and less votes than Columbus, Ohio! [18]

When asked at a Bronx Democratic dinner about how he was going to handle the issue of his being Catholic and voter worries that the Vatican might have a new-found stake in American politics, Kennedy remarked:

> I sat next to Cardinal Spellman at dinner the other evening, and asked him what I should say when voters question me about the doctrine of the pope's infallibility.
> "I don't know, Senator," the Cardinal told me. "All I know is he keeps calling me Spillman."[19]

---

17. *Ibid.*, p. 75
18. *Ibid.*, p. 123
19. *Ibid.*, p. 130

Chapter 1. John Fitzgerald Kennedy: Introduction to the Dream

Eisenhower would open a press conference wearing a drab gray suit and stumble through the reading of a prepared statement to the press; Kennedy, by contrast, rarely read to his audiences at press conferences. In fact, on one memorable occasion, he opened with the following remark about a recent successful space launching:

> The chimpanzee that is flying in space took off at 10:08. He reports that everything is perfect and working well.[20]

When introducing Arthur Krock at a dinner, he said:

> I'm glad to see my old friend Arthur Krock here. Mr. Krock has been to every major dinner in history — except the Last Supper — and he had a relative at that one.[21]

Kennedy's wife, in contrast to her predecessor Mamie Eisenhower, seemed comfortable in the star-like role into which she transformed the position of First Lady. She was educated, well bred, and good looking. When the Kennedys went to France, Parisians swooned over Jacqueline; and when she spoke French, an immediate sense of kinship developed which did not spare President de Gaulle. When President Kennedy spoke at a luncheon in Paris, he opened by saying:

> I do not think it altogether inappropriate to introduce myself to this audience. I am the man who accompanied Jacqueline Kennedy to Paris.[22]

Some of his press conference retorts and rejoinders also portray his ease, humor, and genuine likeability:[23]

> Question [from a small boy]: How did you become a war hero?
> Kennedy: It was involuntary. They sank my boat.
>
> Reporter: Do you think you will lose any votes because of your Catholic religion?
> Senator Kennedy: I feel as a Catholic that I'll get my reward in my life hereafter, although I may not get it here.

---

20. *Ibid.*, p. 174.
21. Gardner, Gerald. *All the President's Wits: The Power of Presidential Humor.* New York: William Morrow, 1986, p. 226.
22. Sorenson, *ibid.*, p. 310.
23. Gardner, *ibid.* pp. 222-247.

> Reporter: The Republican National Committee recently adopted a resolution saying you were pretty much of a failure. How do you feel about that?
>
> President Kennedy: I assume it passed unanimously.
>
> Reporter: Mr. President, have you narrowed your search for a new Postmaster General? Are you seeking a man with a business background or a political background?
>
> President Kennedy: The search is narrowing, but there are other fields that are still to be considered, including even a postal background.

When issues of nepotism appeared and Kennedy was asked penetrating questions about giving his brother the post of Attorney General or having a father with such vast sums of money, he replied:

> I see nothing wrong with giving [Bobby] a little legal experience before he goes into private practice.

or on his father:

> I just received a telegram from my father. He says "don't buy one more vote than you need. I'll be damned if I'll pay for a landslide."

A New Idealism

Kennedy inspired a new kind of liberalism in this country and set many on a journey in pursuit of their own ideals and dreams. His progress in race relations was not met with political or legislative success, but the ideals he set forth changed an entire generation:

> Our job is to turn the American vision of a society in which no man has to suffer discrimination based on race into a living reality everywhere in our land.
>
> Next week I shall ask the Congress of the United States to act, to make a commitment it has not fully made in this century to the proposition that race has no place in American life or law.
>
> The rights of every man are diminished when the rights of one man are threatened. [24]

---

24. Sorenson, *ibid.*, p. 184-195

Chapter 1. John Fitzgerald Kennedy: Introduction to the Dream

These were not the tired, dusty phrases of a political hack, but a spark that ignited a new vision of self and country including a newfound altruism. Kennedy became a figurehead for a renaissance in American idealism and commitment.

For of those to whom much is given, much is required. [25]

Americans were gradually falling in love, seduced by a romantic figure who seemed to be saying just what they wanted to hear and in the loftiest phrases. A mystique began to surround the presidency that seemed to touch every American and much of the rest of the world as well.

Photo: The Inauguration

Few Americans were aware the President suffered from Addison's disease or that he needed large doses of cortisone. The drug tended to make Kennedy gain weight and gave his skin an ever-present sun-tanned look. The Kennedys were probably the best-looking presidential couple ever to occupy the White House, and Washington D.C. began to look more like Hollywood than the political center of the country. As one writer put it, John F. Kennedy was everybody's "dreamboat."

From his television debate on, Jack was a star. Crowds flocked to see him. Journalists began writing about the frenzy that swept through audiences and of the female "jumpers," "leapers," "clutchers," "touchers," "screamers," and "runners" who worshipped the new celebrity. "One remembers," White wrote, "the groans and moans; and a frowzy woman muttering hoarsely, as if to herself, 'Oh, Jack I love yuh, Jack I love yuh, Jack — Jack, I love yuh'; or the harsh-faced woman peering over one's shoulder glowering, 'You a newspaperman? You better write nice things about him or you watch out.'" [26]

But Americans did not know they had fallen under a spell. Indeed, at the conscious level Kennedy's intense charisma and charm had not made much of a dent on opinion polls. He was favored as he approached the 1964 election, but over 40 percent of the electorate were not planning to vote for him.

---

25. *Ibid.*, p. 57.
26. Reeves, Thomas C. *A Question of Character: The Life of John F. Kennedy.* Rocklin CA: Prima Publishing, 1992, p. 196.

The signs of any collective American obsession at that time were largely unconscious, but still there were a few. Letters to the White House, compared to those received during the Eisenhower Administration, increased by 50 percent, with *letters from the lunatic fringe increasing 300 percent!* [27]

Another sign of the syndrome was recognized by one of Mrs. Kennedy's clothing designers:

> On Inauguration Day when she wore the pill box hat I designed for her, it was very windy and as she stepped out of the limo she put her hand up to the pillbox to keep it from flying away. She put a slight dent in the hat. The dent appeared in every photograph. Women started putting dents in their pillboxes and designers even started designing them that way... On another occasion, JFK bought her a leopard coat for $3,000. I designed a matching hat. She wore the ensemble for the cover of LIFE. There was such a rush on leopard skin coats that the price jumped to $40,000 per coat and the animal soon went on the endangered species list, where it remains today. [28]

Kennedy's death made time stop. People froze (or were frozen) in their tracks, forced by some unknown process to photographically record where they were and what they were doing on November 22, 1963. Something big had happened, enormous, numinous, archetypal:

> In 1963 the worst tragedy since Pearl Harbor struck at the United States. It was a stunning blow that affected nearly everyone in America and a large part of the world. The night of the tragedy, the big bell of Westminster Abbey in London tolled for one hour, as though the King or Queen had died. 300,000 people marched by torchlight in Berlin, and all radio programming was cancelled in Ireland. Every store in Paris closed up and the Champs Elysees was almost deserted on a Friday night. New York City came to a total stop, and churches in Baltimore and all across the nation filled up with people in mourning. The opera was cancelled in Vienna. Thousands of people gathered on the lawn in front of Bethesda Naval Hospital in utter silence for hours. At the moment President Kennedy was pronounced dead, 68% of all the people in the United States knew of the shooting, and shortly almost every single person in America knew of it, and no one would ever forget what they were doing at the moment they heard of his death. Nine out of ten people, according to studies, suffered deep grief. Four out of five people felt "the loss of someone very close and dear"... Half the people in America wept... No other President's death since Lincoln so deeply affected the country. [29]

---

27. Johnson McMillan, Priscilla. *Marina and Lee.* New York: Harper & Row 1977.
28. Heymann, C. David. *A Woman Named Jackie.* New York: Carol Communications, 1989, p. 255.
29. Grodin, *ibid.,* p. 463-465.

Chapter 1. John Fitzgerald Kennedy: Introduction to the Dream

Kennedy's coffin was on display in the Capital Rotunda. A quarter of a million people paid their respects. Kennedy's numinosity did not ignore Jackie either. By mid-1964 Mrs. Kennedy had received 800,000 messages of condolence.[30] Photographers hounded her, not merely during her grieving but well into the thirtieth year after the assassination. As she once said: "They're like locusts, they're everywhere. I can't even change my clothes in private."[31]

Many years after the assassination, when Jackie had married Aristotle Onassis, "She went diving off the coast of Skorpios, and 10 photographers in diving outfits and underwater cameras with telephoto lenses tried to snap her picture."[32]

Kennedy's death culminated in thousands of journalistic expressions of grief and tributes from dignitaries around the world including Willy Brandt and President de Gaulle; but one telling poem by Molly Kazan comes very close to capturing Kennedy's quintessential mystique and his meaning to most Americans:

> I think
> that what he gave us most was pride.
> It felt good to have a President like that:
> bright, brave, and funny and good looking.
>
> I saw him once drive down East Seventy-second Street
> in an open car, in the autumn sun
> (as he drove yesterday in Dallas).
> His thatch of brown hair looked as though it had grown extra thick
> the way our wood animals in Connecticut
> grow extra fur for winter.
> And he looked as though it was fun to be alive,
> to be a politician,
> to be President
> to be a Kennedy,
> to be a man.
>
> He revived our pride.
> It felt good to have a President
> who read his mail,
> who read the papers,
> who read books and played touch football.
> It was a pleasure and a cause for pride
> to watch him take the quizzing of the press

---

30. Reeves, *ibid.*, p. 4.
31. Heymann, *ibid.*, p. 429.
32. *Ibid.*, p. 527.

with cameras grinding —
take it in his stride,
with zest.
He'd parry, thrust, answer or duck,
and fire a verbal shot on target,
hitting with the same answer, the segregationists in a Louisiana
or a hamlet or a government in South East Asia
He made you feel that he knew what was going on
in both places.
He would come out of the quiz with an "A" in Economics, Military Science,
    Constitutional Law, Farm Problems and the
moonshot program
and still take time to appreciate Miss May Craig.

. . . It felt good to have a President
who looked well in Vienna, Paris, Rome, Berlin
and at the podium of the United Nations
— and who would go to Dublin
put a wreath where it did the most good
and leave unspoken
the satisfaction of an Irishman
en route to 10 Downing Street
as head of the U.S. government.

What was spoken
was spoken well.
What was unspoken
needed to be unspoken.
It was none of our business if his back hurt.

He revived our pride.
He gave grist to our pride.
He was respectful of intellect;
he was respectful of excellence;
he was respectful of accomplishment and skill;
he was respectful of the clear and subtle uses of our language;
he was respectful of courage
And all these things he cultivated in himself.

. . . He affirmed our future.
Our future is more hopeful
because of his work
but our future is not safe nor sure.
He kept telling us that.
This is a very dangerous and uncertain world.
I quote. He said that yesterday.

Chapter I. John Fitzgerald Kennedy: Introduction to the Dream

He respected facts.
And we must now live with the fact of his murder.

Our children cried when the news came. They phoned and phoned and we cried and we were not ashamed of crying but we are ashamed of what had happened.
The youngest could not remember any other President clearly.
She felt as if the world had stopped. [33]

There have been well over 2,500 articles written about John F. Kennedy, along with those 600 books — far more than any president in this century. Perhaps to underscore the nature of the hero archetype, it might be useful to contrast this with "mere popularity." Elvis Presley was terribly popular, more so after his death than while living. But Presley did not embody the archetype. To quantify the difference we can look at the number of articles written about both Kennedy and Presley in the five years after their respective deaths. Kennedy died in 1963, Presley in 1977. (See Figure 1.1).

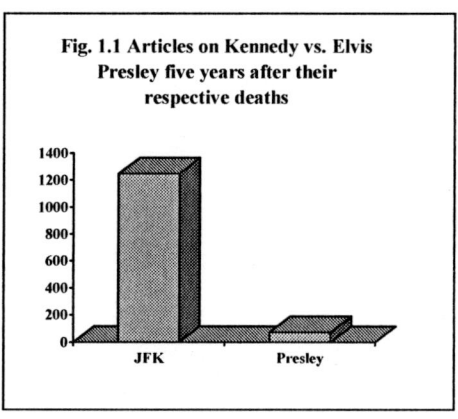

Fig. 1.1 Articles on Kennedy vs. Elvis Presley five years after their respective deaths

This is not merely a quantitative difference, but a qualitative one. It is naive to assume Kennedy was merely "popular." His significance to the American psyche was different, deeper, greater. Indeed in the five years after Presley's death, *which was 20 years after Kennedy's*, there were still more articles written about Kennedy than the King of rock and roll.

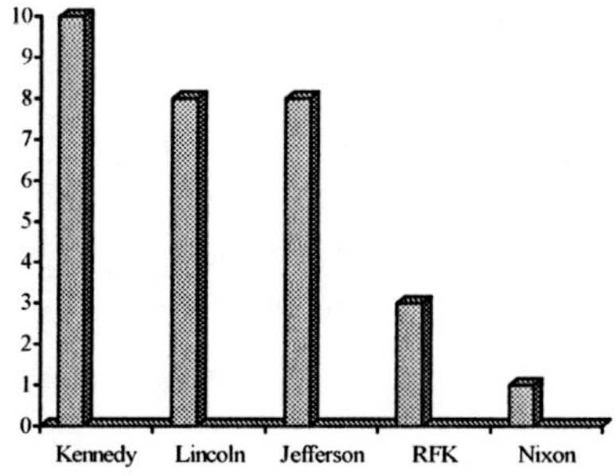

JFK's objective accomplishments or failings would be easily over-shadowed by the records of Harry Truman, Ronald Reagan, even Calvin Coolidge. It is not what Kennedy actually did, but what he represented to the American psyche that is

Fig. 1.2 Schools, hospitals and colleges named after Kennedy, Lincoln, Jefferson and Nixon

---

33. Molly Kazan, cited in Salinger, Pierre and Vanocur, Sander (Eds), *A Tribute to John F. Kennedy*. Chicago: Encyclopedia Britannica Inc, 1964, pp.107-109.

important. He is not a historical or political figure but a *psychological hero*. He is not an objective heavyweight like Albert Einstein, Martin Luther King, or Jonas Salk, because his achievements are exiguous by comparison. But as a *psychological* heavyweight, he is probably the most preeminent American in the twentieth century.

Take, for example, the number of schools, hospitals, junior colleges and universities which are now called "Kennedy." Compared to the "Lincolns" and "Jeffersons," Kennedy is in no measure justified to stand next to these historical figures; but he not only stands next to them, he overshadows them. (See Figure 1.2). [34]

The empirical fact we must struggle with is that John F. Kennedy carries as much psychological weight as Abraham Lincoln and George Washington. In fact, he may easily be one of the four or five most significant psychological figures in American history; and yet, rarely has this aspect of Kennedy been explored. Like Charles Lindbergh, John Fitzgerald Kennedy became an object of American mass psychology, a fixation, an obsession, and it is time we looked not just at the assassination drama and the attendant detective story, but at the psychological and mythological dimension of this story as well. We will address these matters in the final chapter of this book, but by way of introduction, let us get a preview of some of the issues.

KENNEDY AND LINCOLN

The fact that Lincoln and Kennedy were both shot in office is not the basis for their significance. If it were, there would be major monuments to the assassinated Presidents McKinley (1901) and Garfield (1881). Only Lincoln and Kennedy are commemorated with such ardor. Lee Harvey Oswald and John Wilkes Booth are remembered; Leo Czolgosz, President McKinley's assassin, is not. The pattern and vividness of these memory traces suggests that Kennedy and Lincoln have been adopted as *archetypal figures*; McKinley and Garfield seem not to have satisfied the conditions, they seem not to match up to the paradigms.

Many connections have been drawn between John Kennedy and Abraham Lincoln. John Kennedy drew connections himself, frequently invoking Lincoln in his speeches, especially at important, emotionally significant, and historic moments of his presidency.

> If my name goes down in history, it will be for this act. My whole soul is in it. If my hand trembles when I sign this proclamation, all who examine the document hereafter will say: "He hesitated.". . . But Lincoln's hand did not tremble. He

---

34. Data is based on *Patterson's American Education*, 1993, Mount Prospect, IL and *Private Schools of U.S.* Vol. 2. 1968, Market Data Retrieval, Shelton, CT.

did not hesitate. He did not equivocate. For he was the President of the United States. It is in this spirit that we must go forth in the coming months and years [35]

Harry Truman, one of his very first visitors in the White House, asked him if he was ready for such a responsibility. Again, Kennedy invoked Lincoln:

> Mr. Truman asked me if I think I am ready. I am reminded that one hundred years ago Abraham Lincoln, not yet President and under fire from veteran politicians, wrote these words. "I see the storm coming and I know His hand is in it. If He has a place and work for me, I believe that I am ready." Today I say to you, with full knowledge of the responsibilities of that high office, if the people of the nation select me to be their President, I believe that I am ready. [36]

Later, Kennedy strove to link their mutual "missions" in the following remarks:

> In the election of 1860, Abraham Lincoln said the question was whether this nation could exist half slave or half free. In the election of 1960, and in the world around us, the question is whether the world will exist half slave or half free, whether it will move in the direction of freedom, in the direction of the road that we are taking or whether it will move in the direction of slavery.[37]

Mrs. Kennedy promoted a linkage between her husband and Abraham Lincoln, as well, by requesting that his funeral follow the same protocol used for Lincoln's funeral; Kantor notes that, "The President's body was borne by caisson to rest on the same catafalque that had held the remains of Abraham Lincoln."[38] Kennedy followed in Lincoln's footsteps, even to the grave.

The parallels between the Lincoln and Kennedy tragedies are far more intricate and intriguing than we have ever appreciated. Obviously, some parallels and bridges were intentionally drawn, to boost Kennedy's image; but the plethora of coincidental linkages is staggering. Kennedy was shot on a Friday; so was Lincoln. Both were shot in the head, in the presence of their wives. Both were succeeded by a president named Johnson.

These coincidences extend to their assassins, as well. Lee Harvey Oswald and John Wilkes Booth both came from broken homes. Each had a friend named Paine, with whom he spent time just before the assassination. Booth and Oswald were born

---

35. Sorenson, *ibid.*, p. 23.
36. *Ibid.*, p. 94.
37. *Ibid.*, p. 103.
38. Kantor, *ibid.*, p. 129.

100 years apart. Both stayed in New Orleans, visiting their uncles, shortly before the assassinations. Both had 15 letters in their names.

A list of coincidental correspondences is shown in Table 1.1.

Table 1.1 Kennedy-Lincoln Correspondence

- Both Kennedy and Lincoln were succeeded by their Vice Presidents named Johnson. Andrew Johnson was born in 1808, Lyndon in 1908.
- Kennedy and Lincoln both have 7 letters in their names. Andrew Johnson and Lyndon Johnson each have 13. John Wilkes Booth and Lee Harvey Oswald each total 15.
- Lincoln was elected to the White House in 1846, Kennedy in 1946. Lincoln tried and failed to be nominated for the Vice Presidency in 1856; Kennedy tried and failed for the same office in 1956.
- When Lincoln won the presidency, he defeated a man born in 1813 (Douglas). Kennedy defeated a man born in 1913 (Nixon).
- Lincoln, a lawyer, was elected President in 1860; Kennedy, also a lawyer, in 1960.
- Kennedy had been warned by his advisors not to go to Dallas; Lincoln had been warned by his not to go to the Ford Theater.
- Kennedy's security in Dallas was mysteriously weak; Lincoln's security at the Ford Theater was uncharacteristically weak as well.
- Both Kennedy and Lincoln married in their 30s to women in their 20s.
- Each lost a son in the White House.
- Lincoln had two sons, named Robert and Edward. Kennedy had two brothers, named Robert and Edward.
- Both were deeply involved in the civil rights struggle.
- Both were uncharacteristically younger than their Vice Presidents.
- Conspiracy theories over the assassination persisted for both.
- Andrew Johnson was a problem drinker and was suspected of being involved in a conspiracy to kill Lincoln; Lyndon Johnson was a problem drinker and is still suspected in a conspiracy to kill JFK.
- Oswald and Booth symmetries
- Booth was born in 1839; Oswald in 1939.
- Oswald bled to death after being shot with a pistol; John Wilkes Booth was shot with a pistol and bled to death.
- Writings by Oswald, and by Booth, disappeared or were destroyed in the government's possession.
- On assassination eve, Oswald stayed with a friend named Paine. Paine was held for questioning. The night before Booth shot Lincoln, he was with a friend named Paine who was also held for questioning.

Chapter 1. John Fitzgerald Kennedy: Introduction to the Dream

- Conspiracy theorists suggested the real Booth was not buried in his grave and asked that he be exhumed; conspiracy theorists thought the same about Oswald and similarly called for his exhumation.
- Both Booth and Oswald were pegged as mentally unstable fanatics who were lone assassins in search of notoriety.
- Booth's killer and Oswald's killer were later judged to be psychotic.
- Booths' mother thought he was a spy for the Confederacy; Oswald's mother thought Lee was a spy for the U.S. military.
- Booth's father was named after a famous traitor (Brutus); Oswald's father was named after a traitor to the Union, Confederate General Robert E. Lee.

Note: As if to underscore the synchronicity of these two figures, it might be useful to emphasize that Kennedy's secretary, Evelyn Lincoln, was married. Her husband's name was 'Abe.' Sources for this listing include O'Donnel & Powers, Johnny We Hardly Knew Ye (Pocket Books, 1972), p.219;Compendium of Coincidence, (Time, August 27, 1964), p. 19. Sullivan, G., Facts and Fun about the Presidents (New York: Scholastic, 1987); Fortean Times, (John Brown Publishing, 1994), p. 32; Hanchett, William, The Lincoln Murder Conspiracies, (Chicago: Univ. of Illinois Press, 1983).

This type of coincidence or correspondence can be fun, and can be drawn out further and further. "Robert Kennedy," for example, appears in the story of Abraham Lincoln, as a fugitive stranded on "Johnson Island." A New York policeman named John Kennedy attempted to warn President Lincoln of an assassination plot against him. "Lincoln" appears in the Kennedy drama too. John Fitzgerald Kennedy met a real person named "Abe" Lincoln, the husband of his personal secretary, Evelyn Lincoln.

John Wilkes Booth was clearly a traitor to his country. Lee Harvey Oswald, the defector, was also a traitor to his country. Certainly Brutus, the assassin of Julius Caesar, is also a name associated with traitors; he is the historical, archetypal traitor. Brutus is not a very common American name. Few people know anyone named Brutus.

There is more. John Wilkes Booth was an esteemed actor but he had two brothers, one of whom was named Junius Brutus Booth. Indeed, John and his brother played together in a memorable performance of Shakespeare's *Julius Caesar* in March 1865.

Junius Brutus Booth did not change his name to make it more theatrical, nor did he adopt "Brutus" as a name because he was about to play the role in Julius Caesar. He was baptized in that name. Brutus appears on stage rather innocently in the psychodrama we are now studying; he is neither manufactured nor manipulated. Indeed, one wonders what role John Wilkes Booth played when he performed Julius Caesar alongside his brother in 1865, shortly before he assassinated Lincoln. This information is not available, but it would not be utterly surprising if he were cast in the role of Brutus.

The story of the Kennedy assassination now like a surrealistic dream, tantalizing, intriguing. It has taken on a life of its own, as a cultural event, as piece of theater, so troubling to the American psyche that we are compelled to investigate further and even to seek some kind of mystical meaning in it. But we are like lost souls wandering around in some inverted Platonic cave, focusing on the figures without noticing that the atmosphere is in fact created by the disturbing shadows they cast... and shadows are everywhere.[39]

As the event has taken hold in our imaginations, it seems to take on new psychological dimensions that in fact reflect on American society and our sense of who we are as a nation. In order to have the widest and most comprehensive picture of this moment in American history, our last chapter will focus on this dimension. But first, we must examine the myriad pages of assassination literature with fresh eyes and an unbiased, dispassionate objectivity.

---

39. One introductory and intriguing symbolic shadow further illustrates the concept: John Wilkes Booth was clearly a traitor to his country. Lee Harvey Oswald, the defector, was also a traitor to his country. So if we begin a dream interpretation, or start "free associating" to draw out connections, we never cease to stumble on to interesting clues. Certainly Brutus is also a name associated with traitors, the assassin of Julius Caesar, the historical, archetypal traitor.

Brutus is not a very common American name. Few people know anyone named Brutus. If one uses a dream-interpretation approach, and follows out these associations, sometimes we are very surprised indeed. John Wilkes Booth was an esteemed actor, but he had two brothers, one of whom was named Junius Brutus Booth. Indeed John Wilkes Booth and his brother played together in a memorable performance of Shakespeare's *Julius Caesar* in March 1865.

Junius Brutus Booth did not change his name to make it more theatrical, nor did he adopt "Brutus" as a name because he was about to play the role in Julius Caesar. Junius Brutus Booth was baptized Brutus, and took the name of his father, also named Brutus. Brutus appears on stage in this psychodrama rather innocently, unconsciously, if you will, neither manufactured nor manipulated. Indeed it causes one to wonder what role John Wilkes Booth played when he performed Julius Caesar alongside his brother in 1865, shortly before he assassinated Lincoln. This information is not available, but it would not be utterly surprising if he were cast in the role of Brutus in this play.

Chapter 2. Case Closed

"I'm a patsy!"
— Lee Harvey Oswald

At 12 seconds past twelve thirty on November 22, 1963, a convertible limousine carrying President Kennedy, his wife Jacqueline, and Governor and Mrs. Connally of Texas drove down Elm Street in Dallas. The car was traveling at eleven miles per hour to negotiate a difficult turn into Dealey Plaza past the Texas School Book Depository.

> Several shots rang out in rapid succession. According to a Secret Serviceman in the car, the President said, "My God, I'm hit." He lurched in his seat, both hands clawing toward his throat. Directly in front of the President, Governor Connally heard one shot and was then hit himself. He screamed. For five seconds the car actually slowed down. Then came more gunfire. The President fell violently backwards and to his left, his head exploding in a halo of brain tissue, blood and bone. To Mrs. Connally it "was like buckshot falling all over us." As the car finally gathered speed, Mrs. Kennedy believed she cried, "I love you, Jack." From the front seat the Governor's wife heard her exclaim, "Jack . . . they've killed my husband." then "I have his brains in my hand," . . . Mrs. Kennedy repeated time and time again. It was over. Half an hour later, in an emergency room at nearby Parkland Hospital, a doctor told the President's wife what she already knew, "The President is gone." [40]

---

40. Summers, Anthony. *Conspiracy*. New York: McGraw-Hill, 1989, pp. 3-4.

About thirty minutes after the shooting, a deputy sheriff noticed a stack of book cartons on the sixth floor of the Texas School Book Depository. Thus began a collection of evidence which resulted in the attribution of this killing to a sole gunman firing from his sniper's nest in that building, Lee Harvey Oswald.

The following is a list of the "best evidence" collected against him these last 30 years.

EVIDENCE AGAINST OSWALD

Physical Evidence [41]

- Three empty cartridge cases were found in the sniper's nest. A rifle was found shortly thereafter. It was a bolt-action Mannlicher-Carcano Italian rifle of World War II vintage. The rifle, stamped with serial number C-2766, had been ordered eight months earlier from a mail-order company in Chicago, Klein's Sporting Goods Company. The mail order house identified the customer who bought it as A. Hidell at P.O. Box 2915, Dallas, Texas.
- Handwriting on the purchase order made by A. Hidell matched Oswald's handwriting.
- A forged identity card in the name of Alek J. Hidell was allegedly found on Oswald's person when he was arrested.

---

41. Data provided in this section comes from numerous sources. Primary among them are Moore, Jim. *Conspiracy of One.* Fort Worth, Texas: The Summit Group, 1991. Summers, *ibid.*; Oglesby, Carl. *The JFK Assassination: The Facts and the Theories.* New York: Signet, 1992; Groden, Robert J., with Livingstone, Harrison E. *High Treason,* Baltimore: Conservatory Press, 1989.

- Four days after the assassination, the FBI found a palm print on the barrel of the rifle, and the print matched Oswald's right hand.
- Oswald denied using the A. Hidell identity card or ordering the rifle, but he did admit having the P.O. box in Dallas.
- A tuft of cotton fibers was lifted from the rifle barrel which matched the shirt Oswald was wearing at the time he was arrested.
- Oswald had asked a fellow employee, Buell Wesley Frazier, to drive him to Mrs. Ruth Paine's house, where he had left many of his possessions. Oswald and his Russian-born wife Marina were separated and Marina lived with Ruth Paine in Irving (some 15 miles from Dallas), where these possessions and the rifle were kept. On the morning of the assassination, and upon his return to Dallas with Frazier the next morning, Oswald brought a large paper bag to the Depository. When asked by Frazier what he had in the paper bag, he said he had some curtain rods. At the time of the discovery of the sniper's nest, police found a brown paper bag large enough to have held the rifle. Later the FBI found a right palm print and left index finger print on the bag; they matched Oswald's. No curtain rods were ever found at the assassination site. Oswald's alibi was thin.
- The day after the assassination, the police found in Paine's garage two photographs of a man holding a rifle in one hand and two left-wing newspapers in the other. The Warren Commission decided that the man in the photo was Oswald and the rifle in the picture identical to the murder weapon. Testimony from Oswald's Russian-born wife, Marina, verified that she had taken the pictures with his Imperial Reflex camera some months earlier. [42]
- The cartridge cases found at the Depository had been linked to the rifle.
- In early December, Oswald's clipboard was found less than ten feet from where the rifle was found.

Although many witnesses heard fewer than or more than three shots, the majority of witnesses in Dealey Plaza heard three. The Carcano rifle can be operated with 2.3 seconds between shots, and the period of time of firing was 7.9 seconds; it is possible Oswald could have fired three shots in the required time by himself and with no other conspirators.

Oswald was seen on the sixth floor shortly before noon, filling orders for books. Very shortly after the assassination, he was sitting in the second floor lunchroom. Critics have argued that it would have been impossible for Oswald to kill the President and run down to the second floor lunchroom to establish an alibi in such a short

---

42. Oswald said the photos were faked. Canadian photo experts and an English photo expert held that the shadows in the photos were incorrect and that Oswald's chin was not his (Groden, *ibid.*). The House Select Assassinations Committee decided the photos were authentic. Another piece of evidence putatively signaling Oswald's guilt is the neutron activation analysis of bullet fragments found in the limousine. These results lend support to the notion that the fragments also came from Oswald's rifle.

period of time; but Secret Service agent John Howlett duplicated Oswald's route, hid the rifle, and ran down the staircase to the second floor all within ninety-one seconds.

Only one witness partially identified the gunman in the Depository window as Lee Harvey Oswald, forty-five-year-old Howard Brennan:

> He watched spellbound as the gunman fired the final shot and then disappeared from view. Minutes after the assassination, he described the suspect as white, slender, weighing about 165 pounds, about 5' 10" and in his early thirties.[43]

This completes the physical evidence that might be used against Oswald in a hypothetical trial for the crime. However, circumstantial evidence could also be persuasive in convicting this assassin.

Circumstantial Evidence

Oswald rarely, if ever, took taxis. Most curious individuals would have stayed, milling around the assassination scene. Oswald departed from Dealey Plaza quickly, allegedly because there would be "no more work" that day. However, when the bus he was on was stalled in heavy traffic, he hailed a cab to take him past his house. This transfer from bus to cab occurred less than eighteen minutes after the assassination. It would certainly appear that he was on the run.

Oswald's house was on 1026 North Beckley. At 12:54 p.m. Oswald departed the cab at the 700 block of North Beckley and walked three blocks back to his rented room. This suggests Oswald wanted to size up the area and deliberately had the cabbie drive past it before he got out.

Oswald changed clothes in his apartment, grabbed his pistol and left. Officer Tippit was cruising on 10th Street and had passed the intersection of 10th and Patton. He saw Oswald and pulled to the curb asking him to come over to his car. Tippit then opened his door and stepped out of the car, walking toward the front of the vehicle. Oswald allegedly pulled a revolver from his pocket and fired several shots, four of which hit Tippit, killing him instantly. Of twelve witnesses to the Tippit shooting, five or six identified Oswald as the man they saw.

Oswald allegedly left his jacket at the scene of the Tippit murder.

Oswald was arrested in a theater with the revolver still in his possession. The shells found at the scene matched those of Oswald's pistol (four ejected .38 caliber shells were found under a bush near where the officer died). When arrested in the Texas Theater, Oswald reached for his pistol with his right hand and punched the

---

43. Moore, *ibid.*, p. 62.

Chapter 2. Case Closed

arresting officer between the eyes with his left. This is unusual behavior for a man innocent of any wrongdoing.

Texas Theater shortly after Oswald's arrest

When he was arrested in the theater, Oswald exclaimed, "Well, it's all over, now." [44] He was in police custody by 1:51 p.m. that day, en route to headquarters.

David Belin, who served as assistant counsel to the Warren Commission, wrote in November 22, 1963 — "You Are the Jury": "Thus, we have the scientific evidence that unequivocally showed that Lee Harvey Oswald killed Officer J.D. Tippit. Even had there been no eyewitnesses to the Tippit shooting, the apprehension of Oswald less than forty-five minutes after the murder with the murder weapon in his possession was certainly strong evidence that Oswald was the killer. And when you add to this evidence the actions of Oswald in the theater in taking out his gun and resisting arrest and the actions of Oswald before he went into the theater that aroused the suspicion of Johnny Calvin Brewer, the case against Oswald becomes exceedingly strong." Belin then, as if he needed their help, invokes the aid of eyewitness testimony in the Tippit killing: "And when you add to all of this the positive identification by the six eyewitnesses who were taken to the Dallas Police Department: W.W. Scoggins, who saw Oswald pass within twelve feet of his cab; Ted Callaway and Sam Guinyard, who saw Oswald running from the scene with gun in hand; Helen Markham, who saw the murder from across the street and Barbara Jeanette Davis and Virginia Davis, who saw Oswald cut across the front yard of their house — there could be no reasonable doubt that the murderer of Dallas Police Officer J.D. Tippit was Lee Harvey Oswald." Counsel Joe Ball put it plainly when he said that in all his courtroom experience, he had "never seen a more open and shut case." [45]

If we assume that Oswald's shooting of Officer Tippit is an open and shut case, it becomes exceptionally good circumstantial evidence that he also may have killed Kennedy. There is more:

Oswald, according to his wife, attempted to assassinate General Edwin Walker in the months prior to the assassination of Kennedy. Such evidence, if true, adds

---

44. Bonar Menninger, *Mortal Error, ibid.*, p. 16.
45. Moore, *ibid.*, p. 68

weight to the idea that Oswald was unstable and violent. On the day he attempted to shoot Walker, he left a letter for Marina, which said:

> I left you as much money as I could, $60 on the second of the month, and you and June can live for two months on $10 a week. . . If I am alive and taken prisoner, the city jail is at the end of the bridge we always used to cross when we went to town. [46]

He left his wedding ring in a porcelain cup on the day of the assassination of Kennedy. He never took it off before.

He left his wife $170 on the morning of the assassination, as much if not more money than they had ever had in disposable cash up to that time. He usually only went to visit his estranged wife on weekends. However, the day before the assassination, local Dallas newspapers first published the President's route; employees of the Texas School Depository were excited and buzzing that the President would be passing them the next day. That evening Oswald went to Marina's house — uncharacteristically on a weekday — allegedly picked up his rifle and left early the next morning, describing the package he was taking as "curtain rods."

Today, the evidence against Lee Harvey Oswald would be persuasive enough for an indictment. Although there were no unassailable eyewitnesses to the murder of the President directly pointing to Oswald (Brennan could not identify Oswald in a lineup) there is strong physical evidence linking Oswald to the location of the crime scene, to the weapon used in the killing, to the purchase of the weapon, and to a second murder that same afternoon where eyewitnesses positively identified him as the assailant. Oswald's weapon was on his person when he was arrested, and the pistol was used in the murder. The sum total of evidence against, both physical and circumstantial is not just poppycock. Probably FBI agent James Hosty, in his 1996 memoir, gave one of the best and most articulate "summations" for the prosecution:

> Anyone who has examined the evidence carefully as I have over many years cannot help but come to the conclusion that Oswald was the lone gunman. . . purchasing the rifle under an assumed name; trying to kill General Edwin Walker in April 1963; going to Mexico in September and October, where he contacted V.V. Kostikov, ostensibly a vice consul at the Soviet Embassy . . . coming to the Paines' home and retrieving his rifle the day before the assassination and carrying it disguised as curtain rods when he hitched a ride to work on November 22, 1963 — and. . . his post-assassination path to Oak Cliff, where he murdered Officer Tippit in cold blood — an act witnessed by five people — and then, in the movie theater, tried to take a second shot at an officer with the same

---

46. Johnson, *ibid.*, p. 263

gun he used to kill Tippit. With all this evidence and more, for the life of me, I don't understand why some people still don't think Oswald did it, or that there was a second gunman... As I said, the evidence is there for anyone to examine. [47]

While we take agent Hosty's remarks as an appropriate summation of the prosecution's case, we must also realize that in the same book where Hosty makes his assessment, he admits to multiple examples of destruction of crucial evidence and the cover-up of lots more, while citing in his text unreferenced sources which are not accessible for "everyone to examine." Indeed, some evidence has not been made public as late as thirty-eight years after the event.

Officer Tippit

When Mark Furman, the LA police officer in the famous OJ Simpson trial, testified that he found the "bloody glove," he was asked if he had ever said the word "nigger." He denied that he used it, under oath; but subsequently he was exposed by a tape recording of an interview he had held months earlier where he is heard saying the "n word" numerous times. This apparent perjury convinced the jury that if he was willing to lie under oath about the "n" word, perhaps he was also willing to lie under oath about the bloody glove; and thus "reasonable doubt" existed. OJ was set free largely on that basis.

In like spirit, if Hosty, according to his own admissions, was party to the destruction of evidence, why should we not consider that "reasonable doubt" exists with respect to his prosecutorial conclusions as well?

DR. PEPPER OR COCA-COLA: THE OBSESSION BEGINS

The publication of conspiracy texts leaves the dispassionate observer astonished at the high level of detail that has been developed. Consider, for example, the issue of Coca Cola in the second floor lunchroom at the Texas School Book Depository as a symptom of the obsessive neurosis the murder mystery has evoked.

One author, Anthony Summers, believes that Oswald could not have shot the President by virtue of the fact that he was seen by two witnesses sitting in the second floor lunchroom at 12:15 p.m., fifteen minutes before the motorcade passed the Depository.[48] In fact, Oswald naively asked a fellow workmate why the crowd was gather-

---

47. James Hosty, *Assignment Oswald.* New York: Arcade, 1996, p. 254.
48. A total of four witnesses say they saw Oswald in the second floor lunchroom between noon and 12:15. Summers, *ibid.*, p. 554, n. 76.

ing outside and was told that the President was coming. Later, after the assassination, motorcycle patrolman Marion Baker ran into the Depository with his gun drawn, climbed the stairs, confronted Oswald in the second floor lunchroom — about one and a half minutes after the shooting — and then proceeded upstairs. This happened after 12:31 p.m.

To Summers, it was highly unlikely that Oswald could have been in the lunchroom at 12:15, run upstairs to shoot the President, and then run back down to be seen again in the lunchroom at 12:31 to assure himself of an alibi.

Summer's argument is well founded. The published program of the President's itinerary indicated that he would pass the Depository at 12:25 p.m. The President was five minutes behind schedule. The motorcade passed at 12:30. Oswald would not have known that fact and would have had to be in place five minutes earlier.

To attempt to establish an alibi by first placing himself in the lunchroom at 12:15 and hoping to place himself there again after the killing at 12:30 without having exact and specific knowledge of when the President's motorcade would actually pass is difficult and improbable. Assassins do need some set-up time, especially when they are targeting a head of state.

Mrs. Arnold reliably placed Oswald on the second-floor lunchroom before the shooting, and patrolman Baker reliably placed him there after the shooting. Thus, the first of an infinite number of pieces of evidence begins to contradict the Warren Commission findings that Oswald was the killer. [49] However, Jim Moore, a pro-Warren Commission author, draws precisely the opposite conclusion:

> After the encounter with Baker and Truly in the lunchroom, Oswald (displaying icy calm, even though Baker was holding a revolver at Oswald's midsection) put a nickel in the soda machine and selected a Coca-Cola. It may be that this single action on Oswald's part holds the key to his guilt. Oswald habitually drank Dr. Pepper. There can be only one realistic explanation for a miser like Oswald to fail to select his soft drink of choice — he was nervous. [50]

---

49. Summers, *ibid.*, pp. 80-81. Gerald Posner in *Case Closed* argues that William Shelley, Eddie Piper, and Carolyn Arnold were all mistaken and were contradicted by other witnesses. Posner alleges there is no credible evidence Oswald was on the first or second floor in the fifteen minutes prior to the assassination (p. 226). Nonetheless, he and others have interviewed 3 witnesses who placed him on the first and second floor prior to the shooting, and their testimony was not included in the Warren Commission report. In establishing a case of "reasonable doubt," one must take into account these witnesses who contradict the official view, the fact that no one incontestably identified Oswald as the sniper in the window, at least in the opinion of Jesse Curry, and that no one saw Oswald running down the stairs from the sixth floor as he is reported to have done in the official version of the event.

50. Moore, *ibid.*, p. 53.

Moore's deductions are interesting, but Priscilla Johnson's *Marina and Lee* tells a different story; not only did Oswald frequently drink Coke, he liked Coke, and was not as thoroughgoing a habitué of Dr. Pepper as Moore would have us believe. [51]

Will this discussion of beverages and running times down the seventy-two steps at the Depository finally give us an answer to the murder mystery of the century? Maybe; but we should also observe that such a knot of hard-to-verify details can drive us very quickly into an obsessive neurosis, forever ruminating over what may be trivia without any hope of coming to a final conclusion and closing the books on this case

Many, like author Gerald Posner, have argued that indeed it is time to close the case. To him, the evidence is clear and unambiguous, and all the obsessive talk about Coca Cola and Dr. Pepper merely obscures the "obvious" truth that Lee Harvey Oswald, alone, shot the President of the United States.

Before we accept Oswald's guilt, however, it is time to present the case for the defense. We are happy to report that the judge in this case has allowed any and all pertinent evidence — which suggests that the Warren Commission version of this case is not as clear cut and solid as it seems. In the next chapter, we will bring into focus the best evidence collected by conspiracists for these last 40 years.

---

51. Johnson McMillan, Priscilla. *Marina and Lee.* New York: Harper & Row 1977, p. 210.

Chapter 3. Reasonable Doubt

Ironically, it was President Johnson — the man who succeeded John Kennedy and appointed the Warren Commission — who eventually dropped the heaviest official hint that Lee Oswald was more than he appeared to be. In a 1969 interview for CBS Television, Johnson remarked: "I don't think that they [the Warren Commission] or me or anyone else is always absolutely sure of everything that might have motivated Oswald or others that could have been involved. But he was quite a mysterious fellow, and he did have connections that bore examination." That was quite an understatement, but the former President felt he had said too much. He asked CBS to withhold that section of the interview on the grounds of "national security." CBS obliged and suppressed Johnson's remarks until 1975. [52]

Jack Ruby denied the public a trial, which might have determined the killer or killers of President Kennedy. It is doubtful that Lee Harvey Oswald could be convicted of the murder of the President. Perhaps he could be convicted of murdering Officer Tippit, insofar as eyewitness testimony could be provided to place him at the scene, to corroborate that he pulled the trigger, to identify the weapon as his own, and to show that the bullets used were fired from the pistol he was carrying. There were witnesses who saw two men at the Tippit shooting and others who could not identify Oswald specifically; but the weight of evidence would certainly have given the prosecution a very good chance at conviction.

---

52. Summers, Anthony. *Conspiracy* New York: McGraw-Hill, 1989, p. 93.

The same impeccable evidence, however, does not exist with respect to the assassination of Kennedy. The only witness to have identified Oswald as the shooter in the sixth floor window of the Depository failed to identify the color of Oswald's shirt properly.

EVIDENCE FAVORING OSWALD

- Oswald said he changed his shirt after leaving his apartment to go to the movie theater. Depository witnesses also identified the color of Oswald's shirt as reddish in color, while he had been arrested after the Tippit murder in a white shirt. Strangely, a tuft of cotton fibers found in the rifle butt that was found in the Depository matched Oswald's white shirt — the shirt he was wearing at the time he was arrested, *not the shirt he wore at the Depository that morning.*[53] This suggests evidence was planted.
- The rifle was oily, but no oil was found on the brown paper bag allegedly used to carry the rifle into the Depository. Oswald's print was found on the bag, but the absence of any oil from the weapon was unusual.[54]
- Oswald's palm print was found on the rifle barrel, not initially but after the FBI worked on it in Washington. The location of the print was such that it could only have been made while the rifle was disassembled. Indeed, the print was not positively identified as Oswald's until after his death. His mother contended that the FBI planted the print after visiting his coffin. Earlier, Dallas laboratory tests had failed to find any of Oswald's fingerprints on the weapon. More recent (1993) information suggests a print was lifted in Dallas (that is, found and identified), and by virtue of the process used, the same print was not visible to the FBI laboratory in Washington.[55] This matter is still a source of some confusion. Neither were any prints found on the spent shells nor on the live round remaining in the chamber. Was Oswald wearing gloves when he placed the bullets in the chamber? No gloves were ever found. And if he was so meticulous, why did he leave his rifle at the scene?
- Oswald said that he did not own the gun, yet the photographs found in his garage show him holding the assassination weapon. Marina Oswald testified that Oswald owned that rifle and that she had taken that photograph herself with Oswald's camera. Oswald, as mentioned in the prior chapter, said that someone had pasted his face on to the photograph and that it was a fake.

Chapter 3. Reasonable Doubt

Marina Oswald thus represents a highly important witness for the prosecution, but her testimony is dismaying. Her "recollection" of events has been documented as faulty to the extreme. For example, she said to the Warren Commission that she and Lee arrived in the United States by airplane. Clearly, she must remember the first day

---

53. In Summers, *ibid.*, p. 56. One crucial piece of evidence linking Oswald to the rifle was a tuft of cotton fibers found in the butt of the rifle. It was examined microscopically by the FBI laboratory and was reported to match the fibers in the shirt Oswald was wearing at the time of his arrest. However, before this information was developed, Oswald had said that after leaving the Depository and before his arrest, he had gone home and changed shirts. "He said, according to reports of his interrogation, that the shirt he discarded was 'reddish colored' or 'red.' No such shirt was ever traced. So far as is known, he owned only brown, light brown and blue shirts (XVI.515). What's more, he was remembered as wearing a tan shirt by a neighbor who saw him leave for work on the day of the assassination (II.250). Yet, Officer Baker's testimony (III.263, 257) does seem to corroborate Oswald's statement that he had changed into a darker shirt. It is not quite clear what color shirt Oswald wore to work that day. While the matter remains unresolved, it clearly was not white or light-colored — and that is the color shirt reported by those observing a window gunman. (The shirt Oswald was wearing when arrested is preserved at the National Archives). *Ibid.*, p. 555.

However, Jim Moore, the pro-Warren Commission researcher, reports that Oswald's bus transfer ticket was found in his shirt pocket when he was arrested. This transfer ticket has proved of considerable interest and significance to Kennedy researchers. For example, if one poses the question, "Where was Oswald going after the assassination?" some very clever answers have appeared. First, it has been argued that he was actually going to meet a contact in the Texas Theater. Others have said that Officer Tippit actually beeped his car horn at Oswald's house and Oswald's confrontation with him had something to do with a glitch in the plot that Oswald was only partially privy to. (Officer Tippit freelanced as a security guard for a notorious John Birch Society member). A third theory holds that Oswald was on his way to Jack Ruby's house, which was on the same street where Tippit was murdered, approximately 2/3 of a mile away. One of the more intriguing theories suggested that his bus transfer could have taken him to a Greyhound station, where he might have caught a bus for San Antonio and the Mexican border, a journey he allegedly had once made previously.

Thus, the shirt Oswald was wearing is of considerable importance. If he changed shirts, as he alleged, it would be rather suspicious that the FBI laboratory would find fibers in the rifle butt which matched his shirt at the time of the arrest, since this would not have been the shirt worn by the person who fired the Mannlicher-Carcano rifle; in other words, it indicates a conspiracy to set up Oswald as a patsy for the murder.

This discussion leads us in infinite directions: (a) Oswald changed shirts (thus rendering suspicious the forensic evidence tying fibers in his second shirt to the rifle). (b) Oswald lied about his shirt and did not, in fact, change it. (That would explain why his bus transfer ticket was still in his pocket — but, then, the color of his shirt does not match eyewitness accounts of the gunman in the sixth floor Depository window). (c) Oswald did not lie about changing his shirt — why would he need to fabricate such a detail? — and he also switched the transfer ticket from one shirt to the new one. This would be a consistent explanation, but again, it would contradict forensic evidence tying his shirt to the rifle. Furthermore, it would ask us to try to determine his ultimate destination; if he switched transfer tickets from one shirt to the next, he intended to use that transfer ticket in some way. Where was he headed?

she touched down and entered the new land that would become her home. Mrs. Oswald, in fact, arrived in the United States by ship. (See Table 4.6 for a more complete list of her inconsistencies).

Thus, Marina, the single witness who could verify Oswald's ownership of the weapon, is easily impugned. The only other evidence linking Oswald to the rifle is the order form filled out under the alias "A. Hidell." Handwriting experts have shown it to be Oswald's script, but surely other handwriting experts could be found to allege the opposite if Oswald were to be tried for this crime.

- A chemical test of Oswald's right cheek (and hands) proved negative, indicating he either did not fire the rifle or he washed his face prior to his arrest. Oswald spent very little time in his apartment on Beckley Street and changed shirts but did not wash his face, he said.
- The bullet found on the stretcher at Parkland Hospital was not on Governor Connally's stretcher but that of a little boy who was entering the hospital, suggesting the so-called "pristine" bullet was planted.[56]
- 1999 investigations studied the bullet this pristine bullet which allegedly killed both JFK and injured John Connally. Commissioned by the National Archives, a scientific study on the nose of the bullet discovered "paper fibers and nontextile material that could not have come from Kennedy or from the shirt of Connally who was allegedly hit along with Kennedy."

Eyewitnesses Favoring Oswald

A second example of material evidence that would serve to exonerate Oswald involves eyewitness accounts, which place him elsewhere. Kennedy was shot at 12:30 p.m. At 11:50 a.m., co-worker Givens saw Oswald in the domino room of the first floor of the Depository. Bill Shelly, a foreman, saw Oswald about ten minutes before noon in the same room. At noon, Eddie Piper spoke to Oswald on the first floor. (This evidence was not contained in the Warren Commission Report.) Carolyn Arnold, secre-

---

54. Warren Commission lawyer Wesley Liebeler noted that no one clearly saw the rifle nor could identify the rifle which was alleged to have been stored in the Paines' garage. This is the rifle that is said to have been carried into the Depository disguised as a bundle of curtain rods. According to Liebeler, "Not one person alive today ever saw that rifle in the . . . garage in such a way that it could be identified as that rifle." Summers, "The Ghosts of November," *Vanity Fair*, December, 1994, p. 98.

55. Livingstone, Harrison E. *Killing the Truth*, New York: Carrol & Graf, 1993.

56. A discussion of this issue is given in a new text by Harrison E. Livingstone: *Killing the Truth*, New York: Carrol & Graf, 1993, pp 60-611.

tary to the Vice President of the Book Depository, told the FBI that she saw Oswald in the lunchroom on the second floor.

> Oswald was sitting in one of the booth seats on the right-hand side of the room as you go in. He was alone as usual and appeared to be having lunch... It was about 12:15. It may have been slightly later. [57]

These comments also were not contained in the Warren Commission Report. At 12:31-12:32 p.m., Oswald was confronted in the second-floor lunch room, finishing a Coke, by superintendent Truly and Dallas Police Officer Marrion L. Baker.[58]

Thus, if Oswald were put on trial, there would be witnesses Truly, Baker, Arnold, Piper, Shelly and Givens putting Oswald on the first and second floor of the TSBD both *before and after* the shooting. If a "conviction" requires proof beyond a reasonable doubt, this phalanx of witnesses would certainly march in this direction.[59]

In terms of "material evidence," therefore, the case against Oswald is weak. Witnesses place Oswald elsewhere both before and after the killing. Nitrate tests fail to verify that he fired a rifle. Even the Warren Commission was unable to determine "motive" and, if a trial were held then, many witnesses, could have been brought forward to show Oswald genuinely liked Kennedy. As Former Chief of Dallas Police Jesse Curry once said,

> We don't have any proof that Oswald fired the rifle, and never did. Nobody's yet been able to put him in that building with a gun in his hand. [60]

Perhaps Oswald was hired by outsiders to deliver a rifle to the Depository building, to be used by contract killers on the sixth floor while he dutifully waited in the lunchroom. Perhaps he killed Tippit while "on the run" in a state of panic. There are a number of "perhaps" arguments, but the hard, material evidence, which would convict him of the assassination of President Kennedy, is absent. Even at the time it was anything but an open and shut case, and since 1963, the evidence that "something else"

---

57. North, Mark *Act of Treason* New York: Carroll & Graf, 1991, p. 377.
58. *Ibid.*, p. 388.
59. While Oswald was under arrest, he claimed that he was eating in the first floor lunchroom at the time the President was shot. "He said, accurately as it turned out, that two specific fellow workers had walked through the room at one point. If Oswald was not in that room, it is remarkable that he correctly described two men out of a staff of 75." Summers, "The Ghosts of November," *ibid.*
60. Groden, Robert J., with Livingstone, Harrison E. *High Treason*, Baltimore: Conservatory Press, 1989, p. 237.

was going on has gathered such support from all corners that it stands today as the leading hypothesis to explain these events.

There is, of course, circumstantial evidence that points the finger at Oswald. He was an expatriate. He may have tried to shoot General Walker, if his wife's testimony can be believed. He applied for a passport in June 1963. He may have killed Officer Tippit. He left his wedding ring on the dresser for Marina on the morning of the assassination, a ring he never took off; and he left money for her as well, $170 — a meager sum, but still more than she had ever seen before.

But there is also a body of circumstantial evidence that points almost as surely in the opposite direction: Oswald liked Kennedy. No witnesses report otherwise. He kept a *Life Magazine* photo spread on the Kennedys on his coffee table. Oswald had fathered a baby that was born in October, and he loved his children — of that there seems little doubt.

In October 1963, Oswald had written to the IRS that his withholding exemptions should be altered so that his *subsequent* checks from the Depository would allow him more net pay. This is clearly peculiar behavior for someone who does not plan to be around after November 22, much less for someone who had premeditated the murder of a head of state.

As for General Walker's attempted assassination, the bullet found in Walker's home did not match the Mannlicher-Carcano rifle Oswald allegedly used. [61]

Lee Harvey Oswald will likely remain a mystery to us. Our next task is to review the evidence that some conspiracy may have existed in the killing of America's 34th President. The literature on this topic is so voluminous it is easily the subject of an entire book, not a single chapter. Millions of pages of evidence, from the Warren Commission reports and appendices to the House Select Committee on Assassinations (HSCA) inquiries, are summarized here. Every attempt has been made to make this readable. The level of detail, however, may prove exhausting. In no case was significant evidence or data ignored for the purposes of a smooth, easy read. The table in the middle of this chapter, for example, seems to go on endlessly; yet it is important to present the seminal research without cutting corners.

---

61. Bob Goodman, *Triangle of Fire*, San Jose, CA: Laquerian Publishers, 1993, p. 241.

Chapter 3. Reasonable Doubt

One minute after the assassination, spectators continue to run towards and look at the grassy knoll. Over sixty witnesses said shots came from in front of the motorcade.

BEST EVIDENCE FOR A CONSPIRACY

(1) A Fourth Shot

Witnesses

Of the 178 witnesses in Dealey Plaza whose statements were available to the Warren Commission, sixty-one believed at least one of the shots came from in front of the motorcade.[62] Photographic evidence from films shot at the moment show a number of spectators orienting themselves or looking toward the area of the grassy knoll to escape or shield themselves from subsequent shots. One of these witnesses, Jean Hill, who was standing directly across the street from the grassy knoll, said she saw a man moving rapidly away from the knoll toward the railroad tracks immediately after the shots rang out.[63]

---

62. Summers, *ibid*
63. Bonar Menninger, *Mortal Error, ibid.*, p. 51.

Exit Wound in the Back of the Head

A preponderance of Dallas physicians and medical personnel who treated the President was convinced that the fatal shot was from the front, and the hole in the back of the President's head represented an exit wound. (See Table 3.1 below).[64] Motorcycle patrolmen who were to the left and rear of the President's car were splattered with blood and brain tissue — an *extremely unlikely* possibility if the shot came from behind. Robert Groden's research on the strange autopsy results on the President (at Bethesda Naval Hospital in Washington) is significantly at variance with the recollections of Parkland Hospital staff in Dallas. The following table lists the witnesses Groden and Livingstone supply in Dallas who *contradict* the official autopsy findings out of Bethesda.

Table 3.1 Autopsy evidence was impugned by the following witnesses present at Kennedy's admission to Parkland Hospital in Dallas [65]

Dr. Kemp Clark	Dr. Fouad Bashour
Dr. Robert McClelland	Dr. Charles Baxter
Dr. Richard Dulany	Nurse Margaret Hood (Henchcliffe)
Nurse Patricia Gustafson	Dr. Marion Jenkins
Dr. Ronald Coy Jones	Dr. Adolph Giesecke Jr.
Nurse Doris Nelson	Dr. Malcolm Perry
Dr. Paul Peters	Dr. Robert Grossman
Dr. Gene Atkin	Dr. Jackie Hunt

Groden's conclusion from the review of witnesses at Parkland is summarized as follows:

---

64. Since this gathering of names, Livingstone (in *Killing the Truth*, 1993) has added another witness, Diana Bowron, a British nurse who was with JFK's body the entire time it was in the trauma room at Parkland. Ms. Bowron contests the locations for the wounds in the autopsy photos with those she saw. She said there was a gaping wound in the back of the head, suggestive of a frontal shot, and little brain was left in the skull. Strangely, some of the most recent evidence about inconsistencies in autopsy photos, their origin, and their veracity comes from Eisenhower Medical Center's David Mantik, who subjected copies of government photos to a technique called optical densitometry. The result shows "powerful and quantitative evidence of alteration to some of the skull X-rays. They appear to be composites." Summers, "The Ghosts of November", *ibid.*, p. 97.

A shot striking the President where the autopsy report placed it, at or near the hairline of the back of the head, would not, and indeed could not, have blown out the portion of the head which was in fact blown away. [66]

Other commentary from other sources corroborates these arguments:

According to Dr. Robert N. McClelland, "the right posterior portion of the skull had been extremely blasted... Dr. Ronald Coy Jones described "what appeared to be an exit wound in the posterior portion of the skull... Dr. Gene Akin said that the "back of the right occipital-parietal portion of his head was shattered, with brain substance extruding." [67]

These statements from Parkland personnel clearly support the notion that the official Bethesda autopsy is suspicious and that a frontal shot seemed likely.

Groden's 1989 research on Parkland hospital inconsistencies has been corroborated by the most definitive study of this controversy. Under President Clinton, the Assassination Records Review Board was charged with the release of over 60,000 additional documents withheld from the public for over 30 years. This Board published five major findings, one of which speaks clearly to the issue of the autopsy.

Doctors who conducted the autopsy on President John F. Kennedy may have performed two brain examinations in the days following his assassination, possi-

---

65. Groden, *ibid.*, pp. 40-53. Another piece of evidence gathered from medical witnesses at Parkland Hospital deals not with the autopsy inconsistencies but with the magic bullet and fragments thereof. (Recall that the magic bullet theory suggests that the Kennedy and Connally were hit by the same bullet, later found in almost pristine condition on the stretcher at Parkland Hospital.) Anthony Summers reports that far more bullet fragments were removed from John Connally *than could have possibly been attributed to this pristine bullet.* Nurse Audrey Bell, the operating room supervisor, told Summers that she handled "four or five bullet fragments" after their removal from Connally's arm. The smallest, she recalled, was a big as the striking end of a match, the largest twice that size." Dr. Pierre Finck, one of two autopsists, confirms that there were too many fragments found to have come from the so-called "magic bullet." These two Parkland witnesses raise very serious questions regarding whether the bullet found on the stretcher at Parkland could possibly have been the source of both Kennedy and Connally's wounds. A recent, pro-government position on this issue is given in Posner's *Case Closed,* but it does not effectively deal with Bell's and Finck's testimony. According to Summers, "... the Parkland medical staff handed 'more than three' other fragments to a patrolman guarding Connally's room. X-rays, moreover, show that one fragment remained buried in Connally's thigh. The doctors chose to leave it there, and it was still in his body when he died in 1993. Did *all those* fragments really come from the magic bullet? If not, there was more than one assassin in Dealey Plaza." (Source: "The Ghosts of November, *ibid.,* p. 92, 97).
66. *Ibid.,* p. 53. The quote which follows this is from: "Archive Photographs Aren't of JFK's brain, Report Says," *San Francisco Chronicle,* Nov 10, 1998, pA3.
67. Menninger, *Mortal Error, ibid.,* p. 53.

bly of two different brains . . . brain photographs in the Kennedy records are not of Kennedy's brain and show much less damage than Kennedy sustained. [8]

Clearly, the assumption that these suspicious autopsy issues have tried to cover up a frontal shot cannot be easily rejected out of hand.

Ballistics Inconsistencies

An interesting ballistic analysis (an analysis of the character of the bullets and the type of wounds they inflicted) has led one researcher, Howard Donohue, to conclude that different ammunition was involved; that evidence supports the idea that there was more than one shooter. For example, the bullet that coursed through JFK's neck, entered Gov. Connally and wound up on a stretcher in Parkland Hospital, the so-called "pristine bullet," is a full metal-jacketed bullet specifically designed not to fragment or expand.

> But precisely for this reason he could not understand how exactly the same kind of bullet, fired from exactly the same weapon six seconds later, could have exploded in a hail of lead that shattered the President's skull. . . the second round appeared to have acted not as a bullet encased in a thick metal jacket would have but more like a frangible, soft or hollow-nosed missile with a thin metal jacket traveling at extremely high velocity. . . The startling fact was that the bullet that hit Kennedy's head had not behaved like a full metal-jacketed round at all. A great number of tiny lead fragments was characteristic of a completely different kind of bullet. . .

> . . . The bullet that hit him in the head disintegrated completely. We saw nearly forty fragments throughout the right cerebral hemisphere and embedded in the interior of the skull. A lot of them were no bigger than the point of a pen, and the largest was about the size of the nail on your little finger. [68]

Despite the evidence that one of Kennedy's wounds was caused by a heavy metal-jacketed bullet that coursed through his body undamaged, while the other was caused by a frangible bullet that disintegrated on impact, the Warren Commission determined that the Carcano ammunition used by Oswald — all three spent shells found at the Depository — came from the same lot of full metal-jacketed 6.5-millimeter ammunition manufactured by East Alton Illinois-based Western Cartridge Co.

---

68. Menninger, *ibid.*, p. 49 & p. 64.

Ballistics/Autopsy Inconsistencies

There is a further problem in reconciling the ballistics evidence with official autopsy evidence. The official bullets, which hit Kennedy and were certified as coming from Oswald's rifle, were heavy metal jacketed 6.5-millimeter rounds. However, one entrance wound in Kennedy's skull measures only 6 millimeters by 15 millimeters. How Oswald's 6.5 millimeter bullet could cause an entry wound *smaller in diameter* than the bullet itself is an inconsistency that the Warren Commission had to acknowledge. A smaller caliber bullet — like an AR-15 .223 bullet, suggested by one author — might explain the contradiction.

The Warren Commission, intent on keeping the Oswald-as-lone-assassin theory intact, chose instead to suggest that the bone where the entry wound occurred may have "shrunk." Most medical experts doubt this hypothesis, and one pathologist reports that an entrance wound is "always slightly larger than the caliber of the bullet causing it."[69] These findings, of course, suggest that at least one bullet which pierced Kennedy's skull did not come from Oswald's rifle.

Acoustic Evidence of a Fourth Shot

The significance of the putative fourth shot should not be underestimated. Even in an arena this rich in hypotheses that stretch credulity, no one suggests that a lone gunman could have fired more than three shots in the time that elapsed. Indeed, the three-shot theory is already ambitious: it requires Oswald to fire off three rounds in sufficient time to correlate properly with the Zapruder film. In its original tests, the Warren Commission used three professional marksmen and Oswald's rifle to try to duplicate this feat.

> Only one was able to fire three shots within the required amount of time. And none of the group had fired at a moving target.[70]

Later, CBS hired eleven marksmen to try a duplicate effort. Only one was able to *better* the performance. This implies that either Oswald, using this weapon, was the quintessential marksman, or that not all the shots were fired by one gunman. Now, if a fourth shot were fired in this same interval of time, *no one has ever duplicated* that feat, and the existence of a fourth shot surely implies that there was more than one shooter.

---

69. Menninger, *Mortal Error*, New York: St. Martin's Press, 1992, p. 6
70. Menninger, *ibid.*, p. 207

The best evidence that a shot came from in front of the President (from the grassy knoll) comes from the HSCA inquiries held in the late 1970s. JFK archivist Mary Farrel, of Dallas, gave to HSCA Chief Counsel Blakey an audiotape made from a motorcycle patrolman's Dictabelt. Farrel was uncertain what the recording might prove, since its quality was so poor, but she hoped a well-equipped acoustics laboratory might make more sense out of the recording. The HSCA sought recommendations from the Acoustical Society of America and selected the firm of Bolt, Beranek and Newman to analyze the recording. The firm concluded in 1978 that four detectible shots had been discerned from the tape.

> This was a sensational discovery. It was one more shot than the Warren Commission had found, but much more significant was the fact that the third shot followed far too quickly after the second to have been fired by Oswald's weapon. The tape seemed to prove that at least two gunmen fired in Dealey Plaza.[71]

A second, corroborating acoustical analysis was then sought, and two other Acoustical Society of America scientists, Professors Mark Weiss and Ernest Aschkenasy of Queens College, reviewed the evidence. Weiss and Aschkenasy studied echo patterns and concluded that not only were four shots fired, but that the third shot came not from the Depository but from the grassy knoll. The House Select Committee on Assassinations concluded its mandate shortly thereafter and issued its report with the conclusion *that evidence for a fourth shot, and thus a conspiracy, was valid.*

The Justice Department and National Science Association later reviewed this evidence, however, and contradicted it. They said a "delay effect" was noted on the tape, invalidating those conclusions of the committee. More recent reviews (Posner) also challenge the findings of a fourth shot, yet the tell-tale visual "fingerprint" of a fourth shot which has over twenty points of correspondence linking it to a gunshot (and simultaneously differentiating it from any other possible noises, motorcycle backfires, etc.) has not been explained away. That data, in turn, was gathered from the grassy knoll.

Further Evidence of a Fourth Shot: The Zapruder Film

A final piece of evidence suggesting that a fourth shot occurred comes from the Zapruder film. Abraham Zapruder, using his home movie camera, filmed the assassination in its entirety and sold it to *Life Magazine* for $25,000. Only still photos of the

---

71. Oglesby, Carl. *The JFK Assassination: The Facts and the Theories.* New York: Signet, 199, p. 18.

film were ever permitted to be shown to the public until the mid-1970s. One Kennedy researcher noticed that the frames of the Zapruder film had been altered, actually reversed, and when confronted, the FBI apologized that this had occurred — calling it a "printing error." It was precisely this printing "error" that obscured for over a decade the fact that the President is thrown violently *backward* as part of his head explodes, and that the shot that killed him seems to have come from the front.

Revisionism

Great efforts have been made to allege that the President was killed by only one gunman, and thus very difficult matters needed to be explained. For example, if only three shots could have been fired, Connally had to have been hit by a bullet that also hit JFK. The Warren Commission concluded that the first shot did this remarkable feat.

But John Connally disputed this theory and held to his view for years. Still, the Warren Commission and the "magic bullet" theory gained official credence and challenged Connally's own memories. If only three shots could be fired and they had been fired by Oswald, then Connally had to have been hit by the same bullet that hit Kennedy.

There are numerous problems, here. First, the theory has it that Kennedy is shot in the throat by the same bullet which entered Connally. However, "Connally looked normal and did not crumple from his wound until nearly two seconds later."[72] A more specific analysis of the Zapruder film reveals more problems with this single-bullet theory:

> First, a frame-by-frame study of the film showed that Connally was indeed not hit until between 1/2 and 1 1/2 seconds after Kennedy was. Given that the minimum firing time between Carcano shots was 2.3 seconds, the governor's wound came too late to be from the same bullet and too soon to have been a second bullet from the same rifle.

Connally's own testimony to the Warren Commission poignantly makes this point as he attempts to tell Senator Arlen Specter why he believes he was hit by the second shot, not the first shot as the Warren Commission insists:

---

72. Menninger, *ibid.*, p. 2b and pp 40-41.

Photo of the so-called magic or pristine bullet. According to the single bullet theory, the pristine bullet coursed through JFK and Connally's torso and wrist and later found in virtually undamaged condition on a stretcher at Parkland hospital. The bullet to the right is identical to the one Oswald is said to have used and was shot into the wrist of a cadaver. Clearly the two bullets show dramatically different effects.

Source: Warren Commission documents.

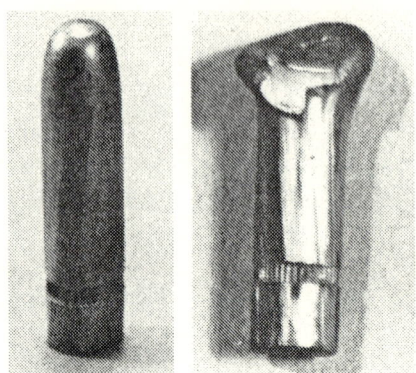

> Well, in my judgment, it just couldn't conceivably have been the first one because I heard the sound of the shot. In the first place, I don't know anything about the velocity of this particular bullet, but any rifle has a velocity that exceeds the speed of sound, and when I heard the sound of that first shot, that bullet had already reached where I was, or had reached that far, and after I heard that shot, I had the time to turn to my right and start to turn to my left before I felt anything. It is not conceivable to me that I could have been hit by the first bullet, and then I felt the blow from something which was obviously a bullet, which I assumed was a bullet, and I never heard the second shot, didn't hear it.[73]

Connally's subjective reactions are corroborated by an analysis of the Zapruder film:

> When the governor comes into view from behind the sign, he turns slightly to his right and then again calmly faces forward, hat in hand, seemingly unhurt. It is not until frame 238, a second and a half later, that Connally reacts to his wound. His shoulder collapses, his cheeks puff out, his hair flies. Critics therefore asked, if a single shot had penetrated Kennedy and Connally, how could this mysterious time lag between the two men's reactions be explained.[74]

The single-bullet theory and all its ramifications have many evidentiary hurdles to mount if they are to be even marginally persuasive. But the Warren Commission appears to have had an incentive to stick to the assertion that there was one shooter with only three shots. These inconsistencies have become more apparent over the years, as people have had more opportunity to think through the twists and turns of logic.

---

73. *Ibid.*
74. *Ibid.*

Other difficulties also had to be explained, particularly, why the President fell backward in the limousine at the rate of many hundreds of feet per second when he was supposed to have been shot from behind. The rationale provided was that a "neuromuscular reflex" propelled the President backward. One UCLA physicist, looking at this conclusion, made the following comments:

> Newton's second law of motion [namely, that the rate of change of momentum is proportionate to the impressed force, and is in the direction in which the force acts] has remained inviolate for three centuries. Not even the advent of relativity and quantum mechanics has disturbed its validity. No physical phenomenon is known that fails to obey it. One of the most immediate consequences is the conservation of momentum; basically the law says that an object hit by a projectile will be given a motion that has the same direction as that of the projectile ... Thus, if someone is shot, and the shot strikes bone, the general direction of recoil will be away from — not toward — the marksman. [75]

In other words, if Kennedy was thrown backward, the shot had to come from his front. Furthermore, a sizable piece of skull was found 10 to 15 feet to the left rear of the limousine.

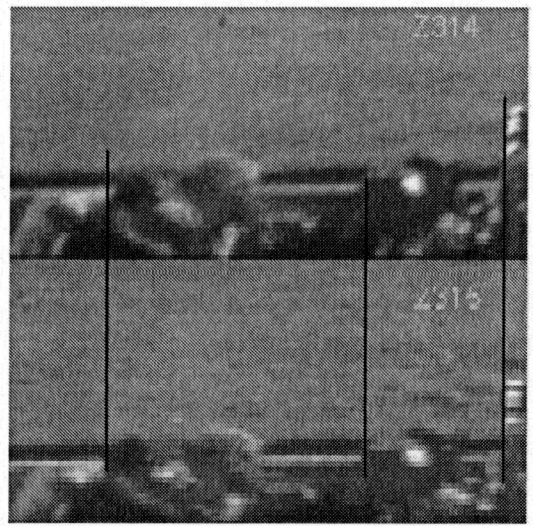

Two motorcycle patrolman had their windshields covered with debris, also to the *left rear* of the car, and a portion of President Kennedy's occipital region was found 25 feet to the left-rear of the vehicle's path — all quite inconsistent with a shot fired from behind.[76] Recall also the famous photo of Mrs. Kennedy crawling out the back of the limousine to retrieve a piece of the President's skull.

Photo: Long-censored photos show President fell backward from frames 314 to 315 of the Zapruder film

---

75. North, *ibid.*, p. 384.
76. *Ibid.*, p. 387.

If tissue was found on the inside of the windshield of the car, as it was, this surely points to a shot coming from behind. Similarly, if a piece of skull was found behind the car, and considerable material was, including a sizeable portion of Kennedy's skull, then it is equally logical to assume this tissue came from a frontal shot.

Thus, in the last generation of inquiry, research on the Kennedy assassination has produced an impressive array of evidence pointing to the existence of a fourth shot and very likely a frontal shot. This represents the first set of evidence suggestive of a conspiracy: (a) 68 witnesses testify that they heard a shot from the grassy knoll; (b) 12 medical personnel at Parkland Hospital testify that their recollections of damage to the back of the President's head contradicted Bethesda autopsy findings and appeared to be an exit, not an entry, wound; (c) two acoustical studies show the presence of four, not three, gunshots; (d) physical debris, skull and brain tissue were found considerably behind the Presidential limousine, suggesting a frontal shot; (e) film evidence and Connally's testimony show both men could not have been hit by the same bullet, thus implying that more than the permissible number of three bullets may have been involved; (f) ballistics evidence suggests different kinds of bullets, frangible vs. heavy metal jacketed, were involved; and (g) photographic evidence shows the President thrown violently backward, likely as a result of a frontal projectile. This represents the best *physical* evidence of second shooter from the grassy knoll area of Dealey Plaza.

(2) Deaths of Witnesses

Many have heard rumors of the loss of lives shortly after the Kennedy assassination and the death of prime witnesses who testified or were to testify before the Warren Commission. Sometimes these deaths are listed in the dozens. Based on the deaths of twenty-one individuals, one actuarial firm calculated that the probability of their combined occurrence was some one trillion to one. Others have called such estimates ridiculous and arbitrary. More tabloid-like exposes have developed lists of names that reach over 200 "unusual deaths."

In a summary of recent literature on the topic, Table 3.2 provides a relatively conservative listing of individuals connected with the Kennedys or Oswald. Any death that seemed to be either directly or indirectly related to the assassination and its major participants is listed. A few of the examples are described below, to give the reader a sense of how names were included.

Chapter 3. Reasonable Doubt

Table 3.2 Deaths associated with the Kennedy Assassination
Deaths are coded M [murder], S [suicide] A [accidental] or N [natural]

1. Action Jackson [M]
2. Banister, Guy [N]
3. Beers, Jack [Unknown]
4. Benavides, Eddy, [M]
5. Bennet, Karen [M]
6. Bogard, Albert [S]
7. Boggs, Hale [A]
8. Bowers, Lee [A]
9. Bowie, A.D. [Unknown]
10. Cabell, Charles [N]
11. Cadigan, James [A]
12. Cain, Richard [M]
13. Carlin, Karen [M]
14. Cheramie, Rose [A]
15. Chesher, Bill [N]
16. Chetta, Nicholas [N]
17. Craig, Roger [S]
18. Crawford, John [A]
19. Davis, Thomas [A]
20. deMohrenschildt, George [S]
21. delVale, Eladio [M]
22. Delaune, Henry [M]
23. Ferrie, David [S,A]
24. Garner, Darrell [A]
25. Gatlin, Maurice [A]
26. Giancana, Sam [M]
27. Goldstein, David [N]

28. Granello, Salvatore [M]
29. Harvey, William [N]

30. Hoffa, Jimmy [M]
31. Howard, Tom [N]
32. Hunt, Dorothy [A]
33. Hunter, William [M]
34. Ingram, Hiram [N]

43. Martin, Frank [N]
44. Martino, John [N]
45. McGann, George [M]
46. McLane, Alfred [A,M]
47. Meyer, Mary Pinchot [M]
48. Milteer, James [A]
49. Moceri, Leo [M]
50. Monroe, Marilyn [S]
51. Nichols, Louis [Unknown]
52. Nicoletti, Charles [M]
53. Oswald, Marguerite [N]
54 Paisley, John [M]
55. Pawley, William [S]
56. Perrin, Robert [Unknown]
57. Pitzer, Lt. Wm. Bruce [S]
58. Plumeri, James [M]
59. Prio, Carlos [S]
60. Roberts, Earline [N]
61. Rogers, Edwina [M]
62. Rogers, Fred [M]
63. Roselli, John [M]
64. Ruby, Jack [N]
65. Russell, Harold [A, M]
66. Saenz, Mona [A]
67. Shaw, Clay [N]
68. Sherman, Dr. Mary [M]
69. Smith, Mrs. Earl T. [Unknown]
70. Staples, Lou [S]
71. State Dept. officer, unnamed [S]
72. Sullivan, William [A]
73. Suydam, Hank [N]
74. Underhill, Gary [S]
75. Wald, Jerry [Unknown]
76. Walle, Marilyn Moore [M]

35. Johnson, Clyde Rev. [M]	77. Walthers, Buddy [M]
36. Kilgallen, Dorothy [S]	78. Ward, Hugh [A]
37. Killam, Thomas Henry [M]	79. Warren, Earl [N]
38. Koethe, Jim [M]	80. Whaley, William [A]
39. Kupcinet, Karyn [M]	81. Wisner, Frank [S]
40. Lowenstein, Allard [M]	82. Worrell, James [A]
41. Macdonald, Betty [S]	83. Yaras, Dave [M]
42. Marcello, Carlos [N]	84. Zangretti, Jack [A] [a]

a. Based on 78 deaths in which cause of death was determined. Most of the deaths in the Kennedy sample occurred in the 1960s and 70s; thus, 1970 norms were used for this chart. Source: New York Times Encyclopedia Almanac, 1970, p. 403. Some deaths were insufficiently documented or otherwise too tangential to be included. One such death was that of Henry Marshall, Agricultural agent, who investigated wrongdoing in the case of President Johnson's friend, Billy Sol Estes. Marshall was found shot to death on a Texas road. The death was ruled a suicide, despite Marshall having been shot 5 times in the head (!). It is a death relevant to the Johnson-based conspiracy theory, but it is not listed here because it occurred before the assassination. Likewise, the death of Benjamin Lewis in Chicago in 1962, is generally attributed to Sam Giancana as a result of his vendetta against Robert Kennedy; but it too is prior to the assassination (See North's text). Jose Aleman, a reluctant witness before the HSCA, who recanted his testimony that Santos Trafficante knew of a contract on JFK, committed suicide in 1983. His death was not included in the list and subsequent statistical analysis, but probably should be. The author learned of this suicide after data analysis had been completed.

Attempted murders also have not been included. Antonio Veciana, a Cuban, told HSCA investigators that the CIA officer involved in the assassination and in numerous activities involving Howard Hunt and Frank Sturgis was named Maurice Bishop. Veciana was shot in the head in late 1979 but survived (Summers, Conspiracy, p. 499). Richard Rudolf Carr saw a heavyset man in the Depository leave in a Rambler station wagon; the FBI told him to keep quiet. He was going to testify in the Jim Garrison inquiry. His apartment in Dallas was searched; later two sticks of dynamite were found under his car. Finally, two men attempted to kill him in Atlanta and he shot them both. The story is quite fascinating and is found in Groden, p. 140.

Another suspicious death which could have been included in this table but was obtained after the statistical analysis had been completed, was that of Dallas policeman Maurice "Monk" Baker. Baker shot himself to death on December 3, 1963 a few weeks after the assassination. He was a friend of Jack Ruby and lived in Oak Cliff on North Beckley, the street where Oswald lived. Source: Livingston, Killing the Truth. Other sources for the list in Table 3.2 come from Crossfire (Jim Marrs), Conspiracy (Anthony Summers) and High Treason (Groden) among others.

Mary Pinchot Meyer

Mary Meyer or Mary Pinchot Meyer, for example, is not a name often cited in the assassination literature, but perhaps ought to be. Kennedy, as will be shown later in this text, had numerous mistresses in the White House. One of his last was Mary Pinchot Meyer, Bobby Kennedy's next-door neighbor. After JFK had broken off ties with Judith Exner, the Mafia-connected bedmate of Sam Giancana, he took up with Mary Meyer.

Mrs. Meyer visited Kennedy in the White House secretly about 20 times between January 1962 and November 1963, sometimes two to three times per week when Mrs. Kennedy was traveling. More than one source says Meyer smoked marijuana with Kennedy in the White House shortly before a major conference on narcotics.[77] She was related to Ben Bradlee of the *Washington Post*, who admitted that he read of Meyer's clandestine visits to the White House in her diary. White House employee Traphes Bryant also kept a diary about these and other White House liaisons.

Mrs. Meyer was murdered in 1964. As of this writing, her murder is still unsolved. Her death was included in this table because it is either directly or indirectly related to the Kennedys or the assassination, and this was the criterion used.

Rose Cheramie

Another death more often cited on these lists is that of Rose Cheramie:

> ... a narcotics addict who was hospitalized near Eunice, Louisiana, during the night of November 20, 1963. A policemen who took custody of her, former Lieutenant Francis Fruge, told me in 1978 that Cheramie said she had been pushed from a car by two men, apparently of Latin extraction. On the way to a hospital, Cheramie — Fruge told me — mentioned that she had heard the two men discussing a plot to kill the President in Dallas. Fruge thought little of this — given that his charge was suffering from withdrawal symptoms — until he heard the news of the President's death. He then arranged to interview Cheramie in hospital as soon as possible. In essence her story was that, as a result of associations while working for Ruby, she was involved in a drug run from Louisiana to Houston, Texas. It was before her two companions dumped her, said Cheramie, that she overheard them discussing an assassination plot. She was also to claim that Ruby knew Lee Oswald. In 1979 an Assassinations Committee report corroborated some aspects of the story. In particular, a former doctor at the hospital, Victor Weiss, recalled being told by a Dr. Bowers that Cheramie had stated before the assassination that President Kennedy was going to be killed. It is Cheramie's supposed comments before the assassination which are of course the most significant aspects of the episode.[78]

Cheramie's two companions appear to be a Cuban exile named "Osanto" and exile activist Arcacha Smith, and linkage with the CIA and David Ferrie occurs between these names. Cheramie did have an obvious relationship to the Kennedy matter. Her death, therefore, is included in this table. A driver who ran over her while she was lying in the road killed Cheramie in 1965 under mysterious circumstances![79]

---

77. Carol Felsenthal, "Portrait of a Marriage," *Vanity Fair*, February, 1993, p. 174.
78. Summers, *ibid.*, p. 591.
79. *Ibid.*

Jerry Wald

Robert Kennedy wrote an early exposé of organized crime, entitled, *The Enemy Within.* Hollywood was considering making a movie of the book, but there were pressures from organized crime not to go ahead with the project. The producer of this controversial film unexpectedly died in his Beverly Hills home, and the film was cancelled. He was 49 years of age. Although this death occurred before the assassination of the President, it is included here as having a direct or indirect link to the Kennedys and a possible Mob involvement.[80]

Dorothy Kilgallen

Many of this author's generation remember Ms. Kilgallen from her frequent television appearances and her daily newspaper column. She had attended the Jack Ruby trial, and as a gossip columnist she had numerous inside sources on Washington matters, similar to the Jack Anderson-Drew Pearson columns with which contemporary Americans are perhaps more familiar.

Ms. Kilgallen told a friend in November 1965 that she had just received information that was going to break the assassination mystery "wide open." She died five days later, and her death ruled a suicide. Her close friend, Mrs. Earl T. Smith also died of "indeterminate causes" two days after Ms. Kilgallen. Ms. Kilgallen's case notes on the Kennedy assassination were never found. Both Mrs. Smith and Ms. Kilgallen's death are listed in the table. Not only had Mrs. Kilgallen been privy to facts about Jack Ruby, but she may also have been prepared to make revelations about Jack and Bobby Kennedy's affairs with Marilyn Monroe.[81]

---

80. For more on Mafia pressures to suppress this movie and the possibility that Wald's death may have been related, see Ronald Goldfarb's *Perfect Villains Imperfect Heroes*, New York, Random House, 1995.

81. Summers, Anthony. *Goddess: The Secret Lives of Marilyn Monroe.* London: Penguin, 1985. A related piece of testimony comes from Marita Lorenz, one-time mistress of Fidel Castro and later a CIA operative with anti-Castro forces in Miami. Lorenz relates a rather chilling conversation she had with Frank Sturgis in 1977. "We were walking down York Avenue," she says, "and Sturgis was bragging about all his exploits. So I asked him, 'Did you kill Alex?' He said 'Alex took too many pictures.' Then he told me, 'We can kill anybody we want. Just blame it on national security.' He said columnist Dorothy Kilgallen 'got whacked' because of her intention to publish a book which included information from her exclusive prison interview with Jack Ruby." With Sturgis spilling the beans so freely, Lorenz cranked up her nerve for the $64,000 question. "I asked him about Kennedy. He says, 'So what if I fucking did it? Who's gonna prove it? I have a fucking alibi. I was home watching television.' And he starts laughing: ha, ha, ha. And he says, 'You missed the big one, Marita,'" (*Vanity Fair*, November, 1993, p. 102).

Chapter 3. Reasonable Doubt

David Ferrie and E. del Valle

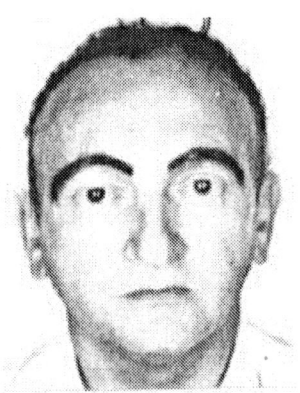

Ferrie (see photo) had severe alopecia and therefore had virtually no body hair. He wore a wig and penciled in his eyebrows. Ferrie was raised a strict Roman Catholic, had studied for the priesthood, and later became a very active homosexual and pedophile. He was a pilot and had smuggled guns to Castro in the 1950s. Some conspiracy literature argues that he was the pilot who brought Carlos Marcello back from Guatemala after Robert Kennedy had deported him. Ferrie was closely allied to the Cuban anti-Castro movement and frequently seen entering Guy Banister's office in New Orleans on Camp Street, the same address that Oswald used when he passed out his "Fair Play for Cuba" literature. When Oswald was arrested for the Kennedy assassination, he was allegedly carrying Ferrie's library card (although that matter has been disputed).

Ferrie was questioned by the FBI shortly after the assassination, not only because of the library card but because an associate of Guy Banister, Jack Martin, had phoned in a tip implicating Ferrie in the killing of President Kennedy. The FBI released Ferrie.

He later came under the suspicion of Jim Garrison, the New Orleans District Attorney. Garrison indicted him in 1967 for the conspiracy to murder President Kennedy. When he heard of the indictment, Ferrie called Garrison's office and said,

> You know what this news story does to me, don't you. I'm a dead man. From here on, believe me, I'm a dead man.

Four days after the indictment, Ferrie was indeed found dead — victim of a massive brain hemorrhage. He left a typewritten note, however, *with a typewritten signature.* The note said,

> ... to leave this life for me, is a sweet prospect. I find nothing in it that is desirable, and on the other hand, everything that is loathsome.[82]

---

82. *Ibid.*

The nature of his death remains questionable; it is listed as a suicide, although murder is also a distinct possibility. That same day, *less than 30 minutes later,* Ferrie's friend and employer E. del Valle (see photo) was found dead in a parking lot in Miami. He had been shot in the heart and his head split open with a hatchet.[83]

State Department Officer

A curious state department officer who is unnamed in the literature went to Mexico to check out a story by an Elena Garro. Garro alleged that Oswald and two companions had attended a party at the home of her relative, Sylvia Duran, a secretary from the Cuban consulate in Mexico City. The Warren Commission tried to investigate the story, and Ms. Garro said she had wanted to come forward with her story shortly after the assassination but that she was "sequestered" in a hotel by a Manuel Calvillo. Garro later refused to testify. One author has indicated that she is suspected of numerous liaisons with CIA sources. A State Department officer tried to investigate the Garro matter in 1964, apparently on his own initiative. He was dismissed, and eventually committed suicide. No further information is given about this death or even his name, but it likewise has been included in the above table.[84]

Other Deaths

Table 3.2 listed 84 deaths related either directly or indirectly to the Kennedy assassination. In very brief synopsis, here is a partial summary of those cases: Marguerite Oswald, Oswald's mother, died of natural causes. Earl Warren, Earline Reynolds, (Oswald's landlady), Jack Ruby, and Guy Banister, the leading suspect in Jim Garrison's New Orleans inquiry, also died of natural causes. Hiram Ingram, Dallas Sheriff, said he had knowledge of a conspiracy. He died of cancer in 1968. William Harvey, a leading CIA suspect who worked on anti-Castro covert assassination activities, died during heart surgery. The photographer who developed the tramp photos from Dealey Plaza died of a heart attack the week after their publication.[85] These are

---

83. Weberman, Alan J. and Canfield, Michael. *Coup D'Etat in America: The CIA and the Assassination of John F. Kennedy.* San Francisco, CA: Quick American Archives, 1992. The quotes in the section on David Ferrie come from Bonar Menninger, *Mortal Error: The Shot the Killed JFK.* New York: St. Martin's Press, 1992, p. 90 and 61 respectively.

84. Summers, *Conspiracy, ibid.,* p. 601

Chapter 3. Reasonable Doubt

the major deaths by natural causes listed in the table. However, there are numerous accidental deaths, murders and suicides that deserve more serious attention.

William Whaley, the cab driver who helped Oswald get away from Dealey Plaza, died in a freak car accident in 1965. James Worrell said he heard a fourth shot and saw a man in a dark sports coat run out of the back of the Depository; he died in a motorcycle accident in 1966. Karyn Kupcinet said she had foreknowledge of the Kennedy assassination, and was a friend of Jack Ruby; she was murdered two days after the assassination. William Hunter, a newsman, wrote a story about Jack Ruby and a year after the assassination he was found shot through the heart in Long Beach, California. Jim Koethe had been at Ruby's apartment the night Ruby shot Oswald. Koethe was later killed with a karate chop to the throat as he came out of a shower in his Dallas apartment, ten months after Kennedy's murder.

James Richard Worrell said he was standing directly below the sixth floor window when he heard a shot. He said "I looked up real quick and saw the barrel fire again. I looked to see where it hit and saw President Kennedy hit. . . Then I looked up and saw it fire a third time. I was 'moving out' by then and didn't see where it hit. I heard four shots, I don't care what they say." After James had run around the Depository, he crossed the street and paused for a moment to catch his breath after a mad dash from the corner. He then leaned against a building. "I saw somebody strike out the back door . . . I just saw his back and couldn't say who it was. He came out and bolted alongside the building parallel to Elm and then he cut to his right. Worrell estimated he had been about 200 feet from this man and was the only one who had reached the rear of the building at that time. . . He described the man he had seen. . . "He looked about 5 feet 7 to 5 feet 10. He looked like he weighed from 155-165 pounds and he had dark hair, a dark sports coat." (This is clearly not Oswald.)

Worrell met his death in 1966 in a motorcycle accident. One of his friend said James' motorcycle was parked on the kickstand and the motor was still running when they found him. James had been found lying in a ditch. Worrell's death is listed in this text and others as a so-called "suspicious death." (Source: Bob Goodman, *Triangle of Fire*, San Jose, CA: Laquerian Publishing, 1993, pp. 122-123.)

---

85. Jack Beers of the *Dallas Morning News* took two photographs of the tramps arrested after the assassination. Weberman says the tramp photos were altered. Beers died of a heart attack a week after the photographs were published (Feb. 16, 1975); Weberman, *ibid*, p. 73.

Wanda Joyce Killam, who worked for Ruby, found her husband, Thomas Henry Killam, murdered four months after the assassination; his throat was cut. Marilyn Moore Walle, a dancer employed by Jack Ruby, had planned to write a book on the assassination; she was shot to death September 1, 1966. Another of Ruby's strippers, Teresa Norton (*aka* Carlyn Bennet), was shot to death in Houston ten months after the assassination. Harold Russel, a witness to Officer Tippit's murder, said he was "going to be hit;" he was killed by a policeman in 1967. Lee Bowers, the railroad control tower official behind the grassy knoll, died in a car crash in 1966.

Many individuals involved with the Jim Garrison investigation also died (besides David Ferrie, Clay Shaw, and Guy Banister). Nicholas Chetta, for example, the New Orleans coroner, performed the autopsy on David Ferrie and was prepared to testify at the Garrison investigation; prior to testifying, in 1968, he died of a heart attack. His brother-in-law Dr. Henry Delaune was murdered less than a year later. Dr. Mary Sherman, similarly connected to David Ferrie, was found shot in the head and set afire.

Gary Underhill, a former CIA agent, left Washington shortly after the assassination. He said that the Far Eastern Group of the CIA was involved in the President's murder. He was shot execution-style in the left side of his head six months after Kennedy's death. The death was ruled a suicide, even though Underhill was right handed.

There is an incredible list of Mafia-connected murders linked directly or indirectly with the Kennedys. Johnny Roselli, the Mafia figure who is said to have quietly arranged a Kennedy divorce and had been in on the CIA-Mafia plots to kill Castro, was found quartered and floating in a drum off the coast of Miami. Sam Giancana who had personal contacts with Kennedy and visited him in the White House was shot to death; also murdered were Action Jackson, Salvatore Granello, Jimmy Hoffa, John Martino, Leo Mocieri, and Charles Nicoletti. Jack Ruby called a Hoffa thug named Barney Baker shortly before the assassination; Baker, in turn, contacted Dave Yaras of Miami on November 21. Yaras was later murdered as well.[86]

Each of these stories is really a novel in its own right, the seeds of a great murder mystery (or serial murder mystery), full of intrigue, suspicion, drama, innuendo and, obviously, conspiracy. However, such an anecdotal approach is of very little value in proving or disproving anything. Is there some pattern or meaning to these deaths? Is

---

86. Aside from the calls Ruby made to Barney Baker, the calls Barney Baker made after he talked to Ruby represent another set of connections. Baker called David Yaras in Miami on Nov. 21, 1963. Yaras had been suspected by Bobby Kennedy of corrupting a Teamsters' local in the Miami area. Yaras had numerous arrests for burglary and murder (Kantor, *ibid.*, p. 74). (Marrs, Jim. *Crossfire: The Plot that Killed Kennedy.* New York: Carroll & Graf, 1989.)

there some way we can understand these deaths beyond merely gossiping about them or drawing out inappropriate or even arbitrary connections?

Consider the warning of pro-Warren Commission author Jim Moore. Moore says Dorothy Kilgallen died of an overdose of drugs and alcohol, and the simple fact that she had attended Ruby's trial was no basis for including her on the list of "suspicious deaths." In addition, Moore states that few have bothered to explain why "fringe" witnesses are being placed on such lists while those really connected with the crime are ignored:

> Howard Brennan, who saw Oswald fire the fatal shot, lived twenty years after the assassination. I can pick up my telephone and call Oswald's wife. The detective handcuffed to Oswald when the assassin was shot by Jack Ruby, J.R. Leavelle, is a personal friend. Phil Willis, who may have taken the most important photo related to the assassination, is still alive and well. Jack Ruby's brother still makes newspaper headlines here in Dallas.[87]

Moore's objections should be heeded as we pursue this topic. Statistics are often misleading, and a naive interpretation of the evidence will not prove whether there was a conspiracy. Deputy Sheriff Roger Craig killed himself; he was a major figure in the assassination inquiry. A CIA officer in charge of a high-ranking KGB defector who crossed sides to say that Oswald was not a Soviet mole killed himself under mysterious circumstances. These pieces of evidence are the stuff of enticing television programs, but they do not constitute any serious evidence proving a conspiracy. We could also make a table of witnesses to the assassination *who are still alive*, and such a table would neither make news headlines nor be of much interest.

Statistical Analysis

The assemblage of data in the table takes on significance only through statistical analysis. If these deaths were related to the Kennedy assassination only as "coincidences" or artifacts of some sort, the statistical analysis would at some point reveal the lack of genuine connectedness. *It does not.*

"Cause of death" is a major variable. Of the 84 names listed, cause of death was identifiable in 78. There were 29 murders, 19 accidental deaths, 13 suicides, and 17 deaths from natural causes. When these deaths are compared to mortality rates in the general population, they add up to one of the leading pieces of circumstantial evidence that Kennedy was killed as part of a conspiracy. By comparison, if we put together lists of 78 individuals randomly selected from obituary columns across the nation, sta-

---

87. Moore, *ibid.*, p. 87.

tistically we could expect to need over 10,000 such samples before we could find one that would show murder rates 37 times the national average, accident rates 2.5 times the national average, suicide rates 17 times the national average and natural causes of death less than a third the national average.

We can compare these statistics with the 1970 national norms.[88] The murder rate in the general population was under 1%, but the murder rate of this 78-person sample is 37%. About 9% of deaths in the United States were caused by accidents; in this sample, the rate is more than double that, 23%. Perhaps 1% of the United States population dies by suicide, but this sample shows 17%. Probably the most important statistic is the least dramatic — namely, natural causes. The national average was 89% from natural causes (heart attack, cancer, etc.); but in this sample only 22% died of natural causes. This is not only startling; *statistically, it is enormously atypical and significant.*

Figure 3.1 makes this point more clearly. The individuals who make up this sample have only one thing in common: They are directly or indirectly related to the Kennedys and the assassination. The measure by which we calculate "differences" from what is normally expected is called Chi Square. The

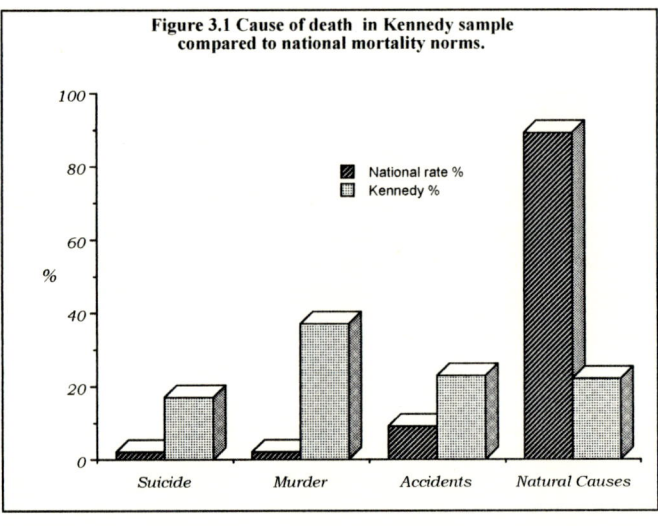

Chi Square statistic reveals that the Kennedy sample is tremendously at odds with national norms. The probability that this variation could simply be the result of coincidence, chance or random occurrence is less than one in 10,000. This suggests that there is some anomalous factor, something extraordinary, that would account for the distribution of the causes of these deaths.

Sheriff Roger Craig's suicide in 1966 may have been the result of depression and alcoholism, unrelated to the Kennedy matter. David Ferrie's death may have been caused by a brain hemorrhage and have had nothing to do with the ruminations of Jim Garrison's conspiratorial obsessions with the Kennedy killing. Marilyn Monroe's sui-

---

88. *World Almanac*, New Jersey, Funk & Wagnalls, 1975.

cide may have been the result of a long, slow, and gradual unfolding of a personality disorder, which had little to do with Kennedy's assassination or any international or national conspiracy. But statistical analysis of these and the other deaths in question shows that they share an anomalous feature that is statistically significant; they share some common characteristic that sets them apart from "normal" deaths.

However much we might like to explain away each death individually or idiopathically — and Gerald Posner's *Case Closed* makes the best attempt at that — the global relationship of these deaths points to something aberrant, to something far outside the realm of chance. These deaths *in toto* are wholly at odds with the pattern of death that occurs in the United States, and that discrepancy is the single best circumstantial evidence that Kennedy's death involves a conspiracy. The *cause* of death of individuals who had a direct or indirect linkage to the Kennedys sketches a pattern that is so unusual, so atypical, so statistically significant, that it suggests a conspiracy.

There are many unstudied and un-researched parameters in this table of suspicious deaths. Average age at time of death, for example, in a random sample of 78 Americans in that time period would have been close to the mid-60s and 70s; but very few of the people in this sample reached their normal life expectancy. Jerry Wald was 48; Marilyn Monroe, 36; Jack Ruby, 54; James Worrel, 23. The mean age at time of death is a dozen years earlier than what might be expected based on actuarial data. This is striking — in fact, shocking.

If the sample were "normal" or "neutral," that is, if the fact of being linked to the Kennedy assassination did not increase the likelihood that they would have an early death, then we can compare the sample to any other set of people who just happen to share a relationship (however indirect) to any other person or event. Say we had a list of individuals who directly or indirectly knew Elvis Presley. Let us further assume that 78 of these friends, neighbors, acquaintances, doctors and advisors had died over the last two decades. One might have committed suicide, another in a car accident, etc.; but when we gather together the causes of death of these 78 persons, we would not expect to see any significant variation from the normal distribution of causes of death in the general population (and if we did find such a discrepancy, we would look further to find out why — did these individuals on average use more alcohol than the average American, or show any other characteristic that might lead to earlier deaths?). The Kennedy data shows deaths that are in *extreme* statistical variance with the pattern of death in the United States, and it is this fact that has eluded researchers up to this point as a *sine qua non* of conspiracy theory.

The whole is bigger than the sum of its parts. Marilyn Monroe allegedly died by suicide prior to the Kennedy assassination; it seems rather ludicrous to consider her death part of the assassination conspiracy. William Sullivan, a major advisor to J.

Edgar Hoover and an individual suspected of being part of the FBI's own cover-up operations, died in a hunting accident. Lieutenant Commander William Pitzer, who had been present at Kennedy's autopsy and had taken photos of the autopsy committed suicide in 1966.[89]

> Pitzer's family and friends believed that he had been murdered, that he had no reason to commit suicide, and had been badly frightened by repeated threats because of what he knew.[90]

Marilyn Monroe had no association with Mr. Sullivan and probably never met Commander Pitzer. One by one, their deaths can be explained. However, taken together, their deaths all belong to a very skewed, significantly atypical statistical sample that is extremely unlikely to occur at random or by coincidence, and that in itself must raise questions.

Unusual Accidents

Figure 3.1 reveals even more fascinating oddities. Let's focus on "accidental death." Nationwide, about 9% of deaths per year are expected to arise from accidents, mostly auto accidents. But here, accidental deaths represent 23% of the entire sample — three times the national average; and they are statistically atypical and unusual, even freakish, in nature.

Hugh Ward, the partner of Guy Banister (whom Jim Garrison had tried to indict for the murder of President Kennedy), belongs to this group. He was killed in a private plane crash just before Garrison could question him.

Maurice Brooks Gatlin, another associate of Guy Banister, was the legal counsel to the Anti-communist League of the Caribbean. He fell out a window in Panama in 1964. Just an accidental death, but one which would cause a statistician or an investigator to begin raising an eyebrow.

James Milteer, the ultra right-wing fanatic who was planning the assassination of the President, according to information gathered by FBI wiretapping, died when a heater exploded.

---

89. In 1998, the Assassination Records Board concluded its business and released some 60,000 additional documents. Many were still heavily redacted, but of the five major findings from this release, the Review Board "found evidence that a second set of autopsy photographs — their whereabouts still unknown — was made of the wounds suffered by President Kennedy." This information raises questions about the circumstances surrounding Pitzer's death. See "Secrecy Faulted on JFK Killing." *San Francisco Chronicle*, September 29, 1998, p A4.

90. Groden, *ibid.*, p. 96.

William Sullivan, the FBI official already mentioned, died when someone mistook him for a deer and shot him.

Thomas Davis, a gunrunner who had a connection to both Jack Ruby and the CIA, told his wife that he knew who killed Kennedy. He died by electrocution while trying to steal wire from a supply dump.[91]

John Crawford was a close friend to both Jack Ruby and Wesley Frazier (the man who gave Oswald a ride on November 22, 1963 to the Depository). Crawford died in a private plane crash.

Even those few that are listed as vehicular accidents are strange: Rose Cheramie was run over by a car "while lying on the road." A Dallas bus hit Mona Saenz, the Texas employment clerk who interviewed Oswald, 17 months after the assassination.[92] That appears to be the only "normal" accidental death. All the others are unusual enough to raise suspicion. The deviations from statistical probability in this sub-sample alone paint a picture that is very far from "normal" in any sense.

Airline disasters, particularly commercial airline fatalities, are extremely rare. The probability in 1973 of dying in a commercial airline accident was 1/10,000. In the Kennedy sample, Congressman Hale Boggs and Dorothy Hunt both died — in two separate crashes. Both airline accidents were considered suspicious and were investigated by the FAA. Hale Boggs was the only Warren Commission member to reject the Commission's findings, and he demanded that a footnote be placed in the report before he signed it. He signed it, but the footnote was never included.[93] Dorothy Hunt was the wife of E. Howard Hunt, the Watergate conspirator and former CIA agent. Hunt was the CIA station chief in Mexico City at the time Oswald allegedly went to Mexico before the assassination. One conspiracy researcher alleged that Dorothy Hunt was carrying papers that implicated Richard Nixon in the JFK assassination. The plane crash that took her life occurred at the time of the Watergate episode that involved her husband.

It matters little if the conspiracy researchers are correct about plots to kill Hale Boggs or any plot to kill Dorothy Hunt, or what Hunt may have been doing or not

---

91. Another admission regarding the Kennedy assassination came from an elusive figure, Thomas Eli Davis III. Jack Ruby had stated to Ray McKeown that he was planning on entering a deal with Davis. Davis was a charming, tall Texan who was entangled in anti-Castro efforts. Davis got involved in CIA activities. He had been in jail in Algiers, charged with gunrunning. In September 1973, Davis was attempting to steal three-quarter-inch copper wire from an abandoned rock yard when he was electrocuted and died. Davis's widow, his third wife, said he rarely told her about where or what he was doing, but he did say to her that, "he knew the man who killed the President" (Kantor, *ibid.*, p. 46).

92. Marrs, *ibid.*, p. 559.

93. TV commentator Cokie Roberts is the daughter of the late Hale Boggs.

doing on the day Kennedy was shot. What is argued here is the dizzying improbability of these two events occurring in a single sample of 78 people.

If an epidemiologist were hired to look at the pattern of death in a particular neighborhood to see if there were any toxins or unusual environmental pollutants which might be affecting the community's health, the first thing he or she would do would be to investigate causes of death and patterns of mortality. If children were dying from kidney failure at rate 10 percent greater than the national norms, or developing leukemia 20 percent more frequently than expected, a warning would be issued immediately and experts would try to find out what was wrong; they would seek to isolate the particular toxin that was affecting the community. In the Kennedy context, there is also something "wrong," and "conspiracy" is the best term anyone has come up with to describe the unlimited possibilities of just what that is.

In the Kennedy sample, the patterns of mortality and accidental mortality are incredibly skewed from normal expectations; no epidemiologist would call this data a statistical fluke. To walk away from this sample and dismiss it as some kind of statistical artifact would be quintessential epidemiological malpractice.

(3.) Death of Witnesses Prior to Government Hearings

In 1977, the House Select Committee on the Assassination of President Kennedy (HSCA) was formed under the chairmanship of Henry Gonzalez; it issued its final report in 1979. It called a number of witnesses, many of whom were never called by the Warren Commission. Prior to this, the Senate Intelligence Committee held similar hearings. In the course of these investigations, many of the witnesses died — in fact, an astonishing number, and rarely were the causes of death natural. Our third criterion of "best evidence" that the Kennedy assassination involved a conspiracy involves the untimely death of these individuals. Each is briefly described. These deaths have already been listed in Table 3.2 but insofar as they cluster about specific dates tied to these hearings, they are treated here more directly.

George deMohrenschildt

Lee Harvey Oswald made a friend after he had returned from the Soviet Union. He was Russian-born Dallas resident Baron George deMohrenschildt. The deMohrenschildts helped the Oswalds re-orient to the United States after their arrival, and Oswald and the "Baron" often had quiet chats about politics and the international situation at the deMohrenschildts' residence. According to deMohrenschildt, Lee was an admirer of Kennedy and never said anything hostile or derogatory about the President in all the time he knew him.

Chapter 3. Reasonable Doubt

DeMohrenschildt had numerous prior involvements with the CIA and U.S. Army Intelligence. He was an eccentric and toward the end of his life appeared to become increasingly emotionally labile. The Baron did not believe Oswald shot Kennedy and had prepared a manuscript entitled *I'm a Patsy*. An investigator for the Assassinations Committee called to arrange an interview, but on the morning it was scheduled to take place, the Baron was found dead in his home, shot through the mouth with a 20-gauge shotgun. [94]

Carlos Prio

Prio was alleged to be a top Mafia figure and had been the President of Cuba from 1948 until 1952, when
he was deposed. He had also been linked to Jack Ruby and former Watergate conspirator and CIA operative Frank Sturgis. He was listed as a witness the Assassinations Committee wanted to interview. A week after Baron deMohrenschildt's suicide, Prio also killed himself.

> Prio was seated in a chair, with a pistol beside him, outside the garage of his Miami home. The verdict was suicide. [95]

Charles Nicoletti

The Assassinations Committee staff had also listed Charles Nicoletti as a witness to interview. Nicoletti was involved in the CIA plan to execute Fidel Castro. He may have been connected to Eugene Hale Brading, who was held for questioning on November 22, 1963. On the day *before* the Assassinations Committee planned to contact Nicoletti, he was found in a Chicago parking lot with three bullet wounds in the back of his head. His foot was jammed against the accelerator, causing the engine to overheat. The car burned and obliterated any possible fingerprints or other material evidence that could have been of use in solving this murder.

---

94. Summers, *Conspiracy*, ibid.
95. *Ibid.*, p. 493.

Sam Giancana

Chicago Mafia boss Sam Giancana began as a driver for Al Capone. By the early 1960s, he had ascended to be one of the most powerful Mafia dons in the United States. He received between $65,000 and $300,000 in monthly proceeds from gambling operations in Las Vegas alone,[96] but he had his hands in many more criminal activities as well. His girlfriend, Judith Exner, was also involved with President Kennedy, and Giancana is alleged to have had many contacts with JFK's father Joseph Kennedy.

Giancana putatively attempted to kill Fidel Castro; the Senate Intelligence Committee had asked to question him about the CIA's scheme to get Castro. A few days after that interview, Giancana was found dead, shot once in the back of the head and six times in a neatly stitched circle around the mouth. Obviously, someone did not want Sam "Mooney" Giancana to talk any more than he had already.

Leo Moceri

Moceri told a government agent that Giancana and Hoffa were murdered in order to stop them from talking about CIA-Mafia plots and associations. Moceri was an Ohio syndicate figure who had had one meeting with a government agent. After his second meeting, Moceri vanished, and his car was found abandoned. Moceri, like Nicoletti, had been in Dallas and allegedly was associated with Eugene Hale Brading.[97]

John Roselli

Roselli was a Las Vegas gangster alleged to have taken a leading role in CIA assassination plots. Hoffa, Trafficante, Roselli and Carlos Marcello were very disturbed over Bobby Kennedy's attacks on organized crime. Numerous rumors persisted that a Mafia contract had been ordered on the President, primarily to remove Bobby from his aggressive role as Attorney General. Roselli had informed the government that he believed his former associates in the Castro assassination schemes had gone on to murder President Kennedy. Shortly

---

96. Goldfarb, *ibid.*, p. 130.
97. Craig, John R. & Rogers, Philip A. *The Man on the Grassy Knoll*. New York: Avon Books, 1992, p. 194.

after these meetings, Roselli dined with Santos Trafficante. When the Senate Intelligence Committee sought to reach Roselli, he was out of reach in Costa Rica. Roselli was last seen alive on a boat owned by an associate of Trafficante. In July, 1976, Roselli's body was found floating in a container near Miami, shackled, stabbed, quartered, and squashed into an oil drum.

Regis Kennedy

Kennedy was a senior agent in the FBI assigned to New Orleans; but he informed the Assassinations Committee in 1978 that Carlos Marcello, the alleged Mafia boss in New Orleans, was not affiliated to organized crime and was a tomato salesman. Regis Kennedy died shortly after testifying before the Committee. Kennedy is said to have confiscated a film of the assassination taken by what conspiracy researchers call "The Babushka lady." (The film was seized before anyone ever viewed it, and was never recovered.) "Regis Kennedy directed one of those [sleuths] assigned to investigate the original allegation that Marcello had uttered threats against the President's life. He died in 1978." [98]

William Sullivan

William Sullivan was one of J. Edgar Hoover's top aides, originally, then had a falling out with the Director. He was scheduled to be questioned by the Assassinations Committee in 1978. As mentioned earlier, he was found shot dead having been mistaken for a deer. He had been head of the FBI's Division Five, which handled the King and Kennedy investigations.

William Pawley and John Paisley

Pawley was a former American diplomat who had allegedly collaborated with Mafia figure John Martino in the CIA operation to prove that Soviet missiles were still in Cuba. Pawley was instrumental in persuading Clare Boothe Luce of *Time-Life* to finance anti-Castro operations. During the Congressional inquiry into the Kennedy assassination, Pawley shot himself.

John Paisley was a CIA operative who had been in charge of KGB defector Yuri Nosenko. Nosenko was the KGB agent in charge of Oswald when Oswald lived in the USSR. Paisley died under mysterious circumstances at the time of these hearings, but his death ruled a suicide. [99]

---

98. Summers, *ibid.*, p. 497.

John Martino

Martino is revealed in an FBI report to have been a close personal friend of Santos Trafficante.[100] An associate of William Pawley, Martino died at this same time of an apparent heart attack; his wife disputed that conclusion. Martino claimed personal knowledge of the plot to kill the President. He said,

The anti-Castro people put Oswald together. Oswald didn't know who he was working for — he was just ignorant of who was really putting him together. Oswald was to meet his contact at the Texas theater (the movie house where Oswald was arrested) in what appears to have been a setup to kill him while he would try to escape. There was no way we could get to him. They had Ruby kill him.[101]

All these witnesses were to testify, had already testified, or were to be called back for additional testimony. Their deaths are all listed in the table; they cluster about a very specific period of time, the hearings before the Senate Intelligence Committee and HSCA. No statistical argument is raised here, but the curious nature and the timing seems noteworthy. Only one came from natural causes (heart attack), and even that was disputed.

---

99. Paisley was a CIA executive whose wife alleges that he had been placed in charge of Soviet KGB defector Yuri Nosenko. Nosenko said he administered the Oswald file for the KGB and asserted Oswald was not a Soviet agent. Other CIA personnel thought Nosenko was a Soviet plant (Helms, Angleton). In 1978, the House Assassinations Committee broke the story of Nosenko's defection. A week later, Paisley's boat was found — empty. A body washed to shore, which was badly bloated; it was identified as Paisley; and it had been weighted down with ballast. The death was ruled a suicide. Paisley's son found his father's apartment badly disturbed and ransacked. Further, Mrs. Paisley sharply disputes the matter, even alleging that the body that floated to shore was not that of her husband. Her husband had a beard, whereas the badly bloated body was bald and had no beard; furthermore, it was not the right height. This death occurred at the time of the HSCA hearings. Ogelsby, *ibid.*, p. 169. CIA agent Victor Marchetti said that Paisley was murdered because he was "about to blow the whistle." (Groden, *ibid.*, p. 330.)

100. Summers, *ibid.*, p. 426.

Table 3.3 Suspicious Deaths of HSCA and Senate Intelligence Committee Witnesses

Name	Cause of Death	Association	Date
George deMohrenschildt	Suicide	CIA	1977
Carlos Prio	Murder	Mafia	1977
Charles Nicoletti	Murder	Mafia	1977
Sam Giancana	Murder	Mafia	1975
Leo Moceri	Murder	Mafia	1975-76
John Roselli	Murder	Mafia	1976
Regis Kennedy*	Natural causes	FBI	1978
William Sullivan	Shooting accident	FBI	1978
William Pawley	Suicide	State Dept.	1977
John Paisley	Suicide/Murder	CIA	1977
John Martino	Natural causes	CIA?	1977

* Regis Kennedy's death would be considered curious, not suspicious, due to the coincidence with his HSCA interview.

101. Groden, ibid., pp. 145-146. The story of John Martino has taken on greater significance in recent years. Martino was a close friend of Trafficante. He also had contacts with the CIA and FBI agent William Robertson. Martino had been in touch with former US ambassador William Pawley, a champion of Cuban exiles. Martino also worked closely with Trafficante's liaison with the CIA, John Roselli. Anthony Summers interviewed Martino's widow in Miami, aged 80. Her oldest child, Edward, lived with her. The following account is given by Summers: "on November 22, 1963, 'John insisted he wanted to paint the breakfast room,' Florence recalled. 'We were supposed to go out to the Americana for lunch... But it was on the radio about Dallas... We were talking about President Kennedy; and he said 'Flo, they're going to kill him. They're going to kill him when he gets to Texas.'" Florence questioned her husband briefly, got no meaningful response, and went out for a while. She was home again by the time Edward, who was 17, heard the news of the assassination on television. "'When I called them in,' he remembered, 'my father went white as a sheet. But wasn't like 'Gee whiz'; it was more like confirmation. Then John was on the phone... 'Florence remembered. 'He got I don't know how many calls from Texas. I don't know who called him, but he was on the phone, on the phone, on the phone...'"

Martino also met with a Newsday reporter, John Cummings, a few times. He said that "there had been two guns, two people involved." Cummings stayed in touch with Martino until his death in 1975. He said to Cummings that he was ailing, and Cummings came to his home. "He told me he'd been part of the assassination of Kennedy. He wasn't in Dallas pulling the trigger, but he was involved. He implied that his role was delivering money, facilitating things... He asked me not to write it while he was still alive."

Martino's version is that Oswald was involved with another shooter who was in the Texas Theater when Oswald was arrested. "There was a Cuban in there. They let him come out. They let the guy go, the other trigger."

A further claim came out of this conversation with Cummings. Martino told him "he had himself met Oswald several weeks before the assassination, in Miami. He said an FBI agent named Connors asked him to come to a boat docked in Biscayne Bay, and introduced him to Oswald by name. The impression John got was that Oswald didn't know his ass from his elbow, didn't know what he was involved in."

Summers also indicates that numerous pages, which refer to Martino, have been withdrawn from the Kennedy-assassination collection at the National Archives at the insistence of the CIA and FBI. (Summers, "The Ghosts of November," Vanity Fair, December, 1994, p. 112.

This clustering of deaths in the mid-1970s is a third piece of "best evidence" that it is not ridiculous to speculate that there was a conspiracy to kill President John Fitzgerald Kennedy. It is doubtful that American history can produce any other comparable concentration of deaths of witnesses called before a government committee.

(4.) The Cover Up

"There's other things involved that are detrimental to other things."[102]
— Regis Blahut, CIA officer,
explaining why he was stealing autopsy photos, 1978

Three pieces or groups of data have been presented thus far to suggest that a conspiracy is a justifiable conclusion: (1) There is physical evidence suggestive of a frontal shot to the President; (2) The causes of death of over 78 individuals connected with JFK or the assassination are statistically anomalous; and (3) A startling sum of eleven deaths are clustered about two sets of government hearings on the Kennedy assassination in the mid-1970s.

The fourth pillar supporting the theory of the existence of a conspiracy is more psychological in nature. It is fair to assume that if one invests a great deal of time and energy defending oneself and/or covering up one's tracks, there is probably something genuine to defend against or to cover up. The fact that there was a cover up after the assassination indicates that something existed that needed to be shielded from view; a significant cover-up effort becomes an indirect piece of evidence that a conspiracy existed.

Data on 62 individuals linked to a cover-up, who withheld information, or who failed to come forward is provided in Table 3.4, below. This database is so large and wide in scope it is almost impossible to summarize. Cover-up activities, witnesses who refuse to testify or speak, or actions taken by others to withhold information can be found from Hollywood to Washington, from the CIA to the darkest circles of the underworld. In the following table only the most reliable data has been included and many wilder, more irresponsible assertions have been omitted.

The table is generally representative of what is contained in the most widely recognized "conspiracy" texts. The information is merely summarized here; this author does not maintain that it is inherently corroborated or valid. A discussion follows, analyzing some of the ways this data might be sifted to render some meaningful conclusions and to try to determine what is bona fide and reliable.

---

102. Summers, *Conspiracy*, ibid., p. 426.

Table 3.4 Significant individuals named in the literature as withholding information or engaged in disinformation about the assassination

1. Alsop, Joseph. Newspaper columnist, aware of Kennedy infidelities (some of which occurred in his own home), did not disclose such information for many years after Kennedy's death. [a]
2. Angleton, James; CIA counterintelligence agent alleged by H.R. Haldeman to have erased all connections between CIA and Oswald (Groden, p. 333); suspected of shredding a document which showed Howard Hunt (of Watergate fame) present at Dallas on November 22, 1963.[b] Angleton also crossed paths with Mary Pinchot Meyer. Mrs. Meyer visited the White House on numerous occasions and was mysteriously murdered in 1964. James M. Truitt, a close friend of Mrs. Meyer and a correspondent for the *Washington Post*, reported that her diary had been destroyed by CIA official James Angleton.[c] Angleton is also thought to have withheld information on the death of John Paisley.  A final incident was that of Winston Scott, former CIA station chief in Mexico. Scott was furious about the premature closing down of the Mexico-Oswald investigation, placed a memorandum in his safe, alleged held a photo of Oswald in Mexico City (not apparently Oswald). Upon Winston Scott's death, Angleton personally removed the contents of Scott's safe.[d] The CIA denied it possessed such a photo before the Warren Commission or the HSCA in 1978. Angleton also alleged to have had access to or possessed a photo of J. Edgar Hoover having oral sex with his longtime companion, Clyde Tolson; Angleton aware that mob figures used this information to "fix" Hoover from persecuting mob--never revealed to Warren Commission or subsequent inquiries.[e]
3. Anonymous; a senior FBI agent who wished to have his identity concealed, admitted to author Summers that the FBI removed telephone numbers from Marilyn Monroe's bill. "I was on a visit to California when Monroe died, and there were some people there, Bureau personnel, who normally wouldn't have been there — agents from out of town. They were on the scene immediately, as soon as she died, before anyone realized what had happened. I subsequently learned that agents had removed the records." [f]
4. Arledge, Roone, past president of ABC, and executive producer Av Westin both played a role in censoring a "20/20" documentary on Marilyn Monroe and her relationship to Kennedy. The specific parts they wanted cut were references to Kennedy and Giancana, and Kennedy's relationship with Judith Exner (Campbell), among others. Suppression of this program became national news. [g]

Table 3.4 *Significant individuals named in the literature as withholding information or engaged in disinformation about the assassination*

5. Belin, David, Chief Counsel to the Warren Commission; numerous witnesses accused Belin of changing their testimony for the final report, including Dallas policeman Roger Craig. He was apparently responsible as well for failing to include Hale Boggs' objection to the Warren Commission conclusions in the form of a footnote in the final draft, as Boggs requested. Belin was once chairman of lawyers for Nixon-Agnew. [h]
6. Bissell, Richard; withheld information on CIA plots to kill Castro. One of those fired by Kennedy after the Bay of Pigs fiasco, along with Allen Dulles and General Cabell. Bissell was CIA's deputy for planning, had recruited Roselli, Giancana and Trafficante to assassinate Castro offering $150,000 bounty. [i]
7. Blahut, Regis; CIA liaison officer with HSCA — fired for trying to steal autopsy photo from HSCA files.
8. Bradlee, Ben; publisher of the *Washington Post*. Knew of Kennedy's liaisons with women, including Mary Pinchot Meyer, yet never revealed this information at the time of the assassination or during later government inquiries. Was aware that James Angleton of the CIA broke into Meyer's apartment after her death and similarly did not come forward with this information at the time of the Senate and House investigations.
9. Buckley, William F; conservative columnist, historically negative toward any conspiracy theory of the assassination. Conspiracy literature cites Buckley as allegedly having undisclosed CIA ties, and ties with Howard Hunt (the operative), and, through Pantipec Oil, having worked "on a deep-cover operation in Mexico in the early 1950's. Buckley's parents owned Pantipec Oil." Buckley also may have been associated with deMohrenschildt, Oswald's friend in Dallas who killed himself shortly before being interviewed by HSCA.[j] Whether Buckley withheld information or sincerely was opposed to the perceived paranoia of conspiracists is a matter of debate.
10. Burkley, George; Navy admiral to whom autopsy notes were ultimately forwarded; also was present at autopsy and aware of photographic evidence. The President's missing brain, failure to preserve film and photos taken at autopsy, pressures on Dr. Humes to destroy his notes. . . all of these issues had a connection to Admiral Burkley's authority over autopsy doctors. Burkley has never been called to "answer any questions about anything." [k]
11. Cabell, Gen. Charles; fired by Kennedy; was involved in CIA plots to kill Castro; his brother, Earle Cabell, was mayor of Dallas at the time of the assassination and was in the motorcade with the President. Cabell is cited in many texts as a suspect in the assassination. Cabell may have been the CIA operative who canceled the air strikes in support of the Bay of Pigs operation for which Kennedy ultimately took blame; other texts dispute this assertion.[l] Assertions of Cabell's role in withholding any information are not considered reliable.
12. Castro, Fidel. His Cuban counsel in Mexico City, Luisa Calderon, allegedly heard Oswald make death threats against JFK. After the assassination she returned to Cuba, and although Castro has submitted to questions about the assassination, he has never made Calderon available for interviews about her experiences (See J. Hosty, *ibid*).
13. Cesar Diosdado, a known anti-Castro exile with allegedly important CIA contacts. Refused to talk to HSCA investigators.

Table 3.4 *Significant individuals named in the literature as withholding information or engaged in disinformation about the assassination*

14. De Brueys, Warren; New Orleans FBI agent denied he had contact with Oswald; facts were subsequently proven otherwise.
15. Dulles, Allen, former CIA Director, member of Warren Commission; refused to testify for Garrison on Clay Shaw, David Ferrie; kept mum on CIA-Mafia plots to kill Castro during Warren Commission hearings; also kept mum on the work of the Cuban Study Group that reviewed the ill-fated Bay of Pigs operation in 1961.[m]
16. Egerter, Ann; CIA employee who handled Oswald's files for the last 3 years of his life. She refused HSCA requests to interview her in the mid 1970s and was threatened with a subpoena. Finally, she gave that interview, but "the verbatim record of her testimony is still classified." Newman's *Oswald and the CIA* (1995) considers her quite informed but one of the more unwilling people he has encountered.
17. Flynn Charles, FBI agent who had over 9 meetings with Jack Ruby beginning in March 1959; did not disclose that he used Ruby as an informant; this information was released only in 1975.[n]
18. Ford, Gerald; past U.S. President, member of Warren Commission, thought to be a liaison between the Warren Commission and Hoover; FBI senior agent William Sullivan said "He was our . . . informant on the Warren Commission."[o] Ford, therefore, was very likely privy to the angry letter Oswald wrote to FBI agent Hosty, which was not revealed at the time of the hearings. (Gordon Shanklin managed the cover-up of the Oswald-Hosty correspondence, but Ford was probably aware of it.) The correspondence was only released to the public 11 years after the Warren Commission closed its business (1975).[p] Ford reportedly was privy to Jack Ruby's 9 contacts with the FBI in 1959-1960, information that was withheld from the public. Recently released records — held secret for over three decades — show that Ford played an "editorial" role in shaping the final Warren Commission report. Harold Weisberg, a longtime critic of the Commission, commented on Ford's editorial recommendations that "what Ford is doing is trying to make the single-bullet theory more tenable. The official story is that the bullet did not hit bone, but it did. They are trying to make it seem that the bullet traveled downward, but it didn't."[q]
19. George Lardner, correspondent for the *Washington Post*: consistently critical of most conspiracy literature; has been accused of disinformation aimed at discrediting any suspicions of connections between Ferrie, Oswald and Garrison.[r]
20. Gervais, Pershing: alleged by Jim Garrison to have been bribed by the government to accuse Garrison of allowing pinball gambling — for a bribe. Garrison was acquitted; saw it as an attempt to silence him.[s]
21. Gill, G. Wray; personal attorney for gangster Marcello, in New Orleans; also represented David Ferrie, who was arrested on August 11, 1961 for indecent behavior with a 15-year-old boy; many writers on this topic consider that he had significant information about these individuals that has ever been publicly revealed.

Table 3.4 *Significant individuals named in the literature as withholding information or engaged in disinformation about the assassination*

22. Hall, Loran; CIA connections with Cuban activities; gave disinformation about Odio evidence. (Hall later admitted the original story was false and it was retracted; however, the original disputation of the Odio evidence was included in the Warren Commission final report.[t])
23. Helms, Richard, former CIA Director admitted withholding information on Clay Shaw's involvement with CIA; thought to have withheld significantly more information from the public on CIA-Mafia plots to kill Castro, Project ZR-RIFLE, Howard Hunt's presence in Dallas, and other matters. He also 'stonewalled' Warren Commission inquiries into Jack Ruby. One CIA document No. 150-59 reported that Jack Ruby had visited American mobster Santo Trafficante in prison in Havana; this document was kept secret for 13 years; Helms was Director of the CIA during much of this time (1966-1973).[u] Helms is also strongly suspected in withholding evidence on David Ferrie from both the Warren Commission, Jim Garrison's inquiry, and the Senate Intelligence Committee. In the mid 1970s' Helms admitted Ferrie had ties to the CIA; this has also been corroborated by former CIA agent and author Victor Marchetti.[v] At the time of the assassination, Oswald was carrying Ferrie's library card. Guy Bannister's associate, Jim Martin, called the FBI to inform that Ferrie played a role in the assassination. Ferrie's association with Cuban anti-Castro exiles as well as Ferrie's investigation by the FBI four days after the assassination were not disclosed by the Warren Commission, nor to the public. Helms is thought to have played role in that deception then and later. Helms was the first CIA director to be sentenced to a maximum of two years in prison for lying to Congress. 
24. Hendrix, Hal, Scripps Howard journalist also alleged as a key CIA contact, offered information on Oswald the day of the assassination; pleaded guilty to withholding information from a Senate Committee investigating CIA. Journalist Seth Kantor saw and spoke to Ruby at Parkland Hospital, but Ruby denied it, and Kantor's testimony was rejected by Warren Commission. Kantor investigated, tried to get copies of his own phone records made in the hours after the assassination. He was unable to obtain them until 1975 and discovered the reason they were withheld for so long was that he had called Hal Hendrix at 6 pm on the day of the assassination, and Hendrix's number was the 'national security' matter that was the likely source of the censorship.[w] On the day of the assassination, Hendrix already had a great deal of information on Oswald and was disseminating it to the media.

Table 3.4 *Significant individuals named in the literature as withholding information or engaged in disinformation about the assassination*

25. Hoover, J. Edgar; withheld information on Mob contracts on Kennedy from the Warren Commission. A personal friend of Lyndon Johnson, Hoover also withheld information on Billy Sol Estes activities in relation to Johnson after the FBI was required to investigate the murder of U.S Agricultural employee, Henry Marshall, who was connected to this inquiry into Estes; Marshall was shot investigating cotton allotments to Estes, a very close associate of Lyndon Johnson.[x] Hoover also withheld numerous wiretaps of gambling figures and underworld persons including the President's mistress, Judith Exner, Sam Giancana, and Las Vegas gambling interests.[y] Another death threat against the President recorded on May 3, 1962 was withheld from the Attorney General as well.[z] Memo from Hoover in 1960 about Oswald's identity papers was also withheld from Warren Commission.[aa]
26. Hosty, James, destroyed note sent to the FBI by Oswald. Hosty said his superior, Gordon Shanklin, ordered him to do so. Hosty, now retired, said that 'bombs are yet to drop on this case.' Hosty claimed that reports on Oswald in Mexico had been removed from the FBI's Dallas office after the assassination.[ab] [Note in John Newman's *Oswald and the CIA* Hosty apparently submitted to an interview and revealed significant information about William Pawley, Hunt, the CIA and Sylvia Odio.] Long held to be a major figure in the cover-up, Hosty finally wrote his memoirs in 1996. He corroborates that significant cover-ups occurred with information cited in this section. Further Hosty corroborates much in the conspiracy literature identifying individuals implicated in various elements of the cover-up: mentioned prominently is Gordon Shanklin who told Hosty about the Oswald note to the FBI "Here, take these. I don't want to ever see them again." Hosty destroyed the note. See Hosty *Ibid.*, p 59. Hosty also implicates the following individuals in various aspects of the cover-up: the FBI's Johnnie Mohr, close to Hoover, Gerald Ford, Jim Malley, Harlan Brown, and Jim Gale (FBI confederates), and the CIA's Winston Scott.
27. Humes, James. J. M.D; primary forensic pathologist who worked on Kennedy autopsy at Bethesda; Dr. Humes had not performed autopsies to any extent prior to this. According to Dr. Michael Baden who reviewed the autopsy results "the qualifications of the pathologists. . . the failure to inspect the clothing . . . .the inadequate documentation of injuries, lack of proper preservation of evidence, and incompleteness of the autopsy" were areas of major deficiency. Dr. Humes admitted that his preliminary draft notes of the Autopsy Report he burned in his fireplace.[ac] Another less credible source cites Commander Humes was involved in the discovery of a fourth bullet. See chi. 4, note 121. Humes's explanation of these allegations is that he burnt his notes of the autopsy because they were stained with blood and likely to be put on public display.
28. Isaac, Don Levine; CIA employee, who spent an intensive week with Marina Oswald prior to her testimony before the Warren Commission, allegedly prompting and/or coaching her responses.

Table 3.4 Significant individuals named in the literature as withholding information or engaged in disinformation about the assassination

29. Johnson, Lyndon; U.S. President. Argued with Kennedy on Thursday evening Nov. 21, 1963 in Kennedy's hotel suite. Wanted the seating arrangements changed for the morning motorcade. Johnson wanted his friend, John Connally, governor of Texas, to be in another car and his nemesis, Senator Ralph Yarborough, to be seated in Kennedy's car. Kennedy refused. Johnson denied the story, but it has been documented by Kennedy advance-man, Jerry Bruno; Johnson may have also withheld far more information on the Billy Sol Estes and Bobby Baker scandals in which he was embroiled at the time. [ad]
30. Kaack, Milton. New Orleans FBI agent investigated Oswald prior to assassination but did not inform Warren Commission When approached by Kennedy researcher, Summers, Kaack responded by telephone in 1978 "No. No. I'm not talking. You won't get anything out of me," and hung up. [ae]
31. Kennedy Aides and Associates. Many individuals associated with Kennedy have published allegedly historical treatments of his Presidency and life withholding highly significant information about both national security, anti-Castro assassination efforts and personal data such as his Addison's disease, promiscuity, etc., while many had knowledge of these matters. These idolater-publicists, often referred to as the "Camelot school," are Arthur Schlesinger, Kenneth O'Donnell, David Powers, Ted Sorensen, Pierre Salinger, Walt Rostow, Evelyn Lincoln, and Theodore White. [af]
32. Kennedy family, Jacqueline Bouvier and Edward; family members likely far more familiar with Kennedy associations with Exner, Giancana, and Joseph Kennedy's connections with the Mafia than have ever revealed to the American public. Mrs. Kennedy is alleged to have known about her husband's liaisons with her press secretary, Pamela Turnure; may also have known Baron deMohrenschildt, friend of Oswald. Mrs. Kennedy was personally responsible for attempts to suppress numerous articles and books on Kennedy or forcing, through litigation, suppression of William Manchester's family-commissioned book, particularly the portion describing the argument between Lyndon Johnson and Kennedy the day before the assassination. Caroline Kennedy has also been quoted as asking the media to leave her father's memory alone. Kennedy's only son has also taken a position that inquiries are of no interest to him. Also, when Robert Kennedy left office, he took with him 50 boxes of documents which are now stored at the Kenned Library. "No other Attorney General walked off the job with such a trove of government paperwork" It is alleged that documents pertaining to Operation Mongoose, Frank Sinatra, Sam Giancana and others may be there. Several historians have requested permission to examine this material (Richard Reeves, Nigel Hamilton, Seymour Hersh, and others), but Max Kennedy, son of Robert, has steadfastly refused to open these papers for inspection. [See 'The old man and the CIA,' *The Nation*, March 26, 2001, pp 15-18.] The Kennedy Library houses secret files as well including a 500 page 'oral history' by Jackie Kennedy never yet released as well as medical data on JFK only released in 2002. It revealed that JFK took incredible amounts of medications: testosterone, anti-anxiety drugs, Stelazine, codeine, Demerol, Methadone for pain, librium, thyroid hormone, procine and hydrocortisone [SJMN: "Medical files show hidden pain in White House," November 17, 2002, p. 27A.

Table 3.4 *Significant individuals named in the literature as withholding information or engaged in disinformation about the assassination*

33. Kennedy, Regis; FBI agent in Dallas. Beverly Oliver (known in the literature as the "Babushka Lady") claims she took an 8mm film of the assassination which she alleged FBI agent Kennedy took it from her. The film disappeared.[ag]
34. Lardner, George, correspondent for the *Washington Post*, consistently negative about the Garrison inquiry. Allegedly Lardner was with David Ferrie, Garrison's principal witness, the day Ferrie died.[ah] Considered a CIA propaganda asset by Mark Lane.
35. Lawford, Peter. President Kennedy's brother-in-law allegedly arranged numerous soirees for the President while Kennedy was in office; withheld considerable information on the Kennedys until his death, partially revealed by his third wife to author Anthony Summers; unavailable for testimony on the death of Marilyn Monroe and was sequestered at the Kennedy estate in Hyannisport at the time of the inquest.
36. Lawrence, David; of the *Herald Tribune*; disinformation; provided information on Oswald apparently before the authorities possessed such details of his life. His article appeared in the Christchurch Star (New Zealand) within the first moments following the assassination.[ai] Prouty suggests Lawrence couldn't have known what he knew at that time and implies Lawrence had advance knowledge on Oswald. Author Gerald Posner disputes this assertion.
37. Luce, Clare Boothe, wife of the chairman of *Time Inc*, often associated with CIA-supported activities, involved in anti-Castro activities, even funding some, and owner of the Zapruder film which was altered and suppressed for over 10 years.[aj] On Dec 6, 1963 *Life* published a memorial edition of the Kennedy assassination captioned "All of Life's Pictures," yet key frames of the Zapruder film were withheld.[ak] Husband Henry Luce participated in killing an important story about Marina Oswald. [See J. Hosty, *Ibid.*, p. 223].
38. McCone, John; former Director of the CIA admitted that he knew of Maurice Bishop, the mysterious figure in Kennedy assassination literature. McCone said he believed that Bishop was a senior agency employee, that he had met him 2-3 times, but that he could not identify who he was. Bishop was a pseudonym and his name appears in virtually all Kennedy assassination literature in which CIA complicity and the Cuban connection is involved. McCone's admissions are considered meager.[al]
39. McMillan, Douglas, FBI agent, compiled reports on Frank Sinatra and his dealings with Sam Giancana as well as Kennedy, Sinatra and Marilyn Monroe. McMillan was described as reluctant to come forward.[am]
40. Merletti, Lewis, Director of the U.S. Secret Service, admonished two agents for speaking to a reporter about JFK's extramarital activities in the White house. The two spoke to Seymour Hersh 35 years after the assassination but, despite the lapse in time, the director felt that this "damaged the agency's professionalism," Source: *The News*, Mexico City, Jan. 17, 1998, p. 9.
41. Moore, Dallas Walton; a CIA agent who knew and cleared George deMohrenschildt to associate with Oswald when he first came to Dallas; this fact was never disclosed to the Warren Commission.[an]

Table 3.4 Significant individuals named in the literature as withholding information or engaged in disinformation about the assassination

42. New York Times; published numerous "disinformation" pieces on the Kennedy assassination. One notable example is that after "The Pentagon Papers" were published the Times wrote that "President Kennedy... bequeathed to Johnson a broad commitment to war." Fletcher Prouty replies that "This is contrived and incorrect. The Times all but ignored President Kennedy's important National Security Action Memorandum #263, October 11, 1963, that, as official policy, ordered 1,000 men home from Vietnam by the end of 1963, and all U.S. personnel out of Vietnam by the end of 1965. [ao]
43. Newcomb, Pat; friend of Marilyn Monroe, described as a person who knew more about Monroe's association than anyone else. "To this day, Newcomb clams up when asked about the Kennedys." [ap]
44. Nixon, Richard; ordered attorney General John Mitchell to withhold ballistics evidence from the Kennedy Assassination "on the grounds of national security."[aq] Denied being in Dallas on the day of the assassination, but later admitted it.[ar] Nixon's whereabouts on November 22, 1963 were "deleted" in articles he wrote. A humorous discussion of his final admissions that he was there is given in Prouty, pp. 119-120.
45. O Leary, Jeremiah of the Washington Star, considered a pro-CIA journalist who staunchly holds to the Warren Commission interpretation of history and accused by some conspiracy researchers as promulgating disinformation. [as]
46. O'Neal, Birch an assistant to James Angleton, the CIA counterintelligence molehunter. John Newman's *Oswald and the CIA*, a review of recently released records, states "O'Neal is possibly the person most knowledgeable about Oswald's CIA files alive today. Now in his eighties, O'Neal has so far refused to comment. (p. 58)".
47. Oswald, Marina; lied or suffered severe amnesia about numerous aspects of the case, most notably incorrectly remembering how she arrived in the U.S. Said initially said she had no knowledge of her husband using the name "Hidell" later admitted signing the name A.J. Hidell to Oswald's Fair Play for Cuba ID card. Guy Banister's secretary, Delphine Roberts, said Marina and Lee visited Banister's office. Marina said she had no recollection of ever visiting it.[at] Other deceptions and inconsistencies documented in Table 10.4.
48. Phillips, David, CIA chief of Western Hemisphere Division in Mexico City; allegedly said no photos of Oswald visiting Soviet embassy in Mexico city existed. Tapes of conversations inside the embassy were "routinely destroyed" said Phillips. Was considered such an unreliable witness the HSCA considered indicting him for perjury. [au]
49. Quigley, John, FBI special agent interviewed Oswald in New Orleans on Aug 10, 1963. "In his report of the interview Quigley later wrote as though he arrived at the police station (to question Oswald) unbriefed, with no knowledge of Oswald's history. At one point the report says flatly, "I did not know who this individual was." This is contradictory to what we now know. In 1961 after Oswald's arrival in the Soviet Union, the FBI in New Orleans, the city of his birth, had reviewed his Navy file. The agent who handled the case then had been — John Quigley" [av] Quigley had numerous contacts with Oswald as reported by North as well (pp. 296).

Table 3.4 *Significant individuals named in the literature as withholding information or engaged in disinformation about the assassination*

50. Rogano, Frank; attorney for Jimmy Hoffa and is reported to have knowledge that Hoffa, Carlos Marcello, and Santos Trafficante plotted the JFK hit.[aw] Stayed mum until early 1990s and then wrote a 'tell-all' expose.
51. Rankin, J. Lee; chief counsel for the Warren Commission. Rankin had been told that the FBI had contacted Jack Ruby nine times in 1959-1960; when J. Edgar Hoover was being asked questions at the Warren Commission hearings, Rankin failed to ask Hoover about any of these contacts. According to Kantor "obviously the decision to keep the Ruby-FBI contacts quiet already had been reached."[ax]
52. Rather, Dan; CBS; first and only journalist to view Zapruder film in mid-70s who incorrectly said President "fell forward" with considerable violence — disinformation. [ay]
53. Rocca, Raymond; CIA agent. Jack Ruby had told his psychiatrist that he was" framed to kill Oswald." and told Dr. Werner Teuter, the psychiatrist to read Buchanan's book. Buchanan on page 295 reveals that Tippit was part of a right-wing plot and how the CIA worried about the upcoming publication of Buchanan's text in the United States. Rocca was the CIA individual who was assigned to investigate Buchanan and/or discredit his work. William Buckley published an article attacking Buchanan's book as well. Rocca resigned during the CIA Domestic Operations scandal. [az]
54. Roselli, John; Mafia figure (deceased) who allegedly was passing false information on to Jack Anderson on Oswald's acting as Castro's agent in the killing of Kennedy.[ba]
55. Salinger, Pierre, Kennedy's press secretary, TV journalist, has not publicly revealed Kennedy's liaisons and promiscuity while in the White House although he was aware of some of this activity. Appears as well to have withheld information about the frequency with which President Kennedy used a cane and crutches.[bb] He is also privy to conversations between Washington and the USSR after the assassination which have been withheld from public awareness and which were described as "compelling" if ever made public. [See J. Hosty, Ibid).
56. Shanklin, Gordon; ordered FBI agent Hosty to destroy Oswald's note. Said CIA had delivered from Mexico only a photograph and typewritten reports. However, FBI Director Hoover made mention in a five page document to the fact that these agents had listened to a sound recording. What happened to the recording remains a mystery. Shanklin was warned before the Judiciary Committee that he might be open to prosecution for perjury. Shanklin is also suspected in the destruction of Oswald's Military Intelligence file submitted to the FBI by Lt. Col. Robert Jones of the 112th Military Intelligence Group shortly after the assassination. [bc]
57. Sinatra, Frank; frequent partygoer with JFK, also allied to Mob figures, and Marilyn Monroe. Did not reveal what he knew of these matters in any significant detail prior to his death.
58. Sturgis, Frank; CIA linked anti-Castro militant, Watergate burglar, spread false story to Jack Anderson linking Oswald to pro-Castro intelligence. James Buchanan wrote an article on Oswald's Miami Fair Play for Cuba actions; the story was false, and Buchanan said Sturgis was the unnamed source of the story; Sturgis denied it; Sturgis is deceased. [bd]

Table 3.4 Significant individuals named in the literature as withholding information or engaged in disinformation about the assassination

59. Surgeon General, U.S. Navy, threatened all present at the Kennedy autopsy with court martial if they revealed the nature of the events surrounding the Kennedy autopsy. "You are warned an infraction of theses orders makes you liable to Court Martial proceedings under appropriate articles of the Uniform Code of Military Justice." [be]
60. Tolson, Clyde, never married bachelor and close associate of J. Edgar Hoover at FBI; Tolson and Hoover widely suspected of being homosexual; privy to most of Hoover's secrets including the ELSUR wiretap recordings of a contract hit on President Kennedy which was never revealed by Hoover to the Secret Service, JFK or the attorney General. Deceased. [bf]
61. Wade, Henry, Dallas District Attorney. Warren Commission investigator, Griffin, had been assigned the Jack Ruby portion of the investigation. He felt that Sergeant Dean in charge of basement security where Oswald was shot had made false statements. Griffin felt that Ruby may have come in to the basement area where Oswald was shot by another entrance. Dean bitterly complained. Pressure from Henry Wade's office got Griffin off the back of Sergeant Dean. "Griffin was confined to Washington through April and May, and was still stuck there on June 7, the day others went to Dallas to meet with Ruby" e.g. Gerald Ford, Chief Justice Earl Warren. [bg]
62. Westin, Av; ABC TV executive producer; see discussion of Roone Arledge.

a. Heymann, C. David. A Woman Named Jackie. New York: Carol Communications, 1989.
b. Weberman, ibid., p. 331.
c. Reeves, Thomas C. A Question of Character: A Life of John F. Kennedy. Rocklin CA: Prima Publishing, 1992, p. 8.
d. Summers, ibid., p. 522.
e. Summers, Vanity Fair March 1993.
f. Summers, Goddess, ibid., p. 382.
g. Summers, Conspiracy, p. 421.
h. Grodin, ibid., p. 223.
i. Grodin, ibid., p. 311; see also Reeves, ibid., p. 257.
j. Weberman, ibid., p. 29.
k. Grodin, ibid., p. 87.
l. Prouty, Fletcher. JFK: The CIA, Vietnam, and the Plot to Assassinate John F. Kennedy. New Jersey: Carol Communications, 1992, p. 158. See also Grodin, ibid., p. 311.
m. Summers, ibid; Prouty, ibid.
n. Summers, ibid., p. 443
o. North, ibid., p. 449.
p. Kantor, ibid., p. 175.
q. See: "Ford actively edited report on JFK slaying," SJMN, Thursday July 3, 1997, p. 6A.
r. Ogelsby, ibid., p. 266.
s. Ibid., p. 288.
t. Summers, ibid., p. 390.
u. Kantor, ibid., p. 186.
v. Weberman, ibid., p. 44.
w. Kantor, ibid.
x. North, ibid., p. 94; p. 150.

y. Ibid., p. 119; p. 131.
z. Ibid., p. 144.
aa. Craig & Rogers, ibid., p. 234.
ab. Summers, ibid.
ac. Ibid., p. 9; Grodin, ibid., p. 87.
ad. Zirbel, Craig. The Texas Connection. New York: Warner Books, 1991.
ae. Summers, ibid.
af. Reeves, ibid.
ag. Groden, ibid., p. 122.
ah. Groden, ibid., p. 362.
ai. Prouty, ibid., pp. 308-309.
aj. Lane, Mark Rush to Judgment. New York: Holt, Rinehart and Winston, 1966; also Summers, ibid., p. 425.
ak. North, ibid., p. 470. The Luce Family and spokespersons for Life sharply dispute that the Zapruder film ever showed the president falling forward or that Clare Boothe Luce had any role in obtaining or publishing the pictures. Richard B. Stolley, the Life reporter who found and purchased the Zapruder film, told me that: (a) there was no issue of Life entitled "All of Life's Photos," and that (b) any assertion that crucial Zapruder frames were deliberately omitted was untrue. Mr. Stolley was apparently acting on behalf of the Luce family when he replied to my query.
al. Summers, ibid., p. 512.
am. Summers, Goddess, p. 333.
an. Summers, Conspiracy, p. 197.
ao. Prouty, ibid., p. 116.
ap. Summers, Goddess, p. 351
aq. Groden, ibid., p. 331.
ar. Groden, ibid., p. 345. 78
as. Lane, ibid.
at. Summers, Conspiracy, p. 314.
au. Ibid.
av. Summers, ibid., p. 280.
aw. Ogelsby, ibid., p. 314.
ax. Kantor, ibid., p. 187.
ay. Summers, ibid.
az. Weberman, ibid., p. 176.
ba. Groden, ibid., p. 356.
bb. Reeves, ibid., p. 294.
bc. Summers, ibid., pp. 60-62.
bd. Summers, ibid. p. 423.
be. Groden, ibid., p. 88.
bf. North, ibid.
bg. Kantor, ibid., pp. 20-21.

How to Look at this Data

Much Kennedy assassination literature is unreliable. Much of it is self-published, or virtually so, and has not been verified or vetted to any degree by any outside editor. Good reason exists to question the integrity of some of the data presented, and some of the scholarship as well as the motives of the sources of information. Consider, for example, a sentence taken from a widely read text, *Coup D'Etat*, by Weberman and Canfield:

> With Nixon in power, Nazi sympathizers held high positions in the Republican party ... Nixon's men funneled money to the Nazis and Nixon himself voiced admiration for Albert Speer. [103]

Where did they get that from? What is the basis for such speculation? The sometimes overpowering bias of various writers obviously requires we maintain a healthy distance and skepticism about the assertions that come from these sources. The suggestions of a cover-up that is revealed in our table above, therefore, need to be sifted through in an effort to separate gossip, rumor, and innuendo from genuine hard evidence.

What follows is a distillation of the most incontrovertible evidence of a cover-up developed from Table 3.4.

The Hard Evidence of a Cover-Up

1. FBI: Probably the first, if not the most reliable, evidence of cover-up activities involved FBI agent Hosty. Acting under the direction of his superior, Gordon Shanklin, Hosty destroyed a letter written to him by Lee Harvey Oswald, complaining of Hosty's attempts to talk to Oswald's wife, Marina. The destruction of this letter was revealed years after the Warren Commission report.[104] In addition, two entries were deleted from Oswald's notebook: the telephone number of J. Edgar Hoover's personal secretary, Mrs. Grant, and agent Hosty's name.[105] Although members of the Warren Commission may have known about the deletion of Hosty's name from the notebook, this fact was not revealed to the public.

Also disturbing is the evidence of FBI cover-up activities in withholding information on Jack Ruby's "informant" status from 1959 onward. Ruby met with FBI agents nine times, and admitted this fact to Warren Commission counsel Rankin; Hoover asked that in the interests of national security, the information be withheld; it was.[106]

---

103. Weberman, *ibid.*, p. 93.
104. North, *ibid.*, p. 425.
105. *Ibid.* p. 426.
106. *Ibid.*, p. 519.

Another element to the FBI cover-up is a memo written by J. Edgar Hoover himself about Oswald, as far back as 1960:

> Hoover successfully hid one of his own memos to the State Department from the Warren Commission, and it did not surface until many years later after he was dead. Dated in June of 1960, when Oswald was in the Soviet Union, Hoover warned that someone might be using Oswald's identity. Evidence existed of an Oswald imposter even before Kennedy became president. Hoover had personally signed this memo. Imagine how embarrassing it would have been if this had come out. [107]

There are numerous other instances of FBI activity to cover up evidence in this case, but this is one of the most incontrovertible examples, well documented, and admitted by Agent Hosty himself. It is incontrovertible confirmation that cover-up activities were carried on within the FBI, and that in itself is reason enough to question the credibility of the Warren Report.

2. CIA: Regis Blahut. The "under-publicized" story of Regis Blahut is another irrefutable piece in the puzzle. Most Americans are aware that significant evidence on the Kennedy assassination has been concealed, lost, destroyed; a summary of the lost data is provided by Summers:

> The brain, along with other autopsy materials, including X rays and photographs, was apparently first delivered to President Kennedy's former secretary for safekeeping. Safe it was not — at least from the point of future investigators. In 1966, after the materials had passed into the care of the National Archives, it was discovered that the President's brain was missing. Also absent were tissue sections, blood smears, and a number of slides. Nor have any photographs of the interior of the President's chest survived, even though the chief autopsy doctor and an official photographer remembers them being taken. In 1979 the Assassinations Committee failed to discover any trace of the missing brain or of the other material. It favored the theory that the President's brother Robert Kennedy disposed of it to avoid tasteless display in the future.[108]

A far more telling incident occurred in June, 1978, however. The Assassinations Committee Chief Counsel possessed X-rays and ballistic evidence that were housed in a separate safe in a special room for the time the HSCA was holding its hearings.

---

107. Craig & Rogers, *ibid.*, pp. 234-235.
108. Summers, *ibid.*, p. 10.

They could not be examined, even by the staff concerned, without the chief counsel's personal permission. This was granted separately on each date of access, and items studied were meticulously logged in and out. One day in June, 1978, however, an interloper found a loophole in the precautions. A staff member, on legitimately taking photographs to a nearby office, left the safe closed but not locked. By the time the researcher returned, the safe had been opened and the sensitive material seriously disturbed. A folder had been taken out of the safe and one photograph of the dead President ripped out of its cover. There was an immediate investigation with disturbing results. A fingerprint check showed that the only unauthorized person who had handled the files was a CIA employee. He was Regis Blahut, a liaison officer who had been assigned to supervise and assist with secret CIA material stored in the Committee premises. He worked in a secure area quite separate from the room where the photographs were held and had no business being in that room at all. Blahut was interrogated both by Committee staff and by superiors at the CIA. At first he denied the whole thing, and then — faced with the incontrovertible evidence — Blahut simply maintained there was an innocent explanation. In one brief conversation with a reporter, he said darkly, "There's other things involved that are detrimental to other things." He declined to elaborate, and the CIA told the Committee Blahut had acted out of "mere curiosity." Blahut was fired . . . One of the pictures which had attracted his specific interest was a photograph of the late Presidents head. The pictures of the head are, of course, at the center of controversy over the source of the shot or shots that caused the President's fatal head injury. . . . The matter was to have been further investigated in Congress, but has since been quietly forgotten. [109]

When we add into this drama the 1998 disclosure on the part of the Assassination Records Board that an entire set of autopsy photographs have been missing, it adds considerable credibility to the view that a conspiracy was at work:

> New testimony released yesterday about the autopsy . . . says a second set of pictures was taken of Kennedy's wounds — pictures never made public . . . believed taken by White House photographer Robert Knudsen during or after the autopsy at the National Naval Medical Center in Bethesda, Md. Added David Lifton, author of *Best Evidence*, "It's of tremendous significance that there's another camera and its existence and its product have been concealed all these years. We've got a credible paper trail about another camera and film, but no pictures."[110]

From the burning of autopsy notes in a fireplace to the purloining of autopsy results, scientific evidence of tainted "composite" photographs, disclosed government

---

109. Summers, *ibid.*, p. 11-12.

110. "Secret Set of JFK autopsy photos alleged in testimony." *San Francisco Chronicle*, Aug 1, 1998, p. A5.

admissions that autopsy photos are missing and clear evidence that CIA personnel attempted to steal autopsy photos from a Congressional Committee — all this points to a conspiracy.

3. CIA: Document No. 150-59. Among the hardest facts pointing to a CIA cover-up, the "best documented" case seems to be document No. 150-59. It was withheld from the Warren Commission and kept secret for 13 years. The document reported that Jack Ruby had visited American mobster Santos Trafficante while he was in prison in Havana under Castro.[111]

Trafficante was linked in numerous texts to Mob plots to assassinate the President, and his linkage with Giancana is copious. Had the American public been made privy to JFK's sexual liaison with Judith Exner, her closeness with Giancana, Giancana's connections with Trafficante, and, in turn, Trafficante's relationship with Ruby, it is doubtful many would have believed that a single deranged assassin named Lee Harvey Oswald killed President Kennedy.

4. FBI: Destruction of Oswald's military intelligence file. Gordon Shanklin suspected. Somewhat less thoroughly documented is the destruction of Oswald's Military Intelligence file. Shortly after the news of Oswald's arrest was made public, Lt. Col. Robert Jones of the 112th Military Intelligence Group (based in San Antonio, Texas) urgently requested information from his men at the scene of the crime. He had been advised that an "A.J. Hidell" had been arrested. Jones claims that a file he had on Lee Harvey Oswald was cross-referenced with A.J. Hidell. This file contained information about Oswald's past, his time spent in the Soviet Union, and his arrest for passing out leaflets for pro-Castro organizations. Jones called the FBI in Dallas and spoke to Agent Gordon Shanklin. He wrote a report summarizing the day's activities, but apart from forwarding the file on to Shanklin, that marked the end of his activities.

Jones was interviewed by the Warren Commission and found to be a credible witness. When the Assassinations Committee sought to review the file in 1978, they were told the file had been destroyed in 1973 "as a matter of routine." The committee wrote that "without access to this file, the question of Oswald's possible affiliation with military intelligence could not be fully resolved."[112] Similarly, the Committee noted that Shanklin's credibility was "seriously impeached" by this action.[113]

---

111. Kantor, *ibid.*, p. 186.
112. Summers, *ibid.*, p. 62.
113. Summers, *ibid.*, p. 63.

5. Cover up of JFK's personal life: The compendium of cover-up activities related to Kennedy's personal life and activities is also now "hard evidence." We do not know who is most culpable here, but it is indisputable that many writers, historians and Kennedy associates purported to write objective biographies while egregiously withholding highly significant information about this period — from Pierre Salinger to Ben Bradlee of the *Washington Post*.

Kennedy's liaisons with women in the White House, his machinations with Giancana in particular, his argument with President Johnson the night before the assassination, his awareness of and/or participation in plots against Castro, even his singular luncheon meeting with J. Edgar Hoover — where he was confronted about his affair with Judith Exner — were withheld, omitted, unmentioned, distorted or rationalized away. We must also include CIA Counterintelligence Chief James Angleton's admission that he destroyed the diary of one of Kennedy's mistresses shortly after her murder in 1964. (Angleton said he destroyed the material not out of national security interests or any loyalty to JFK, but because of his concern for the surviving family members.) How these personal relationships played into the assassination is unknown, but to consider them irrelevant is quite another matter.

6. Cover up of neutron activation tests.[114] Neutron activation analysis allows for precise definition of ballistics evidence. At the time of the assassination, this process was new and few had heard of it; but if we had the results of the tests that were performed, they could tell whether the bullet fragments in Kennedy's brain came from the same source or different sources.

> In 1973 a previously unknown letter from J. Edgar Hoover to J. Lee Rankin, chief counsel for the Warren Commission, surfaced. The letter, dated July 8, 1964, revealed that in addition to spectrographic analysis, another kind of test had been conducted on the bullet fragments. This was an extraordinarily precise and, at the time, relatively new procedure known as neutron activation. The process involved irradiating organic or inorganic materials — in this case the bullet fragments — with nuclear particles. The specimens would then emit gamma rays which could be counted, compared, and analyzed to reveal the exact composition of the substance down to parts per billion. The process was and remains vastly superior to spectrographic analysis and is so accurate it is often referred to as "nuclear fingerprinting."
> ... Hoover's 1964 letter blandly noted that "minor variations" were found in some of the Dealey Plaza bullet fragments, including those recovered from the limousine as well as those removed from Kennedy's brain, but that the differ-

---

114. Quotations on neutron activation tests come from Menninger, *Mortal Error*, ibid., pp. 123-125.

ences were not sufficient to permit positive differentiation and or identification . . . A number of assassination researchers jumped on this statement as proof of misrepresentation by the FBI director since, they said, variations of *any kind* revealed in the precise neutron activation process unequivocally demonstrated the samples originated from difference sources.

These specific test results, beyond Hoover's suppressed letter, were never disclosed.

> Indeed the fact that the government had only inadvertently revealed that neutron activation tests had been conducted, that they had never disclosed the results of these tests, that they hadn't even revealed the results of the less sophisticated spectrographic tests . . . The fact that one investigation of Kennedy's skull and X rays showed forty tiny bullet fragments embedded in the brain, yet the tissue samples, scrapings, the brain itself as well as the slides were "not available at the National Archives in the years that followed and no one seemed to have any clue where they'd gone," . . .

All the above casts doubt on the government/Warren Commission conclusions. In sum, evidence that spectrographic evidence as well as neutron activation tests on fragments in Kennedy's brain were completed but never released is widely accepted as strong evidence of a government conspiracy to cover-up important evidentiary material.

(One might also consider softer evidence. Documents that were held secret for over three decades show that Warren Commission member John McCloy disagreed with the writing of the final report, objected to the magic bullet theory, and felt that the evidence "against it" was not fully stated. That the government would hold what appears to be an innocuous memo secret for so long shows the degree to which a forced unanimity was sought in the promulgation of the Warren Commission Report.[115]

These pieces of "hard evidence" for a cover-up are presently not disputed. They occurred; they have been documented, and they do not constitute rumor, innuendo or hearsay evidence. They are in themselves neither benign nor merely tangential to an objective inquiry regarding the death of President Kennedy. They indicate that government agencies were involved in the matter of the assassination: the FBI and the CIA. (In late 1995, the government released documents that show the FBI also withheld the fact that it had sought information from the Swiss government about Oswald's presence there before his defection to the USSR and prior to the assassination.)

---

115. "1964 memo," *San Jose Mercury News*, August 11, 1997, p. 4A

SUMMARY

This chapter attempted a fresh and unbiased look at the evidence supporting a 'conspiracy' in the killing of John Fitzgerald Kennedy. Each conspiracy theorist tends to assemble his or her own 'best evidence,' and this chapter has tried to get as close to all this evidence as possible. If we do not disabuse ourselves of the notion that Lee Harvey Oswald killed President Kennedy and Officer Tippit, and we do not dismiss the notion that he may indeed be the lone assassin of the President, there is still a vast body of literature with which any objective scholar must deal. That evidence, in toto, is summarized below.

Physical Evidence Favoring Oswald

- His shirt was changed prior to his arrest, and yet cotton fibers linking that shirt to the rifle butt were presented as evidence by the FBI.
- Prosecuting attorneys — far more than defense attorneys — have for years used nitrate test evidence to support the firing of a weapon, yet nitrate tests on Oswald's cheek came up negative.
- No witness unambiguously put Oswald in the window firing the weapon, but two witnesses put him in the second floor lunchroom at 12:15 p.m. and again at 12:31 pm. (Kennedy was shot at 12:30). Given that the motorcade was five minutes late from its published arrival at Dealey Plaza, there is considerable doubt that Oswald could have effectuated this assassination and yet be in the lunchroom fifteen minutes prior to and one minute after the killing while simultaneously being able to correctly identify the two individuals (out of a staff of over 75) who walked into the lunchroom during these critical 15 minutes.
- Plentiful evidence exists that Oswald liked President Kennedy, and the issue of motive has never been established, even the Warren Commission concluding this was a motiveless crime.

A Fourth Shot

Substantial evidence exists that a fourth shot struck the President. And a fourth shot could not possibly have been fired from Oswald's rifle. This evidence includes:
- Over 61 witnesses in Dealey Plaza heard shots from the grassy knoll.
- The acoustic study of a Dictabelt convinced scientists that a fourth shot occurred (with a 95% probability of occurrence).
- Autopsy photographs and testimony from over 13 medical personnel present at Parkland Hospital in Dallas showing the President was struck from the front,

- The Zapruder film, long censored from the American public by *Life Magazine*, shows the President accelerating backward as the result of the frontal headshot.

The evidence for a frontal shot on the President is substantial and persuasive; it is an important clue that others in addition to or in place of Oswald may have been involved.

Pattern of Suspicious Deaths

A second rich source of evidence for a conspiracy is statistical, and involves the study of over 84 deaths occurring with individuals directly or indirectly related to the Kennedys and the assassination in Dealey Plaza.

- In 78 of these cases, cause of death could be established. The pattern of these deaths is statistically significant and at extreme variance with the natural profile of mortality etiology in the United States.
- The probability these deaths could have arisen by chance is less than one in ten thousand. From an empirical analysis of this data, it is far more absurd to assume the deaths arose from random and unrelated causes than to assume they arose from a systematic process, i.e., a conspiracy of some sort, which obtains to this assassination event. Corroborating this finding is a sub-sample analysis of the accidental death of two individuals in this study, which similarly show a probability of occurrence of one in 33,000 that such deaths could have occurred by chance alone.

Deaths Associated with Congressional Witnesses

- In addition to this statistical data, another table presenting eleven deaths, mostly of Mafia figures contacted by the Senate Intelligence and House Assassinations Committees in the mid-1970s. This also points dramatically to an underworld conspiracy of silence on this matter. Virtually no set of Congressional inquiries in all of U.S. history can detail such an enormous clustering of witness deaths occurring either shortly before or shortly after testimony was either sought or taken.

Cover-up Actions as a Predictor of Conspiracy

- The pattern of "cover-up" that has manifested itself over the last 30 years also suggests a conspiracy. Some 60 individuals are cited in the literature as having allegedly engaged in theft of documents, disinformation, withholding and/or deceit is presented.

- The FBI's complicity in destroying evidence is incontrovertible, including evidence of Oswald's contacts with the FBI and his contact with Agent Hosty, the obliteration of J. Edgar Hoover's personal secretary's number in Oswald's notebook, as well as FBI destruction of Oswald's military intelligence file in 1973 which had been sent to agent Gordon Shanklin of the FBI by Lt. Col. Robert Jones of the 112th Military Intelligence Group.
- CIA theft of autopsy photos of the President's head by CIA liaison officer Regis Blahut in the late 1970s; undisclosed sets of autopsy photos never made public and lost, CIA withholding of highly significant information linking Jack Ruby to Santos Trafficante and the Mafia, and significant withholding of information concerning JFK's personal life by associates, former aides, and by CIA Counterintelligence Chief James Angleton.

Many other instances of cover-up also exist, but just these hardest pieces of evidence alone are clearly sufficient to point to a cover-up of information which goes to the core of a conspiracy involving members of the intelligence community, and the FBI.

CONCLUSION

Reviewing this information, we draw the same conclusion as the House Select Assassinations Committee. We do not yet know who is involved in any conspiracy, to whom any alleged conspiracy may be attributed; but that there was a conspiracy in the killing of President Kennedy is a well-founded conclusion.

To hold otherwise, to cling to the notion of a single assassin, is scientifically untenable. That the pattern of these 78 deaths happened by "coincidence," as a statistical anomaly, has one chance in ten thousand of being valid. The argument that a fourth shot did not occur has less than a 5% chance of being accurate. To say that FBI cover-up activities were motivated out of director Hoover's vanity and urge to protect the "image of his agency," or that Regis Blahut stole an autopsy photograph merely because he was "curious," would smack of a neurotic denial syndrome more than an objective assessment.

Indeed, the absurd "crackpots" whose speculations are the most outlandish and scientifically unforgivable are not paranoid malcontents; they are precisely those mainstream protagonists of the status quo, i.e., those who have historically backed the Warren Commission findings.

This is the group that holds stubbornly to what is improbable, unsupported and rationally untenable, namely the assertion that Oswald acted alone, that no conspiracy ever existed, and that magic bullets, strange neuromuscular spasms, and sheer coincidence should be the working concepts used to explain the contradictory data.

Chapter 3. Reasonable Doubt

There is simply too much contradictory data to dismiss on those terms, and too much psychic energy is needed to engage the denial process for very long. Holding to such a position now can only be called "mainstream lunacy." The world has been asked to naively and innocently accept, as "unfortunate" trifles, that the president's brain was never examined, his throat wound was ignored, autopsy physicians were sworn to secrecy (even in retirement), his brain is mysteriously missing from the National Archives, and a lieutenant commander who took autopsy photos committed suicide; and that otherwise we have seen the accurate and credible results of a serious post mortem examination.

The world is asked to simply accept the government's assertion that Oswald acted alone but without any discernible motive; that the 68 witnesses in Dealey Plaza should be ignored; that the Dictabelt acoustic analysis by two preeminent firms be dismissed; that censorship of the Zapruder film be understood as in the national interest; that debris from the President's brain flying 25 feet to the left rear of the limousine was a logical "neuromuscular" reflex reaction to being shot from behind; and that the "magic bullet" which coursed through Kennedy and Connally mysteriously appeared on a stretcher of a child at Parkland Hospital, showing neither damage nor any residue of tissue or blood from either man. While that bullet did all its damage and remained unblemished, we are asked to believe that another bullet exploded on impact, leaving over 40 fragments in Kennedy's brain; and that another one left a hole in the President's skull which was *smaller* than the diameter of the bullet itself . . . and yet all the bullets were from the same gun and the same assassin.

Furthermore, for a generation the public has been asked to dismiss the notion of a "conspiracy to cover-up" the assassination as nothing more than a symptom of cynical and paranoid writers trying to make money by exploiting this national tragedy. The fact that Sam Giancana testified before the Senate Intelligence Committee and then was found slain with bullet holes neatly stitched around his mouth should not convey to the average American that "silence is golden" when it comes to discussing any conspiracy. The deaths of so many other witnesses should also be ignored.

That Jack Ruby was an FBI informant, that he had visited Santos Trafficante in Havana, that Oswald had FBI contacts repeatedly and that none of these facts were presented at the time of the Warren Commission. . . all of this should similarly be disregarded as we "put the past behind us."

Judge Burton Griffin, who was a counsel to the original Warren Commission, made an abrupt turn-around in 1977 about the credibility of the Warren Report with the following comments:

> I feel that the CIA lied to us, that we had an agency of Government here which we were depending upon, that we expected to be truthful with us, and to cooperate with us. And they didn't do it. The CIA concealed from us the fact that they were involved in efforts to assassinate Castro which could have been of extreme importance to us. Especially the fact that they were involved in working with the Mafia at that time . . . [Judge Griffin feels the same about the FBI, and says] What is most disturbing to me is that two agencies of the government, that were supposed to be loyal and faithful to us, deliberately misled us.[116]

A long list of non-believers followed: Bobby Kennedy harbored suspicions and confided to former White House aide Richard Goodwin that "if anyone was involved, it was organized crime."[117] Bobby said that if he were elected President he would reopen the investigation. Warren Commission members Hale Boggs, Senator John Sherman Cooper, and Senator Richard Russell also expressed their doubts about the conclusions. On a recently released tape, withheld for over three decades, Senator Russell flatly says to Lyndon Johnson, "I don't believe it." Johnson replies, " I don't either." [118]

The public doesn't, either. A CBS poll taken in November, 1993 revealed that 81% of Americans believe there was a cover-up, and 89% believe JFK died as a result of a conspiracy. Only 52% felt that way shortly after the assassination. [119]

Another non-believer to add to this list is the discreet personal secretary of JFK, Evelyn Lincoln. Shortly before she died, she wrote that she felt her boss was killed by a conspiracy. [120]

Still, the most impressive anecdotal evidence supporting a conspiracy comes from none other than J. Edgar Hoover, the imperturbable supporter and advocate of the conclusions on the Warren Commission. Hoover died in the mid-1970s, but in 1994 a researcher, Anthony Summers, released a stunning story purporting to describe a conversation between Hoover and a trusted friend. The friend asked Hoover who killed JFK, and Hoover's astonishing reply was:

> If I told you what I really know, [he replied,] it would be very dangerous to this country. Our whole political system could be disrupted. [121]

---

116. Summers, *Conspiracy, ibid.*, p. 532.
117. Goldfarb, *ibid.*, p. 297.
118. Anthony and Robbyn Summers, "The Ghosts of November," *Vanity Fair*, December 1994, p. 92.
119. *Ibid.* A more recent CNN poll conducted by CNN and broadcast on the History channel on November 18, 1998 continues to show a majority of Americans (73%) believe JFK died as the result of a conspiracy.
120. Liz Smith on Evelyn Lincoln, "Grapevine," *San Jose Mercury News*, May 12, 1997.
121. Summers, Anthony & Robbyn, "The Ghosts of November, *Vanity Fair*, December, 1994, p. 100.

Chapter 3. Reasonable Doubt

It seems that a conspiracy in the assassination of John Fitzgerald Kennedy is a very plausible, rational, and tenable conclusion to draw. The next task that faces us is to look at the origin of the conspiracy, to review the most salient theories, and to see if anything conclusive comes from our efforts.

Chapter 4. Conspiracy

> *The people have a right to the truth as they have a right to life, liberty, and the pursuit of happiness.*
> — Epictetus

Conspiracy theories have now fallen into "schools." Some assert it was a "get-even-with-Bobby" vendetta, featuring the Mafia in the lead role. There is a more Dostoyevskian drama, emphasizing the themes of retaliation and perfidy, spotlighting the CIA and angry anti-Castro Cubans. A more traditional view sees a "coup d'etat" staged by Lyndon Johnson. And finally, we have what might be called the "what-goes-around-comes-around" theme, played out by Fidel Castro — who is said to have endured eight separate assassination attempts before striking back. This chapter will confine itself to examining the most persuasive theories.

1. The Johnson Theory

> "I looked it up: One out of every four presidents has died in office. I'm a gamblin' man, darlin', and this is the only chance I got."
> — Lyndon Johnson in a conversation with Clare Boothe Luce, after accepting the Vice Presidential nomination in 1960. [122]

---

[122]. Reeves, Thomas C. *A Question of Character: A Life of John F. Kennedy*. Rocklin CA: Prima Publishing, 1992, p. 179.

Actually, each theory sounds plausible, in itself. It is only when you pause and look at what the theory does not explain that shortcomings emerge. One of the most recent theories that is both convincing and yet has quite a few unfilled holes comes from Craig Zirbel, author of the *Texas Connection*.

Essential Ideas

Lyndon Baines Johnson gained the most from the assassination of President Kennedy. He rose to power from the comparatively impotent position of Vice President. Prior to Kennedy's victory, Johnson had been majority leader in the Senate, one of the most powerful men in government. Graduating to the Vice Presidency actually placed him in a position in which the office could be exploited *far less* than his prior positions in government; but he made up for the lost time.

When Republican Senator Barry Goldwater was asked his recollections of LBJ, he hesitated; then he crowed, finally, that Johnson had made more money as president than any other president in history. Johnson left an estate valued at approximately $20 million. He is known to have used his office on many occasions for his own private gain. Securing FCC licenses for broadcast stations in Austin, Texas, for example, gave him a virtual monopoly in that television area:

> And despite Austin's size and position as the Texas state capital, the FCC for decades refused to allow any other televisions stations in Austin (aside from LBJ's), thereby protecting Johnson's television monopoly in the region.[123]

As Vice President, he was handicapped. There were few important appointments he could make — except for the Secretary of the Navy. Johnson nominated Fred Korth. Korth, in turn, strongly agitated for the largest defense contract ever awarded by the Pentagon: the $6 billion contract for the TFX fighter plane, to be built by General Dynamics, in Texas. Korth was later indicted for conflict of interest in this matter.

Johnson's major appointment, in other words, was a clear act of patronage, and a criminal one, to boot.

Not only did Johnson lose some of his power base as Vice President, there were clear signs that Kennedy was not going to have him on the ticket in 1964. In fact, the last words Kennedy dictated to his secretary, before his assassination, were to that effect.

Further, Johnson's own political career was increasingly threatened as Kennedy's presidency marched forward. Three scandals came close to implicating

---

123. Zirbel, Craig. *The Texas Connection*. New York: Warner Books, p. 102.

Johnson during this time: the TFX scandal, the Billy Sol Estes scandal, and the Bobby Baker case. The three pushed Johnson's career to the edge of dissolution.

Billy Sol Estes, a personal friend of Johnson, was arrested in March of 1962 and charged with defrauding the government. He had been blessed with government contracts to store surplus grain in his warehouses. Johnson attempted to intervene on January 31, 1961, defending Estes' practices. Agricultural agent Henry Marshall was assigned to investigate. On June 3, 1961, Marshall was found dead in a ditch in Franklin, Texas, with five bullets in his head from a bolt-action rifle. The local justice of the peace declared the death a suicide. Marshall's widow remonstrated against "Texas justice" for years afterward.

Billy Sol Estes refused to talk, and thus protected Johnson from exposure. LBJ's personal legal counsel became Estes' principal attorney. Estes was convicted; yet, on appeal, the decision was overturned. Eventually, he was sentenced to a fifteen-year prison term for fraud.

While Estes did not ultimately escape jail, he was never charged with the murder of Agent Marshall, which was later determined not to have been a suicide. Marshall's body was exhumed and tested. The results showed that in addition to the five bullets to his head, before his death Marshall also received a severe blow to his head, and was asphyxiated with carbon monoxide. While this did not solve the question of who killed Marshall, 23 years after his death it was at least determined that the suicide story was a cover-up for murder.

In March of 1984, one year after his release from prison, Estes was subpoenaed to testify before a grand jury concerning the death of Agent Marshall in 1961. Because grand jury testimony is secret, only reports of his testimony and not actual transcripts are available. However, the reports of Estes' sworn grand jury testimony show that, decades after the murder, Estes linked Vice President Johnson and two other men to the execution of Henry Marshall. While it is entirely possible that Estes in his old age decided to lie about the event, it is also possible that after years of silence — with Johnson dead, and nothing to fear — Estes perhaps decided to tell the truth.[124][125]

---

124. Another death related to the Belly Sol Estes scandal was his accountant, George Krutilek. Interviewed by FBI agents on April 2, 1962, on April 4th Krutilek was found dead in the town of Clint, Texas with a hose from his exhaust stuck in the window. The El Paso County pathologist held that he did not die from carbon monoxide poisoning. (North, *ibid.*, p. 139-140). This death was not listed in the prior chapter's table on suspicious deaths since it occurred prior to the assassination. A source that appears less credible cites even more deaths connected with Billy Sol Estes: employees Harold Eugene Orr and Howard Pratt, deceased under unusual circumstances. A discussion of this matter can be visited at http://users.crocker.com/-acacia/meeting.html.

125. *Ibid.*, p. 141.

Another scandal, which began only months before Kennedy's death, involved Bobby Baker. Baker was known as "Lyndon's boy." Johnson once said of him, "Bobby is my strong right arm. He is the last person I see at night and the first person I see in the morning."[126]

Baker was earning $20,000 a year as secretary to the Senate Majority leader, but he owned a mansion near LBJ, purchased a townhouse for his mistress, had an interest in a North Carolina motel, and also became an owner of a seaside resort called the Carousel. He was also involved in influence peddling related to a vending machine company servicing federal contractors in California.[127]

The media began publicizing stories of Johnson's direct links to Bobby Baker. Johnson acted as if he had never met Baker. The Senate Rules Committee voted to continue pursuing the investigation. Baker resigned on October 7, 1963; Johnson flew to Dallas, and remained there in seclusion; *he did not return to Washington until after November 22.* On the day of the President's assassination, the Bobby Baker scandal was still one of the leading headlines of the *Dallas Herald Tribune* and other papers throughout the country.

If Jack Kennedy had not been murdered, the Baker investigation would not have ended. If Jack Kennedy had not been murdered, the Baker scandal would have either destroyed or tarnished Johnson' image so completely that he would not have been on the 1964 ticket. If the President had not been slain, the truth about LBJ may have put him in prison, as his grandma predicted, rather than into the White House."[128]

> A lobbyist named Winter-Berger was discussing public relations with Speaker of the House McCormack in McCormack's Washington office. Johnson then barged in and began ranting hysterically . . . oblivious to the lobbyist's presence. . . Johnson said: "John, that son of a bitch [Bobby Baker] is going to ruin me. If that cocksucker talks, I'm gonna land in jail . . . I practically raised that motherfucker, and now he's gonna make me the first President of the United States to spend the last days of his life behind bars."[129]

---

126. *Ibid.*, p. 145.
127. Some wonder why JFK asked him to serve as Vice President in the first place. Seymour Hersh, in *The Dark Side of Camelot*, contends Johnson knew of JFK's sexual excesses and threatened to expose him if his name were not on the ballot. SJMN, November 9, 1997, p. 8A. Recent conspiracy literature — perhaps a more questionable source, — alleges Estes implicated Malcolm "Mac" Wallace, an LBJ crony, in numerous murders. "In 1984, grand jury testimony Estes named Wallace as the 1962 killer of Agricultural inspector Henry Marshall. . . Estes identified eight other Wallace victims including President Kennedy." (Electronic Assassinations Newsletter, November 12, 2001; www.assassinationweb.com/shack3g.htm).
128. *Ibid.*, p. 149.
129. North, Mark. *Act of Treason* New York: Carroll & Graf, 1991, p. 516.

Chapter 4. Conspiracy

Zirbel, in *The Texas Connection*, provides a startling array of facts to buttress his case.

- It was Johnson who strongly urged the President to come to Dallas, and Johnson who played a major role in planning the trip, including arrangements for parades, security, and cities to visit.
- On the day before the assassination, Johnson went to Kennedy's suite at the Cortez hotel and had a bitter argument with him. He wanted Kennedy to remove John Connally (who was Johnson's friend) from the President's limousine and have Senator Yarborough (his enemy) sit in Connally's seat instead. The President refused.
- Many of Johnson's strongest supporters in Dallas had made threatening remarks against Kennedy, including oil billionaire H.L. Hunt (not to be confused with E. Howard Hunt) and industrialist Clint Murchison.
- John Connally, Lyndon Johnson, and Kennedy met in Washington on October 4, 1963 to make final arrangements for the trip. The dates and routes were decided and known only to these men. Oswald began his Texas School Book Depository job on October 16, 1963.

The Dallas police, under Chief Curry (a personal friend of Johnson), were negligent to the extreme.

Zirbel makes the following remarks:

> The actions of the Dallas Police Department . . . defy all logic and common sense. Why did they: never follow up on the miracle bullet; fail to explain Officer Tippit's patrol assignment in Oswald's neighborhood; refuse to say why a Dallas police car stopped in front of Oswald's rooming house; not explain why Officer Tippit was seen casually talking to Oswald before Tippit's death; not investigate how and why Oswald killed Tippit; fail to answer how Oswald could have single-handedly stacked over a ton of books to create a sniper's nest; not question why they only could find a few of Oswald's prints in the sniper's area; not ask why the sniper did not fire at a closer unimpeded range; not supply an explanation as to how Oswald's fingerprint could surface on the alleged assassination weapon days later; not allow Oswald to have a lawyer; take no contemporaneous notes of Oswald's interrogations; permit Oswald to be an execution target for Ruby on the late Friday evening; never allow Oswald to publicly talk; not transfer Oswald out of the Dallas jail within 12 hours as required by law; . . . permit the Chief to ignore reliable warning of a possible execution attempt of Oswald; perform a public transfer of Oswald; not use a human police shield to protect Oswald; let Ruby get into a secured area twice with a gun; and have an ambulance ready in advance of the shooting?

As Zirbel says, while the Dallas Police Department has never supplied adequate answers to these questions, Police Chief Curry's personal relationship with Lyndon Johnson may offer some insight.[130]

Jack Ruby also had indicted Johnson in many of his rambling statements made during his incarceration. Here is one such example:

> First, you must realize that the people here want everyone to think I am crazy... isn't it strange that Oswald... should be fortunate enough to get a job at the Texas Schoolbook Depository Building two weeks before... Only one person could have had that information, and that man was Johnson... because he is the one who was going to arrange the trip... The only one who gained by the shooting...[131]

In addition, Johnson had major personality problems, and some of his aides felt he was not merely a buffoon but mentally unbalanced. Two had privately consulted with a psychiatrist about his mental stability.[132] Virtually everything Johnson touched was branded by his megalomania and the LBJ imprimatur. His wife was called Lady Bird Johnson, his daughters Lucy and Lynda (LBJs), his best friend John Connally was called "Little Boy Johnson" (LBJ). His dogs and household as well as his ranch in Texas all fell under the LBJ logo. After he became President, the Space Center in Texas was named the Johnson Space Center. When Johnson visited the Vatican, he presented the Pope with a bust of himself.

---

130. Zirbel, *ibid.*, p. 187

131. *Ibid.*, pp. 206-207. 9. This author has never visited the Johnson estate, but a friend related the following story. On his drive from California to Florida, he passed through Texas; the vastness and emptiness of the landscape impressed him. Suddenly a two-lane road became a major freeway with stunning and impressive directional signs, overpasses, etc. The sign pointed passing drivers to the exit leading to the Johnson ranch. A few miles later, the expressway suddenly ended and the driver was back on a two-lane road passing through vast, empty stretches of landscape. This freeway was likely another of Johnson's pork barrel adventures in the service of his megalomania.

132. The two LBJ aides who sought advice from a psychiatrist about LBJ were Goodwin and Bill Moyers (Heymann, *ibid.*, p. 106.)

Chapter 4. Conspiracy

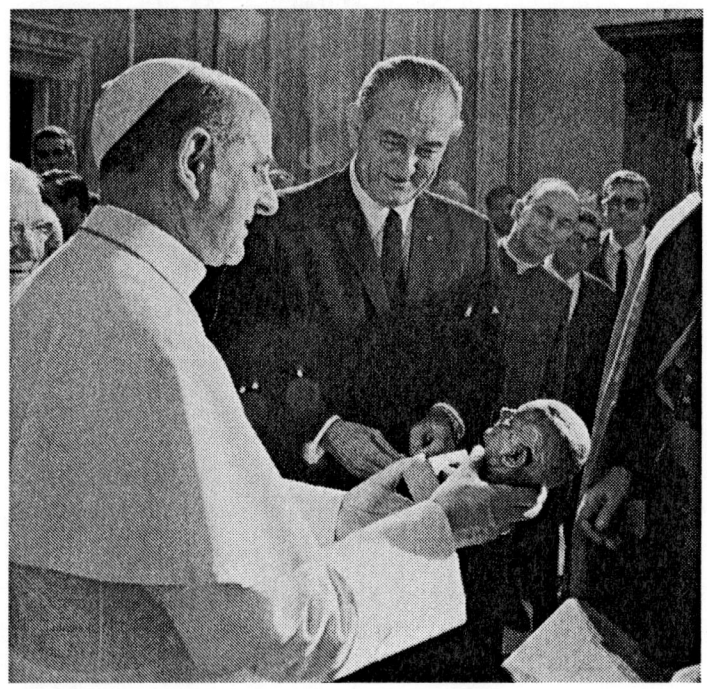

LBJ presents the Pope with a bust of himself.

Besides this megalomania, Johnson's personal behavior was borderline. He had at least two mistresses, each for over 20 years. The first was a woman named Alice Glass, and their affair began in 1938 after he had been married for four years. He also developed a relationship in 1948 with Madeline Brown. Ms. Brown claims that she had a son by him and that Johnson supported her for decades. He also took up with Dr. Doris Kearns for a short time; Dr. Kearns was a professor at Harvard.[133]

Johnson was, at the very least, a problem drinker and many incidents of public drunkenness have been documented. Not infrequently, he would order his secret service men to form a shield around him so that he could urinate outside during a White House gathering.

Since grade school he had told his friends he wanted to be President of the United States. As Vice President, Johnson would have his chauffeur drive him to the White House each morning, whereupon he would walk through the White House,

---

133. Michael J. Sullivan, *Presidential Passions*, New York: Shapolsky, 1991, pp. 79-100.

pass by the Oval office, and then exit the building, walking the rest of the way to his own office. He actually met with President Kennedy for less than two hours in the entire last year of the Kennedy presidency.

> It is well known that Johnson and Kennedy disliked each other. Johnson once derisively asked Bobby if his brother had "got any pussy lately." LBJ was probably also aware of Kennedy's references to him and his wife as "Colonel Cornpone and his little Porkchop." [134]

Strongest Points

The strongest points of the Johnson theory are those involving motive. Johnson had Jackie Kennedy removed from the White House by the Monday following the assassination. Mr. Kennedy's rocking chair was removed at the same time. Johnson wanted to be sworn in as Chief Executive on "Texas soil," so the plane carrying the grieving widow was held up for 90 minutes so that he could be sworn in with a Texas federal judge conducting the ceremony. Johnson took over Air Force One rather than return to Washington in the vice presidential plane.

He told the Warren Commission that Kenneth O'Donnell told him at Parkland Hospital to take Air Force One back. According to O'Donnell, "Later, a lawyer for the Warren Commission pointed out to me that Johnson's testimony that I told him to board Air Force One disagreed with my own testimony before the commission about our conversation at the hospital. He asked me, to my amazement, if I would change my testimony so that it would agree with the Presidents'. 'Was I under oath?' I asked him, as of course, I was. 'Certainly I wouldn't change anything I said under oath.'" [135]

This illustrates the apparent control Johnson had over the Warren Commission and its conclusions, as well as the attempts to forge a consistent document despite the contradictory testimony of the participants.

The Johnson egoism, megalomania, and drive for power are well documented and provide good reason to consider him a prime suspect. His dealings in government for personal profit, his waning political prospects just prior to the assassination, JFK's desire to dump him as Vice President, and his ascent to power after the assassination would lead any outside observer to at least consider Johnson to have both motive and opportunity.

Furthermore, there has been much controversy about the autopsy in Bethesda Naval Hospital vis-à-vis results obtained at Parkland Hospital in Dallas. Many have

---

134. Heymann, C. David. *A Woman Named Jackie*. New York: Carol Communications, 1989, p. 427

135. O'Donnell, Kenneth and Powers, Dave. *Johnny, We Hardly Knew Ye*. New York: Pocket Book, 1972. p. 41.

argued that a proper autopsy should have been conducted in Dallas, not Washington. One Parkland physician, Dr. Earl Rose, had to be physically restrained by Kennedy aides to get the President's body out of Dallas and onto Air Force One. The major decision maker in permitting the body to be taken to Washington was a personal friend of Lyndon Johnson, District Attorney Henry Wade.[136]

Zirbel makes an excellent point in his analysis of the make up of the Warren Commission. If there was anyone in a position of power to defuse, defeat, and squelch any inquiry into Johnson's involvement, it was Johnson himself. An inquiry into the assassination of President Kennedy could have been headed by his brother Robert, the Attorney General. By creating the Warren Commission, Johnson placed the investigation under his own authority and removed it from Bobby Kennedy's control. By making Allen Dulles the CIA liaison on this Committee — a man Kennedy had recently fired — Johnson further rigged the Committee in his own favor. Johnson was never deposed, never considered a suspect, and never had to testify under oath before the Commission.

The theory is compelling.

Another strong point favoring this theory has appeared only recently with the release of documents withheld by the government for over 35 years. Based on these released materials, one conspiracy-based newsletter reports on how LBJ might have had Oswald placed in the Texas School Depository. LBJ knew George deMohrenschildt, Oswald's closest friend in Dallas, and an individual who clearly had associations with the CIA. DeMohrenschildt also had personal associations with LBJ and wrote to him on April 17, 1963. George Brown, LBJ's chief financial sponsor, had previously employed deMohrenschildt. These men and their associates, Sid Richardson, H.L. Hunt (the oil magnate), and Harold Byrd (owner of the Texas School Book Depository) regularly met at the Dallas Petroleum Club. Such associations provide ample room for an LBJ plot to be hatched with Oswald-the-patsy properly placed in the right place at the right time.[137] (Curiously enough, when deMohrenschildt killed himself many years after the assassination, he was writing a book on Oswald called *Patsy*.)

---

136. *Ibid.*, p. 45.
137. Martin Shackelford, "New discoveries in the recently released assassination files." Electronic Assassinations Newsletter, November 12, 2001. (www.assassinationweb.com/shack3g.htm).

Weakest Points

The Johnson theory, however, still does not give us an assassin, nor are believable scenarios provided to explain who was involved. How did Oswald get involved? Who connects Johnson to the assassins? Connally, Korth, the billionaire Hunts, Chief Curry, District Attorney Henry Wade, and wealthy Texans like Clint Murchison are all listed as part of the conspiracy, but documentation is weak.[138]

If Connally were implicated as one of the plotters, it would seem ludicrous for him to be a sole voice disagreeing with the Warren Commission findings that there were only three shots. If Connally conspired with Johnson, and the Warren Commission was simply Johnson's personal "clean up" brigade, then Connally's disagreement with the Commission makes little sense at all. Connally did not waver on his insistence that the magic bullet theory was harebrained.

There are a few errors of substance. Oswald, says Zirbel, would have had to move of a ton of book cartons in the Depository to create his sniper's lair, implying that others would have been needed to create the nest. Author Jim Moore has shown that these book cartons weigh less than 50 pounds each and has himself accomplished the task with ease.

Overall, Zirbel's case against Johnson is very interesting and not easily dismissed. Some curious connections are brought forth. Jack Ruby visited a building owned by Johnson's personal friend H.L. Hunt shortly before the assassination. So did Marina Oswald. Fred Korth, the Johnson appointee indicted for conflict of interest as Secretary of the Navy, had represented Lee Harvey Oswald's mother, Marguerite, in a divorce action. Texas District Attorney Henry Wade and Dallas Police Chief Curry, clearly involved in botching the case against Oswald, were personally close to Johnson.[139] Another investigator turned up evidence recently that the Dal-Tex building, a location many have felt could have housed a second shooter, was owned by a very close personal associate and advisor to Johnson, Morris Jaffe,[140] just as Johnson is alleged to have known the owner of the Book Depository.

---

138. North, *ibid.*, p. 361.

139. In 1995, a letter reportedly written by Jack Ruby surfaced. The 12-page letter, addressed to a Dallas police officer friend named Joe, reiterates Ruby's theory that Johnson was involved in the assassination. "Someday, Joe, you will find out what President Johnson is....One thing is for certain... he couldn't stand a polygraph test." Ruby said Oswald got his job in the Book Depository ten days before Kennedy himself knew he was coming to Dallas. "Who up in Washington was so close to the president to know this information and pass it on to Oswald(?)" Source: "Letter from Ruby," *San Jose Mercury News*, April 15, 1995.

140. Bob Goodman, *Triangle of Fire*, San Jose, CA: Laquerian Publishers, 1993.

For Europeans, who suspected President Johnson had engaged in a coup d'état from the very beginning, it is curious that the American effort to examine this idea took over 30 years before an indictment ever reached the book sellers. [141]

2. The Mob Theory

> Mark my word, this man Kennedy is in trouble, and he will get what is coming to him... He is going to be hit.
> — Santos Trafficante[142]

A second intriguing theory centers on a conspiracy within the Mafia to kill Kennedy. There are many twists and turns of intrigue and machination here, however. In fact, it is precarious to condense the Mob theory into a few short pages, simply because there are so many names, places and associations involved, from "Milwaukee Phil" to "Needle Nose Labriola." A list of individuals reckoned to be part of the conspiracy is provided in Table 4.1, merely to illustrate this complexity.

Essential Points

Kennedy's father, Joseph Kennedy, is said to have made over $100 million in the stock market crash of 1929 by selling short. He had multiple contacts with bootleggers and illegally imported scotch whiskey during Prohibition. When JFK became a Congressman from Massachusetts, Joseph Kennedy maintained a low profile. His son, however, was in touch with him constantly, often many times per day even when he was President. Joe Kennedy was a major force in priming and securing the vote for his son, and was actively involved in all his son's campaigns. To win was far more important than issues or platforms.

One "deal" made behind the scenes was to get the Illinois vote for Kennedy over Nixon. Kennedy beat Nixon with fewer than 200,000 votes nationally, in one of the closest presidential races to that date; the Illinois vote, particularly the Chicago vote, was engineered by notorious Mayor Richard Daley and gangster Sam Giancana. John Kennedy may or may not have been aware of his father's actions on his behalf.

---

141. There is also a possibility that Johnson may have some connections to Carlos Marcello of New Orleans. A Texas mafia figure named Jack Halfen allegedly had contributed a portion of Carlos Marcello's Texas slot machine profits to Lyndon Johnson's political campaigns. Halfen kept 800 feet of movie film showing himself and his wife with the Johnsons on a Texas hunting trip. At the time of the President's assassination, there was a thick investigative file on Robert Kennedy's desk detailing the Marcello-Halfen-Johnson connection; Kennedy was debating whether to pursue it. North, *ibid.*, p. 371.

142. Summers, Anthony. *Conspiracy* New York: McGraw-Hill, 1989, p. 243.

J. Edgar Hoover met with President Kennedy only once He informed the President of his knowledge of Kennedy's extramarital relationship with Judith Exner, and her connections with gangster, Sam Giancana.

> In 1988 Judith Exner, the woman who became the mistress of both President Kennedy and Chicago mobster Sam Giancana, claimed she had been used as a courier between the White House and Giancana, and that President Kennedy had gone so far as to meet Sam Giancana. Going far beyond her testimony to the Senate Intelligence Committee, Exner said, "I lied when I said that President Kennedy was unaware of my friendships with mobsters. He knew everything about my dealings with Sam Giancana and Johnny Roselli because I was seeing them for him." For eighteen months in 1960 and 61 Exner said she repeatedly carried envelopes from the President to Giancana and Roselli. There were, she calculated, some ten meetings between the President and the Chicago mobster, one of them at the White House.[143]

Sam Giancana once said to Judith Exner Campbell, "Listen, honey, if it wasn't for me your boyfriend wouldn't even be in the White House." [144]

Hoover also told Kennedy, in December of 1961, that he was aware of his father's relationship with Giancana and of his contributions to JFK's 1960 campaign. Kennedy told his father, and within a few days Joseph Kennedy had a massive stroke from which he never fully recovered.[145]

In 1961, John Kennedy had been accused of adultery in a California divorce suit. A friend of Sam Giancana, gangster Johnny Roselli, intervened to remove the President's name as a "co-respondent." The enraged husband was paid off and the matter was settled quietly.

Robert Kennedy, the Attorney General and J. Edgar Hoover's boss, had very difficult relations. Bobby had difficulty even reaching his star employee and, frustrated at constantly having to deal with Hoover's secretary, he placed a red phone directly on the Director's desk and ordered him to answer it whenever he called. Hoover bristled, but complied. Hoover's fiefdom was only temporarily interrupted by Kennedy's presence on the scene.

---

143. *Ibid.*, p. 527. White House telephone logs show that Exner called over seventy times from the President's inauguration until March of 1962 (Summers, p. 248). Their affair ended abruptly in March 1962, immediately after FBI Director Hoover had lunch with JFK.

144. Reeves, *ibid.*, p. 214.

145. North, *ibid.*

Hoover did not believe in a "Mafia" and always placed the term in quotes in any communications. Bobby Kennedy, on the other hand, was making a concerted effort to wage a war on organized crime through the Justice Department. He received little assistance from Hoover in the effort. In 1962, the Kennedys convicted over 101 Mafia figures and had hundreds more scheduled for trial (more than all the prosecutions under the prior Eisenhower administration). Racketeering prosecutions were up by 300% over 1961 rates, and 700% over 1960 rates. The Mob was, of course, upset; Hoffa and Giancana were prime targets.[146]

The Kennedy attack on the Mafia, therefore, was a double-edged sword. It is odd indeed, if true, that Giancana helped the President win Illinois and yet Robert Kennedy was massing a phalanx of federal agents to put Hoffa, Giancana, and Marcello behind bars. When RFK served on the McClellan Committee investigating organized crime, prior to the election of his brother to the presidency, Giancana was placed in the position of having to take the Fifth Amendment over thirty three times.

Table 4.1 lists individuals whose names are mentioned in conspiracy texts with respect to the Mafia aspect of the assassination.

An added factor here is that President Kennedy and Bobby were both attempting to force J. Edgar Hoover to resign. As late as March 15, 1963, however, Hoover said he had no intention of submitting to their requests.[147]

Hoover Wiretaps

In the interim, through wiretap programs named ELSUR and COINTELPRO, J. Edgar Hoover garnered pivotal information from Mafia figures; the information was held in his personal files and not provided to the Attorney General or the President. Among these starting revelations are the following:

Feb. 28, 1962. Benjamin Lewis was murdered, gangland style, in Chicago. An HSCA exhibit reveals Giancana saying, "That will teach that little fucker, Kennedy, who runs Chicago."[148]

---

146. Anthony Summers interviewed Edward Partin, a Teamster official in Louisiana who gave federal investigators incriminating information on Hoffa. According to Partin, Hoffa was planning to blow up Robert Kennedy's house. Summers arranged to interview Partin for television, but the former Teamster begged off. He had a note delivered, reading, "I am sorry I cannot keep the appointment with you, but for the safety of my family and myself, especially my family (whom I have had to move out of the state and hide), I just don't think it would be fair to them. . . Up until now they have known only fear, death, and the threat of death" (Summers, *ibid.*, p. 253). Partin originally alleged that Hoffa intended the death of the President as well as his brother.

147. North, *ibid.*, p. 243

148. *Ibid.*, p. 619.

Table 4.1. *Individuals mentioned in conspiracy texts with respect to a Mafia aspect of the assassinationy*

Albert Anastasia	Johnny Roselli
Alex Gruber	John "Moose" Murret
Alfred McClane	Jose Aleman
Angelo Emile Brune	Joseph Campisi
Antoine Guerini	Joseph Civello
Barney Baker	Judith Exner Campbell
Benjamin Lewis	Lenny Patrick
Beverly Oliver	Lewis McWillie
Carlo Gambino	Joe Bonano
Carlos Marcello	Joe Tonahill
Christian David	Joe Valachi
Chuck Giancana	Lucien Marti
Chuckie Nicoletti	Meyer Lansky
Dave Yaras	Michael Clemente
David Ferrie	Michele Nicoli
Dean Martin	Mickey Cohen
Diamond Joe Esposito	"Milwaukee Phil"
Duane Nowlin	Moe Dalitz
"Dutz" Murret	Morgan Brown
Eddie "Cockeyed" Dunn	Mugsy Tortorella
Eddie McGrath	"Needle-Nose" Labriola
Edward Becker	"Needles" Gianola
Edward Partin	Nofio Pecora
Eugene Hale Brading	Paul Dorfman
Franc Caracci	Paul Roland Jones
Frank Chavez	Phyllis McQuire
Frank Costello	Richard Cain
Frank Fiorin (Sturgis)	Roscoe White
Frank Goldstein	Robert Maheu
Frank Rogano	Roger Bauman
Frank Sinatra	Sam Giancana
George McGann	Sam Saia
Gilbert Beckley	Sammy Davis Jr.
Guy Banister	Sam Termine
Harold Tannenbaum	Santo Sorge
Irwin Weiner	Santos Trafficante
J.D. Tippit	Skinny D'Amato

Jack Lawrence	Tommy Payne
Jack Ruby	Victor Emanuel Pereira
James Files	Vito Genovese
Jean West	William "Action" Jackson
Jimmy Hoffa	William Pawley
Joe Bonano	
Jimmy Hoffa	

Sources: Scheim, David. *Contract on America*. New York: Shapolsky Books, 1988; Kantor, Seth, *The Ruby Cover-Up*. New York: Kensington Publishing, 1978; Summers, Anthony, *Conspiracy*. New York: McGraw-Hill, 1989.

May 2, 1962: A wiretap tape of Mafia leader Michael Clemente of the Genovese family in New York says:

> Bob Kennedy won't stop today until he puts us all in jail all over the country. Until the commission meets and puts its foot down, things will be at a standstill.[149]

May 3, 1962. Conversation between Gilbert Beckley, functionary of Eddie McGrath, and a woman identified as Jeane.

> What is this Russia, you know what they did, they went over to Gil's and said do you know that Gil is living with a girl in New York City, why don't they come in and say this to me?. . . I'll say since when is fucking a federal offense, and if it is a federal offense I want the President of the United States indicted because I know he was whacking all those broads Sinatra brought him out. . . If I could just hit Bob Kennedy. . . . some kind of bomb that will explode I would gladly go to the penitentiary for the rest of my life, believe me.[150]

Justice department informant Edward Partin attended a meeting with Jimmy Hoffa in Washington D.C. His report, summarized for FBI files and withheld from the Attorney General by Mr. Hoover, says, in part,

> Hoffa had talked about assassinating Robert Kennedy. The first plan, the one Hoffa's then leaning toward, involved fire bombing Hickory Hill, Robert Kennedy's Virginia estate, with extraordinarily lethal plastic explosives. The place will burn after it blows up. The second plan was a backup scheme. Robert Kennedy would be shot to death from a distance away; a single gunman would be

---

149. *Ibid.*, p. 143.
150. *Ibid.*, p. 144.

enlisted to carry it out — someone without any traceable connection to Hoffa. Somebody needs to bump that son of a bitch off... Bobby Kennedy has got to go.[151]

July 17, 1962: Philadelphia FBI ELSUR wiretap records Angelo Bruno in a conversation about Carlos Marcello of New Orleans.

>Bruno reveals that Marcello had again approached Sinatra through Trafficante, calling upon him to use what influence had had with President Kennedy's father. Reportedly the attempt had only made matters worse. This recording reconfirms the close relationship shared by Marcello and Trafficante. The transcript is sent by AIRTEL to Hoover.[152]

August 3, 1962. An FBI report on Frank Sinatra's Mob associations is sent to President Kennedy. President Kennedy breaks all contacts with Sinatra from that moment forward. Sinatra is reportedly so angry that he personally destroys the helicopter-landing pad he had installed at his Palm Springs home for JFK's occasional visits. Some time later, Sinatra meets with Giancana and Roselli.[153]

September, 1962. Santos Trafficante[154] is told by Carlos Marcello that a contract has been put out on Kennedy.[155]

>During the summer and fall, Marcello associate Trafficante is recorded by ELSUR on four occasions, the Mafioso expressing tremendous bitterness toward the Kennedys over the disruption of his gambling operations. The Attorney General is not informed.[156]

April 1963. Hoover receives information showing President Kennedy leaving the house of Pamela Turnure at 1 a.m. Turnure is Mrs. Kennedy's press secretary. Hoover keeps the information, but does not share this material with the Attorney General or the President.[157]

May 9, 1963. Robert Kennedy finally succeeded in indicting Jimmy Hoffa for jury tampering.[158]

---

151. *Ibid.*, p. 152
152. *Ibid.*, p. 168.
153. *Ibid.*, p. 172.
154. John Roselli, Sam Giancana and Santos Trafficante were recruited by the CIA to assassinate Castro. They mutually had an interest in the prior gambling, drug, and prostitution operations they had enjoyed prior to Castro. Castro took power in 1959 (Reeves, *ibid.*, pp. 256-257).
155. *Ibid.*, p. 185
156. *Ibid.*, p. 185
157. *Ibid.*, p. 160
158. *Ibid.*, p. 249.

Robert Kennedy was also on the trail of Santos Trafficante (see photo). He considered Trafficante's Sicilian family as the key element in Mafia circles in Tampa. Trafficante once confided his feelings to Jose Aleman, to whom he had loaned over $1 million of Teamsters funds: Trafficante told Aleman that Kennedy would not make it to the election. He was going to be hit.[159]

As late as 1978, Aleman was afraid to come forward. The HSCA had publicly praised his courage. However, Aleman says that he informed the FBI of the impending fate of the President prior to the assassination. He told his FBI contacts that something was going to happen. The FBI, says Aleman, did not take him seriously until it was too late. (A few years after these events, Aleman took his own life.) The FBI denied the accuracy of this story, but Mark North suggests, in his book, that Hoover wanted this hit on Kennedy to take place and did nothing to stop it.

Marcello

Carlos Marcello, born Calogero Minacore, was the head of the Mafia (or Cosa Nostra) in the southern United States. His syndicate was estimated to be grossing $1.1 billion annually — in effect, it was the largest industry in the state of Louisiana.[160] He lived on a 3,000 acre estate outside New Orleans called Churchill Farms.[161] On April 4, 1961, Marcello was arrested. On the personal orders of Bobby Kennedy, he was seized, handcuffed, rushed to the airport, and flown to Guatemala — since his forged birth certificate made him a Guatemalan national. Marcello was disoriented in Guatemala and, walking through the jungle in suit and tie, he fell and broke a rib. He was furious and vowed revenge.[162] He returned surreptitiously to his estate outside New Orleans — once again to fight extradition — and said to three friends,

---

159. *Ibid.*, p. 268. (Note that the Kennedy-Hoffa vendetta became furious and fully public. After a Senate hearing in 1958, when Kennedy was on the McClellan Committee investigating organized crime, Hoffa called Kennedy a "vicious bastard". Leaving one committee session, Hoffa was heard to say "That S.O.B. — I'll break his back, the little sonofabitch." Summers, *ibid.*, p. 245. The next morning Kennedy once again grilled Hoffa in open hearings.

160. Summers, *ibid.*, p.254.

161. *Ibid.*, p. 256.

"Livarsi na petra di la scarpa!" (Take the stone out of my shoe!)... But Marcello left no doubt about his meaning as he talked on in his Sicilian-accented Southern drawl. "Don't worry about that little Bobby sonofabitch," cried Marcello. "He's going to be taken care of." Referring to the Kennedys, he said "The dog will keep biting you if you only cut off its tail," but if the dog's head were cut off, the entire dog would die. "The meaning of the analogy was clear — with John Kennedy dead, his younger brother would cease to be Attorney General, and harassment of the Mafia would cease."[163]

According to the informant who supplied this information (Edward Becker), Marcello mentioned that they would have to take out "insurance" for the President's assassination. By this he meant "setting up a nut to take the blame." According to Becker, that is the way it is done in Sicily all the time.

Marcello had a motto: *"Three can keep a secret, if two are dead."*[164] Marcello died on March 3, 1993 and whatever secrets he may have had, he took them with him — insisting to the end that he was merely a tomato salesman.[165]

The leading theorist of the Mob School is Chief Counsel of the HSCA Committee, Professor Blakey. He has said, "I am now firmly of the opinion that the Mob did it. It is a historical truth."[166]

Who Killed the President?

This theory also does not definitively answer who killed Kennedy, but it comes far closer than many of the others. Christian David's information, given in Chapter 1, provides a plausible hypothesis. Marcello, in this theory, conscripts sharpshooters from the Corsican Mafia. Antoine Guerini, the Corsican boss in Marseilles, accepts the contract. One of the shooters was Lucien Marti, who was shot dead in Mexico in 1972. His two accomplices were never identified and are still alive. Sarti used an explosive bullet; his was the third shot, and it struck the President in the head, killing him. It was fired from the grassy knoll. The fourth shot, according to this source, missed.

---

162. Carlos Marcello was arrested in the early 1970s. When he was released from prison, he quietly retired to Metairie, Louisiana where he progressively succumbed to Alzheimer's disease. He is reputed to have invited the Gambino family of New York to assume control of his operations (Craig, John R. & Rogers, Philip A. *The Man on the Grassy Knoll*. New York: Avon Books, 1992, p. 238.) He died in 1993.
163. Summers, *ibid.*, p. 257.
164. *Ibid.*, p. 258.
165. Craig, *ibid.*, p. 212.
166. *San Jose Mercury News*, March 4, 1993, p. 5B.

Chapter 4. Conspiracy

Christian David was asked who could corroborate the story, and he named Michele Nicoli. Author Steve Rivele finally found Nicoli and met with him over many months. He was extremely reluctant to talk. Nicoli finally told Rivele that Christian David's rendition of the story was correct.

Oswald fits into this theory just as he said: he was a patsy. Oswald was arrested in New Orleans for passing out "Fair Play For Cuba" leaflets; his uncle Dutz, who had contact with two Marcello associates, posted bail. One of those associates was present at Oswald's bail hearing — Nofio Pecora. Pecora not only was one of Marcello's oldest friends but phone records show that, three weeks before the assassination, Jack Ruby was in touch with Pecora as well.

David Ferrie, too, has been linked to the Marcello organization as well as to Oswald. Ferrie was in the courtroom during Marcello's acquittal in New Orleans on the very day JFK was shot, and drove to Texas later that day. Ferrie piloted an aircraft out of Guatemala, returning Marcello to New Orleans after Robert Kennedy ad deported him. And Oswald clearly knew David Ferrie.

These, then, represent the most intimate and immediate contacts Oswald had to organized crime: his uncle Dutz, a bookie for Marcello, another of Oswald's uncles — John "Moose" Murret (also seen by police in Marcello's company),[167] David Ferrie, a close associate of Marcello and Oswald's Civil Air Patrol instructor many years earlier, and finally Nofio Pecora, the Marcello friend who bailed Oswald out of jail and spoke to Jack Ruby three weeks before Kennedy was hit.

It was through this linkage that Oswald was set up to be the patsy for the contract hit. Even if the Sarti assassination connection is untrue, there were other underworld figures present at Dealey Plaza that day. One of them was Eugene Hale Brading. He was arrested at the Dal-Tex building and gave a false name; his true identity was not discovered until the late 1960s. Some argue that Brading was involved. Brading was an associate of Meyer Lansky, the Mafia kingpin to whom Trafficante reported. Brading and Morgan Brown checked into Suite 301 of the Cabana Hotel overlooking the Stemmons Freeway in downtown Dallas, and with associate Morgan Brown left town at 2 p.m. on the day Kennedy was killed.

Another author, however, gives a variation on the Mafia conspiracy:

---

167. Information suggesting that Oswald's second uncle also had underworld ties is recent and comes from Summers, "The Ghosts of November," *Vanity Fair*, December, 1994. David Ferrie's presence at Carlos Marcello's acquittal is corroborated in R. Goldfarb, *Perfect Villains, Imperfect Heroes*, ibid.

In all likelihood the actual assassins of John Kennedy were contract killers brought in from other parts of the country in typical gangland fashion. These people may have been supplied through the cooperation of gambling network functionaries like Saia, Campisi, di Piazza, Nolan, Beckley, Ruby, McWillie, and McGrath who were the common thread between men like Marcello, Trafficante, Giancana, and Lansky.[168]

A third assassination scenario is proposed in a book written by the younger Sam Giancana and Giancana's godson. This plot involves virtually everyone, principally Sam "Mooney" Giancana, but Johnson and Nixon as well. In this text the assassins were Charles Harrelson and Jack Lawrence (Marcello's men), two unnamed Cuban exile friends of Trafficante, plus Richard Cain, Chuckie Nicoletti, and "Milwaukee Phil," Giancana's men from Chicago. Cain fired the shots from the sixth-story window while other "soldiers" on the team, Roscoe White, J.D. Tippit, Frank Fiorini (Sturgis) also participated.[169] (In this rendition Roscoe White, not Oswald, killed officer Tippit.) Ruby's role was to take out Oswald after his arrest and clean up what Tippit failed to do, namely to hit the patsy, Oswald. According to the younger Giancana:

> "On November 22, 1963," Mooney stated with chilling authority, "the United States had a coup; it's that simple. The government of this country was overthrown by a handful of guys who did their job so damned well... only one American even knew it happened. But I know. I know I've guaranteed the Outfit's future... once and for all. We're set here in the United Sates. So it's time to move on to greener pastures.[170]

A derivative of this scenario was presented by Hoffa's personal attorney, Frank Rogano, on the television program *Hard Copy*, on the occasion of Carlos Marcello's death in March 1993. In this presentation Jimmy Hoffa asked Marcello to hit Kennedy. After the assassination, Marcello communicated to Hoffa through Rogano, saying, "You owe me . . . You owe me big!" Rogano also reported at another time that shortly after the assassination Hoffa took Rogano aside and said, "I told you they could do it. I'll never forget what Carlos and Santos [Trafficante] did for me." [171]

Allegedly there are tapes in which Marcello is recorded ordering the contract. In this variant of a Mob hit, Oswald continues to be the patsy, conscripted for the assignment by his uncle Dutz from New Orleans who was a father figure to Oswald, and at the same time a lieutenant of Marcello and a bookie. This differs from Giancana's rev-

---

168. Summers, *ibid.*, p. 260.
169. North, *ibid.*, p. 372.
170. *Ibid.*, p. 538.
171. Ronald Goldfarb, *ibid.*, p. 285.

elations, but is nonetheless consistent. The program did not name the assassins, however. (See page 116.)

Yet another assassination scenario has appeared with the discovery of convict James E. Files. Files is currently sitting in Joliet State Penitentiary and alleges that he was the grassy knoll gunman, hired by Chuckie Nicoletti; Johnny Roselli and Nicoletti were in the Dal-Tex Building. According to his story, JFK was hit from behind by Roselli and from the front by Files. Roselli arrived at 6:30 a.m. that morning on a private flight from Miami, flown by Robert "Tosh" Plumlee, a CIA pilot. Mr. Plumlee testified before the Senate Foreign Relations Committee on August 2, 1990 and his testimony was held as Top Secret. Plumlee's testimony appears to corroborate Files assertions.[172]

Strongest Points

Here are the strongest elements supporting the theory that the Mob was behind the assassination.
- Oswald as the "patsy" makes eminent sense in this model. He is not the assassin at all — thus his presence in the lunchroom *before and after* the hit. The Mob does not typically use highly visible, vocal players for its contract hits; and Oswald had recently appeared on New Orleans TV, debating the cause for Cuba. But as a patsy, he was perfect.
- Oswald's panicky behavior after the assassination supports the theory. He rushed home, took a cab past his own house, went inside, grabbed his revolver, and ended up shooting Officer Tippit. Rather than acting like an assassin on the run, it seems he realized that he had been set up and that the police would be looking for a "commie kook" in a matter of minutes, thus the panicky behavior.
- Robert Kennedy's persecution of Marcello, Trafficante, and Giancana create the motive. President Kennedy's association with Giancana, plus his father Joseph's past relationships, define a scenario in which the Kennedy brothers may not have been fully cognizant of the paradoxes in their own behavior. John was sleeping with Giancana's girlfriend, while Bobby was trying to put "Mooney" in jail. Joe Kennedy had used Giancana to secure the Illinois vote, but Bobby arrested him at O'Hare International Airport. Roselli helped Kennedy cover up an embarrassing divorce suit and had worked with the CIA plots against Castro, but Bobby similarly persecuted him. The extremely private and elusive Trafficante had been involved in CIA sponsored plots to murder Castro and was rewarded — in his eyes — by nothing short of harassment and persecution by the relentless tactics of Bobby Kennedy.[173] The Mob, in other words, had been double-crossed!
- Thus the Marcello-Hoffa-Trafficante-Giancana basis of this plot adds up motive, method and opportunity. Ample evidence exists as well that clear threats

---

172. http://mcadams.posc.mu.edu/arrb/index67.htm
173. Giancana, Sam and Giancana, Chuck. *Double Cross*. New York: Warner Books, 1992, p. 468.

were made by these individuals; Hoover's silence on the matter raises an issue of FBI complicity.

- Hoover collected scandalous information on Martin Luther King's sexual behavior as well as Kennedys. Hoover was decidedly racist and became extremely agitated when Kennedy condoned the 200,000 person, civil rights "March on Washington." He did not like the Kennedys, did not like the racial overtones of the liberal administration, and certainly did not like being pressured into retirement in his generation-long job. There is good evidence that the Mafia also had compromising information on Mr. Hoover, which he did not want exposed, so Bobby's campaign against the Mob threatened Hoover at an even more personal level.
- The Mafia assassination theory, therefore, also involves Hoover's collusion and offers to explain much of the FBI-based cover-up of essential facts as well as FBI efforts to stonewall the various committees which attempted to examine the evidence themselves, including the Warren Commission.
- The clear pattern of deaths of Giancana, Roselli, and so many other Mob figures who were called upon to testify (eight of whom were murdered shortly before or after their testimony) also supports this scenario. Many others who have been named in this section were also murdered: Richard Cain, Action Jackson, Chuckie Nicoletti, Milwaukee Phil, and Dave Yaras.
- And if the goal of the assassination was to immobilize Robert Kennedy by killing the source of his power, it actually accomplished its aim. The Justice Department crusade against organized crime came to a halt.
- The minute that bullet hit Jack Kennedy's head, it was all over. Right then. The organized crime program just stopped, and Hoover took control back. Kennedy (Robert) himself said, "Those people [The FBI] don't work for us anymore." One FBI agenda admitted to biographer Anthony Summers, "The whole Mafia effort slacked off again." Less than two weeks after the assassination on December 3, 1963, an FBI bug revealed a cynical remark by one Chicago hood to Sam Giancana: "In another two months from now, the FBI will be like it was five years ago. They won't be around no more."[174]
- A final strong point in the Mob-hit theory is the role of Jack Ruby in the killing of Oswald. The best "patsy" is a dead patsy, and in this scenario Oswald had to be silenced. Ruby's background was largely whitewashed by the Warren Commission; indeed, the Warren Commission concluded that it "*could not establish a significant link between Jack Ruby and organized crime.*"[175] Ruby operated a striptease club; his association with organized crime is not at all difficult to establish.

Following is a partial list of Ruby's more significant contacts, which have come to light in research since the 1964 Warren Commission report.

---

174. Goldfarb, *ibid.*, p. 303.
175. Arthur Schlesinger reported that when Bobby Kennedy learned that the CIA had used Giancana, Bobby was visibly upset. Bobby allegedly learned about the CIA relationship to Giancana in May of 1962 (Reeves, *ibid.*, p. 260).

Table 4.2 Jack Ruby's Underworld Connections and Contacts [176]

- Jacob Rubenstein started out as a courier delivering sealed envelopes for Al Capone in Chicago.
- Jack Ruby, still in Chicago, was associated with the corrupt Scrap Iron and Junk Handler's Union founded by Leon Cooke. Cooke was later murdered and Ruby's picture appeared in the *Chicago Tribune* in connection with the unsolved killing.
- Ruby's rap sheet included nine arrests in 16 years in Dallas.
- Ruby visited mobster Santos Trafficante in prison in Havana in 1959 on more than one occasion.
- On October 12, 1963, Ruby called Irwin S. Weiner in Chicago and talked for 12 minutes. Weiner was Jimmy Hoffa's financial counselor.
- Two weeks later, Ruby called Barney Baker. "An FBI rap sheet on Baker says he was Hoffa's bagman and muscleman." He had been paroled from Sandstone Prison on June 7, 1963. (After Ruby's call, Baker called hitman Dave Yaras in Miami.) [177]
- On November 12, Paul Rowland. Jones and Alex Gruber held meetings with Ruby, both associated with organized crime and ex-convicts. Jones was guilty of attempted bribery, and convicted in Kansas of murdering a state's witness. Gruber had been convicted many times of grand larceny. He is alleged to have been the Mafia paymaster at this time. Gruber had a police record, was born in Chicago, met with Ruby a few days before the Kennedy assassination, and had a long-distance conversation with Ruby minutes after Kennedy was pronounced dead at Parkland Hospital.
- On November 14, Ruby called Chicago gangland gunman, Lenny Patrick. Patrick had a long record, was a convicted bank robber, and had been arrested many times on suspicion of being a triggerman in numerous gangland killings.

---

176. *Ibid.*, p. 58; 205; 309.

177. Before Baker called David Yaras in Miami, Baker called Victor Emanuel Pereira, on Oct 9, 1963. "Pereira was in business principally with two people. One was Earl Shieb, who had of a national chain of auto paint shops and was father of Philip Earl Shieb, a machine-gun toting leader in the extreme-rightwing secret military movement, the Minutemen. The other partner was Eugene Hale Brading, who hooked up with Pereira in El Paso, Texas in 1950. Note that Eugene Hale Brading was stopped for questioning. On the day of the assassination, Milteer was allegedly photographed in Dealey Plaza at the assassination site. Milteer, like Eugene Hale Brading, was closely associated with the Minutemen. (Groden, p. 414). Others dispute Milteer's presence.

"Carlos fucked up!" Frank Rogano's revelations in 1992

Nick Pileggi, a Mafia historian, brought Frank Rogano's revelations to a focus for a PBS Frontline documentary. Rogano was Jimmy Hoffa's attorney and later became closely involved with Santos Trafficante and Carlos Marcello. Rogano confirms that Hoffa, Trafficante, and Marcello all had independent motives for wishing Kennedy removed. Hoffa had been under two indictments at the time of the assassination. Marcello had been deported by Bobby and was furious. Trafficante too was under investigation. Trafficante, Marcello, and Rogano met at the Royal Orleans Hotel in New Orleans and Rogano told both men that Hoffa wanted Kennedy hit. Rogano's impressions were that Trafficante and Marcello acted as if the matter were already in progress. Ed Becker, a Las Vegas promoter, also recalls being with Carlos Marcello in New Orleans and discussing the Kennedys. Marcello said "that's gonna be taken care of." Becker left that afternoon meeting with Marcello and said "it really frightened me; it really did."

On the day Kennedy was assassinated, Rogano came to his office in New Orleans and all his secretaries were crying. He was told that Jimmy Hoffa was on the phone. Hoffa said to him in an ecstatic voice. "Did you hear the good news? They killed the sonofabitch!" That evening Rogano met Trafficante at the International Inn in New Orleans accompanied by his wife Nancy. Nancy Rogano left the dinner. Trafficante wanted to toast the assassination, was very happy, and Mrs. Rogano, feeling he had something to do with it, couldn't take the party atmosphere and left.

Four days before Trafficante died in 1987, Rogano went to speak to him. He asked Santos who killed Hoffa. Trafficante, knowing that Rogano was very close to Hoffa, confessed that "My hands were tied." Hoffa had to be taken down. Rogano then asked Trafficante the much larger question about JFK. Trafficante replied "Carlos fucked up." To Rogano that meant Carlos Marcello should have killed Bobby instead of having killed Jack.

Professor Blakey of Notre Dame believes Rogano's story to be the single most credible explanation of the assassination. He says that three independent witnesses corroborate much of what Rogano says, FBI informant, Jose Aleman, who killed himself in 1983, Johnny Roselli, a mob figure murdered in 1976, and Ed Becker, the Las Vegas promoter, still living. Rogano's version, however, does not reveal the actual assassins.

Subsequent researchers have found an inconsistency. Rogano says he met with Trafficante on March 13th in Tampa. The widow of one of Trafficante's associates, however, says he was in his north Miami Beach home then. Jack Hodus, a pharmacist, also places the mobster in Miami on that day. Hospital records show Trafficante treated for dialysis the prior day; thus Rogano's alleged meeting with Trafficante is questionable. Rogano replies in turn that he has three other witnesses to this event which he will produce if necessary or if he is sued for libel.

Sources: PBS Frontline, David Fanning Executive Producer, WGBH, "JFK, Hoffa and the Mob." 1992. Also Summers, "The Ghosts of November, Vanity Fair, December, 1994, p. 106.

* A curious footnote is that Rogano said that Alan Dorfman of the Teamsters gave John Mitchell, the Attorney General under Richard Nixon, between $100-200,000 for the release of Hoffa from prison. Despite Bobby Kennedy's heroic efforts to put Hoffa away, he was released from prison on December 23, 1971.

Chapter 4. Conspiracy

- Ruby was a longtime friend of Lewis McWillie, a gangster whom he visited in Havana where McWillie worked as a pit boss in the Tropicana gambling casino.
- Ruby met with Joseph Campisi the night before the assassination at the Egyptian Lounge. Campisi was the number-two man in Marcello's Dallas organization. Campisi acknowledges "a longstanding personal relationship with the New Orleans Mafia leader."[178] Campisi and his wife were Ruby's first visitors after his arrest.[179]
- Jack Ruby met with gangster Johnny Roselli twice in Miami in 1963.[180]
- Frank Caracci, convicted on 3 counts of conspiracy to bribe a Federal tax agent, met with Ruby on one occasion in New Orleans.[181]
- Frank Chavez, arrested for attempted murder, is listed in a recently discovered FBI report linked to Jack Ruby.[182]

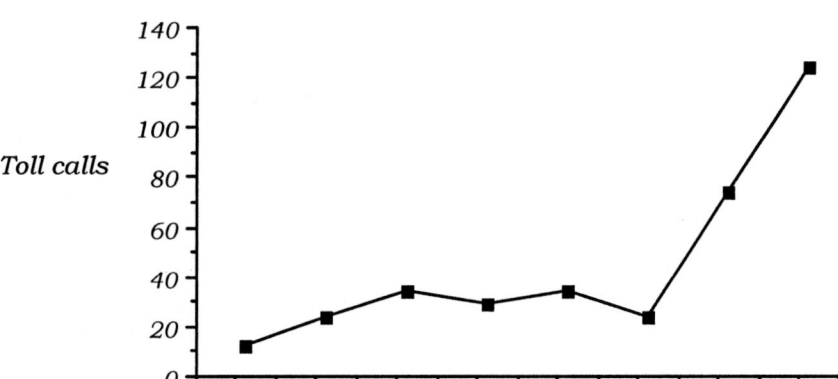

Ruby's Toll Calls in 1963

Gerald Posner in Case Closed, like the Warren Commission, attempts to make the case that Ruby was not significantly involved with the underworld. The citations in Table .2 clearly speak to the contrary. The HSCA also listed ruby's toll calls in its final report. Obviously Ruby's behavior changed from September through to the assassination. Not only did his use of the telephone dramatically increase, but his contacts with mobsters accelerated significantly. (Source: HSCA exhibit F545.)

Just eleven days before the assassination, Ruby signed a power of attorney over to his lawyer. Ruby was deeply in debt and needed a cash infusion quickly:[183] The IRS

---

178. Summers, ibid., p. 452.
179. Craig & Rogers, ibid., p. 193.
180. Scheim, David *Contract on America*. New York: Shapolski Books, 1988, p. 104.
181. Ibid., p. 103.
182. Ibid., p. 102

was seeking over $39,000 in back taxes at the time that he shot Oswald. The IRS had given him this bad news that June.

In fact, Ruby actually had two chances to kill Oswald, perhaps even three — the first being a "silent" press conference where Oswald was paraded in front of reporters but not permitted to answer questions. "Nowhere in its 888-page report to the public did the [Warren] Commission include Ruby's admission to the FBI, a month after the crime, that he was carrying a loaded, snub-nosed revolver in his right hand pocket during the Oswald press session in the assembly room."[184] On Sunday, Ruby again gained entrance into the allegedly "secured" area where Oswald was to be moved to the county jail. It was there that Ruby shot him,[185] according to Robert Blakey, an expert from the House Assassinations Committee.

> The most plausible explanation for the murder of Oswald by Jack Ruby was the Ruby had stalked him on behalf of organized crime, trying to reach him on at least three occasions in the forty-eight hours before he silenced him forever.[186]

Weaker Points

- Oswald got his job in the Texas School Book Depository through Ruth Paine's contacts. No genuine connection between Paine and the Marcello group stands out. Thus, what did the Mob have to do with placing Oswald at the TSBD to serve as the patsy?
- Ruby sent a Western Union telegram at 11:17 to one of his strippers. After finishing, he walked across the street and down the ramp and ran into Oswald as he was being transferred. He shot him spontaneously, it would appear. If he had stayed in line at Western Union another 30 seconds, he would have missed Oswald altogether. And, if Oswald had not asked to change shirts just before leaving his cell, he would have been transferred while Ruby was still at Western Union.

---

183. He also told his tax lawyer on November 19, 1963 that he expected to receive money soon to cover his debts. Ruby's first use of a safe was also in November. Source: Harrison E. Livingstone, *Killing the Truth, ibid.*, p. 91.

184. Kantor, *ibid.*, p. 101.

185. *Ibid.*

186. Goldfarb, *ibid.*, p. 281. In addition to this source, corroborating anecdotal evidence comes from James Files, previously mentioned as one of the alleged grassy knoll gunmen. Files, currently in prison for murdering a policeman, says that on the morning of the assassination, he drove Johnny Roselli to meet Jack Ruby. Later Files fired the fatal headshot. According to Files, Ruby was in on the plot from the beginning (Source: author's personal correspondence with Files.)

Ruby himself would say, in the last interview he gave before he died of cancer, that there was no way he could have been part of any calculation to bring him there at just the instant Oswald passed — unless "it was the most perfect conspiracy in the history of the world. . . the difference in meeting this fate was thirty seconds one way or the other." [187]

- If Oswald was privy to any Mob-related undertaking — to any degree — his bank account did not show it. There were no large infusions of cash. Indeed, Oswald applied for unemployment compensation twice in 1963 after losing two separate jobs. (He was fired from the Reily Coffee Company on July 22, 1963 and went to Dallas on October 3; got a room at the YMCA, and applied at the Texas unemployment office for help in finding a job.[188] When he needed bail after his New Orleans arrest, the $10 fine was paid by his uncle Dutz. Oswald's complicity in this affair does not seem to have earned him any pay-off. Oswald appeared to be dirt poor at the time of the assassination. His tax returns are still held secret, but private researchers have not been able to show Oswald to be in possession of even moderate sums of cash during this time.

In some of the Mob-based theories, Oswald is reputed to have known Ruby. In fact, one researcher suggesting that when Oswald was walking toward the Texas theater, he was really walking to Jack Ruby's house less than a mile away. Marina Oswald scoffs at that hypothesis:

> How could Lee have known Ruby, she asks. He didn't drink, he didn't smoke, he didn't go to nightclubs and besides he was sitting home with me all the time.[189]

The various bestsellers promoting Mob-based assassination scenarios reveal confessions of various parties, and there is considerable inconsistency when these books are taken together. One report says Hoffa ordered the hit through Marcello and that Oswald was a minor figure set up as a patsy by his uncle "Dutz." Another says that Giancana ordered the hit and that Oswald was "CIA all the way."

These are the major observations that undermine the Mob-hit theory. There are a few downsides to this theory, but not many. Even Bobby Kennedy considered it a very compelling possibility. Clearly, this theory is a leading alternative to the explanation offered by the Warren Commission. Like the Johnson model, the Mob attack on Kennedy shows motive, method, and opportunity. Further, the deaths of so many

---

187. Norman Mailer provides an interesting discussion of this aspect of the conspiracy in *Oswald's Tale*, New York: Random House, 1995, p. 734.
188. North *Ibid.*, p. 320.

Mafia figures who were scheduled to talk to investigating committees add up to another bit of circumstantial evidence that is not easy to ignore. When Sam Giancana was found shot to death with five bullet holes around his mouth, Santos Trafficante said, "Now there are only two people who know who shot Kennedy. And they aren't talking."[190]

3. THE CIA THORY

> Time magazine and CNN conducted a survey . . . in January 1992. The poll revealed that 73 percent of the American people believed there had been a conspiracy to assassinate the president, and that 50 percent of the American people believed that the CIA was responsible for the murder.[191]

A third, equally telling model involves the CIA. This theory is difficult to expound: A certain person is said to have known or associated with another, who, in turn, worked for Mister X, a former employee of Mister Y, and so on, *ad infinitum*. The theory reads like a Russian epic novel, and guilt by association is everywhere.

Frank Sturgis, for example, worked at the Tropicana Hotel in Havana and thus has a Cuban connection. Sturgis' real name was Fiorini, and his contacts with the Tropicana and Jack Ruby's friend, Lewis McWillie (who also worked at the Tropicana), give both gentlemen a connection to Santos Trafficante and the Mob. Sturgis, however, worked for E. Howard Hunt, and so had a CIA connection. Hunt was a senior officer in the CIA; he, in turn, worked for Nixon as a Watergate "burglar."

---

189. Johnson McMillan, Priscilla. *Marina and Lee*. New York: Harper & Row 1977, p. 454-55. On August 10, 1963, Oswald was arrested for passing out FPCC leaflets in New Orleans. He needed bail, so he called his Uncle Dutz. Dutz's daughter called Emile Bruno, an associate of two Syndicate deputies of Carlos Marcello; Bruno posted bond for Oswald (North, *ibid.*, p. 296). Another figure was Nofio Pecora, who joined Uncle Dutz at the hearing where Oswald's fine was paid on August 12, 1963.

Sam Termine, another underworld figure, was friendly with Oswald's mother, Marguerite. Termine had served as a bodyguard and chauffeur for Carlos Marcello and was a close friend of Dutz. Dutz was married to Marguerite's sister, Lilian, and was involved in illegal bookmaking activities. He was an associate of Sam Saia; the IRS identified Saia as one of the most powerful gambling figures in Louisiana; he was very close to Carlos Marcello. Thus Oswald may connect to Marcello through his uncle and his uncle's associations with Emile Bruno, Nofio Pecora, Sam Termine, and Sam Saia.

Lee Harvey Oswald's mother said, "Just because Mr. Murret worked for those people, and may have known Marcello, that doesn't mean anything about Lee." Summers, *ibid.*, p. 312.

190. FBI surveillance tape cited in Summers, *ibid.*, p. 500.

191. Lane, Mark. *Rush to Judgment*. New York: Holt, Rinehart and Winston, 1966, p. xx

Chapter 4. Conspiracy

(Both Hunt and Sturgis were arrested in Watergate.) Thus, in the end we can link Sturgis to Trafficante, Nixon, the Mob, the CIA, even to Jack Ruby.

This approach suffers in that it follows the logic of McCarthyism. An individual falls under suspicion because he knew someone who knew someone else who was implicated in some kind of wrong doing by yet another third party.

This theory is so complex and interwoven that it is very difficult to keep the facts and personalities in any kind of perspective. Some of Tolstoy's novels help the reader along by listing all the characters up front, and it might help if we did the same. There are generally considered to be 39 major players involved in this scenario.

Table 4.3 Important Figures In The CIA Assassination Model

- 1. Banister, Guy, former Chicago FBI and Military Intelligence agent, heavily involved with anti-Castro Cuban exiles; accused by Jim Martin of plotting the death of the President. Operated out of 544 Camp Street in New Orleans. Banister was also a member of the John Birch Society and of the paramilitary Minutemen; he abhorred the United Nations and was a rabid anti-communist. He also had ties to the CIA. Banister died of a heart attack. He kept a file on Lee Harvey Oswald in his agency, but that file was destroyed.[192]

- 2. Richard Bissell & Tracy Barnes. Bissell was a high-ranking CIA officer fired by JFK after the Bay of Pigs. Tracy Barnes was an associate of Bissell. Barnes is described as a "veteran of CIA covert operations in Guatemala." Barnes was involved in covert operations against Castro and was connected to E. Howard Hunt. Although many conspiracy texts mention Bissell, few cite Tracy Barnes. Newman's *Oswald and the CIA* (see bibliography) does not link Tracy Barnes in any significant way other than to corroborate that he worked for the CIA under Bissell. A text by Robert Morrow (reviewed in footnote 130, Ch. 4) is paradoxical. On the one hand it is an extraordinarily dramatic fictionalized work, and one would be hard pressed to believe it was true. On the other hand, there are very "testable" assumptions one of which, for example, is the mention of Tracy Barnes as Robert Morrow's CIA case officer. Morrow's book alleges that Tracy Barnes ordered four surplus Mannlicher-Carcano rifles for use in the assassination!

- 3. Bringuier, Carlos: anti-Castro Cuban who fought with Oswald as he passed out FPFC leaflets; was arrested with Oswald in New Orleans; an associate of Guy Banister and David Ferrie. They met when Oswald entered Bringuier's

---

192. Summers, *ibid.*, p. 292.

store in New Orleans, posing as an *anti*-Castro freedom fighter and soldier of fortune. Oswald gave Bringuier his Marine Corps manual and attempted to convince him that he was trained in guerrilla warfare and willing to train Cubans to fight *against* Castro.

- 4. Bishop, Maurice: shadowy figure within CIA, alleged by Antonio Veciana to have had a leading role in setting up Oswald. Veciana was involved in Alpha 66, the largest active anti-Castro operation the CIA has identified. His CIA contact called himself Maurice Bishop. Several CIA officials, including John McCone, did admit to knowing that Bishop was a CIA senior agent. Some have suspected the CIA Cuban officer in Mexico City, David Phillips (see photo), was Bishop (Veciana says he was not). Others have speculated that Bishop was Howard Hunt. Maurice Bishop played roles in the assassination attempts on Castro, and in efforts to remove Salvador Allende in Chile. When

David Phillips, thought by some to be Maurice Bishop

questioned by HSCA, David Phillips said he had never heard the name of Maurice Bishop. His testimony was not convincing. "Phillips reacted to unexpected questions by lighting a second cigarette moments after his first, and on one occasion lit a third while the first two smoldered in the ashtray."[193] HSCA was considering perjury charges against Phillips, but never pursued them. Subsequent to these hearings and before his death, Phillips said he felt "rogue CIA officers" were responsible for killing JFK. Phillips is also cited later in this section as having been party with Howard Hunt in the overthrow of a leftist Guatemalan president in 1954.

- 5. Bosch, Orlando: implicated by Marita Lorenz as one of the conspirators in the assassination of JFK. A major Cuban exile leader with Pedro Diaz Lanz, and a member of the secret Operation 40 unit, an assassination squad originally formed by the CIA in 1960.[194]

- 6. Cabell, General Charles involved in anti-Castro CIA operations, the Bay of Pigs, and fired by Kennedy after the fiasco. It is alleged that General Cabell was rabidly right wing, and that his brother Earl, mayor of Dallas, was instrumental in arranging the motorcade route. One text asserts Earle was part of the conspiracy to kill Kennedy.[195] A somewhat fictionalized text on the assassination, *First Hand Knowledge*, also accuses General Cabell of criminal involvement in continuing to counterfeit Cuban currency to destabilize the Cuban economy in direct violation of Kennedy's order specifically discontinuing all counterfeiting operations. Barry Goldwater is said to have known about it. (See Ch. 4, 132n). Harrison Livingstone,

---

193. *Ibid.*, p. 511.
194. See Lane, *ibid.*, and Groden, *ibid.*
195. Giancana, *ibid.*, p. 465.

in *Killing the Truth*, says General Cabell also had a hand in controlling events at the autopsy. (p. 547).

- 7. Cain, Richard, operative of the CIA and simultaneously connected to the Mafia; implicated by Giancana as one of the shooters in Dallas. [196]
- 8. Cubella, Ramon/Ramon Cubelo: disaffected Cuban agent who worked for the CIA. On November 22, 1963 CIA operative and alleged friend of the Kennedys, Desmond Fitzgerald, had given him a poisoned pen for an attempt on Castro's life.[197] (See note 130).
- 9. June Cobb: an American woman employed at Fidel Castro's Ministry Office in Havana, worked in many capacities having connections with Castro, the CIA, Marita Lorenz, and anti-Castro Cubans. She was also linked to Alexander Rorke, Gerry Patrick Hemming, and Frank Sturgis. Newman's *Oswald and the CIA* suggests Cobb might have been a double agent, but precisely what could have been her role in the assassination drama — beyond innuendo and multiple associations — is unclear.
- 10. DeMohrenschildt, George. Russian friend of Oswald in Dallas. Connected to the CIA, described in earlier chapters. He befriended the Oswalds, joined with the Dallas Russian community in helping them, but reported to J. Walton Moore of the CIA on his contacts — a fact that has only been disclosed in recent years. deMohrenschildt shot himself to death as soon as he learned the HSCA wanted to interview him.
- Moore was the Dallas CIA Domestic Contacts Service chief at the time of his association with him. DeMohrenschildt had other CIA contacts, however, which have only come to light in the last ten years. Nicholas M. Anikeef acknowledged that he had a close and continuous friendship. Still, in 1992 Anikeef "stubbornly refused to disclose what part of the Agency he had worked for, even when told it is publicly known. Anikeef was branch chief in the Soviet Russia Division" (Newman, p. 279). DeMohrenschildt also had a business contact in Haiti named Charles Thomas. Thomas was a CIA covert action operative. (Newman, p. 391). Generally, the government's position is that George deMohrenschildt was a Russian émigré who innocently helped the Oswalds in Dallas. Underneath this official veneer rests a different set of facts. DeMohrenschildt had three CIA contacts at the time he was associating with Oswald: Walton Moore, Charles Thomas, and Nicholas Anikeef. These latter two names only became known since the release of JFK records in 1992.
- 11. Diaz Lanz, Pedro: Cuban exile implicated by Marita Lorenz as on the JFK assassination team. Lanz was the former Chief of the Cuban Air Force. [198]
- 12. Del Valle, Eladio: anti-Castro Cuban affiliated closely with David Ferrie; alleged to have engaged in numerous CIA contract actions; del Valle was murdered

---

196. *Ibid.*
197. Giancana, pp. 460-465.
198. Groden, *ibid.* The source for information, Homerio Echevarria, comes from "Secret ties," Reuters, cited in *The News*, Mexico City, December 21, 1995, p. 10.

on the same day that David Ferrie died after Ferrie had been indicted by Jim Garrison for the murder of JFK.

- 13. Dulles, Allen: former head of CIA, fired by Kennedy, then appointed by Johnson as a member of the Warren Commission. Conspiracy texts link Dulles to numerous acts of cover-up. Dulles played a role in overthrowing the left-leaning Arbenz government in Guatemala. One of his agents for this operation was E. Howard Hunt. Two weeks before the assassination, Oswald wrote a letter to a Mr. Hunt (we have at least two Mr. Hunts involved in various scenarios) and had checked out a library book describing the Arbenz operation in Guatemala.
- 14. Echevarria, Homerio: came under suspicion for the assassination from the FBI's Chicago field office; an anti-Castro Cuban. In 1995, a secret memo was released showing that Echevarria's father, Ebelia, had ties to the FBI. This information was held secret for 32 years. (See note 63).
- 15. Ferrie, David anti-Castro right-wing soldier of fortune, CIA contract agent, and affiliated with the Marcello crime syndicate. Accused by Jim Martin, Banister associate, of plotting to kill the President. Ferrie was making telephone calls from an ice rink in Galveston on the day of the assassination, and may have been a co-conspirator. A New Orleans witness who knew both men says, "Marcello thought Ferrie was very intelligent."[199] Over the years, debates have raged over whether David Ferrie ever had contact with Oswald. The only evidence supporting such contact was that Oswald was in the Civil Air Patrol and Ferrie had once served as an instructor. Gerald Posner, in *Case Closed*, argues that Ferrie and Oswald's connection is sheer fantasy. Subsequent to Posner's work, however, an author produced a photo showing Oswald and Ferrie together in the Civil Air Patrol in 1956. Another source believes David Ferrie was the most important single individual to know the truth of the assassination conspiracy. Ferrie, a homosexual pedophile, lived with Raymond Broshears from August 1965-1966. Broshears, whose testimony has been impugned, said Ferrie admitted to him his participation in the conspiracy, said that four shooters were involved (from the grassy knoll, from behind, and from a sewer opening) and that Oswald did not kill the President. Ferrie died, mysteriously, right after Jim Garrison indicted him.
- 16. Hall, Loran: provided disinformation testimony against Silvia Odio's evidence; part of a right-wing brigade of anti-Castro Cubans, associated with Frank Sturgis, said under immunity from prosecution that he was approached to be part of a plan to kill the President. Hall knew Trafficante in prison in Cuba and left Cuba with him when released by Castro. Hall's alias was Lorenzo Pascillo. He also worked in the Capri Hotel, in Havana, controlled by Trafficante.
- 17. Harrelson, Charles Voyde: (Father of Woody Harrelson of TV *Cheers* fame) Harrelson was on probation for armed robbery and embarked on a new career in the execution-for-hire business. He knew Jack Ruby. In 1980, Harrelson had taken an overdose of cocaine and confessed to killing Kennedy and a Judge Woods. He

---

199. Summers, *ibid.*, p. 309. Also see Bob Goodman, *Triangle of Fire*, San Jose, CA: Laquerian Publishers, 1993, p. 207.

was successfully prosecuted for the contract killing of Woods and is currently in prison. He is alleged to be a CIA contract agent who worked with Charles Rogers as one of the two grassy knoll gunmen. [200]

- 18. Harvey, William: A major suspect in planning the assassination of Kennedy, according to author Anthony Summers. Harvey (who died in 1976) was a member of the CIA's Executive Action Program, and closely in touch with people like Lucien Sarti. He was head of Task Force W, which was involved with anti-Castro operations, and with mobsters Roselli and Trafficante. His boss was John McCone, Director of the CIA. Harvey hated Bobby Kennedy and appeared mentally unstable. He was transferred to Italy because, during the height of the 1962 missile crisis, he sent commando teams into Cuba without the President's knowledge. As late as June 1963, Harvey was still meeting with Roselli in the U.S. and had even visited anti-Castro camps in Florida. "The feeling of some of the CIA people we talked with,' says one (HSCA) staffer, 'was that Harvey was heavily involved with the organized crime figures. The feeling was that he was out of control and may have worked with organized crime figures to murder JFK. He behaved as if he was all-powerful. . . He may have been the key in accomplishing the assassination.'" [201]

- 19. Helms, Richard. Former Director of CIA; is alleged to have attempted to cover up Hunt's presence in Dallas plus the "Company's" relationship to Guy Banister, David Ferrie, and Clay Shaw; highly uncooperative with the Warren Commission in the eyes of many conspiracy writers. Associated with James Jesus Angleton, Director of Counterintelligence, and known to have incarcerated KGB defector Yuri Nosenko. Angleton destroyed important assassination-related documents and a tape of Oswald held in the personal files of CIA Mexico station chief Winston Scott. Angleton removed Scott's personal effects and no such tapes were ever found. Angleton also destroyed the diaries of Mary Meyer, a JFK mistress and former wife of CIA official Cord Meyer, Jr. Angleton admitted to the destruction of these diaries. Helms was more than likely aware of at least some of Angleton's activities as well as the alleged debriefing of Oswald by CIA Domestic Contacts Division agent Andy Anderson, a fact which the CIA denied and which Helms most recently denied in a 1993 interview on Frontline.

- 20. Holt, Chauncey Marvin: alleged to have ties to organized crime and the CIA; Holt helped provide forged documents to "'set up" Oswald and worked with Charles Rogers and Charles Harrelson (the two grassy knoll gunmen) who allegedly killed JFK. Holt has been an informant and was said to be one of the three tramps arrested in Dealey Plaza.[202]

- 21. Hemming, Gerry Patrick: alleged that he had been offered a CIA contract to assassinate the President by Guy Banister. Implicated by Marita Lorenz as one of the members of the JFK assassination team. Hemming was a leader of Interpen,

---

200. Craig & Rogers, *ibid.*
201. Summers, *ibid.*, p. 529.
202. Craig & Rogers, *ibid.*

an anti-communist, anti-Castroite group of mercenaries. Hemming was also, through Interpen, an associate of Frank Sturgis and Loran Hall. Elsewhere Anthony Summers mentions a "Gerry Hemming," a man who knew Oswald and had worked with Naval Intelligence; whether it is the same person as Gerry Patrick Hemming is unknown.[203] Other authors, e.g. Gerald Posner, mention a Gerry Patrick Hemming connected to the same military base in Japan to which Oswald was assigned.

- 22. Hunt, Howard CIA station chief in Mexico City in August-September, 1963, when Oswald visited the area. Hunt was linked to 544 Camp Street in New Orleans. Hunt is alleged to have been the "old man tramp" arrested at Dealey Plaza on the day of the assassination. Photographic forensic evidence by Weberman and Canfield is startling. Hunt holds these allegations are defamatory, has sued, and says that he was in Washington, DC at the time of the assassination. The litigation resulted in Weberman's ability to depose Hunt and ask some telling questions. Hunt dropped his $12 million lawsuit. To Weberman, "by withdrawing his suit with prejudice against him, he essentially admitted that he was in Dallas on the day of the assassination." [204]
- 23. Lopez, Edwin Juan: attorney for HSCA, author of the highly secret Lopez report alleging that Oswald was represented by an impostor in his visits to the Cuban and Russian consulates in Mexico City.
- 24. Lorenz, Marita: former anti-Castro exile and fighter testified under oath that Frank Sturgis drove with her from Miami to Dallas in November 1963.
- 25. Maheu, Robert, former employee of Howard Hughes, later operated a detective agency, allegedly had close ties to CIA and Charles Cabell; implicated by Giancana as part of the Kennedy assassination conspiracy.
- 26. Marchetti, Victor: former CIA assistant director, says he is "absolutely convinced that Ferrie was a CIA contract officer and involved in some rather nefarious activities." [205]
- 27. Mertz, John Michael: French mercenary and assassination expert alleged to have been on the CIA hit squad with Jean Soutre; that is highly speculative accounting by an unreliable conspiracy author.
- 28. Novo, Guillermo: one of two anti-Castro Cuban brothers implicated as one of the Dealey Plaza assassins by Marita Lorenz. [206]
- 29. Novo, Ignaci: one of two anti-Castro Cuban brothers implicated as one of the Dealey Plaza assassins by Marita Lorenz. [207]
- 30. Odio, Silvia and Annie: important witnesses linking Oswald to anti-Castro Cubans; see text.

---

203. Weberman, *ibid.*, Summers, *ibid.*, and Lane, *ibid.*
204. Weberman, *ibid.*, p. 224. Quote which follows is from p. 326.
205. Summers, *ibid.*, p. 300.
206. Lane, *ibid.*
207. *Ibid.*

- 31. Pawley, William. Owner of sugar interests in Cuba. The CIA had used Pawley in 1952-54 and again in 1959. Pawley had connections to anti-Castro Cubans and to Clare Boothe Luce. He was suspected by FBI agent James Hosty of being connected to right-wing interests and the Sylvia Odio incident. Pawley killed himself about the time of the 1977 HSCA investigations. Also associated with Mafia figure John Martino (See John Newman pp. 110, 350).
- 32. Phillips, David: CIA agent, suspected of being Maurice Bishop. Shortly before he died, he informed a former HSCA staff worker that, "JFK was done in by a conspiracy, likely including rogue American intelligence people." (The remark was made in 1986; it is significant because Phillips was virtually mute under questioning many years earlier during the HSCA inquiries.) [208]
- 33. Roberts, Delphine, the secretary of Guy Banister, interviewed by author Anthony Summers. Roberts remained taciturn during the Warren Commission inquiries, but indicated to Summers that Oswald frequently came to Banister's office on Camp Street and that Oswald and David Ferrie had spent considerable time together. [209]
- 34. Rorke, Alexander: implicated by Marita Lorenz as part of the assassination team made up of Cuban exiles and CIA agents lead by Frank Sturgis (Lane); Anthony Summers, however, shows Alexander Rorke as having died prior to the JFK assassination.
- 35. Rogers, Charles Frederick: wanted for the butcher-style murder of his two parents in Houston; currently at large. Alleged to have been the grassy knoll gunman and a CIA contract operative operating under various aliases; also alleged to be one of the three tramps arrested near Dealey Plaza. Rogers lived with his parents in Houston and disappeared for many weeks after the assassination. His parents received strange calls leading them to believe their son had had a hand in the assassination. Upon his return home, the parents confronted him with their suspicions (which they had also previously shared with two neighbors). Rogers allegedly killed both his parents and tried to dispose of their bodies. Remnants were found, but Rogers was never seen again. See the discussion of Carlos Rigal in

---

208. Summers, *ibid.*, p. 518.

209. *Ibid.*, p. 304 Delphine Roberts, Guy Banister's mistress and secretary throughout the Kennedy assassination period, decided to talk. "She stalled questions from the New Orleans District Attorney in 1967 and tried to elude the Assassinations Committee staff in 1978; however, Summers interviewed her, finally. She said Oswald and Banister knew each other very well. "Oswald came back a number of times. He seemed to be on familiar terms with Banister and with the office... There were various leaflets up there pertaining to Fair Play for Cuba. They were pro-Castro leaflets. Banister just didn't say anything about them one way or the other. When Oswald was passing out FPFC leaflets in the street next door, Banister said, "Don't worry about him. He's a nervous fellow, he's confused. He's with us, he's associated with the office...." It is by no means certain that Delphine Roberts has told the whole truth or revealed all she knows. What she has said was divulged with reluctance, and she has refused to talk at all in the past," (Summers, pp 295-.296).

Robert Morrow's text (note 132) as a possible connecting alias. Rogers had connections to both the military and CIA.[210]

- 36. Shaw, Clay: a shadowy figure indicted by Jim Garrison for the murder of John Fitzgerald Kennedy. Shaw, allegedly acting under the alias Clay Bertrand, tried to find Oswald an attorney. Shaw was found innocent of conspiracy to kill JFK, but in the late 1970s CIA Director Helms allegedly admitted Shaw had CIA connections. Shaw, like associate David Ferrie, was a homosexual. Gerald Posner argues that Clay Shaw was entirely innocent of any association with the assassination and that Garrison destroyed him. Shaw is deceased. Others from the conspiracist school assert Clay Shaw was involved in Richard Helm's QK/ENCHANT and a member of the secret project ZR/CLIFF under William Harvey's super-secret Staff D, along with the ZR/RIFLE assassination program (See assassinationweb.com/shack3g.htm).

- 37. Smith, Sergio Arcacha: an extreme right-wing anti-Castro militant, representative of the Cuban Revolutionary Council, also connected to 544 Camp Street, Guy Banister's office. Smith said privately to Anthony Summers that he was controlled by the CIA.[211] He was once in the employ of oilman H.L. Hunt, as well. Jim Garrison tried to get him extradited to New Orleans, but Governor Connally of Texas refused Garrison's request and Smith remained under the protection of Texas authorities. Smith was associated with E. Howard Hunt, according to Harrison Livingstone in *Killing the Truth* (1993).

- 38. Sturgis, Frank (formerly Fiorini): fought alongside Castro, became disenchanted; he became a soldier-of-fortune; also connected with Trafficante. Later Sturgis was a Watergate conspirator along with Howard Hunt; this team was originally put together under Nixon. Sturgis is alleged by Weberman and Canfield to be one of the "tramps" arrested in Dealey Plaza. Rather stunning photographic similarities are provided between Sturgis and one of the tramps. Sturgis died in 1993. He was a CIA anti-Castro Cuban exile; he leaked two stories, one to Jack Anderson, the other to author James Buchanan. In each he was an "unnamed source" who said Oswald was a pro-Castro agent. Sturgis denied his involvement as the unnamed source, but both Jack Anderson and James Buchanan independently said he was.

- 39. Veciano, Antonio: anti-Castro leader and CIA agent; head of Alpha 66, a violent Cuban exile group seeking to murder Castro. Said his main CIA contact was Maurice Bishop. Veciano was shot in the head but survived to testify at the HSCA; still fears for his life.[212]

The CIA theory is not monolithic. One approach points to anti-Castro Cubans, another to the power brokers of the Vietnam War. We have the Jim Garrison version,

---

210. Craig & Rogers, *ibid.*

211. Summers, *ibid.*, p. 297. See also Harrison Livingstone, *Killing the Truth*. New York: Carroll & Graf, 1993, p. 490-91.

212. Groden, *ibid.*, p. 192

the Weberman-Canfield scenario, the intrigues proposed by Mark Lane, and another scheme presented by Craig and Rogers. Garrison was the New Orleans prosecutor who indicted individuals for the assassination. Weberman and Canfield are two researchers who authored *Coup D'Etat in America.* Craig and Rogers base their work on three informants, two of whom remain secret. Mark Lane has been an avid Kennedy researcher since 1963. The works of Summers, Groden, Livingston, Posner, Newman, and Mailer are also included.

Essential Points

- Oswald had close ties to the military. His half-brother was a career Air Force officer. His brother, Robert, served with the Marine Corps. Oswald's cousin, Dorothy Murret, allegedly had a CIA connection. Oswald stayed with her when he was in New Orleans.
- Oswald became a Marine, studied Russian, and served at the Atsugi base in Japan. Top-secret U2 flights originated there, and Oswald had a security clearance. More than one researcher says Oswald had access to secret details about the U2's high-flying capability: It could fly at an unprecedented 90,000 feet on secret photographic missions. During the Eisenhower years, U2 flights regularly invaded Soviet airspace, flying well into the heartland of the country. Francis Gary Powers was the first pilot shot down — just before the failed summit meeting between Eisenhower and Khrushchev in 1960. That was soon after Oswald defected.
- Oswald got a hardship discharge from the Marines in 1959, by claiming his mother was ill. He then defected to Russia. At the U.S. Embassy in Moscow, he renounced his U.S. citizenship. The Soviets sent him to Minsk, Byelorussia, where he worked in a radio plant and married a pharmacy student named Marina Prusakova. With his apparently desultory personality, however, he changed his mind about the USSR rather quickly and sought to return to the U.S., wife in tow. To the surprise of many, he experienced almost no difficulty coming back, despite his security clearance, his defection, and the renunciation of his citizenship. The State Department even granted him a loan.

Some researchers believe that Oswald's intelligence connections go all the way back to the Marines, that he learned Russian in Japan in order to carry forward with a risky intelligence mission, that he defected to the USSR as a CIA plant and in Minsk collected data on life in the Soviet Union for the CIA. Anthony Summers shows Oswald was granted access to the two top floors of the American Embassy in Moscow, where only individuals with clearances were ever permitted.[213] Each year evi-

---

213. Oswald's access to the top-secret sections of the U. S. Embassy comes from the same source. As noted earlier, I know from personal experience that access to the top two floors of the embassy was tightly restricted.

dence accumulates that Oswald had unexplainable military and intelligence connections.

Not all CIA-conspiracy proponents accept the idea that Oswald's leftist Fair-Play-for-Cuba image was a CIA cover. It was, however, the position of his mother Marguerite, and of Mark Lane in his books *Rush to Judgment* and *Plausible Denial*. In Minsk, Marina (who called her husband "Alik" — "Lee" sounded too Chinese, to her),

> . . . noticed that he had photographs and a ground plan of the radio plant. Marina was horror-stricken. . . So Alik was a spy after all. . . To make matters worse, he would not let her near the papers and refused even to say what he was doing.[214]

George deMohrenschildt befriended the Oswalds upon their arrival in Dallas. DeMohrenschildt, a descendant of Russian nobility, had worked for the Office of Strategic Service (OSS) during World War II, and was close to people connected with Pantipec Oil (as were Howard Hunt and William F. Buckley). He was friendly with the Shah of Iran and a personal friend of "Papa Doc" Duvalier, the corrupt leader of Haiti. In the early years after the assassination, the role played by Baron George deMohrenschildt appeared to be that of a casual friend, someone who enjoyed political palaver with Lee, and a representative of the Dallas Russian community which took an interest in helping them.

This image changed at the time of deMohrenschildt's suicide in the mid-1970s. Shortly before killing himself, he admitted to writer Edward Epstein that he was asked by CIA's Walton Moore to contact and befriend the Oswalds.[215]

> In the summer of 1962 deMohrenschildt heard more about this defector. One of Moore's associates handed him the address of Lee Harvey Oswald in nearby Fort Worth and then suggested that deMohrenschildt might like to meet him. . . [whereupon] deMohrenschildt called Moore again. . . Some help from the U.S. Embassy in Haiti would be greatly appreciated by him, he suggested to Moore. Although he recognized that there was no quid pro quo, he hoped that he might receive the same sort of tacit assistance he had previously received . . . "I would

---

214. The quote is from Priscilla Johnson-McMillan's *Marina and Lee*, New York, Harper & Row, 1977, p. 116. Some have asserted this text is not credible and question Johnson-McMillan's objectivity. See Anthony and Robbyn Summers, "The Ghosts of November," *Ibid*.

215. Epstein paid for this interview. DeMohrenschildt had been suffering from psychiatric difficulties. On the morning of the interview with Epstein, an investigator for the House Select Committee on Assassination (HSCA) also wanted to talk and left his card at the residence. DeMohrenschildt went upstairs and shot himself. He had written a book on Oswald, entitled *I'm a Patsy*, which his wife turned over to the HSCA shortly thereafter. Quotations on contacts with Walton Moore are from Mailer, *ibid.*, p 44 and 481 respectively.

never have contacted Oswald in a million years if Moore had not sanctioned it," he explained to me. "Too much was at stake."

A search of J. Walton Moore's CIA files on these events yielded even more information supporting these contacts:

> . . . the documents found in deMohrenschildt's CIA file showed that there was far "more contact between Moore and deMohrenschildt than was stated." In fact, they revealed that Moore had interviewed him numerous times over a course of years and prepared reports based on this information. Moore himself testified that he had "periodic" contact with deMohrenschildt for "debriefing purposes" and, although maintaining he could not recall any discussion about Oswald, acknowledged that these contacts may have extended to 1962. [216]

Unlike the impression created for the Warren Commission, the CIA was not wholly ignorant of Lee Harvey Oswald. It had a connection to him through deMohrenschildt, who kept J. Walton Moore closely apprized of events almost immediately after Oswald's return to the U.S.; deMohrenschildt seems to have known that Oswald made an attempt on the life of General Walker. Did Moore and the CIA know too? [217]

It was also deMohrenschildt who introduced the Oswalds to Michael and Ruth Paine, and Ruth Paine, in turn, who helped Oswald get a job at the Texas School Book Depository. Paine was alleged to have had a CIA connection through the Agency for International Development, a suspected CIA front organization where her father was employed. Michael worked for Bell Helicopter, and had a security clearance. [218]

Oswald went to New Orleans, the city of his birth, and stayed with his cousin Dorothy Murret. He got a job at the Reily Coffee Company across the street from 544 Camp Street. When Oswald passed out Fair Play for Cuba leaflets, he used the Camp Street address. It is this fact that put Jim Garrison on the scent of the assassins:

> In fact, almost everyone who had an office in or was associated with 544 Camp Street could be traced to Howard Hunt. [219]

---

216. Weberman, *ibid.*, p. 22.

217. DeMohrenschildt had two other CIA contacts at the same time as he was liaising with Moore; these were Charles Thomas and Nicholas Anikeef of the Soviet Russia Division of the CIA.

218. Gerald Posner (*Case Closed*) believes the Paines' involvement with Oswald was innocent and unfortunate; others suggest that since their background is still classified, there must be something of interest there. Warren Commission documents 212, 218, 258, 508 as well as documents 600-629 were classified with respect to the Paines and their relatives. Source: Jim Garrison. *A Heritage of Stone*, New York: G.P. Putnam's Sons, 1970, p. 134.

- Oswald passed out leaflets for fair treatment of Cuba using the Camp Street address, but the office was actually run by Guy Banister, a former FBI and military Intelligence agent. Banister and Oswald present quite an unusual juxtaposition of left- and right-wing politics to be occupying neighboring offices.
- At the time of the assassination, Banister struck his longtime friend and associate, Jack Martin. Martin, in turn, called the FBI and reported that David Ferrie, an associate of Banister, was involved in the Kennedy assassination.[220] When the FBI questioned Banister, he gave his address as 531 Lafayette, the side entrance to 544 Camp. The only admission Banister ever made to the FBI was that Arcacha Smith of the Cuban Revolutionary Council had an office there. Smith was also the head of the Cuban Democratic Revolutionary Front, and these two anti-Castro organizations had contacts with Howard Hunt of the CIA. Recently released documents show that the CIA funded the CRC, but that Kennedy stopped CIA support for it as of May, 1963.[221]
- On November 22, 1963, a man named Clay Bertrand called attorney Dean Andrews and asked him to represent Oswald. Who was trying to arrange an attorney for Oswald, and why? Jim Garrison claimed the shadowy Clay Bertrand was really Clay Shaw, a well-connected businessman affiliated with the International Trade Mart in New Orleans. Garrison indicted Shaw as part of a conspiracy to assassinate the President, but was unable to prove Shaw was Bertrand. Shaw was eventually acquitted of all charges. Over a decade later, Victor Marchetti, a former assistant to the Director of the CIA confirmed that Clay Shaw was indeed Clay Bertrand. Why, one might ask, was Clay Shaw, a CIA intelligence operative, trying to secure an attorney for Lee Harvey Oswald?
- Richard Helms, later the Director of the CIA, also admitted that Clay Shaw had ties to the CIA, but did not clearly link Shaw with the Bertrand pseudonym. Banister, Ferrie and Shaw became Jim Garrison's leading conspirators in the assassination. This is the essence of the Garrison theory. The facts that Ferrie died mysteriously four days after Garrison indicted him, that Banister died within ten days of the conclusion of the Warren Commission hearings, and that CIA Director Helms and assistant Director Marchetti, many years after Shaw was acquitted, admitted Shaw was a CIA agent prevent us from dismissing Garrison's theory out of hand. Since the government released records, evidence mounds that Clay Shaw was involved in CIA activities QK/ENCHANT and an assassination program called ZR/RIFLE.[222]
- Oswald engaged in some odd behavior in the summer of 1963, in New Orleans. He appeared in an establishment run by an anti-Castroite Carlos

---

219. *Ibid.*, p. 35. Gerald Posner, author of *Case Closed*, however, believes Oswald chose this address only to rile Banister and Arcacha Smith.

220. *Ibid.*, p. 36

221. See John Newman's *Oswald and the CIA*.

222. See Electronic Assassinations Newsletter at http://www.assassinationweb.com/shack3g.htm.

Chapter 4. Conspiracy

Bringuier. He told Bringuier that he wanted to be an anti-Castro freedom fighter and gave Bringuier a copy of his Marine Corps training manual. Later, Bringuier saw Oswald passing out leaflets for the Fair Play for Cuba Committee. Bringuier punched him during the demonstration. (He and two other Cubans were arrested for disturbing the peace as a result of the brouhaha.[223]) Oswald was arrested as well. Researchers argue the entire fist fight was "staged" in order to develop Oswald as a pro-Castro firebrand instead of the anti-Castro freedom fighter he really was:

> Oswald's arrest provides us with more information about the nature of activities on behalf of Castro. He threw away the leaflets after the press showed up and photographed him, and he requested to see an FBI agent when he was in jail . . . Oswald sent clippings about the incident to the chairman of the Fair Play for Cuba Committee to enhance his credibility with them. [224]

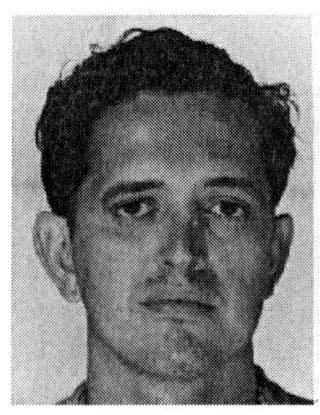

Oswald's connection to right-wing causes and anti-Castro Cubans leaves a very fragile trail of evidence beyond his contact with Bringuier (photo, right). Bringuier, however, was linked to David Ferrie, and David Ferrie to Banister and Arcacha Smith, according to a 1961 New Orleans police report. Bringuier was one of the last people to see David Ferrie alive. When Ferrie killed himself, he left a typed note. (Skeptics find it curious that a man should type what appears to be a suicide note despite dying of a brain hemorrhage.) As mentioned in a prior chapter, Ferrie's friend and employer Eladio del Valle was found shot dead on the same day Ferrie died. Del Valle headed the anti-Castro Free Cuba Committee. Ferrie appears to have lent his library card to Oswald and came into money both before and after the assassination. [225]

---

223. Bringuier was also head of *Cuban-Americans for Nixon-Agnew*. Weberman, *ibid.*, p. 42.
224. *Ibid.*, p. 41.
225. *Ibid.*, p. 44. Note that Ferrie had an office in New Orleans and that Eugene Hale Brading (associated with Hoffa and the right-wing Minutemen) had an office next door. *Ibid.* p. 62. Oswald applied for his passport on June 24, 1963 and received it on June 25 (North, *ibid.*, p. 283).

Not only did Oswald solicit Bringuier in the summer of 1963, in June he applied for a passport to leave the country. A prior defector from the U.S., a man under scrutiny by the FBI, and undesirably discharged from the Marines had no difficulty getting a passport within 24 hours. This, in turn, fuels those conspiracists who think Oswald had some covert intelligence function all along.

- By September 27, 1963 Oswald allegedly checked into the Hotel Commercio in Mexico City, traveling there by bus. (E. Howard Hunt, the CIA agent (and future Watergate burglar) is alleged to have been the station chief in Mexico City at the time of Oswald's trip. Very little is known about Hunt's activities during 1962-63. This period is totally omitted from his autobiography and all that is known about it is that he was the CIA Chief of Station in Mexico City during August and September, 1963. [226])
- While in Mexico, Oswald went to the Cuban Consulate and showed clippings about his pro-Castro activities to an official there. He spoke to Silvia Duran (and drew a floor plan of the embassy in his notebook). The Cuban officials told Oswald he could get a visa to Cuba if he first got a visa from the Russians. He became furious, and yelled at the Cuban counsel. He then called upon the Soviet Embassy and was told there would be a delay of four months. Rebuffed by both, he returned to Dallas. His strident behavior, however, made an impression on the staffs of both embassies. Was that its purpose?

This story is by no means over. It twists and turns at every corner, laced with innuendo, impostors, suspicions, and intrigue. So that we can avoid getting lost in a morass of detail, here is a brief review of the facts that have emerged so far: (1) Oswald attempted to pose an anti-Castro soldier of fortune in his contact with Bringuier. (2) Bringuier knew and associated with David Ferrie, and Oswald knew Ferrie. [227] (3) Ferrie, Banister, Hunt, and Shaw were connected to the CIA. (4) The CIA was apprized of Oswald's comings and goings all along by George deMohrenschildt, a man who posed as a friend of the Oswalds' in Dallas, yet met regularly with a CIA contact named Walton Moore — facts never revealed to the Warren Commission nor by the Warren Commission. (5) Let us also recall that Oswald had a military intelligence file that was "inadvertently destroyed" before the Warren Commission could see it.

With this behind us, the stew of intrigue thickens even more.

---

226. *Ibid.*, p. 78.
227. This point was hotly contested by Gerald Posner, but since his book was released, PBS Frontline researchers discovered a photo of Oswald and Ferrie in the Civil Air Patrol together: a devastating blow to Posner's attempts to evangelize Warren Commission conclusions.

The Odio Incident and Loran Hall

As the Warren Commission was winding down, a credible witness, Sylvia Odio, reluctantly came forward to disturb the momentum the investigation was gathering. She declared that Oswald was the lone assassin and had leftist, pro-Castro sentiments. Many have considered the Odio incident as the best proof of a conspiracy to kill the President.

In late September, 1963, Silvia and Annie Odio were living in the Crestwood Apartments in Dallas. They were wealthy daughters of a prominent Cuban family that had been involved in revolutionary politics. Their father supported Castro, but was a democrat, and when Castro's revolution devolved into Marxism-Leninism, Mr. Odio worked against the regime. Castro imprisoned him on the Isle of Pines in 1963.

Silvia, 26, and Annie 17, were part of the growing exile community in Dallas. Silvia helped form *Junta Revolucionaria*, or JURE. This group was against Castro and Communism, but was made up of nonviolent social democrats. Other Cuban exile organizations sardonically referred to JURE as "Castroism without Castro."

The doorbell rang. Two Latinos and an American stood at the door as Annie opened it a crack. They said they were supporters of JURE; they also knew her father's underground name in Cuba, so Annie let them in.

The two Latinos identified themselves by their *noms de guerres* as "Leopoldo" and "Angelo." The third man, much younger, was an American introduced as "Leon Oswald." Leopoldo said the three had just come from New Orleans. They were familiar with recent plots to kill Castro.

They wanted the young women to translate into English a number of fundraising letters addressed to American businessman. Something made Silvia Odio feel uneasy. Her father had warned her to take the utmost care in the Byzantine intrigues of exile politics, and she was leery of dealing with strangers. She told her visitors she wanted no part in a campaign of violence. The meeting did not last long and ended inconclusively. The men left, in their red car, supposedly about to embark on another long journey. [228]

About forty-eight hours later, "Leopoldo" called Odio at home.

> He brought up the request for help again, but he also seemed keen to discuss something else. "What did you think of the American?" he asked. Odio, thinking how quiet the American had been, said she had not really formed an opinion. Then Leopoldo made a number of remarks which — even at the time — Odio found chilling. He said of Oswald, "Well, you know, he's a Marine, an ex-Marine,

---

228. Summers, *ibid.*, p. 387.

and an expert marksman. He would be a tremendous asset to anyone, except that you never know how to take him." Listening to this, Silvia Odio wondered what she was expected to say. She knew even less when Leopoldo went on. "He's kind of loco, kind of nuts. He could go either way. He could do anything — like getting underground in Cuba, like killing Castro... The American says we Cubans don't have any guts. He says we should have shot President Kennedy after the Bay of Pigs. He says we should do something like that."[229]

When President Kennedy was shot, Silvia Odio fainted and was taken to a hospital. Annie, after seeing the President's killing on the television, said to herself, "My God, I know this guy and I don't know from where... Where have I seen this guy?" Both sisters realized that the American who visited their apartment in September was Oswald. They were terribly frightened and decided not to say anything to anyone about it.

> "We were so frightened, we were absolutely terrified," Sylvia remembered. "We were both very young and yet we had so much responsibility, with so many brothers and sisters and our mother and father in prison, we were so afraid and not knowing what was happening."[230]

But they did tell a friend, Lucille Connell, who told someone else; and finally the FBI was called. By the time the word got around, it was late summer of 1964. A Warren Commission lawyer wrote that Silvia Odio was checked out thoroughly, that the evidence was "unanimously favorable... Mrs. Odio is the most significant witness linking Oswald to the anti-Castro Cubans."[231]

What made Odio's testimony unassailable was that prior to the assassination, she had written her father in a Cuban prison about the visit, about the assassination comments, and about the American. Odio's father received his daughter's letter and was very concerned. He wrote back to her:

> Tell me who this is who says he is my friend — be careful. I do not have any friend who might be here, through Dallas, so reject this friendship until you give me his name.[232]

---

229. Ibid., p. 388
230. Mailer, *Oswald's Tale*, ibid., p. 631.
231. Ibid., p. 390.
232. Ibid., p. 391.

Odio retrospectively dated Oswald's visit to between September 24 and 29, 1963; *this was the time Oswald was supposed to have been in Mexico!* The Warren Commission had to struggle with the veracity of the Odio testimony just at the time it was concluding its business.

Suddenly, J. Edgar Hoover reported that his agents had found Loran Hall, "a participant in numerous anti-Castro activities," who said he was the man who had visited Odio along with two of his colleagues. Hall said that one of his friends *looked like Oswald.* Hoover was satisfied that Odio was mistaken in her judgments. The Warren Commission report went to the printers with Loran Hall's story impugning Odio as part of the final copy.

When FBI agents traced down the two other men Hall named as his companions, both said Odio's story was untrue. Finally, and after the Warren Commission Report was already released, Loran Hall admitted he had lied.[233] Years later when the House Assassinations Committee tried to investigate this matter,

> Hall was highly reluctant to give evidence to the Assassinations Committee. When he eventually did so, on a basis that assured him against prosecution arising from his testimony, Hall maintained he had never claimed to have visited Silvia Odio. In its final report, however, the Assassinations Committee called his original tale "an admitted fabrication." [234]

Hall is a disinformation source and, therefore, one who could lead us closer to the origin of the conspiracy. Unfortunately, Loran Hall is linked to virtually everyone. He was a leading member of "Interpen," a tough anti-Castro group made up of exiles and CIA contractors. He was a member of the International Anti-Communist Brigade that trained Cuban exiles at Lake Ponchatrain outside of New Orleans — a camp where Oswald is supposed to have traveled with David Ferrie. Hall had a connection with Santos Trafficante, was detained in Cuba with him, and released at the same time. (Trafficante, of course, was a key CIA-Mafia liaison for assassination plots against Castro.) Finally, Hall had been arrested towing a trailerload of arms to the Interpen training camp at No Name Key in Florida, part of the anti-Castro guerrilla activity Kennedy was trying to stop.[235]

---

233. *Ibid.*
234. *Ibid.*, p. 392
235. Weberman, *ibid.*, p. 134.

Silvia Odio holds to her story.[236] She was shown photos of Loran Hall and his two associates and said these were definitely not the men who visited her. Annie says the same thing. Their father stands by Silvia's pre-assassination letter to him. Odio also told her priest about the incident, and through painstaking research, Weberman and Canfield tracked him down in a Florida nursing home, corroborating her testimony yet again.

Silvia Odio, the daughter of a Cuban millionaire, attended Catholic school in Philadelphia. She received a law degree from the University of Illinois and speaks four languages. The FBI spent much time looking into her past mental health record, particularly her proclivity to fainting spells. The agent who interviewed Odio and helped to put the Hall fabrication in place was James Hosty, a man whose name has appeared earlier regarding destruction of evidence, erasures from Oswald's notebook, etc. (No mention was ever made in the Warren Report that Hall retracted his statement or said it was a lie.) [237]

The reason many consider the Odio testimony extremely weighty evidence of a conspiracy involving anti-Castro elements was that Odio positively identified Lee Harvey Oswald *posing as an anti-Castro mercenary.* She has written no bestsellers, never sought publicity or monetary gain, and her testimony has been consistent and corroborated.

Loran Hall's effort to discredit the Odio sisters adds to the intrigue. Hall is still alive. He testified under immunity from prosecution before the HSCA that "right-wing radicals in league with CIA operatives offered him money to take part in the Kennedy assassination. He has claimed that there have been attempts to kill him and that the FBI distorted his original replies about the Odio episode." [238]

---

236. Posner takes the position that Odio is not credible and that Oswald had no connection with Ferrie, Bannister and Shaw. A lengthy review of this controversial text as well as these allegations and counter-allegations is provided in Ch. 6 as a sidebar.

237. *Ibid.*, p. 137. One answer to the Loran Hall fabrication, that is still consistent with a CIA plot, is that after the assassination the "cabal" decided it was better to peg Oswald as a lone assassin rather than as a member of a communist conspiracy. The Loran Hall testimony was offered to help establish the "lone nut" approach. Interestingly, Allen Dulles, the former CIA director who sat on the Warren Commission, passed out a book to each member. The book was a historical accounting of prior presidential assassins, and the thesis was that each assassin was a lone nut acting on his own passions. Dulles' distribution of this book show that the CIA was already invested in the "lone nut" hypothesis. There is a further amusing anecdote: One of the cases the book described was an attempt on the life of President Roosevelt in Florida. The assassin missed Roosevelt, and hit the former mayor of Chicago instead. Giancana's book explains that the man who was the "lone nut" in that assassination attempt was in fact in debt to the Mob — he never intended to kill Roosevelt at all, only the other passenger, whom he indeed succeeded in killing.

238. *Ibid.*, p. 492.

That is what Loran Hall (see photo) said to the HSCA in the 1970s, but in a taped interview he said somewhat more:

> There's only two of us left alive — that's me and Santo Trafficante. And as far as I'm concerned we're both going to stay alive because I ain't gonna say shit.[239]

Thus the tale of a cabal of anti-Castro Cubans and right-wing CIA contract agents — and perhaps Mob affiliates — is not easy to dismiss. Anti-Castro Cubans felt betrayed by Kennedy during the Bay of Pigs invasion. The Cuban missile crisis was resolved — in their minds — by Kennedy again betraying their cause by making a secret deal with Khrushchev never to invade Cuba. When Weberman and Canfield interviewed anti-Castroite Frank Sturgis, he echoed the feelings of anti-Castro guerrillas:

> Yeah, I figured he made a deal. In that we had to cut back. I felt that was wrong. He deserted the people. I felt that was wrong. That's why all the news people had me in the newspapers. Hey, I can show you clippings where they say I was involved in the assassination of President Kennedy![240]

The secret deal with the Kremlin and pressures from the Kennedy administration to close anti-Castro training bases, Operation Mongoose, and all other Everglades covert actions enraged anti-Castro exiles. Since the CIA bankrolled most of these organizations, this may have become the seedbed for the assassination.

Mexico City

There is a problem with Oswald's trip to Mexico in September, 1963. Possibly Silvia Odio was mistaken with respect to the dates Oswald visited her, but considerable evidence shows Oswald, or someone posing as Oswald, visited the Cuban and Russian consulates. The Assassinations Committee investigated this matter with

---

239. The nature of the interview, who taped it, and to whom the interview was given, are not clear. The source of this information is Summers, "The Ghosts of November," *Ibid.*
240. *Ibid.*, p. 235.

Edwin Juan Lopez serving as the principal researcher for the HSCA. The 280-page "Lopez Report" was classified, and is still classified; but Lopez himself, risking violation of his oath of secrecy, said he believed Oswald was impersonated in Mexico City. A summary of this evidence on the Oswald imposter is given by Ogelsby:

> (1) A CIA photo said to be of Oswald leaving the Soviet embassy is not Oswald's image. (2) A tape recording of Oswald talking on the phone with a Soviet diplomat is not Oswald's voice. (3) A Cuban diplomat who had three angry confrontations with Oswald said repeatedly and in detail that the Oswald of Mexico City was not the Oswald of Dallas. (4) The one eyewitness who said she saw Oswald in the Cuban consulate could not describe him correctly to House investigators. [241]

As the theory goes so far, the CIA or right-wing Cuban exile forces were systematically setting up Oswald as a leftist, pro-Cuban, pro-Soviet, assassin, someone who had applied for a passport to leave the country, visited Silvia Odio to announce assassination plans, applied for visas to Cuba and Russia in Mexico City, and whose obstreperousness would be remembered by all.

We don't know if Oswald went to Mexico or was represented by an imposter.[242] Sylvia Odio may have met Oswald but incorrectly remembered the dates. Originally, Marina did not disclose to the FBI that her husband had been to Mexico — for whatever reasons — but later she said he did make the trip. Her most prized possession from her husband was a miniature straw donkey, which she says he brought her from Mexico.[243]

Anti-Castro Cubans or not, Sylvia Odio or not, Mexico City or not, we have barely scratched the surface of this mercurial conspiracy theory.

---

241. Ogelsby, *ibid.*, p. 218.

242. A number of credibility problems are found in Posner's *Case Closed*. One of his strongest suits, however, may be the evidence he brings supporting Oswald's trip to Mexico. Posner cites Soviet personnel in Mexico City, Nechiporenko, Vatzkov, and Kostikov, Cuban employees Sylvia Duran and Alfredo Diaz, and another witness, Oscar Contreras, all testifying that the man they met in Mexico City was the man they saw arrested for the assassination. Posner's case is convincing, and his evidentiary rationale is impressive. The most recent contrary opinion is found in John Newman's *Oswald and the CIA*. Newman's position is that Oswald simply did not make many contacts himself: he was an imposter, was also at work at the same time. Still another source of evidence on the issue of whether Oswald went to Mexico City is FBI agent James Hosty. In his 1996 memoirs, he says that the photo of Oswald that was submitted for a Cuban transit visa was given to the Warren Commission by Castro, and that the photo is indeed a passport photo of Oswald presented by him to the Cuban Consulate in Mexico City (Hosty, *ibid.*, p. 214).

243. Johnson, *ibid.*, p. 451.

Chapter 4. Conspiracy

The Vietnam Connection

Another version of a CIA-based plan to assassinate Kennedy focuses on the significance of Vietnam in the overall motive. In Oliver Stone's film *JFK*, a mysterious figure provides Jim Garrison with inside details of the machinations of the plotters. The part is played by Donald Sutherland. Sutherland's character is based on the real Col. Fletcher Prouty, who served as Chief of Special Operations for the Joint Chiefs of Staff during the Kennedy years. His book, entitled *JFK: The CIA, Vietnam and the Plot to Assassinate John F. Kennedy*, implicates Richard Nixon but takes a very different approach from Weberman and Canfield:

Had Kennedy lived, asserts Prouty, the U.S. would not have become embroiled in Vietnam. Kennedy's intentions were to remove 1,000 troops from Vietnam initially and to begin a full-scale withdrawal prior to the 1964 elections, to be completed by the end of 1965. [244]

General Charles. P. Cabell, who was fired by Kennedy after the Bay of Pigs fiasco, was a zealous CIA right-winger. Cabell had interests in the Textron Corporation's acquisition of Bell Helicopter Company that profited greatly from the "Huey" and other choppers used in Vietnam. (Michael Paine, Oswald's friend, also worked for Bell Helicopter).

The largest single military procurement contract in history was slated to be awarded under Kennedy: the TFX fighter plane. General Dynamics in Fort Worth, Texas was the leading contender, and Lyndon Johnson's appointee, Fred Korth, was indicted for conflict of interest trying to secure the contract for them. Bell helicopters for use in Vietnam were to be built in Texas. To the chagrin of many Texans, General Dynamics was not given the TFX contract.

Another drama opens with the assassination of Ngo Dinh Diem, the first president of South Vietnam, on November 1, 1963. The assassination was engineered by the CIA. Kennedy himself favored the removal of Diem, but not by murder; he was very disturbed by the news. Diem's murder occurred 21 days before Kennedy's.

Kennedy was frightened about the CIA's power, says Prouty. Its role in the Bay of Pigs and in the Diem assassination, plus his inability to get control over it, bothered him. He authorized a Cuban Study Group, an outgrowth of the Bay of Pigs; the highly secret study (never released) was chaired by Robert Kennedy. The conclusions formed the basis of Kennedy's desire to declare war on the CIA — after his reelection!

As a beginning point in this war on the CIA, Kennedy issued two National Security Action Memoranda (#52 and #55) which placed "Cold War" actions under the authority of the Joint Chiefs of Staff, no longer the CIA:

---

244. NSAM #263; Prouty, *ibid.* p. 116.

"Kennedy asserted a power of the presidency that he assumed he had, but when orders were delivered to the men to whom they were addressed, he discovered that his power was all but meaningless. His directives were quietly placed in the bureaucratic files and forgotten. There have been few times in the history of this nation when the limits of the power of the President have been so nakedly exposed. I was the briefing officer for the chairman of the Joint Chiefs of Staff, to whom NSAM #55 was addressed. I know exactly what he was told about that series of documents, and I know what he said about them during that meeting. During that meeting, I was told to have them put in the chairman's file, where they remained. Gen. Lyman L. Lemnitzer did not choose to be a 'Cold Warrior.'"[245]

On the day of President Kennedy's assassination his entire Cabinet departed for Hawaii on an unprecedented trip to Japan. "No one has explained why the Kennedy cabinet was ordered to Japan at that time."[246] Shortly after the President's death, Vietnam policy was reversed and Johnson began a build-up of forces, which reached over 550,000 men and cost over $220 billion.

> Prouty does not provide a very perspicuous theory but an array of facts, spiced with ample amounts of conjecture and innuendo. The whole effort hangs very loose indeed. It is not easy to deduce whether it was Nixon or Johnson behind the 'high cabal' or how the conspiracy enunciated itself in the person of any specific assassins.

Who Killed Kennedy?

In reviewing the CIA-based theories of the assassination, the question of who actually shot the President generates four very different responses — all quite hypothetical and convoluted.

Scenario No. 1: One approach, suggested by Summers and others, seems to go as follows: A disturbed CIA agent known as William Harvey had been a "can-do" operative involved with anti-Castro activities. Even during the global tensions around the Cuban missile crisis, Harvey sent a team of commandos into Cuba without Kennedy's knowledge or consent. Harvey was disciplined and transferred to Italy as a result. He cozied up to organized crime in his desire to see Castro assassinated — most notably John Roselli and, through him, Marcello, Giancana, and Trafficante, He may have been part of the so-called Corsican contract hit on the President carried out by Lucien Sarti

---

245. Prouty, *ibid.*, p. 169.
246. *Ibid.*, p. 281.

and two other assailants. Harvey may have been the "rogue CIA officer" David Phillips referred to when he died.

How Harvey is supposed to have set up Oswald as the patsy stretches the imagination. A guess might be that it was done through associations with Marcello and David Ferrie,[247] out of the offices of Guy Banister and Arcacha Smith at 544 Camp Street. In this model, Oswald thinks he is part of a covert operation to "infiltrate" Cuba once his pro-Castro credentials have been developed. He starts a fictional Fair Play for Cuba chapter (with one member), gets arrested passing out pro-Cuban leaflets, has a made-for-TV fist fight with an anti-Castro exile (Carlos Bringuier), appears on television debating the socialist cause for Cuba . . . *all as part of an effort to establish Oswald's pro-Cuban facade.* Thus accomplished, he awaits further orders. He had no idea what Banister, Ferrie, and others had in mind for him.

This is one explanation of how the crime was carried forward under the right-wing banner of anti-Castro Cuban exiles and disaffected, rogue CIA officers. Oswald served as the dupe, the patsy, who sat out the assassination in the second floor lunchroom of the Depository building, unaware that sharpshooters had killed the President and left his rifle on the sixth floor to incriminate him.

Scenario No. 2: Weberman and Canfield move in another direction. Richard Nixon is a leading suspect on their list. Nixon was in Dallas on the day of the assassination and lied about it, before finally admitting it. Watergate involved the arrests of Howard Hunt, Frank Sturgis, and others. This was not the first time Nixon used this team, and his involvement in covert activities can be dated to his time as Vice President under Eisenhower.

E. Howard Hunt was in Dallas on November 22, 1963, according to these authors. Frank Sturgis was, too. Both Sturgis and Hunt denied it, but Marita Lorenz testified under oath in 1975 (for the first time) that she had driven from Miami to Dallas in November of 1963 with Frank Sturgis. (Lorenz was once a spy recruited by Sturgis in Castro's Cuba and had been involved in one assassination attempt against Fidel Castro.)[248]

---

247. One of Banister's secretaries, Mary Brengel, was tracked down by Anthony Summers. She told him that one day when she was taking dictation from Banister, he referred to his work in helping Marcello fight deportation. "Mrs. Brengel expressed surprise that her employer was involved with organized crime, and Banister responded curtly, 'There are principles being violated, and if this goes on it could affect every citizen in the United States.' He left no doubt that he was firmly on Marcello's side (Summers, *ibid.* p. 310). This leaves open the connecting links between CIA Harvey, through Marcello, Banister, Ferrie, and ultimately to Oswald.

248. Weberman, *ibid.*, p. 322.

The most persuasive evidence Weberman and Canfield provide are the photographic similarities of Hunt and Sturgis to the tramps who were detained in the railroad yard shortly after the assassination.[249] They identified the third tramp, whose real name was unknown, as "Daniel Carswell."

On the left Weberman compares the CIA's E. Howard Hunt (far left) to a close-up of one of the three tramps (middle photo). In Weberman's text, Hunt's photo appears as an acetate fold-over which seems to exactly fit over the face of the tramp on the right. The match is uncanny.

Right: Photo of the three tramps arrested in Dealey Plaza.

Hunt sued Weberman for libel for his allegations, and Weberman welcomed the litigation because it would finally give him an opportunity to depose Hunt under oath.

Hunt later dropped his suit and this, in turn, continued to fuel conspiracy theories that Hunt was involved.

To summarize, after the assassination three individuals were arrested and later released by the police. They became known in Kennedy assassination lore as "the three tramps" (see photo).

The TV program *A Current Affair* announced that the three tramps had been tracked down. All turned out not to have been involved, but Weberman and Canfield challenge such assertions and allege the tramps were none other than CIA agent Howard Hunt, Frank Sturgis, and Daniel Carswell. The photographic forensic evidence they cite is uncanny, especially in relation to Howard Hunt. Who the actual assassins are, in this theory, however, remains muddy.

---

249. *Ibid.*, pp. 222-223.

Scenario 3: A book by Craig and Rogers — based upon anonymous informants — gives another twist. According to these authors, Charles Frederick Rogers, alias Carlos Rojas, Carlos Rigel,[250] or Ricardo Montoya, was one of the two grassy knoll gunmen. The other was Charles Voyde Harrelson. Both had known each other in Huntsville. Rogers had been pals with David Ferrie and, like Ferrie, was a pilot.

Rogers vaguely resembled Oswald and was the "imposter" who used Oswald's identity papers in Mexico City. The purpose of the trip was to set Oswald up. The only difficulty was that Oswald's Russian was excellent, but Rogers' was very poor. Sylvia Duran, the Cuban Counsel, said that the obnoxious Oswald she had met at the Consulate in Mexico City did not resemble Lee Harvey Oswald. (Posner challenges this.) The Cuban Counsel, Eusebio Azcue, also told the HSCA that the man who was so obnoxious with him was not Oswald.

There was also the incident, investigated and documented by the Warren Commission, of a Lee Oswald who had taken a car for a test drive. He behaved obnoxiously, drove the car through Dallas at high speeds and left an "unforgettable" impression on the car salesman, Albert Bogard. Bogard could not remember what his Oswald looked like, but his boss, Frank Pizzo, said that the Lee Harvey Oswald who had come to the car dealership was not the Oswald arrested for the assassination. Pizzo's descriptions did fit Charles Rogers, however. (It is important to note that the real Oswald could not drive.)

After the assassination, Rogers and Harrelson met Chauncey Holt and planned to take a train out of town. Holt was to meet Eugene Hale Brading and Morgan Brown at the Cabana Hotel and get a plane out of the country. Rogers and Harrelson were to have another plane waiting for them, presumably David Ferrie's; he was at an ice rink in Galveston at the time of Kennedy's death. (Posner says David Ferrie's plane was in no condition to fly at this time.)

The *Grassy Knoll Gunman* gives such detail as to dates, times, motel safe houses, bus numbers, etc., that either the informants were very much in the know or were highly skilled writers of dramatic fiction. They even know of Oswald's preference for Dr. Pepper.

Craig and Rogers report on two witnesses not found in other conspiracy literature: Rev. Elmer Gerhart and his wife Marietta. Both say they met Oswald a few days before the assassination. Oswald contacted Charles Rogers outside their church. The Gerharts reported the incident to the FBI *twice* after the assassination, but nothing

---

250. The name Carlos Rigel appears in two books; in each Rigel is cited as a hit man. The first is Robert Morrow's *First Hand Knowledge* (Shapolsky Publishers, 1992); the second *The Grassy Knoll Gunman* by Craig and Rogers (Avon Books, 1992).

came of it. Charles Rogers was reclusive and lived at home. His parents became concerned when he did not show up for a number of weeks after the assassination. They received mysterious phone calls and began to conclude their son had a hand in the assassination. They confided in Rev. and Mrs. Gerhart. When Charles finally returned home and was confronted by his mother about her suspicions, he murdered both his parents. He dismembered both bodies, attempting to destroy the evidence of the crime, but left town without completely cleaning up the home. Rogers has not been seen since, is still thought to be alive, and is wanted for the murder of his parents in Houston.

Still, the origin of the conspiracy is unclear in this model, and one is left in the murky waters between the CIA, the Marcello organization, anti-Castro Cubans — or some combination of the above. Rogers worked for the CIA as a contract agent and had worked with David Ferrie and Guy Banister. Ferrie had contacts with the CIA and the Mob (through Marcello), and Banister had these same contacts in addition to his membership in the Minutemen. Thus, even if Rogers was the grassy knoll gunman, we still have no idea who hired him.

Scenario 4: Author Mark Lane offers another scenario. Marita Lorenz testified that she left Miami, in one of three cars heading for Dallas. E. Howard Hunt of the CIA financed the effort. The assassination team was led by Frank Sturgis, Gerry Patrick Hemming, two Cuban brothers, and a pilot, Pedro Diaz Lanz; others involved were Orlando Bosch (a fugitive) and Alexander Rorke, Jr. (deceased). Gerry Patrick Hemming — who said that Guy Banister in New Orleans offered him a contract to assassinate President Kennedy at the request of the CIA — gave very scanty corroborating testimony. Hemming said he turned Banister down.

Gerry Patrick Hemming

Lane speculates that the two Cuban brothers were Guillermo and Ignacio Novo — both later sentenced for crimes related to the murder of two Chilean officials in Washington. [251]

---

251. Lane, *ibid.*, pp. xvii-xix.

Chapter 4. Conspiracy

Clues From Oswald Himself

These four different CIA assassination scenarios leave many questions unanswered. Does Oswald's behavior give us any direction?

Oswald's Dyslexia

Oswald mastered Russian but had a spelling deficit, which caused writing errors and dropped a trail of clues along the path we are trying to follow. One important misspelling is the word "concerning." He spelled it with a "d": "concerding." This is an atypical mistake and one that implicates him in the writing of a strange letter that appears after the assassination.

On November 8, 1963, he misspelled this word in a mysterious letter written to a Mr. Hunt. The letter surfaced in 1975 and was sent to Kennedy assassination researcher Penn Jones, by an unknown source. It was studied by the HSCA. Three handwriting experts concluded it was authentic. The handwritten version is reproduced later in this chapter.[252]

> Dear Mr. Hunt,   November 8, 1963
>
> I would like information concerding my position.
>
> I am asking only for information.
>
> I am asking that we discuss the matter fully before any steps are taken by me or anyone else.
>
> Thank you.
>
> Lee Harvey Oswald

Few conspiracy researchers have examined this letter in depth. Some think it was sent to oil billionaire H. L. Hunt of Dallas. Others suspect it was sent to agent E. Howard Hunt. Curiously, the letter surfaced in 1975, not 1963. It was in 1975 that the Watergate matters concluded; Nixon resigned August 9, 1974. The Watergate conspirators were found guilty and were sentenced.

Howard Hunt's wife, Dorothy, died in a mysterious plane crash in December, 1973. Researcher Sherman Skolnick believes that Dorothy Hunt was carrying documents that linked Nixon to the Kennedy assassination.[253]

We do not know if Dorothy Hunt was carrying such documents, but we do know that the plane went down under mysterious circumstances and that Mrs. Hunt was carrying $10,000 in cash, allegedly "hush money" for the Watergate burglars. The

---

252. Summers, *ibid.*, p. 626.
253. Weberman, *ibid.*, p. 69.

Oswald letter surfaced as Howard Hunt was being indicted and sentenced in the Watergate burglary, and shortly after his wife had perished in a mysterious airline disaster.

If we speculate that the letter was to E. Howard Hunt, the Mexico City CIA liaison, a man Oswald may have had contact with only weeks earlier when he was in Mexico, we begin to see the faint outlines of Oswald as a CIA functionary, an aspiring spy, a low-level CIA contract agent or an unwitting fool being set up as a patsy for a crime. Oswald did not know what his function was. He sought clarification — "I am asking that we discuss the matter fully before any steps are taken by me or anyone else" — two weeks before the assassination.

Library Books

Another interesting clue was his most recent reading. Oswald checked out a number of books from the Dallas Public Library on November 6, 1963. The books should have been returned on the 13th to avoid late charges, but one was still overdue months later and was not found among his effects. Eventually, someone anonymously returned it, and who that person is remains one of the infinite number of mysteries surrounding the whole assassination drama. [254] [255]

Oswald checked out James Bond spy thrillers by Ian Fleming, plus an unusual title: *The Shark and the Sardines*, by Juan Arevalo, of Guatemala. This reading list shows us a dual Oswald. On one side, we see someone fascinated by deep-cover spy thrillers full of James Bond/CIA overtones, [256] and on the other side a fan of leftist writers, which persuades us Oswald was still a Marxist, with socialist sympathies — 180 degrees opposite to the right-wing fantasies of anti-Castro Cubans, the Minutemen, Guy Banister, David Ferrie, and the like.

There is a deeper clue, however, in the Arevalo book. Weberman and Canfield tried to show Oswald linking up with the CIA through Guy Bannister, David Ferrie, Howard Hunt, and Frank Sturgis; this Guatemalan book may be a key in supporting their theory: Arbenz, the overthrown Guatemalan leader, was close friends with Arevalo, the author. The Arbenz government was overthrown in 1954 in a CIA operation where David Atlee Phillips and Howard Hunt were implicated:

---

254. Posner asserts the library card issue was a rumor started by Jim Garrison. Garrison in turn based his arguments on selected Secret Service documents; the case of the missing, classified, or non-existent library card remains open.

255. Summers, *ibid.*, p. 624.

256. Oswald's favorite television show as a young boy was, "I led three lives," a serial drama of an FBI informant who had joined the communist party. One émigré noticed a book on his living room table in Dallas, entitled *How to Be a Spy* (Posner, *Case Closed.*)

Chapter 4. Conspiracy

In 1954, in association with a CIA team, including Howard Hunt as Political Action Officer, Phillips played a leading part in the overthrow of the anti-American, left-leaning Arbenz government in Guatemala. It was a remarkably cunning operation in which Arbenz was panicked into resignation as much by propaganda as by actual force of arms. [257]

Oswald's reading is a list of spy thrillers fictional and real — some of them engineered by CIA officers who were now possibly his associates. The list looks like it could have been recommended to Oswald by the very owner of the library card he used, David Ferrie. Recommending the Arevalo book would be tantamount to advising Oswald to read about an event Ferrie's colleagues had carried off with pride and precision nine years earlier. [258]

Look for a moment at chronology: In late September, Oswald supposedly makes a trip to Mexico City, where David Atlee Phillips and E. Howard Hunt have recently been. On November 6, 1963, Oswald checks out a book about the overthrow of a Guatemalan president in which Howard Hunt had played a role, and two days later he writes his "concerding" letter to a Mr. Hunt requesting more information before any further steps are taken. Does Oswald know Howard Hunt? Have they formed any association?

The official versions of history, and particularly of these associations, begin to come apart at the seams. Either that, or we have an incredible array of coincidences:

- Officially, Oswald does not know Hunt, but by an incredible coincidence he checks out a book about a leader Hunt helped overthrow.
- Officially, Oswald does not know Howard Hunt, but he writes a letter to a Mr. Hunt two weeks before Kennedy was killed
- Official versions of history say Oswald does not know David Ferrie, but his picture was taken with him in the Civil Air Patrol with only a handful of other cadets present.

---

257. Summers, *ibid.*, p. 509; see also Weberman, *ibid.*, p. 35. The issue of the overthrow of the Arbenz government has now been corroborated. In 1997 the CIA released 1,400 pages of classified material, some of which indicated that the CIA actively planned assassinations and had specifically tried to train and create military force of exiled Guatemalans to overthrow the Arbenz government. The propaganda efforts against Arbenz were sufficient to topple the regime. "Released records show CIA considered assassinations" (Walter Pincus, *SJMN*, May 24, 1997, p. 22A). *The Shark and the Sardines*, a book about the collapse of the Arbenz government, clearly creates an interesting link between Oswald, who checked the book out, and Hunt, who allegedly was the propaganda mastermind for the CIA project to oust Arbenz.

258. The CIA's Richard Bissell and Tracy Barnes were also connected to the Guatemalan operation (See John Newman, *The CIA and Oswald*)..

- Officially, Oswald does not know David Ferrie, nor Ferrie Oswald; but one of them is demonstrating *for* Cuba in New Orleans on the very same day the other is demonstrating *against it*. . . also in New Orleans.
- Three days after being accused of shooting JFK, Oswald dies; and four days after being indicted by Jim Garrison for the assassination, Ferrie dies.
- Officially Oswald does not know either Ferrie or Guy Banister, but Ferrie frequently visits Guy Banister on Camp Street, and Oswald just happens to use that same address on his Fair Play for Cuba brochures.

The official version of the myth insists on leaving this trail of unlikely concurrences to sheer coincidence; anything else impinges on the credibility of the Warren Commission.

It was just a few months earlier that Oswald walked into Carlos Bringuier's store in New Orleans, posing as an anti-Castro soldier of fortune saying that he wanted to join up to overthrow the communists:

"He told me that he was against Castro and that he was against Communism". . . Then Oswald requested some literature, which Bringuier gave him. . . "After that Oswald told me that he had been in the Marine Corps and that he had training in guerrilla warfare and that he was willing to train Cubans to fight against Castro," said Bringuier. "Even more, he told me that he was willing to go himself to fight against Castro." [259]

Did Lee Harvey Oswald make contact in New Orleans with CIA-sponsored right-wing anti-Castro elements which brought him into association with David Ferrie, Guy Banister, and Howard Hunt? Back in New Orleans when Oswald left his job at the Reily Coffee Company across the street from Banister's office, he made a friend at the garage, Adrian Alba. Within weeks of his departure from New Orleans to Dallas, he told Alba, "I have found my pot of gold at the end of the rainbow." And that was the last Alba saw of him. [260]

Oswald and Ferrie

Keep in mind who David Ferrie was. He worked as a pilot for Carlos Marcello. He was a former pilot for Eastern Airlines and lost his job because of charges of homosexual pedophilia. He was a CIA contract agent — of that, there is little doubt, in the literature, and in 1963 he made such a vile speech (saying that JFK should be shot)

---

259. Posner, *Case Closed*. pp. 150-151. For the coincidental times of Ferrie and Oswald's New Orleans demonstrations, see Summers, p. 301.
260. *Ibid.*, p. 284

Chapter 4. Conspiracy

that he had to be removed from the podium by those who had invited him. Ever a booster and member of the Warren Commission spirit squad, Gerald Posner, spends page after page lambasting Jim Garrison's case against Clay Shaw, David Ferrie and Guy Banister as totally off the track, *because Oswald did not know David Ferrie*. But Posner is the first to concede that the entire assassination drama would be wide open if Ferrie and Oswald could truly be linked:

> The issue of whether Oswald knew the adventurer David Ferrie is equally important, since Ferrie had extensive anti-Castro Cuban contacts and also did some work for an attorney for Carlos Marcello, the New Orleans godfather. [261]

Three people linked Oswald with David Ferrie: Dean Andrews, a New Orleans lawyer; Jack Martin, Banister's associate who contacted the FBI after the assassination; and Delphine Roberts, Banister's secretary and mistress. The reliability of these witnesses has been the subject of debate for two decades, but finally the question was solved with a single photograph. Of the dozens of issues and debates, this is one appears to be ended, with Gerald Posner the loser.

The photo clearly shows Oswald and David Ferrie together in the Civil Air Patrol; it was discovered recently by WGBH television and Frontline researchers, and is now receiving distribution and currency. *Oswald did know Ferrie*, so the whole Pandora's box of CIA conspiracy theory is fully opened.

---

261. Posner, Gerald. *Case Closed*. New York: Random House, 1993, p. 142.

Ferrie, Sturgis, Banister, Oswald, Bringuier, Howard Hunt... every one of these men was anti-Castro, and CIA-linked — *except one*, Lee Harvey Oswald.

With the photo of Oswald and CIA-Mafiosi Ferrie together, the testimony of Sylvia Odio telling us that Oswald posed not as a pro-Castro but as a CIA-sponsored anti-Castro mercenary, Carlos Bringuier's tale about Oswald trying to join up with CIA-connected anti-Castro forces, Oswald's James Bond books, a book about Hunt and the CIA undermining a leftist government — all of this followed by Oswald's letter to Hunt — It looks very much like Lee Harvey Oswald was linked with this CIA-related group, was known to this group, or was seeking to be part of it.

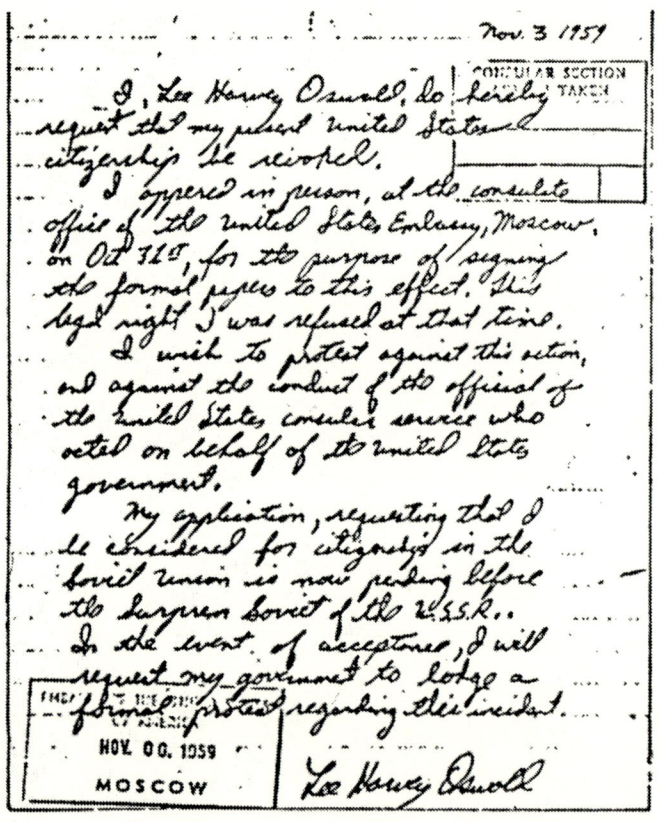

These are samples of two Oswald letters. The first is his original letter to the American Embassy written in 1959 renouncing his citizenship. The letter is found in the original Warren Commission Report on page 24. Note Oswald's spelling deficit can be seen in how he spells Supreme i.e., "Surprem." The second letter only became known in the mid-1970s. It has haunted conspiracy researchers ever since. HSCA investigators said the handwriting similarities show that the Nov. 8, 1963 letter to Mr. Hunt was Oswald's handwriting. It is worth noting how Oswald formed the letter' "I." In most cases he ends construction of the letter without crossing through the major axis of the

Chapter 4. Conspiracy

(47) November 8, 1963. Photograph of a facsimile copy of a handwriten letter to Mr. Hunt.

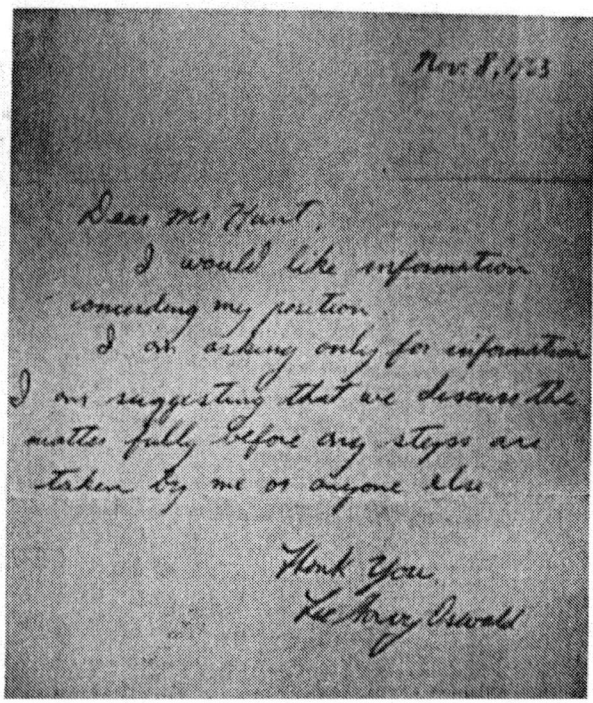

letter. This can be seen in both the 1959 and 1963 samples. It is an unusual feature found in both documents. Furthermore we can still see his spelling deficit in "concerding" in the 1963 letter.

Some argue Oswald's letter was sent to oil billionaire H.L. Hunt, Weberman and Canfield hold that it was sent to E. Howard Hunt, the CIA station chief in Mexico City in September and October, 1963. Hunt was one of the Watergate burglars, was a high official in the CIA under General Cabell, and his wife had recently perished in a mysterious commercial airline disaster in 1973 when the letter surfaced. Hunt is said to have had a close relationship with Guy Banister in New Orleans. How this letter (right) came into the hands of Kennedy researchers is still a mystery, but the HSCA felt the letter was authentically Oswalds'.

Two weeks before the assassination Oswald checked out a library book by Juan Arevalo, *The Shark and the Sardines*, in part about the overthrow of the Guatemalan government in 1954. Howard Hunt was a CIA operative at the time played a role in that governmental overthrow. Two days after checking out the Arevalo book, Oswald wrote this letter to Hunt, and two weeks after that Kennedy was assassinated. The CIA overthrow of the Arevalo government was directed by Allen Dulles, then head of the CIA and later a critical member of the Warren Commission investigating the assassination. Dulles and his brother, John Foster Dulles, were alleged to have ties to United Fruit Company. It is a notable coincidence therefore that the man Oswald writes to [Hunt] was a CIA agent who participated in the same covert operation which Oswald is reading about in his library book, and that the man who would later sit on the Warren Commission to investigate the assassination [Dulles] was Hunt's boss.

"Better For You Not to Know!" [262]

There are a few other signs in Oswald's behavior which point to a CIA conspiracy. These are enumerated in two texts, *Oswald's Tale* (Norman Mailer) and *Marina and Lee* (Priscilla Johnson-MacMillan). Between October of 1962 and April of 1963, his behavior becomes suspicious, secretive, and hard to track. His personal finances wren a factor:

> By the beginning of December there is a likelihood that Oswald is being paid either by deMohrenschildt or by an associate... but whatever the source, the fact is that Oswald, in debt since May of 1962 to the State Department to the sum of $435.71 for family transportation from Moscow to New York, first begins to repay that debt on August 13, 1962. At that time he sends $10 in cash from Mercedes Street and follows it with a money order for $9.71 on September 5, and another money order for $10 on October 10, and still another $10 on November 19, 1962, a picayune total of $39.71 eked out over fourteen weeks. Suddenly, he is able to pay off the rest of his debt — ten times as much — $396.00! — in the interval from December 11, 1962, to January 29, 1963 — that is, in seven weeks: $190.00 in a money order purchased on December 11 (just twenty-three days after he sent $10), another $100 on January 9, and a last money order, purchased on January 29, for $106.00... Oswald earned $305, $240, and $247 in November, December and January, and for living disbursed $182, $165, and $190 in those same months.. As soon, however as we take away $396 for the State Department debt, he is now $118 in arrears, and even this figure depends on there being no other expenditures than those that were noted by the Warren Commission. It is highly unlikely that every cent he spent in those three months was recorded.

In this period, not only are Oswald's finances strange but his whereabouts unaccounted for:

> ... from October 1962 to April 1963, there have to be a hundred, if not two hundred, hours that no one (certainly not Marina) can account for. Who knows what he did and whom he met in that time?

A few times he had anxiety dreams and would talk in his sleep. One such occasion was in February of 1963. When Marina joked about it, Oswald became very upset. In the morning he said, *"Better for you not to know."*

---

262. Quotations in this section come from Mailer, pp. 483-484, and 514. The reference to Oswald's talking in his sleep is from McMillan-Johnson, p. 161, and Mailer, p. 558.

A more telling incident occurred later, the week after he received his passport, June 24, 1963. He had another anxiety attack:

> . . . He shook from head to toe at intervals of half an hour and never once woke up. . . On the following night Marina was watching him read and he looked up at her: . . . she saw a look of sadness in his eyes. He put his book down and went into the kitchen by himself. Marina waited a few minutes. Then she put the baby down and followed him. Lee was sitting in the dark with his arms and legs wrapped around the back of a chair and his head resting on top. He was staring down at the floor. Marina put her arms around him, stroked his head, and could feel him shaking with sobs. . . Finally she said: "Everything is going to be all right. I understand." Marina held him for about a quarter of an hour and he told her between sobs that he was lost. He didn't know what he ought to do. At last he stood up and returned to the living room.
>
> Recalling that night thirty years later, she said that if he had wanted to tell her about his problem he would have, but it was better not to ask. She could still feel his burden. There was something so heavy he had been carrying, and she didn't know what it was. She never knew. It was sad, she said.[263]

Oswald's emotional behavior is not evidence, but it tells us that much is unknown and unexplained, and that five months before the assassination he was teeming with anxiety, fear, and trepidation.

He had just lost his job at the Reily Coffee Company in New Orleans. Was that the reason for these emotions? The following week Oswald seemed improved. He decided that he would ask the Soviet Embassy if he could return, with Marina. On the weekend of June 29th, together they wrote Comrade Reznichenko of the Soviet Embassy in Washington, saying they wanted to go back.

On the surface, his sobbing and night terrors suggest he was feeling like a failure, having lost another job; and we can speculate that perhaps he was lamenting that he had lost every job he ever had since coming from the USSR: a husband who could not provide for his wife and his child, while his second child was expected five months hence.

If the nucleus of all this angst was so conventional, why would he choose not to talk to Marina about it? She knew what he did with General Walker. He obviously trusted her enough to confide such issues to her, but this time he avoided telling her what was going on. That suggests something else was afoot, something too big for him to handle himself, something too big to confide in Marina.

---

263. MacMillan-Johnson, *ibid.*

Strong Points in the CIA Conspiracy Model

Accumulating evidence suggests that Oswald had some kind of military or intelligence function. Although perhaps repetitive, a table attempting to summarize and condense the material may be useful.

Table 4.4 Eight "Soft" Lines of Evidence Connecting Oswald to the CIA and Military Intelligence

- Oswald had a military intelligence file that was destroyed; it was not seen by the Warren Commission nor the HSCA; evidence supports the existence of such a file. (See prior chapter).

- Oswald was seen entering the two top floors of the U.S. Embassy in Moscow. Teachers, wives, and dependents of embassy employees were never allowed to enter these highly restricted floors. Oswald's access to this area suggests he had special clearances.

- As a Marine, Oswald had a security clearance and worked on a top-secret base in Japan. His cousin, Dorothy Murret, with whom he stayed in New Orleans, allegedly had a CIA connection. Oswald knew Michael and Ruth Paine and George deMohrenschildt in Dallas. DeMohrenschildt, particularly, but the Paines as well, had intelligence connections. De Mohrenschildt admitted that he befriended Oswald *for the government* and reported to the CIA about his contacts. This information was not known to the Warren Commission and only came out after De Mohrenschildt's suicide. Documents released in 1992 showed that deMohrenschildt actually had three CIA contacts in 1963: Walton Moore, Domestic Contacts Division, Nicholas Anikeef, from the CIA's Soviet Russia Division, and Charles Thomas, a CIA covert operations agent.

- Oswald was reported seen in the presence of a CIA agent, Charles Frederick Rogers, alias Carlos Rigel, by the Rev. Elmer Gerhart and his wife Marietta. Charles Rogers, confronted by his parent's suspicions of involvement in the assassination, murdered them and has been a fugitive ever since.

- Many individuals provided testimony, some under oath, that they had met Oswald face to face in an intelligence context and associated with right-wing CIA and anti-Castro elements, not leftwing causes. These individuals are Marita Lorenz, Sylvia Odio, Annie Odio, and Carlos Bringuier.

- Marina Oswald initially did not believe her husband was part of any conspiracy. She has since changed her mind and now believes he was. She also now suspects he was involved in intelligence gathering in the USSR, too. Oswald's mother, Marguerite, also believed her son had an intelligence connection.

- Oswald's readings show a high level of curiosity about spying. In Dallas, he had a coffee table book entitled *How to be a Spy*. Two days after checking out a book about Hunt's CIA triumph, Oswald appears to have written a letter to a Mr. Hunt; the letter implies that the two had prior contacts.

Chapter 4. Conspiracy

- Oswald knew David Ferrie in the Civil Air Patrol (his instructor) and likely met Ferrie in New Orleans. There is now photographic evidence showing Oswald and Ferrie together. Oswald was said to have been working for Guy Banister when he was distributing Fair Play for Cuba leaflets. He used Banister's Camp Street address, an address which housed CIA-sponsored anti-Castro organizations, most notably the Cuban Revolutionary Council under Arcacha Smith.
- Jim Garrison was unable to prove that Banister and Ferrie had CIA connections. Years later Richard Helms, Director of the CIA, made admissions that these individuals did have a relationship to the CIA; Victor Marchetti, former CIA Assistant Director, corroborated Ferrie's CIA associations. If Oswald can be linked with Ferrie in 1963, he can be linked with the CIA, anti-Castro Cubans, and/or the underworld — Ferrie and Banister were connected to all three.

The table summarizes essential information about Oswald; but a CIA-based assassination theory has other strong elements to it, apart from him: especially motive. Fletcher Prouty said that President Kennedy, highly disturbed over CIA planning of the Bay of Pigs operation, and over his inability to get control of the organization, sought, after his re-election, to dismantle it. This would be motive enough, within the agency; but motive also comes from CIA-backed anti-Castro Cubans, whose bases Kennedy tried to shut down. The Cubans felt betrayed by his secret dealings with Khrushchev and felt the U.S. would no longer support their efforts to overthrow Castro. The CIA itself, the CIA officers fired for the Bay of Pigs fiasco, and CIA-sponsored anti-Castro exiles all may have shared a desire to remove the President.

The CIA's contacts with organized crime figures strengthen the motive. The Mob lost a great deal of gambling, narcotics, and prostitution revenue when it lost Cuba to Castro, and it was being persecuted on dozens of fronts by Attorney General Robert Kennedy, as well. The relationship of William Harvey, an unstable CIA figure who worked under General Cabell, and Harvey's repeated contacts with John Roselli, Giancana, Marcello, and Trafficante, makes a Mob-CIA plot plausible. Not only was there motive and opportunity, but plenty of assets to carry out such a crime.

The CIA's history of generating disinformation, withholding real information, loss of documents, and recalcitrance in dealing with investigative committees is indicative of something. CIA officer Regis Blahut's attempt to purloin autopsy photos from the HSCA is the most stark example, but equally important is *how strenuously the CIA attempted to disassociate itself from Oswald.* Efforts to deny any contacts, any relationship, any debriefings with Oswald and to spread rumors that he was an agent of Castro through "unnamed sources" (three from the CIA itself) show that the CIA had a compelling interest in creating the impression that Oswald was working for someone else.

Table 4.5 CIA efforts to dissociate itself from Oswald:

1. Frank Sturgis, a CIA contract agent associated with Howard Hunt, and an anti-Castro Cuban exile, leaked two stories to Jack Anderson and author James Buchanan. In each hew as an "unnamed source" that said Oswald was a pro-Castro agent. Sturgis denied his involvement in circulating these rumors, but both Jack Anderson and James Buchanan independently said he was. Sturgis was attempting to show Oswald as a pro-Castro leftist and to deflect any attention away from Oswald as in any way connected to the CIA.

2. John Roselli, a Mafia figure working closely with CIA agent William Harvey, was also a source of disinformation about Oswald. He leaked a story to Jack Anderson that Oswald was a pro-Castro agent. The story boomeranged and Roselli was exposed. (Roselli was murdered shortly after this disclosure.)

3. Loran Hall came forward to say it was he, not Oswald, who visited Sylvia Odio. Hall's story was later admitted to be a lie. Hall was an anti-Castro exile and CIA contract agent who made these admissions under immunity from prosecution.

4. Richard Helms, who became Director of the CIA after the assassination, was suspected of being involved in numerous instances of withholding information from the Warren Commission and other investigative agencies. His most recent denial centered around an alleged "debriefing" by CIA agent Andy Anderson. The CIA long held that despite Oswald's defection to the USSR and his Fair Play for Cuba activities, it did not have any files on him at the time of the assassination. The debriefing memo discovered only in 1993, an event which occurred prior to the assassination, still looms as a contentious issue.

A final strong point is anecdotal and repeated from earlier in this chapter:. Lyndon Johnson's mistress, Madeline Brown, said that Johnson had fathered a child with her after their long association and that, one New Year's Eve, she asked him if he had had anything to do with the assassination. He became visibly upset and in a temper replied to her that it was the "CIA and the oil men." [264] Anecdotal evidence is certainly not the best, but the remark is not easy to disregard either.

Weak Elements

This theory is based chiefly on conjecture and does not give us much more than anecdotal testimony, innuendo, and associations to form a basis for suspicion. The sworn statements of Silvia Odio, Marita Lorenz, and others might provide the basis for prosecution of Howard Hunt, Frank Sturgis (deceased), Loran Hall, Orlando

Bosch, and perhaps James Angleton (deceased) and/or Richard Helms (for obstruction of justice), but there isn't enough to successfully prosecute anyone for the assassination. There is little physical evidence — no bullets, eyewitnesses, or fingerprints — pointing to the CIA.

---

264. *Ibid.*, p. 308. The mistress of Lyndon Johnson, Madeleine Brown, related a chilling anecdote to author Dick Russell on August 4, 1992 regarding this implication. "Before the assassination, according to Brown, 'Lyndon told me that the Kennedys would never embarrass him again. It was not a threat, but a promise." Then, as 1963 passed into history, they were together at a New Year's Eve party. "I said, Lyndon, 'I've got to have my mind put at ease,' Brown remembers, "People are saying you are responsible for the assassination, and I've got to know. Well he had a terrible temper tantrum, as he often did. Then he told me: 'It was the oil people and the CIA.'" (Dick Russell, *The Man Who Knew Too Much*. New York: Carroll & Graf, 1992, p. 606.)

A corroborating source, Harrison E. Livingstone's *Killing the Truth* (New York: Carrol & Graf, 1993) mentions Madeline Brown in the following context: "I know Madeline Brown, a former mistress of Johnson, rather well and find her mostly credible. It is hard for me to believe that she is making up all she says. Brown has, in the past, maintained that LBJ told her that John Kennedy was going to be assassinated in advance of it happening. In my talks with her, she confirms the portrait given in The Texas Connection, and then some. She says that Johnson was a totally amoral man who slept with any woman who came along, betrayed all his women, and who was often drunk and abusive. She said that she believed he worked together with H.L. Hunt and others on the murder." (p. 466).

In my own research, a peculiar event transpired. As the author of this text, I have attempted to base all conjecture and speculation on evidence gleaned from one published sort or another. In the matter of Kennedy mistresses I felt a need to be particularly careful about making claims of affairs, which others had published, and I tried to independently confirm some of these allegations. One text suggested that Pierre Salinger's secretary slept with Kennedy, so I wrote Salinger about this. Salinger denied JFK slept with his secretary, but did acknowledge JFK's womanizing. At the same time, he revealed that one of his employees took up with LBJ after the assassination. His letter to me is excerpted below:

"Dear Dr. Kroth, . . . Kennedy pushed me to have mistresses, which convinced me he was having mistresses. During the campaign, I got side information from journalists (who in those days were not interested in publishing that information) that John F. Kennedy was having an affair with Pamela Turnure, who later became Jackie's press secretary. There were rumors in the White House about Fiddle & Faddle, but I did not get specific information. And, finally, no employee assigned to my office had an affair with the President. One did in the next term with Lyndon Johnson. Best Regards, Pierre Salinger." (Source: Personal correspondence, October, 20, 1995).

Madeline Brown's allegations first given to author Dick Russell, therefore, seem to be corroborated in part, at least, by two other independent sources, Harrison Livingston and Pierre Salinger.

Groden, *Ibid.*, p. 237. Let us not forget another suspected conspirator from the right, Frank Sturgis, the unnamed disinformation source of Jack Anderson's early writings linking Castro to a Soviet plot. We should also remember mobster Roselli as another deep-throat source for articles linking Oswald to a leftist conspiracy originating with Castro. Thus we have suspects H.L. Hunt, Sturgis and Roselli each contributing disinformation to support the hypothesis of a leftist conspiracy to kill the president.

Great harm is done to people named as part of a conspiracy to kill the President of the United States when accusations sit upon such a weak factual base. Issues of defamation and libel certainly could be brought forward. (Hunt did sue Weberman and Canfield for libel, but withdrew his suit. Sturgis threatened Marita Lorenz, but did not seek to litigate while he was alive. Others, like David Phillips, clearly could have initiated defamation suits but did not do so. Some conspiracy researchers, unheeding of the damage they can bring to someone's reputation, argue that failure to sue is even greater proof of culpability. [265]

The entire aura of obsessiveness about this event has caused the original players in the drama to become larger than life. Ruby, the great "Mob chieftain," might really have been just a small-time Dallas striptease hawker who was $39,000 in arrears on an IRS debt. Oswald, the "super-assassin, double-agent, and James-Bond-master-spy," earned $1.25 an hour, and his 1962 tax return revealed an income of less than $1,000. Although Mailer has brought convincing evidence that Oswald's expenditures were greater than his earnings, there is still considerable difficulty showing him ever having more than a few hundred surplus dollars. The characters of our drama tend to be magnified and are probably far less interesting than collective fantasies make them out to be.

A final weak point is that if Oswald was being set up as a patsy for a future assassination in Dallas and had visited Silvia Odio in late September, how did the conspirators know that Kennedy would be in Dallas at that time? No one could have known Kennedy's motorcade route prior to October 4, and that was *after* Oswald met with Odio.

As it presently stands, the theory is still little more than a compilation of allegations, associations and innuendo, pseudonyms, denials, suspicious, and faceless fugitives or sharp-shooter-mechanics who are already either deceased (like Lucien Sarti) or probably deceased (like fugitive Charles Frederick Rogers).

Yet to take the position of Gerald Posner — that this whole line of inquiry should be dropped — is nonsensical. Until a thorough-going inquiry is made into the actions of Richard Helms, Howard Hunt, James Angleton, Richard Bissell, Tracy Barnes, James Hosty, the entire cast of the anti-Castro Cubans and their CIA-associates,

---

265. As an illustration of the damage that can be done to individuals, Mailer's *Oswald's Tale* (p. 479) relates the following: In Dallas the Oswalds were invited to a Christmas party organized by deMohrenschildt. In attendance was a Japanese woman, a leftist, named Yaeko Okui. She and Oswald conversed intensely, and Lee took her address. This made Marina jealous. She spoke Russian with him at the party. Okui has been the subject of speculation by conspiracists — did Oswald have an affair with her? Was she a communist contact? Tracked down by Norman Mailer's research team in 1995, she refused to comment or answer any questions but did say that the party she attended and the subsequent attention she received "ruined her life."

Chapter 4. Conspiracy

Postscript: John Newman's Oswald and the CIA

In 1992 the JFK Records Act resulted in the release of thousands of documents. By 1995 researcher John Newman meticulously analyzed the paper trail on Oswald reviewing some 2 million pieces of paper. There are a few new individuals to include in the already-bulging compendium of names associated with Oswald and these have been added to our various tables in this text on cover-up [Table 3.4] and on CIA personages [Table 4.3]. Newman does not turn any corners on the assassination, nor does he integrate his work with other scholarship. His task is obviously taxing enough. His sense is that some kind of operation was built around Oswald. Here is a brief synopsis of his major findings which may not be incorporated elsewhere in this text.

In November, 1960 the State Department requested a list from the CIA of American "defectors" in Eastern Bloc countries. James Angleton wrote back saying, "our files are being searched for the information you desire, and you will be hearing further from me in a few days. . . . On November 21, Bissell signed this letter with the defectors list attached. The Oswald entry, the tenth on the CIA's version of the defectors list, was classified SECRET. This correspondence occurred in 1960, but in 1964 during the Warren Commission the CIA continued to assert it had no information on Oswald before the assassination. Newman also discovered the CIA had been opening Oswald's mail as early as November, 1959, in a secret program called HT/LINGUAL.

Another interesting research coup was in sorting through all of Oswald's New Orleans behavior. It is here that he cultivates both a pro-Castro and an anti-Castro identity. "Whether Oswald's actions were his own or the result of direction or manipulation, but carrying out both pro-Castro and anti-Castro activities in New Orleans, Oswald was playing a dangerous game. During this spectacle [when Oswald was arrested for disturbing the peace in his confrontation with Carlos Bringuier], Oswald actually insisted on seeing an FBI agent while in jail, to supply him, Oswald said, with information on his FPCC activities. It was a strange place to play the part of informant, an oddity underlined by a strange FBI act: They withheld the fact—for quite some time—that Special Agent Quigley had interviewed Oswald in jail (p. 319).

The Oswald character who emerges in FBI files and from there into CIA files begins in New Orleans by doing two things: infiltrating the FPCC as "Lee Harvey Oswald" while simultaneously forging an undercover identity. In this undercover role, his character, 'A.J. Hidell", a pro-Castro activist, hands out FPCC literature under a false organization title, "Fair Play for Cuba Committee, New Orleans Charter Member Branch," with a false post office box (30016), and a false office address, 544 Camp Street (p. 327).

Newman's greatest contribution seems to be unprecedented, namely that Oswald did go to Mexico City *and so did* an impostor. No conspiracy research has taken this position, to my knowledge. Newman is persuaded both events happened. The reasons are substantial: Newman sorts all of the documentary information and transcripts into a table, interviews witnesses, cites declassified portions of the still-classified Lopez Report, and quotes surviving, fugitive sections of deceased CIA officer Winston Scott's manuscript which James Angleton took from Scott's safe after his death and apparently destroyed. His conclusion is that the Soviet and Cuban consulates were dealing with two Oswalds, the real one and the impostor.

plus CIA-Mafia dimensions of this matter, any recommendation to close this case should be considered suspect.

There may be weak spots in the theory, but it certainly deserves the most serious attention, especially the Oswald-David Ferrie link discovered in 1993. That is perhaps the most significant research breakthrough in a decade. It refutes the work of Gerald Posner almost in its entirety. Indeed, when one considers how many pies Banister and Ferrie had their fingers in, it is not at all preposterous to assume that Oswald, through them, could have been connected to the CIA, the Mob, anti-Castro Cubans . . . or all three simultaneously.

4. The Communist Conspiracy

> *We are prepared to . . . answer in kind. United States leaders should think that if they assist terrorist plans to eliminate Cuban leaders, they themselves will not be safe.*
> — Fidel Castro [266]

There is yet a fourth theory — not a leading one, but one that has intrigued this author particularly since my own personal experience allows me some insight into it. Oswald's relationship to the Soviet Union, his activities, marriage, and departure from that country paint a picture sharply divergent from my own experience there. A first-person account may be of interest, at least in the early part of this section.

In the mid-1960s, I had just received my Masters degree in psychology and not yet earned my doctorate. I thought that teaching abroad might give me valuable experience, and so I applied for numerous teaching positions. I was hired by the Moscow Diplomatic School, an elementary school on Kropotkinskaya Street, part of the U.S. Embassy school system. I earned a salary of $4,500 plus free round-trip transportation from the U.S. I thought it would be a great adventure — my first trip to Europe. I was 24 years old, single, and it was 1965.

Actually, I couldn't speak a word of Russian. I could barely decipher that essential sign, "Pectopah" (restaurant). One cultural shock seemed to follow another. Life in Moscow was extremely difficult for this spoiled American bachelor.

It snowed on October 11, but the heat in my building was not turned on until November. That gave me a personal taste of the effects of "central planning." I slept shivering under an electric blanket for two weeks. It was still snowing on May Day of the following year. For a few days in February, the thermometer dipped to 37 degrees-below zero.

---

266. Reeves, *ibid.*, p. 278.

Chapter 4. Conspiracy

When I went to work, a chauffeur-driven embassy car picked me up in the dark. When I left school at 3:30, the embassy car dropped me off at my apartment, and it was dark again. It seemed as if I had not seen the sun for the entire academic year.

I was told on orientation day that teachers had no diplomatic immunity; we had to be careful of our associations, because the embassy could do little to rescue us if we got in any compromising situations. Fraternizing with members of the opposite sex, if they were not part of the diplomatic community, could get us in serious trouble, and we were apprized early that the embassy would discontinue our contracts and send us home if that happened. "So much for Russian girls!" I thought.

Close to the end of my teaching contract, I fell in love with a Soviet citizen, Anya. We got engaged and sought to be married. Anya is now my fully Americanized wife and the mother of our two children, Anya and Maya; but things did not go quite as easily for us as they did for Lee Harvey Oswald. First, the embassy consular section pointed out that my contract was almost up and said they wanted me out of the country as soon as possible. The consul said my chances of marrying this woman were virtually nil, and if I did succeed in getting the Soviets to permit it, my chances of getting her out of the country *were a solid impossibility*. He said that in the prior year, only three Russians were let out of the Soviet Union who were not on some sort of official mission.

This was the heart of the cold war. It was many years prior to the Helsinki accords, many years prior to the waves of Jewish emigrants, but still six years *after* Oswald had married Marina and emigrated with her to Texas.

Undaunted, I finished up my contract and left in June, 1966, returning from Paris, in August, no longer affiliated with the embassy. I thought my fiancée and I could be married now that I was just a plain old American tourist and not part of a diplomatic mission; not quite.

One of the myriad Catch 22s was that if one wanted to marry a Soviet citizen, it had to be done in the legal residence of the bride. My bride-to-be lived ten miles outside of the Moscow City limits — an area closed to foreigners. Since I could not legally visit the area where the marriage bureau was located, there was no way to permit a wedding.

Another obstacle was that the bride had to have notarized permission from both her parents. Even though she was 24 years old, even if her parents were separated. Furthermore, any notary "authorizing" a Soviet citizen to marry an American was placed in a dicey situation. There were few volunteers, notaries or otherwise, to help us out. After thirty exasperating days, my visa expired and I had to leave the country, unsuccessful and disappointed. I returned to the U.S. to start my doctoral program and vowed I would figure out this system and return.

It took us another year, and reams of letters, until finally we received permission to be married. With help from a Moscow attorney, I received permission to enter her "forbidden city" in the Moscow suburbs and we were married. Over a year had passed, and two trips in and out of the USSR were necessary to get that far; but we finally succeeded. *Permission to leave* was an entirely different story. It was now September, 1967.

Permission to leave the cloistered fortress of Soviet Russia involved OVIR, the dreaded passport agency. OVIR would refuse an application to leave the USSR on virtually any technicality.

Again, permission from one's parents was necessary. Notaries were necessary. A "letter of recommendation" from one's employer was necessary. Can you imagine writing a "letter of recommendation" for a miscreant, a traitor, who was planning to leave Brezhnev's USSR for good, in the arms of an American?

Another 6-8 months passed. My wife secured a pejorative letter of recommendation from her job, her mother's notarized permission, and, from my side, a few letters from congressmen and senators (most notably Senator Cranston) requesting humanitarian consideration. My wife was finally given her papers to leave and she did so in 1968.

In the USSR of old, if your husband or wife had served in the military in the prior five years, indeed, if they worked for the telephone company — any reason could be construed as a security reason for refusing to issue an exit visa. Every job in the Soviet Union had some kind of strategic value, according to the logic at OVIR. When I lived in Moscow, there was no telephone directory. Publishing a directory would violate state secrets, we were told. The only telephone book in existence in Moscow was a small handbook published by the American embassy.

These are not exaggerations, however ludicrous it may seem today. In reading the literature about Lee Harvey Oswald, I find myself experiencing high levels of disbelief regarding his Russian years and his marriage to Marina. Oswald married and left the Soviet Union five years before I arrived. The situation could not have been any easier.

The woman who married us, for example, said that she had once married a foreigner to a Soviet citizen under Stalin. She was sent to prison for five years for that mistake. When she was finally "told from above" that she had to marry us, she read off a paragraph in Russian, informed us we were now man and wife and abruptly asked us to leave. In this short ceremony, she broke out in hives and her eyebrows, cheeks, and forehead turned puffy and red. She was shaking from head to toe. Our entire marriage ceremony was a secular, ten-minute reading of a passage in Russian, two signatures, and a taxi ride back to Moscow. It had taken over fifteen months of work to get that far.

Chapter 4. Conspiracy

Oswald's marriage to Marina, the niece of a lieutenant colonel in the Ministry of the Interior, thus raises some issues for me that someone without this kind of experience might overlook.[267]

The following items summarize some of the more "curious aspects" of Oswald's Russian connection. Thus begins a "Soviet" conspiracy theory we will discuss, not one which is very popular or given much currency, but one which has a set of facts worthy of our attention:

Victor Marchetti, the former CIA assistant director, said that in the late 1950s, the U.S. did not have adequate intelligence gathering capability for the USSR. The Office of Naval Intelligence attempted to recruit as many as forty young men who might be sent into the Soviet Union. They were trained at various naval installations, but the operation was managed primarily from Nag's Head, North Carolina.

> In a sudden rash of turncoats, no less than five were Army men stationed in West Germany, and two were former Naval men and employees of the National Security Agency. . . Of the civilians who went to the Soviet Union, one was a former official of the Office of Strategic Services. . . another was a former Air Force Major. . . Then, of course, there was Lee Oswald, fresh out of the Marines.[268]

Oswald may have been such an agent. When I worked as a schoolteacher in the mid-1960s, I had no diplomatic immunity. I was not allowed on to the two top floors of the embassy. This is where the more official embassy business was conducted, and it was highly protected. Two Marine guards stood out in front, and in the ten months I was associated with the diplomatic mission, I was never invited in this area, even though I knew quite a number of people attached to the embassy and, in fact, had their children in class.

It was quite surprising, therefore, to read a recent Anthony Summers piece about Oswald's behavior in Moscow in 1959:

> The official story has it that when Oswald defected he went to the American Embassy in Moscow only once, visiting only the consular office on the ground floor. Yet the widow of the assistant naval attaché, Joan Hallet, who worked as a receptionist at the embassy, says Consul Richard Snyder and the security officer

---

267. Marina's Uncle Ilya, the MVD colonel, was close to retirement. If there is a reasonable explanation for the ease of the Oswald's marriage, it may have been that Uncle Ilya believed Oswald genuinely wanted to stay in the USSR, and thus he supported the marriage. He did not support the Oswald's leaving the USSR, however, and expressed concern that his pension might be affected. See Johnson, *ibid.*

268. Summers, *ibid.*, p. 147.

"took him upstairs to the working floors, a secure area where the Ambassador and the political, economic, and military officers were. A visitor would never ever get up there unless he was on official business. I was never up there." According to Hallet, Oswald came to the embassy "several times" in 1959. [269]

Joan Hallet's story matches my experience. She was "never" up there, *even to visit her husband*, and neither was I. The consular offices were on the ground floor, as she mentioned, and if Oswald did, in fact, enter the two top floors, he certainly had a status *far different* than those of us who did not have high-level clearances. Even after I announced my intentions of marrying a Soviet citizen, a physicist who worked in a Soviet optics factory, the U.S. embassy never thought my particular situation warranted a trip to the two top floors.

After Oswald was arrested in Dallas, he was allowed telephone calls. On Saturday, the day after the assassination, he called Ruth Paine. He also tried but failed to complete another call. It was to a man named "Hurt" in Raleigh, North Carolina. John D. Hurt served in U.S. Military Intelligence during World War II. Oswald's address book showed no known contacts in North Carolina. One member of HSCA was quite concerned about the nature of this attempted call, however. It is possible Oswald entered the Soviet Union as a military intelligence "plant," thus perhaps the North Carolina connection.[270] This is a point of view now held by Oswald's widow, Marina in 1996, although as she says, she has no proof. [271]

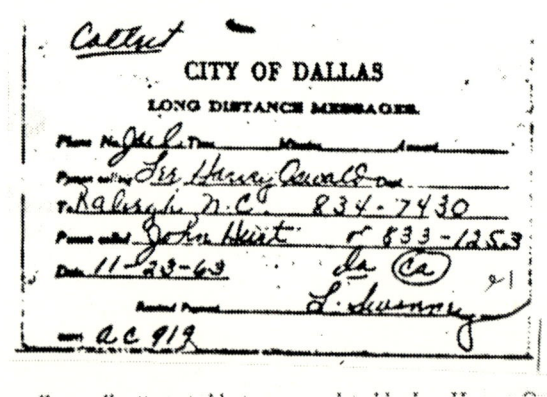

Record of a collect call attempted but not completed by Oswald in the Dallas jail on November, 23, 1963. The call was to a John Hurt in Raleigh, North Carolina. Hurt said he had no idea why Oswald would want to call him. Hurt had a military intelligence background. This phone record was uncovered by independent researchers and not submitted to the Warren Commission. (Source: Weberman and Canfield, p. 287.)

---

269. From Summers, The Ghosts of November, *ibid*.

270. Record of a collect call attempted but not completed by Oswald in the Dallas jail on November, 23, 1963. The call was to a John Hurt in Raleigh, North Carolina. Hurt said he had no idea why Oswald would want to call him. Hurt had a military intelligence background. This phone record was uncovered by independent researchers and not submitted to the Warren Commission. Weberman and Canfield, p. 287.

271. Mailer, *ibid*.

Chapter 4. Conspiracy

Oswald's Soviet Diary

While in Moscow, seeking to renounce his citizenship and remain in the USSR, Oswald learned that the Russians did not want him. He attempted suicide. He was rescued by Rimma Shirokova, his Intourist guide and taken to Botkin Hospital. He spent a week recovering there. This information was supplied by the Soviet Government after the assassination, along with Oswald's "Historic Diary." An excerpt of that diary is given below. Spelling mistakes and other errors are as they appear in the diary:

> 6:00 Recive word from police offial. I must leave country tonight at 8.0 p.m. as visa expirs. I am shocked!! ... My dreams! I retire to my room. I have $100 left. I have waited for 2 year to be accepted. My fondes dreams are shattered because of a petty official, because of bad planning I planned to much!
>
> 7.0 p.m. I decide to end it. Soak rist in cold water to numb the pain. Than slash my left wrist. Then plaug wrist into bathtub of hot water. I think 'when Rimma comes at 8. to find me dead it will be a great shock...somewhere a violin plays, as I wacth my life whirl away...[272]

Again, based on my own experience, this diary seems glaringly inauthentic. Oswald did have a spelling disability, but his IQ was above average. When a Russian speaks English, one of the hardest sounds to pronounce is a short "i". "Receive" is often pronounced "reciv." My wife still has trouble with it after 30 years, despite her incredible fluency in English and having earned an American doctorate. Certain words are automatically mispronounced. To see my wife's habitual mispronunciation in Oswald's diary smacks of forgery; it strongly suggests that the diary was composed by an *English-speaking Russian*.

"*Then plaug wrist into bathtub of hot water.*" Russians also have great difficulty with articles like "a," "an," or "the." "A" bathtub of hot water would certainly do; "the" bathtub would be preferable and perfectly natural for an American, even with a spelling disability. The missing "a" *is a Russian error*, not an American error.

"*I must leave country tonight at 8.0 p.m.*" I must leave "the" country tonight, again not a mistake characteristic of a dyslexic with a spelling disability, but a mistake characteristic of a Russian who is still struggling with the problematic use of "the."

It is also unlikely Oswald would write 8 o'clock as "8.0". Even more unlikely is the maudlin phrase, "somewhere a violin plays, as I watch my life whirl away." It would be uncharacteristic for Oswald to compose such a tear-jerker (and if he did,

---

272. *Ibid.*, p. 154

wouldn't he say, "is playing"?), but it is a very familiar image in that minor-keyed, melodramatic, deep Russian adoration for suffering.

Suspect as well is the term "petty official," so often used in Russian parlance and on the tongues of virtually all Soviet citizens, but not a phrase frequently used by Americans. It sounds especially peculiar and arcane in the vocabulary of a man from the South.

Another article is missing in the entry for February 1:

> I make my first request to American Embassy, Moscow... I stated I would like to go back to U.S.[273]

If the Oswald diary is suspect, curiously reminiscent of a Russian attempting to write in English (and more researchers than myself have considered it so), then one must wonder why it was submitted by the Soviets with Oswald's documents after the assassination.

> Upon studying Oswald's Russian diary,[274] we and others believe that it could not possibly have been written by Oswald, or in fact anyone other than a forger. There are simply too many literary allusions, a vocabulary far too complex, using such words as splendid, abound, unobtainable, especially enthusiastic and so on, all spelled quite correctly, to have been written by someone with such bad grammar and spelling as the diary attempts to portray. Alongside numerous known letters and handwriting samples of Oswald's, the hand-printed diary is clearly fake.[275]

The Soviets said Oswald had no intelligence function. If his diary is as specious as it seems, was this Soviet position a falsehood too?

After the assassination, some wanted to exhume his body to make sure that the signs of this suicide attempt were still there. Oswald's diary has him attempting suicide at 7 p.m., but he was admitted to Botkin Hospital at 4 p.m. the next day, twenty one hours later! Rimma, his Intourist guide, had him admitted. Either the diary itself is suspect and replete with errors or his wound was little more than a scratch — which would be the only reasonable explanation how almost a whole day could pass before he was taken to the hospital.[276]

---

273. Johnson, *ibid.*, p. 93.

274. Contrary to the findings of conspiracists — and this author — the HSCA felt the diary to be genuine.

275. Groden, *ibid.*, p. 166

276. Norman Mailer's inquiry favors the latter interpretations (See *Oswald's Tale*, p. 52).

There are also many other problems with the descriptions, dates and times in his diary. He referred to getting paid, for example, in "new rubles," but the ruble was not revalued until *a year later*.

Rimma gave him a copy of Dostoyevsky's *The Idiot*, when he first arrived. However appropriate the title, at that time Dostoyevsky was very difficult to get and was considered highly anti-Soviet; it was rarely sold in bookstores and would have been an extraordinary gift for a new acquaintance in many ways.

In January, 1960 Oswald was moved to Minsk, 450 miles from Moscow. He was given 5,000 rubles by the Soviet Red Cross. I was in the USSR about 6 years later, and the average monthly salary for a college-educated person was in the neighborhood of 150 rubles. Oswald's payment was the equivalent of three years of salary. And his salary in Minsk was greater than the director of the factory's. [277]

Further, Oswald was given an apartment in Minsk overlooking the river, at a time when people lived doubled up in communal apartments shared by two to four families. Few bachelors had their own apartments — unless they were very high-ranking party officials or KGB. Oswald was treated as a VIP — of that, there is little doubt. Indeed, when I was in Moscow, as a bachelor, I was given a one-bedroom apartment in the embassy compound. The few Russians who ever visited were amazed that a single man could have such splendid accommodations.

There is other evidence that Oswald was given exceptional treatment. He had no domestic passport and was formally a "stateless person," meaning that he had approximately no rights at all. I personally knew a Georgian who wanted to live and work in Moscow; he paid the ruble equivalent of $10,000 to a woman to marry him so he could get the requisite documentation on his domestic passport to legally qualify to live in Moscow. Oswald had no such difficulties. He applied to get married as a stateless person and was granted permission to marry within 10 days.

Only a few privileged sportsmen were allowed to have guns. Oswald, again without benefit of a domestic passport, applied to join a gun club, and in no time at all had a hunting rifle.

Marina Nikolaevna Prusakova: Suspicions Increase

Oswald married a young pharmacist, Marina, with whom he had a child in the USSR. They immigrated to the United States in 1962. While in the U.S., Marina Oswald wrote to a friend named Ella Soboleva, at the address of one Igor Sobolev, a Soviet citizen thought to be an agent of the First Chief Directorate — the senior intelligence branch of the KGB. [278]

---

277. *Ibid.*

Marina's uncle Ilya Prusakov lived in Minsk. He was an engineer and a lieutenant colonel in the Ministry of the Interior. The MVD was a highly sensitive bureau; Prusakov was a party member of high standing. It was unimaginable that someone could get an exit visa in the early 1960s, in only four months' time, with a relative in such a high position. If her uncle had merely been a private in the infantry four years earlier, that would have been sufficient grounds for OVIR to refuse Marina's departure entirely. That Marina was permitted to depart the Soviet Union while her uncle was in the MVD is suspicious in the extreme.

> On Christmas Day, one week to the day after Marina's interview with Colonel Aksyonov of the KGB, Marina was summoned to OVIR. She stopped by on her way home from work and was informed that both she and her husband had been granted exit visas. [279]

When I was in Moscow, each Saturday the faculty from my school would go to the embassy, shop at the PX, buy American cigarettes, have a hamburger at the cafeteria, and share the latest news. One story involved an American book salesman. He left Russia for a book fair in Helsinki, Finland, and wanted to have his picture taken at the border. It was snowing. As he turned around to smile for the camera, he was arrested by Soviet border guards. The snow had obscured the demarcation line between the two countries. They took him directly to a Soviet prison. The embassy tried to locate him, on behalf of his relatives. This "imperialist spy" spoke no Russian at all, and was imprisoned in the Soviet Union for 18 months. Prison life was so unbearable that when he finally got permission to go to the bathroom alone, on a prison train, he slit his throat when the guards were not looking. One Saturday when we were gossiping over our weekly hamburgers, his body was delivered to the embassy grounds for shipment back to the States.

That was the climate back then: a climate of paranoia, fear, suspicion, irrationality, and intrigue. The ability of a young pharmacist — not from the relatively cosmopolitan, international capital of Moscow but provincial Minsk — to secure permission to marry an American defector and simply leave with her husband is mind-boggling. The fact that she lived with her uncle, a colonel in the MVD, and neither his career nor her exit visa was compromised, is baffling.

Norman Mailer makes the point that both Uncle Ilya and his wife Valya told Marina that this would make things difficult for them. A KGB report also shows that Ilya promised the KGB that he would continue working to convince Oswald and his

---

278. Summers, *ibid.*, p. 164.
279. Johnson, *ibid.*, p. 135.

Chapter 4. Conspiracy

wife to change their opinion about going to America. These tidbits make the story more human, but the hard facts remain categorically and exceedingly abnormal. [280]

The poet Yevtushenko got permission to leave the USSR for poetry readings in the West only on the condition that he leave his wife and children behind. It was common practice for the Soviet Union to treat one's spouse and children as hostages in order to guarantee that famous ballerinas, poets, or sports personalities would not defect. For Marina to simply come home one day with a visa is entirely outside the range of the normal.

If the Soviets saw no way to exploit Oswald in an intelligence function and thought he was mentally unstable — and this has been their historic position — then the most likely response would have been to place him in a psychiatric hospital. Under Yeltsin, Americans were discovered who had been tucked away in Soviet mental institutions for the majority of their lives, some since the 1950s. The next most likely reaction would have been to expel or imprison him, but certainly not to let him emigrate with his educated wife, the niece of a colonel in the Ministry of the Interior.[281]

There are other incongruities to mention, but whether they, in toto, add up to a conspiracy theory is another matter.

> After the assassination, Marina was offered lucrative book contracts and apparently signed some. She rapidly became wealthy, remarried, and lived on a 15-acre estate near Dallas — but never wrote her account. In 1963, she barely had money to feed her children, but as early as she 1964 was reported to be worth over $250,000.

Warren Commission counsel Norman Redlich wrote a memo that stated, "the amounts that she has actually received are considerably more than the figures which have been made public." There are several documents about Marina's wealth and relationship with her attorneys that are still classified. [282]

Marina Oswald may have received up to $70,000 in donations from Americans concerned with her fate and future. Perhaps pity and compassion was the source of her wealth. Nonetheless, the overall, composite, historical picture of Marina Oswald

---

280. Just before departure, the KGB met with Col. Prusakov once more. He informed them that he had instructed Marina to conduct herself in the U.S. in a worthy manner and not to partake in any anti-Soviet propaganda. (Mailer, *ibid.*, pp. 234-239 and 214.)
281. Marina applied for her passport on August 21 and received it in hand by Dec. 1. Even U.S. Ambassador Thompson testified to the Warren Commission that it was highly unusual to get it so quickly. Newman, *Oswald and the CIA, ibid.*
282. Weberman, *ibid.*, p. 179

does not come through. There are very many unanswered questions about how she left the USSR, how she obtained her wealth, and most important, why she testified before investigative committees with such unreliability.

Table 4.6 Deceptions and/or Inaccuracies of Marina Oswald

1. Marina told an acquaintance that her husband had defected to the Soviet Union after working at an American exhibition in Moscow. This was untrue.

2. Marina was asked who introduced Oswald to her. (Yuri Mereginsky introduced them.) First, Marina said she did not remember anyone called Mereginsky. The second time, she remembered his name. At a public hearing a few weeks later, Marina's memory had gone wholly blank.

3. Marina Oswald could not remember the time that Oswald had asked for her hand.

4. Originally, Marina said, "Lee - good man. Lee not shot anyone." Later she identified the Mannlicher-Carcano rifle as her husband's and said her husband had wanted to kill General Walker and Richard Nixon. She said nothing about the Walker shooting until confronted with a note found among Oswald's effects.

5. Marina said she stopped Oswald from shooting Nixon by locking him in a bathroom. However, there were no published itineraries showing Nixon coming to Dallas, and Warren Commission investigators found that the bathroom locked from the inside, not the outside.

6. Marina's birth certificate listed her place of birth as "Severodvinsk." Unfortunately, the city had not been named Severodvinsk until 1957; Marina was born in 1941.

7. Marina said she arrived in New York City by plane. She arrived aboard a ship, the S.S. Maasdam, from Holland.

8. Marina had the name Lev Prizentsev, in Leningrad, in her address book. She said he was an older gentleman she had met at a rest home. The CIA found no references to Prizentsev in their computer, but his address at Kondratyevsky Prospect, 63 was the same as a Robert E. Webster, a former Navy man who defected shortly before Oswald and returned at the same time as Oswald, in May 1962.

9. On November 29, 1963 and again on January 17 and 22, 1964, Marina denied any knowledge of Lee's trip to Mexico, although soon afterwards she told what she knew about that, too. She explained her reluctance on this score by saying that she loathed the FBI for pestering her, and, in her bad moods, she could not refrain from showing it.

10. She lied on her visa application, saying she had never been a member of the Communist party, but had in fact been in the Komsomol.

Sources for this table are Johnson, *Ibid.*, pp4. 47, Groden, *Ibid.*, p. 164, Summers, *Ibid.*, pp. 149; 159-160, Posner, p. 115. J. Hosty, *Ibid*, pp. 103-113.

Marina Oswald is an important witness in the State's case against Lee Harvey Oswald. If the State were unable to connect Oswald with the rifle, its case against him would dissolve. The bullets found in General Walker's home could not be matched with the Mannlicher-Carcano. *Only Marina's testimony makes the connection stick.*

The validity of the photographs tying Oswald to the rifle similarly requires that her testimony be believable, since she said she was the one who took them. Had Oswald gone to trial, his defense attorney could easily have impeached this all-important State's witness; she left a legacy of inconsistent testimony trailing behind her.

To believe a woman was introduced to her future husband by a man who's name she forgot, that he proposed to her on a date she cannot remember, that she emigrated from her country but could not recall whether it was by plane or by ship, that she first said he did not go to Mexico (three times) and then said he did because of her "moods" . . . such matters are simply too much for any hypothetical jury to believe. And if her testimony is not judged credible, then the photos of Oswald with the rifle, the attack on General Walker, and the Mannlicher-Cancano rifle all become questionable.

The Yuri Nosenko Affair

Another suspicious episode emanating out of Soviet Russia occurred in 1964, but the Warren Commission made no reference to it. It is a very unusual story.

It used to be unthinkable, unimaginable, that a person could be held without trial, without bail, in fact held hostage in a building for over three years, often deprived of food and water or any contact with the outside world, including reading materials, and that this could all happen inside the United States of America. Yet it happened in the 1960s. The incident is well documented, and the reasons for it are given below:

> Two months after Oswald was killed, a high-ranking KGB officer defected to the United States from Geneva. His name was Yuri Nosenko; he was 36, in the prime of his career in Soviet Intelligence, and held rank in the KGB's Second Chief Directorate, counterintelligence. Nosenko left his wife and children behind and claimed that he had been compromised, that a cable came from KGB headquarters ordering him home, and rather than risking prison he wanted to defect to the U.S. The CIA had no choice but to honor his request.
>
> He then said that he was the person who had handled Oswald in the USSR. According to Nosenko, the KGB knew nothing about Oswald until he was already in Moscow. They did not even know of his Marine Corps background. He said the KGB found him not very intelligent and mentally unstable. When Oswald threatened suicide in order to stay, the KGB "washed its hands" of him. *"The interest of KGB headquarters in Oswald was practically nil."*[283] As for Marina, Nosenko said that she was not very smart either and the Soviets were "glad to get rid of them both." [284]

This was Nosenko's story. The fifteen documents the Soviets forwarded to the Warren Commission obviously exonerated them from any involvement. Nosenko's defection produced the same effect, but senior CIA officers did not believe the story.

U.S. agencies had a capability to intercept all cables between Moscow and Geneva. They checked. *No cable had been sent ordering Nosenko home.* Finally, Nosenko admitted that he had made it up to make the United States accept him.

A second KGB defector, Major Anatoli Golitsyn, told the CIA Nosenko had been in the KGB but was not the lieutenant colonel he made himself out to be. Nosenko gradually admitted this, too, and said he exaggerated his rank to enhance his chances of getting asylum. However, Nosenko had brought documents with him showing him to be a lieutenant colonel. Asked how he came by such false papers, he said it was just a "bureaucratic blunder."

Nosenko said he handled the case of an American military attaché in the early fifties. When asked how the attaché's tour of duty ended, he was mistaken. The attaché was expelled. If Nosenko was the KGB officer-in-charge, he certainly would have known that. He didn't.

Nosenko failed two CIA lie-detector tests.

He provided the U.S. information about two Soviet spies, a British clerk and an American Army soldier. However, CIA analysts felt both of these sources had already been compromised and he was not passing on information of genuine value.

---

283. Summers, *ibid.*, p. 166.
284. *Ibid.*, p. 166.

The CIA team groped its way across this minefield of Soviet falsehood and bluff and looked in vain for a definite motive. They [The CIA] did not know why the KGB would be prepared to jettison an important career officer like Yuri Nosenko. . . None of this dealt with the immediate problem in the wake of the Kennedy assassination. Why was Nosenko spinning his story about the KGB handling of Lee Harvey Oswald? The problem became submerged in feuding within the American intelligence community. It has never been resolved.[285]

J. Edgar Hoover liked what Nosenko had to say, but one faction within the CIA was extremely suspicious and theorized that Nosenko had come to quash suspicions that a Soviet mole existed within the intelligence community. For up to four years, Nosenko was treated more like a prisoner of war than a prize defector. He was kept in a single room, watched 24 hours a day, and often forbidden to lie down during daytime. The HSCA heard of these interrogation techniques, as did a few politicians, and shock waves rippled through Washington. Strange as it might seem, Nosenko never cracked and stuck to his story. [286]

Why would the Soviets send Nosenko on a mission of disinformation? Virtually all intelligence analysts say it is implausible, indeed impossible, that the KGB would not have interrogated Oswald extensively.

Either way, Nosenko's insistence that Oswald was not questioned at all is transparent nonsense. While we can still only speculate at Moscow's reasons for priming Nosenko with a phony Oswald story, embarrassment in the wake of the Kennedy assassination is an inadequate explanation. [287]

Soviet Motives

The Cuban missile crisis concluded a year *prior* to Kennedy's assassination, and it was not until a year *after* that Khrushchev was ousted from power. The Cuban missile crisis looked like a victory for Kennedy. His ratings at the polls shot up. He had proved his maturity. Even Castro felt Khrushchev backed down, and accused the Russian of cowardice. The global perception of the Russian-American confrontation was that the U.S. had won and the Soviets lost.

Kennedy, in fact, had made a deal with the Soviets, agreeing to remove U.S. Jupiter missiles from Turkey in return for Soviet compliance in removing missiles in Cuba.

---

285. Summers, *ibid.*, pp. 168-169.
286. Without ever resolving the contradictions, the CIA later hired him as a consultant. Nosenko accepted!
287. *Ibid.*, p. 176

This fact was not made public. The secret protocol also promised that the United States would stop its efforts to overthrow Castro. However, Kennedy had great difficulty getting control over covert operations, and attacks on Cuba continued well after the missile crisis agreements were in place. Did Khrushchev think he was being betrayed by Kennedy, on top of his humiliation at the hands of the Kennedy administration during the missile crisis? This is the strongest point in the Soviet conspiracy model: motive. Humiliation, embarrassment, and betrayal might have ignited a fire of revenge in Khrushchev.

In almost all other respects, a Soviet conspiracy theory makes no sense. Oswald as a Soviet assassin is a joke. Oswald as a mole called upon to shoot the President on orders from Moscow, à la the "Manchurian Candidate," is absurd.[288]

When the KGB wanted to "hit" a diplomat in England, a man with an umbrella walked behind him, nonchalantly touched his leg, excused himself, and walked on. The diplomat died from shellfish toxin that had placed on the tip of the umbrella. KGB hits were high-tech, very discreet, and often carried out under layers of cover.

To conscript a mentally unstable ex-American defector with a history of leftist leanings and a wife from Russia to shoot the President of the United States would be, at the very least, indiscreet! To have him carry out the assassination using a World War II vintage rifle moves it from indiscreet to stupid, and to select a man who cannot drive a get-away car brings it into the territory of demented.

When Brezhnev wanted to assassinate the Pope — allegedly — he set about it in a manner that could not be traced back to the USSR. The KGB operated through Bulgarian intelligence services and then hired a Turkish extremist as the shooter. Is it likely that the Soviets would have called upon their "mole" in Dallas to carry out such a sensitive assignment? If caught, he would have pointed directly to them, and besides, this "assassin" had never succeeded in shooting anyone before in his life. If he did shoot at General Walker as a rehearsal, he failed.

Indeed, one co-worker in Minsk (Pavel) recalls that Oswald could not put film in a camera without help; he pulled out the wiring in a new radio because he put the batteries in improperly, and couldn't tune in the Voice of America without Pavel

---

288. Those who feel Oswald may have been a Soviet hit man sometimes cite Oswald's contact with Valerie Kostikov in Mexico City. Kostikov was alleged to have been from the KGB assassinations unit. Norman Mailer's *Oswald's Tale* confirms Kostikov was a KGB officer assigned to "wet jobs," i.e. State-approved assassinations. John Newman garnered a precious interview with historically recalcitrant James Hosty, who corroborated this. Hosty said that Kostikov was the "Soviet officer in charge for Western Hemisphere terrorist activities including and especially assassinations. In military ranking he would have been a one-star general. . . . the most dangerous KGB terrorist assigned to this hemisphere," (p. 429). So, when Oswald visited Mexico City, he was not simply visiting the consular at the desk.

showing him how to use a penknife to do it. Oswald was no James Bond, that's for sure. [289]

That Oswald could have been a Soviet mole or a KGB hit man is a farfetched notion that cannot be taken seriously. Lee Harvey Oswald is the best proof that the Soviets were not involved in the assassination of John Fitzgerald Kennedy!

Inconsistencies in Soviet Behavior

But it is also true that Soviet behavior does not compute, and for that reason suspicions are justified. Why did they let him leave? Why was he allowed to take his wife with him? Why did they forge his diary? Why send Nosenko to the U.S. to buttress the case that the Soviets had no involvement, when Nosenko did such a poor job of convincing anyone?

One possible explanation is that the Russians felt vulnerable after the assassination, embarrassed, and wanted to provide evidence for their non-involvement. They forged (or heavily edited) Oswald's diary and *quickly* sent Nosenko over to defuse any anti-Soviet attributions of guilt. Nosenko did not have enough time to prepare (less than two months), and the forged diary was also done in haste. The Soviets wanted all this information in the hands of the Warren Commission, *and it was their haste* that explains why the diary and Nosenko were so unpolished. Not only is this a reasonable explanation, but also it allows us to come to an innocent conclusion. The Soviets had nothing to do with the assassination, but out of embarrassment swiftly created a few documents and witnesses to save face.

If we grant this possibility, it answers a great number of questions; but there are still problems. Why was Oswald treated like a VIP in the USSR and then allowed to return to the US, on a whim, with his wife? Why not put him in a psychiatric hospital, or in prison, or simply send him home alone?

This is a serious question still looking for an answer. The incident of the Helsinki book salesman who slit his throat happened *five years after* Oswald's adventures in Minsk. The cold war was still very, very, cold in those days.

Oswald's VIP treatment in the USSR is easier to explain. After all, he was a defector who may also have provided the USSR with vital information, and he was sympathetic to the communist philosophy. Thus the plush accommodations in Minsk, the 5,000-ruble bonus, even permission to marry. The difficulty is how we explain Oswald's ability to leave.

If he gave the Soviets precious U-2 secrets, enhancing their ability to shoot down Gary Powers, were they so grateful they granted Lee his most whimsical fancy, even if

---

289. See *Oswald's Tale, ibid.* p. 144 for more information on Oswald's life in Minsk.

that was to leave? Ridiculous! If Oswald was an intelligence asset, it is doubtful the Soviets would ever have let him return — *if only to protect the secrets they obtained.* To return Oswald would give the Americans an opportunity to find out what Oswald had told them.

This question has never been satisfactorily answered and, to anyone who has experienced Soviet bureaucracy for both marriage and exit, the explanations which have been given are not typical of cold war Soviet behavior and make little sense.

One possibility exists that might make this sense of the bizarre anomaly, and that is if Oswald were "exchanged" for someone. There is absolutely no proof for this, of course, but if that were the case, it could explain some of the incongruities.

If there was a secret, high-level exchange, Oswald in the USSR for "someone" held in the U.S., then we can understand why he was allowed to take his wife to Dallas. The idea of an exchange also explains why he received State Department help, even though he was a defector who had tried to renounce his citizenship and may have surrendered American secrets.

This hypothesis handles a few inconsistencies, but it also generates a problems of its own. If the U.S. exchanged someone for Oswald in order to find out what he had divulged to the Soviets, why did Oswald not end up in prison once he arrived?

There is another possibility: that Oswald was an "intelligence asset" for the United States, had been on an intelligence mission as some conspiracy researchers think, and perhaps was exchanged, their spy for ours. This would also explain how he was able to take his wife out with him (Soviet acquiescence to the spy swap), but then, once again, new problems are created. If Oswald was a "prized intelligence asset," then why was he treated so shabbily in the U.S. after he got back, having to take menial jobs in Dallas and New Orleans?

Going undercover in the USSR, collecting data in Minsk, and getting out alive in a swap would be risky business worthy of rather substantial rewards. To be working the Reily Coffee Company for $1.25 an hour while receiving an undesirable discharge from the Marines would be a curious reward for valiant service to your country. Oswald applied for unemployment compensation twice after he arrived back in the States.

The "exchange for a traitor" scenario has problems; the "exchange for an 'intelligence asset'" has problems, too; but no exchange at all has even more problems. The mysteries go round and round.

At the core of the problem are two fundamental paradoxes. (1) At the same time that Rudolf Nureyev and others were defecting from the Soviet Union, leaving loved ones behind with the prospect of never ever seeing them again as the price for their freedom, Lee Harvey Oswald *effortlessly* left Russia with the niece of a MVD Colonel.

(2) Our U.S. Marine, with a security clearance, who had formally renounced his citizenship, defected, and possibly given U-2 secrets to the Soviets, *effortlessly* came back to the U.S. . . . without being arrested, interrogated, or debriefed, and with a $480 advance from the State Department.

We may not be able to accept a Soviet conspiracy theory as rational or credible;[290] and so we leave this model behind us in our journey — but for the sake of intellectual honesty, we have to admit that we cannot explain these two paradoxes.

5. THE CUBAN COMMUNIST CONSPIRACY

The Soviet conspiracy theory is admittedly weak, but a communist conspiracy originating in Cuba is quite another matter. Castro lived through eight CIA assassination attempts; maybe he thought that was enough!

> The source, a Washington lawyer, reported that one of his clients had sensational information. It was that Fidel Castro, learning of the American plots against his own life, had retaliated by having President Kennedy murdered. In March 1967, the allegation came to the attention of President Johnson, and he ordered an FBI inquiry. Agents interviewed the lawyer, who said his client had learned from "feedback furnished by sources close to Castro" that the Cuban leader had "employed teams of individuals who were dispatched to the United States for the purpose of assassinating President Kennedy." The investigation failed to come up with hard facts or names, but President Johnson was clearly impressed. He later confided to one newsman, "I will tell you something that will rock you. Kennedy was trying to get Castro, but Castro got him first." [The lawyer's client who sparked off the new Castro rumor, unidentified publicly until 1976, was none other than John Roselli, the Mafia gangster who had helped the CIA in its plots to kill Castro.][291]

A French journalist, Jean Daniel, was with Castro when he heard the news of Kennedy's assassination. Castro was very upset. He mumbled, "This is bad news," three times in Spanish. He said that changed everything, the Cold War, relations with Russia . . . "[it] all will have to be re-thought." Daniel's reaction was that Castro was genuinely astonished and set back by the news.

Let us be skeptical for a moment and rephrase the communist conspiracy model in Cuban terms to see how the data organizes itself.

---

290. Another reason supporting Soviet lack of involvement in the assassination is that, if they were involved, it would have been logical for them to go on military alert after the assassination, and they never did (Hosty, *ibid.*, p. 221).

291. *Ibid.*, pp. 409-410.

Postscript Another Soviet/Cuban Twist: James Hosty's Account

Conspiracists long considered FBI agent James Hosty, the man who interviewed Oswald before the assassination, as a key figure in the cover-up. Hosty finally wrote an accounting some 33 years later, *Assignment Oswald*, New York, Arcade, 1996. The following is a brief summary:

Hosty corroborates what most of the conspiracy community always suspected, namely that a systematic cover up and destruction of documents within the FBI about Oswald, Ruby, etc., all are not fabrications. His text is full of such admissions.

Hosty raises important points about the ease with which Marina Oswald left the country. Marina lived with her uncle, Ilya Prusakov. "Prusakov's apartment was in a complex set aside exclusively for high ranking members of the KGB and MVD; thus Marina was now exposed almost exclusively to these people.... Then another series of astounding events occurred. Marina supposedly learned that Lee desired to return to America shortly after their wedding. After a brief resistance, she agreed to go with him. In amazingly short order, the Soviet immigration agency, known as OVIR, which was part of the MVD and known to be under the control of the KGB, approved Marina's exit visa. It was all too easy for Marina to leave the Soviet Union, especially as the niece of an MVD lieutenant colonel" (pp. 113-115).

In a similar case, an American, James Mintkenbaugh, lived in the Soviet Union in the late 1950s. When he said he wanted to return to the United States, the KGB approached him to ask if he would marry a young Soviet woman and take her back with him to America. Hosty makes a similar suggestion about Marina Oswald with the suggestion she may have been originally targeted to be a "sleeper" agent.

On Nov. 19 Oswald probably read the *Dallas Times Herald* article that Kennedy was virtually inviting a Cuban coup. As a staunch supporter of Castro, that was Oswald's last straw. He picked up his rifle and proceeded with the assassination of JFK. (Hosty believes Oswald was the lone assassin.)

Hosty adds that on Oswald's September visit to Mexico City, he talked to the head of the KGB assassinations unit, Mr. Kostikov with "information so hot" that the Russians would allow the Oswalds to settle in a city of their choice in the USSR. He also said to the Cuban embassy that "he was going to kill that son of a bitch John Kennedy" (p. 215)..."[W]ithin hours of the president's death, a CIA telephone wiretap picked up Cuban intelligence official, Luisa Calderon, telling someone that she had known beforehand that Kennedy was going to be killed." Luisa Calderon, a Cuban intelligence official returned to Cuba and is apparently the only person Castro never allowed to be interviewed by the HSCA.

Hosty's theory is that Oswald wanted to impress the Soviets and Cubans by killing JFK and return to the USSR. Hosty does not believe the Soviets or Cubans would have co-conspired with such a malcontent to carry off the assassination. Hosty's theory is interesting except that some of his most salient quotes, especially those attributed to Calderon, seem based on unreferenced documents, apparently CIA materials Hosty has been exposed to but which are unavailable to anyone. One flaw in his theory is that Oswald already hated JFK on Sept 23, when he left for Mexico, but the Dallas article about Kennedy inviting a Cuban coup did not appear until November 19. Indeed, there is a dearth of evidence that Oswald hated JFK, and Hosty's suggestions do not add much to this compilation. Other facts also do not compute, in this theory. For example, when Oswald left New Orleans for Dallas in September, he walked out on his rent. It is not plausible that an assassin in search of an effective cover would call attention to himself in this way.

Hosty's text is laudable for its admissions about the cover up, but it seems to have been conditioned by all-too familiar and historic anti-communist rhetoric, which skews many of its interpretations in that direction.

Chapter 4. Conspiracy

Castro conveniently had a Western journalist present at the time that the news broke so the journalist could *credibly* inform the world of Castro's surprised reaction. Castro also made statements to a hushed public hearing *which he recorded*, vehemently condemning the murder of Kennedy. When the HSCA requested an audience with Castro, he fully cooperated in 1978 *and played this recording*: a very interesting public relations move designed to further insure his innocence of any complicity.

John Roselli, the gangster, who disseminated the rumor about Castro killing the President, was himself murdered for talking too much shortly after it became known that he was the source of the rumor. Was he hit by one of Castro's agents?

Add to this scenario that Castro had a relationship with Mafiosi Santos Trafficante, who had smuggled guns to him during his fight against Batista. Even though Castro had Trafficante imprisoned, his prison accommodations were plush, and he was allowed to leave Cuba with relative ease. Is it possible that Castro sought Trafficante's help in hitting Kennedy, and that both Castro and the Mob wanted Kennedy hit for their own, unique reasons?

Castro was the object of assassination and poisoning attempts and may have believed Kennedy could not be trusted to honor his commitments to Khrushchev. In his anger, he found an unexpected ally in the Mafia, which wanted nothing more than to see Kennedy and his brother Bobby put out of commission.

An obscure conspiracy text written in Russian and published in the U.S. makes this very point (*Kennedy, Oswald, Castro, Khrushchev*, by Igor Efimov). In Efimov's view, Castro began a sinister relationship with the Mafia through Trafficante.

In 1982, four Cuban officials were indicted on drug smuggling charges; one of them was a Cuban admiral. Castro was not above being involved in the U.S. drug trade, and his ties to the drug cartels (as well as suspected ties to the deposed drug-dealing Panamanian leader, Manuel Noriega) also suggest that Cuba maintained significant Mafia connections. It is Efimov's conjecture that Castro, through agents Pino Machado and Moleon Cassera, plotted the assassination of Kennedy and may have used the Trafficante connection to accomplish it.

One piece of evidence from the Mafia that supports this hypothesis is that the Mafia never was very serious in its so-called association with the CIA in trying to hit Castro. The Mob merely went through the motions. Mobster John Roselli said the whole CIA-Mafia relationship was a sham:

> All this activity was a charade. . . all those fucking plans concocted by the CIA never proceeded farther than Santos (Trafficante). He simply agreed to go to jail for them allowing them to think that fellows risked their lives infiltrating Cuba, that their boats are sewn through by bullets and all such fucking shit. [292]

---

292. Summers, *ibid.*, pp. 168-169.

Perhaps it is not the CIA-Mafia connection that is of interest, but the far less publicized Castro-Mafia link that needs to be examined.

Efimov relates another alarming tale, namely that on the day of the assassination, Castro's man in Dealey Plaza was Miguel Cassas Saez, a friend of Castro's brother Raul. Saez departed Dallas for Mexico City. An Air Cubana plane out of Mexico City was delayed in departure for Havana for five hours until Saez allegedly arrived and boarded. He sat in the pilot's cabin for the entire flight to Havana on the day of the assassination.[293]

To amplify Efimov's theory, we might suppose that John Roselli was killed not by Castro's agents, but by the Mafia. Suppose that Roselli, through his attorney, was sincere in his attempt to "leak" information that Oswald worked for Castro. Most conspiracy texts consider this to be disinformation, an attempt to point the finger at Castro instead of the CIA. That is the conventional conspiracist interpretation of Roselli's behavior. *But what if Roselli was telling the truth?* Maybe what he leaked through his attorney was true, and that Castro was indeed behind the hit. If Trafficante hit Kennedy not only for his own reasons, *but for Castro as well,* then killing Roselli to keep him quiet about the actual Cuban-Mafia plot could be seen as a logical Mafia maneuver. The last time anyone ever saw Roselli alive was on Trafficante's boat.

Castro may have had a double-agent, Rolando Cubella, informing him that the CIA was trying to kill him. Cubella was originally a CIA hit man and met with his CIA contact, Desmond Fitzgerald, in Paris on November 22, 1963, the very day Kennedy was assassinated.[294] Cubella was tapped by the CIA to assassinate Castro and accepted the assignment. Before meeting with Fitzgerald, however, Cubella made great efforts to make sure that Robert Kennedy knew of the arrangement to kill Castro. He was assured that Desmond Fitzgerald was very close to Bobby. Why did Cubella need such reassurance? Did he want to make absolutely certain that the Kennedys were behind the attempts on Castro's life?

If Cubella needed to know that Bobby had approved of the hit against Castro — and Cubella was sending this information back to Castro — it is plausible that Castro

---

293. This getaway plane's behavior is partially corroborated in Hosty's *Assignment Oswald,* ibid.

294. See Chapter 4 Appendix on page 191.

was seeking "confirmation" that indeed Kennedy, not just the CIA, was behind the attempts on his life.

Certainly Castro knew that a secret peace overture initiated by Kennedy was in the offing, through William Attwood (but it is also possible that Ramon Cubella informed him that the Kennedy brothers were simultaneously planning his assassination). If Castro was presented with such paradoxical information, he might have concluded that his only option was to proceed with his own retaliation plans and assassinate JFK.

Strong Points

- One of the strongest elements of this theory is motive. Even after the Bay of Pigs, the nuclear showdown in the Cuban Missile Crisis, the intervention of the Russian Big Bear, JFK's secret agreement to remove missiles from Turkey and his promises not to invade Cuba (or try to kill Castro) . . . Cubella's "contract" was *proof* to Castro that nothing would stop the Kennedy brothers from trying to kill him. The only logical step was to hit back. On November 22, Kennedy, not Castro, would get what was coming to him. [295]

- A second strong element here is John Roselli's death, so soon after he leaked information about Castro's involvement. If one can suppose a Castro-Mafia "shared desire" to eliminate Kennedy, one can also see that the Mafia had the means to carry this off more easily and could operate more effectively on American soil than Castro. (Remember also that the Mafia had access to the Lincoln bedroom right up through April of 1962, when Judith Exner Campbell was consorting with the President.)

- The Mafia does not "whack" its soldiers for spreading disinformation, but it does put a contract out on someone who is singing like a bird. Roselli said that Castro killed Kennedy, and then Roselli was killed. It is surprising how conspiracy researchers have overlooked the obvious possibility that Roselli died *because he was telling the truth!*

Weak Points

- If we conjectured that Castro with the U.S. Mafia conspired to hit Kennedy, Oswald makes no sense here. He is an unlikely member of any government's coterie of hit men. Oswald may have been a sharpshooter, but the KGB or the Cubans would have used someone with more experience, and would have equipped him with far better shooting gear.

---

295. *The Johnson White House Tapes, 1963-64*, by Michael Beschloss, reveals that Johnson thought Castro was to blame for JFK's death, but that any retaliatory strike would invite a nuclear confrontation with the Soviets. Johnson did not see a mafia element in the Castro connection, however. (See "LBM blamed Castro for JFK's death," SJMN, October 6, 1997, p. 8A.)

Oswald points to the left, to "fair play for Cuba," to a pro-Cuban position. This is a devastating argument against the Castro-hit theory. There is no cover, no subterfuge; the man charged with the crime looks too much like a Castro sympathizer who was on television passing out leaflets in support of Castro back in New Orleans.

So either Castro was not involved or, if he was, then Oswald was in no way supposed to be a patsy for the crime. Why is Oswald there? How did he get there? Either we reject the Cuban origination of this plot or our next best assumption would be that Oswald, one of the triggers, was just not supposed to be caught. Perhaps he was supposed to be on the plane that left Dallas, headed to Mexico City, and then went on to Cuba, the same one that carried his alleged co-hit man, Miguel Saez, to Havana. If Oswald was an actual assassin, then this model still makes some sense. (John Martino, a murdered Mafioso, said Oswald went to the Texas theater to "meet someone." The Texas theater was a reconnoiter point and part of the getaway plan which Officer Tippit foiled. [296])

- If the Cubans were behind the assassination, then Oswald's employment at the Texas School Book Depository is another major weak point. How would Castro have known in advance that Kennedy would be in Dallas on November 22? Oswald took his position at the Depository on October 16. The only way out of this dilemma is that we suppose that Castro was in league with the Mafia; without a Mafia source, it is unlikely that Castro would have such early information on the travel itinerary to Dallas.

- Another downside to this theory is the legacy of murder and strange accidental deaths. Why would Cuba or the KGB murder ten Mob figures associated with the Kennedy assassination investigation in the mid-1970s? How would Castro get the CIA and FBI to cooperate in stalling investigative committees, killing witnesses, destroying documents or classifying information they wanted kept secret? Most of the evidence developed in Chapter 3, pointing to a conspiracy, would be hard to explain if one assumed the origin of the conspiracy was in Havana.

- In 1963, Castro and the Mob did not have much in common. An association between the two might be logical in the 1980s, when cocaine cartels were operating from Columbia, Panama, and throughout the Caribbean — and when a Cuban admiral was arrested for drug dealing — but back in 1963, Castro and the Mafia were not on the friendliest of terms. Cubans and Mafiosi make inimical bedfellows, despite their shared desire to see the Kennedys eliminated.

- A recently released declassified document from the National Security Agency reports that the U.S. had the capacity to intercept up to 1,000 messages a day from Havana. Cuban army and navy units had been placed on alert on the evening of

---

296. Martino was a friend of Trafficante and had some CIA contacts. According to Martino, Oswald was on his way to meet his fellow-trigger at the Texas Theater, but officer Tippit got in the way. When Oswald was arrested, the other "trigger" was in the theater and escaped. Martino, however, said the man Oswald was to meet was a CIA anti-Castro Cuban, not an agent of Castro. Summers, "The Ghosts of November" *Vanity Fair, ibid.*

November 23, 1963. (If Castro killed JFK, they would likely have been placed on alert *before*, not *after* the assassination.) Secondly, Castro appeared "frightened, if not terrified," after the assassination and felt it could trigger a U.S. invasion of the island. While that is only circumstantial evidence, it is inconsistent with the view that Castro was the mastermind of the plot. [297]

In sum, there are many intriguing aspects to a Cuban plot and particularly a Cuban-Mafia plot, but it is still very hypothetical and sketchy to warrant much credibility.

White Hand And Black Hand: The CIA and the Mob

The theories presented in this chapter generate a panoply of potential conspirators, co-conspirators, disinformation and cover-up figures, plus a horde of assassins. We have treated these theories as relatively separate and discrete, but there is room to develop synergies. We have tried the Cuban-Mafia connection; what about the Mafia and the CIA?

Underworld figures had significant contacts with the CIA. Giancana, Roselli, and Trafficante had all been enlisted by the CIA to assassinate Castro. According to the Giancanas, the Mob was referred to as The Black Hand while the CIA called itself The White Hand:

> Mooney [Sam Giancana] stood up from his chair, cigar in hand, and marched across the room. When he reached Chuck [Giancana], he lowered his voiced and hissed. "Maybe this will help." He fixed Chuck in a steely, impenetrable gaze. "We took care of Kennedy. . . together." . . .There was a deadly silence in the room as Mooney [Sam Giancana stalked back to the comfort of his chair. Chuck felt as if his mind had just gone blank, become an empty slate of shock . . . He finally knew for certain what he'd secretly feared all along; his brother had been right — the government and the Outfit were really two sides of the same coin. But hearing the truth — and hearing it directly from Mooney — left him speechless . . . Mooney said that the "alleged lone gunman," Lee Harvey Oswald, like Ruby, had ties to both the CIA and the Outfit [Mafia]. Oswald had been connected to the New Orleans Mob from the time he was born; his uncle was a Marcello lieutenant who had exerted a powerful influence over the fatherless boy. Early in life, Oswald had formed a powerful alliance with the U.S. intelligence community, first as an impressionable young man during a stint in the Civil Air Patrol with homosexual CIA operative David Ferrie — a bizarre, hairless eccentric whom Mooney said he and Marcello frequently used to fly drugs and guns out of Central America. And later, when serving in the Marines during the late fifties, when Oswald attended a series of intensive intelligence training sessions run by the Office of Naval Intelligence in a top secret Japanese spy base. The short of it, Mooney said, was that Lee Harvey Oswald was a CIA agent. . . He was not a Castro sympathizer nor Communist at all. . . . "In truth," Mooney said,

---

297. George Larner, "Castro feared invasion," SMJN, Aug. 20, 1997, p. 10A.

"Lee Harvey Oswald was a right-wing supporter of the Kill Castro Bay of Pigs Camp... CIA all the way.

... Mooney said that the entire conspiracy went "right up to the top of the CIA." He claimed that some of its former and present leaders were involved, as well as a 'half a dozen fanatical right-wing Texans, Vice President Lyndon Johnson, and the Bay of Pigs Action Officer under Eisenhower, Richard Nixon."... Mooney said both Richard Nixon and Lyndon Johnson knew about the whole damned thing. [298] [299]

Table 4.7 The CIA-Mafia Link

Organized Crime Figure	CIA Associate	CIA Associates Once Removed[a]
Marcello	David Ferrie	Arcacha Smith, Hunt, Cabell, Helms
Guy Banister	Arcacha Smith, Hunt	Helms, Cabell
John Roselli	William Harvey	Helms
Sam Giancana	William Harvey	Helms
Trafficante	William Harvey	Helms
Trafficante	Frank Sturgis	Hunt, Cabell, Helms
Trafficante	Loran Hall	Sturgis, Hunt, Helms

a. General Cabell, never interviewed by the Warren Commission, was the supervisor of Howard Hunt (Groden, Ibid., p. 315). Table developed from conspiracy literature.

Although much of the Giancana text tends toward the fantastic, perhaps we should not so easily dismiss the idea that the CIA and the Mafia, together, may have played simultaneous and mutually advantageous roles. Table 4.7[300] shows at least some of the potential connecting links between Mob figures and CIA personnel.

Of course, one wonders what the motive might have been for a combined CIA-Mafia plot against Kennedy. The motives for the Mob are well established. The Mob, at least in the person of Sam Giancana, felt double-crossed by the Kennedys. However, CIA motives have never been well established other than resentment over the moves Kennedy made to dismantle the organization after the Bay of Pigs fiasco.

A few right-wing former CIA officials were embittered by Kennedy's action with Khrushchev and his failure to proceed properly during the Bay of Pigs invasion. Allen Dulles, General Cabell, and Richard Bissell were three CIA figures fired by Kennedy over the Bay of Pigs. Kennedy also removed General Walker. General Walker and General Cabell, in turn, were affiliated with right-wing organizations and figures, from the John Birch Society to the Minutemen and right-wing oilman H.L. Hunt. William Harvey, the rogue CIA operative who became cozy with organized crime, was

---

298. Ibid., p. 176.

299. Ibid., pp. 409-410. Also, Cuban television reported that "the same group of mobsters and right-wingers that tried repeatedly to kill Fidel Castro" was behind the assassination of President Kennedy. Three American mobsters and two anti-Castro Cubans were identified as responsible. Source: San Jose Mercury News, November 29, 1993, p. 2A

300. Efimov, Igor. *Kennedy, Oswald, Castro, Khrushchev.* Tenafly, N.J.: Hermitage, 1987, p.

Chapter 4. Conspiracy

demoted and transferred for unauthorized covert operations against Cuba. Perhaps, when we view this list of disgruntled, demoted, or demoralized CIA figures, we can construe a motive, and to that extent there is some merit in thinking both organized crime and embittered elements of the CIA could have joined white and black hands in this historic unfolding of events.

Robert Morrow has a related text on the CIA-Mafia link, *First Hand Knowledge: How I Participated in the CIA-Mafia Murder of President Kennedy*. New York: Shapolsky Publishers, 1992. Morrow, a CIA agent, allegedly broke his silence to write this work. On close inspection, this book is simply far too dramatic, if not fictionalized, to merit serious, scholarly attention. There is a scene, for example, of Morrow picking up $250,000 in cash from a Bimini bank, being followed by two tails, picking up a stray motorcycle with the key conveniently left in the ignition, and fleeing to the airport where a waiting plane takes him off the island. In another scene, Morrow arrives in Puerto Rico at the lavish home of a U.S. Congressman and is greeted by a sultry house guest, Francoise, who later meets him for a rendezvous in Miami — where she is murdered. (No police inquiries are ever reported.) Morrow makes a daring flight with David Ferrie deep into Cuba, measures wave emanations from a hard Soviet missile silo, and then steals off to Florida from a deserted airstrip. Ferrie is wounded and faints, yet Morrow, not only an expert scientist, inventor of the VCR and accomplished counterfeiter but also a pilot, takes the controls from Ferrie and finishes the mission. The James Bond-like elements of this text suggest that much of it was written with a Hollywood screenplay in mind. Oswald is treated as a government plant during his stay in Minsk and is alleged to have been working for the U.S. all the time. (Unfortunately, Morrow does not seem bothered about the difficulty in explaining that Oswald's total income from this high-risk adventure amounted to less than $2400, by Morrow's own accounting.)

On the other hand, he includes a considerable amount of ostensibly factual material. Some of the essential points of his work in linking CIA and Mafia forces to the plot against Kennedy are summarized below. They have not been included in the body of this text because they are simply too suspect. However, many of the points are subject to verification. In case the entire text is not sheer fantasy, the author's allegations and assertions are listed below:

Robert Morrow has a related text on the CIA-Mafia link, *First Hand Knowledge: How I Participated in the CIA-Mafia Murder of President Kennedy*. New York: Shapolsky Publishers, 1992. Morrow, a CIA agent, allegedly broke his silence to write this work. On close inspection, this book is simply far too dramatic, if not fictionalized, to merit serious, scholarly attention. There is a scene, for example, of Morrow picking up $250,000 in cash from a Bimini bank, being followed by two tails, picking up a stray motorcycle with the key conveniently left in the ignition, and fleeing to the airport where a waiting plane takes him off the island. In another scene, Morrow arrives in Puerto Rico at the lavish home of a U.S. Congressman and is greeted by a sultry house guest, Francoise, who later meets him for a rendezvous in Miami — where she is murdered. (No police inquiries are ever reported.) Morrow makes a daring flight with David Ferrie deep into Cuba, measures wave emanations from a hard Soviet missile silo, and then steals off to Florida from a deserted airstrip. Ferrie is wounded and faints, yet Morrow, not only an expert scientist, inventor of the VCR and accomplished counterfeiter but also a pilot, takes the controls from Ferrie and finishes the mission. The James Bond-like elements of this text suggest that much of it was written with a Hollywood screenplay in mind. Oswald is treated as a government plant during his stay in Minsk and is alleged to have been working for the U.S. all the time. (Unfortunately, Morrow does not seem bothered about the difficulty in explaining that Oswald's total income from this high-risk adventure amounted to less than $2400, by Morrow's own accounting.)

On the other hand, he includes a considerable amount of ostensibly factual material. Some of the essential points of his work in linking CIA and Mafia forces to the plot against Kennedy are summarized below. They have not been included in the body of this text because they are simply too suspect. However, many of the points are subject to verification. In case the entire text is not sheer fantasy, the author's allegations and assertions are listed below:

● General Cabell ordered Morrow to continue counterfeiting Cuban currency to destabilize the Cuban economy. If true, Cabell's behavior is treasonous since Kennedy issued orders specifically discontinuing all counterfeiting operations against Cuba. Barry Goldwater is alleged to have known about the counterfeiting operation.

● Richard Helms, not yet Director of the CIA, authorized an assassination attempt on Castro via Rolando Cubelo. He operated through Desmond Fitzgerald. The meeting with Cubelo occurred in Paris on Nov 22, 1963. Helms informed neither the Attorney General, the head of the CIA, nor the President of his actions. Cubelo's code name was AM/LASH. (This is partially confirmed in Efimov's Russian text cited earlier.)

● Some new names appear in this text which are not found in other works. Thomas Luchese, a Mafia don, played a role in the Mafia-CIA plot against Kennedy.

● Tracy Barnes was Robert Morrow's CIA case officer. He ordered Morrow to purchase four 7.35 surplus Mannlicher-Carcano rifles intended for use in the JFK hit. Barnes's name rarely appears in conspiracy literature.

● Another major player was Marshall Diggs, former Comptroller of the U.S. Treasury, who supplied Robert Morrow with much of the information contained in this book.

● Carlos Marcello, Guy Banister, and Clay Shaw are also implicated along with Mario Kohly, a leader in the Cuban resistance movement. Clay Shaw is said to have had close ties to Jack Ruby.

● David Ferrie, an active CIA agent and the private pilot of Carlos Marcello, is one of the key players in masterminding the plot against Kennedy. His close associate Eladio del Valle (who was murdered in Miami on the same day that Ferrie died), is much more fully developed in this text than in most others. Del Valle was an active anti-Castro Cuban who worked for the CIA.

● Morrow also indicts Santos Trafficante, Meyer Lansky, CIA agent William Harvey, Richard Bissell, and Robert Maheu as have other conspiracy texts. According to Morrow, William Harvey became the coordinator for CIA plans for assassinating Fidel Castro. "Harvey would meet regularly with John Roselli, Santos Trafficante, Sam Giancana, Robert Maheu, and Eladio del Valle," (p. 146).

● He also states that one of the shooters in the ambush of the President, on the CIA hit squad, was French mercenary and assassination expert John Michael Mertz, also called Michel Roux or Jean Soutre. "The FBI found out that a John Mertz, Sara Mertz, and Irma Rio Mertz flew from Houston to Mexico City on November 23, 1963," (p. 174). Another assassin was Carlos Rigel, a hit man of French origin, whose CIA code name was QJ/WIN. Clay Shaw is alleged to have recruited other hit men from the Minutemen. For aforementioned reasons, none of these names have been included in Table 4.6

● Marcello initiated the contract on Kennedy in April, 1963. Ferrie was one of the principal planners. Jose Aleman, an FBI informant, was told by Trafficante of the impending hit. This information went to Aleman's FBI contacts, George Davis, and Paul Scranton, and Hoover learned of the plot on November 4, 1963. He did not inform the Kennedy brothers of his information.

- Morrow corroborates that a meeting occurred in Dallas between J. Edgar Hoover, Richard Nixon and Clint Murchison on the eve of the assassination. The topic of discussion was what would happen if Kennedy were assassinated. (This information is described in Chapter 6 of this work but comes from sources other than Morrow.)

After the assassination, Commander James J. Humes was in charge of the Bethesda autopsy. He discovered a fourth bullet in the President's body (found in the chest cavity). This discovery was not made known and autopsy notes were burned. The bullet was handed over to FBI special agents Francis X. O'Neill and James W. Sibert. Morrow says that "O'Neill and Sibert his escorts took the shell, signed a receipt for it, and gave it to Humes. Humes, in turn, gave the signed receipt to the Secret Service where it remained secreted until it was uncovered in 1977 through a freedom of Information Act suit filed by Washington attorney Mark Lane," (p. 248).

- President Johnson had a mistress in Washington D.C. — Mary Margret Wiley, his secretary. She married Lyndon's sidekick, Jack Valenti, now the president of the Academy of Motion Picture Arts & Sciences.

- This book is unique in suggesting an interesting "motive" for the assassination. Morrow suggests that the reason Kennedy was killed was to inspire the American government to attack Cuba. Oswald was set up as a pro-Castro figure; the thought was that having a pro-Castro Marxist tabbed with the murder of the President might lead to a declaration of war against Cuba. The Mafia, CIA, and anti-Castro Cubans were very interested in that outcome.

- Another interesting element of this possibly-fictionalized book is the discussion of the murder of Presidential mistress Mary Pinchot Meyer. No text has really ever addressed how her murder might be related to the assassination, but Morrow says that her former husband, Cord Meyer, a CIA agent, gave Mrs. Meyer numerous sources and access to CIA persons and documents. Mrs. Meyer allegedly became friendly with Bobby Kennedy after the assassination and wanted to pass on information to him. That is why she was murdered.

- Morrow lists numerous other murders and deaths that could easily be researched. None has been included in the tables in the present text, but might be included in the future, pending verification. Here is a partial listing:

- Two deaths associated with Johnson and the Billy Sol Estes case are referenced in this text (not included in the statistical tabulations); Morrow adds a few more names. Harold Eugene Orr, president of an Amarillo Text company, was found dead of carbon monoxide poisoning and had played a key role in Estes' finance frauds. Howard Pratt, the Chicago office manager of one of Estes' fertilizer suppliers, was similarly found dead of carbon monoxide poisoning.

- Francoise Manet, a consort of Morrow's, was murdered by Cuban agents in a Miami hotel (June, 1961).

- Two of Castro's agents were murdered in reprisal, one unnamed, the other called Callas. Carlos Rodriguez Quesada murdered Callas for the CIA. In turn, Quesada was murdered by John O'Hare, a CIA mercenary. O'Hare killed Quesada and Gilberto Rodriguez Hernandez because they were suspected of forwarding information to the Kennedy Administration regarding the counterfeiting operation. None of these deaths have been listed in the tables presented in this text. Further research verifying these murders might eventually lead to their inclusion.

SUMMARY

We conclude our attempt to present a review of all the major conspiracy theories with one caveat. It is important to keep in mind that conspiracy research literature is heavily laden with defamation, innuendo, and guilt by association, and that factual, hard evidence is lacking to the extreme.

Table 4.8 seeks to create a composite picture of the leading conspiracy literature on the Kennedy assassination.

Table 4.8 Summary of names in published conspiracy theories

Model	Alleged Conspirators	Alleged Assassins
President Johnson	Lyndon Johnson, H.L. Hunt, John Connally, Fred Korth, Chief Curry, District Attorney Wade, Clint Murchison	Roscoe White? Harry Wetherford Malcolm Wallace
Mafia	Meyer Lansky, Carlos Marcello, Santos Trafficante, Tony Arrcado, Sam Giancana, John Roselli, Jimmy Hoffa	(a) Lucien Sarti plus 2 accomplices (or) (b) Eugene Hale Brading, James Files, Johnny Roselli, Charles Nicoletti with Jack Ruby to Silence the Patsy (c) Charles Harrelson, Jack Lawrence, Richard Cain, Nicoletti, "Milwaukee Phil," Roscoe White, & JD Tippit with Ruby to silence Oswald
FBI	J. Edgar Hoover, Gordon Shanklin	No assassins identified; only role was to protect the contract hit on the President from detection; aid and abet setting up Oswald
CIA anti-Castro Cubans	David Phillips, William Harvey,* General Cabell	(a) Ferrie (getaway), Howard Hunt, Frank Sturgis, Daniel Carswell
	Arcacha Smith, Carlos Prio	(b) Eugene Hale Brading, Morgan Brown, Loran Hall
	James Angleton, Allen Dulles*	Charles Frederick Rogers, Charles Harrelson, Chauncey Holt, Lee Harvey Oswald
	Richard Helmls, Richard Bissell*, Guy Bannister, Clay Shaw, H.L. Hunt, Carlos Bringuier, Gen Edwin Walker, Richard Nixon, Orlando Bosch, Pedro Diaz, James Milteer	(c) Gerry Patrick Hemming, Pedro Diaz Lanz, Frank Sturgis, Alexander Rorke, Guillermo Novo and Ignacio Novo
USSR and/or Castro	Nikita Khrushchev	(a) arranged through Trafficante via Marcello for Castro; hit man Miguel Cassas Saez
	Castro Pino Machado/ Moleon Cassera	(b) Lee Harvey Oswald, perhaps aided by Valerie Kostikov (KGB assassination unit)

* Fired or transferred by Kennedy after Bay of Pigs invasion. Note: Two assassins not listed above come from a source deemed too fantastic and unreliable for inclusion. The assassins were alleged to be part of a CIA conspiracy, French mercenary, John Michael Mertz and Jean Soutre. See also discussion in Ch. 5 for another Mafia hit man, James Sutton aka James E. Files who confessed to shooting JFK from the front while Nicoletti hit him from behind from the Dal-Tex building.

Chapter 4. Conspiracy

Appendix

An intricate controversy emerges from some of the substance of this text when compared to the work of Anthony Summers. It concerns the activities of two men, William Attwood, the U.S. Ambassador to the UN, and Ramon Cubella, a high-ranking Castro official who was an agent of the CIA.

In September, 1963, an African diplomat contacted Attwood and informed him that Castro wanted to talk to Kennedy. Given the extreme risk of appearing to be soft on Castro or seeming to be seeking a rapprochement with him, Kennedy instructed Attwood to approach these discussions with great respect for secrecy. Attwood was in contact with the Cubans as late as November 19; only RFK and the President, along with very few others, were aware of these discussions. The meetings were coordinated through the help of an ABC correspondent, Lisa Howard.

While these steps were being taken, the CIA was involved in another, quite opposite, set of actions. In late September 1963, the CIA contacted Cubella and sought to enlist him in an effort to kill Castro. Efimov argues that Cubella was a double agent and was informing Castro of these machinations against him. Anthony Summers, who interviewed Cubella, disagrees and asserts that Cubella never informed Castro of his CIA connections.

The CIA asked Cubella to assassinate Castro and assured him that any coup against Castro would be recognized by the U.S. Government. Cubella wanted to make sure that he was dealing with people who were directly connected to President Kennedy; the CIA reassured him that Desmond Fitzgerald would be his contact man and that Fitzgerald was a personal friend of RFK. In fact, RFK knew nothing of these events and Desmond Fitzgerald was a CIA official. He met with Cubella in Paris on November 22, 1963 (!) and gave him a poison pen with which to assassinate Castro.

It is here that stories diverge. Cubella says that the CIA pen was returned and that he did not want to personally assassinate Castro. Others (Efimov) argue the pen was requested by Cubella and that it contained a very lethal poison. Summers says the pen held a bullet in its chamber, not poison.

Ultimately, Castro arrested Cubella, but he was never charged with any crimes prior to 1964. He was sentenced to prison for 30 years (that would argue against his being in Castro's favor, and a double-agent). However, Cubella was released in 1979 and lives now in Spain.

What appears certain is that CIA Director Helms, Fitzgerald and other CIA officials did not inform the President or RFK of these plans to assassinate Castro, and this underscores the degree of autonomy the CIA held in these years — particularly since these events occurred after the Cuban Missile Crisis.

From a psychological perspective, it is of interest to note the paradox of these events. On November 19, JFK sent William Attwood to seek detente with Castro. On November 22, the CIA sent Cubella off to kill Castro.

We know for certain that Castro was aware of Attwood's efforts, but we do not know if Castro was aware of the CIA-Cubella plot to kill him at this time. For a discussion of this interesting twist to the whole conspiracy matter, the reader is directed to Summers, *ibid.*, pp 344, 395, 401-402 and Efimov, Igor, p. 258.

A yet-more-recent-datum to add to this is that Manual Artime, a Cuban exile leader favored by the Kennedys, stated that both RFK and JFK, contrary to what has been said, did in fact have knowledge of this Cubella plot to assassinate Castro, code-named AM/LASH. If true, then the Kennedy brothers were playing both ends against the middle, negotiating a peace through Mr. Attwood and initiating an assassination plot against Castro all within a few days of each other and similarly within a few days of the assassination of Kennedy. The Cubella plot has been bandied about by Kennedy researchers for quite a few years, but some recent information tends to corroborate this last version. In 1994 two researchers learned from former Secretary of State Dean Rusk that he, too, learned of the coup operation against Castro after the president's death. Rusk seems to imply that the Kennedy brothers knew of both the coup and the peace effort *and were behind both.* Asked if this was not "the height of duplicity," Rusk replied, "It was just an either/or situation. That went on frequently." All the same, Rusk admits that the Kennedys were "playing with fire," (Summers, "The Ghosts of November," *Vanity Fair*, December, 1994, p. 105).

Chapter 5. Paradox

There was the door to which I found no key,
There was the veil through which I might not see.
    — Omar Khayam

So far, we have attempted to stay close to the published literature. Reasonable conclusions are limited: (1) Lee Harvey Oswald may have shot President Kennedy, but he may not have. (2) Some mysterious set of events has lurked behind the scenes, and the full facts of the Kennedy assassination have not become known. (3) A conspiracy from some quarter is a very sound and reasonable hypothesis. Any other scenario is unlikely, problematic, and contrary to the best evidence on the subject. (4) The most likely conspiracies involve the Mafia or the CIA and anti-Castro Cubans. A plot originating with President Johnson, the Soviets, or a conspiracy born in Havana are plausible but have significantly more difficulties to overcome to be more credible.

Interpreting The Facts

Once the homework is done, speculation must take over. Having added up what can be known for sure, the next step is to draw out implications and associations, engaging in creative thinking. Let us try to look at the material without being limited by any inherited, vested interest of one conspiracy "school" or another. Maybe we can find something others have missed.

The Cover Up

Table 3.4 listed 62 of the most important individuals alleged to have been associated with hiding or distorting information regarding the assassination over the last 38 years, from James Hosty (the FBI agent who tore up Oswald's letter) to Clare Boothe Luce (who published "All of *Life's* Photos" while withholding the most significant frames of the Zapruder film). By taking a closer look at the cover-up, we ought to be able to get closer to the source of the conspiracy.

Figure 5.1 ties each of the cover-up sources with the agencies or areas from which they originated. The media has been a leading source of cover-up and disinformation; but it is also a source of genuine, valid, and compelling information. After all, many mainstream sources as well as the underground literature on the Kennedy assassination have published very incisive pieces. Thus, this media sample is probably an artifact of information dissemination and not to be weighed too heavily. In other words, the media disseminates information; our question is, who generated it in the first place?

Another disclaimer is that the Mafia does not regularly use publicists and has limited disinformation capabilities. Its modus operandi is to enforce silence through intimidation and murder. Mafia-related murders, therefore, have been included as examples of cover-up even though they were not originally listed in the table in Chapter 3. If the intent is to enforce silence, then such murders ought to be tabulated.

Categorizing the leading sources of deception (by commission and omission) leads us back to the FBI, the CIA and the Mob, again, *and shows that each is about equal to the others*. If there is a conspiracy of silence (and disinformation) — and we exclude the media from our focus — then these three are the major players.

This approach does not tell us much. We already know that the FBI, the CIA and the Mob have an interest in keeping the truth about many events buried. But it does tell us something new: The conspiracy to cover up the truth about this event originated *from inside the United States*.

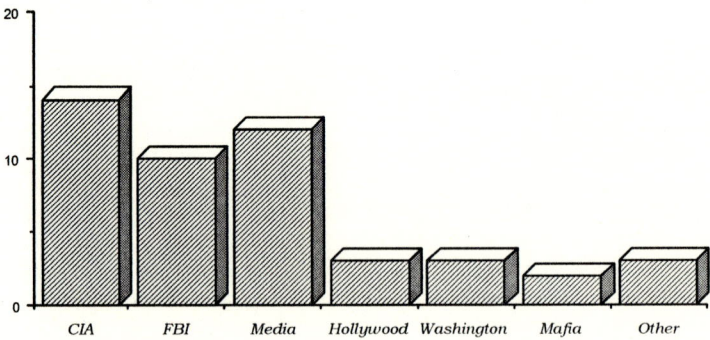

Figure 5.1 Distribution of Cover-up Sources (including Mafia Murders)

> "Cover-up" includes murdering people to prevent them from talking. Included in the figure are the Mafia-related murders of Sam Giancana, John Roselli, Carlos Prio, Jimmy Hoffa, Charles Nicoletti, Leo Moceri, Richard Cain, Salvatore Granello and Dave Yaras. Not included are three others cases that perhaps fit the bill. Circumstances make two of the "suicides" questionable (Paisley and Pawley) and the heart attack (Martino), as well. All of the murders had some connecting point with the Kennedy assassination.

Dealey Plaza

Another way to look at this information might be to place the names of all the assassins in some order. How many possible assassins were there in Dealey Plaza on November 22, 1963? (See figure 5.2). Joseph Milteer, the ultra right-wing leader of numerous racist groups, who had been on the phone to FBI informant William Somersett (see frontispiece) was reported as knowledgeable of the upcoming assassination. Some said he was photographed in Dealey Plaza among the spectators; others dispute that. Howard Hunt, Frank Sturgis, and Daniel Carswell are alleged by Weberman and Canfield to have been the tramps arrested in the railroad yards and Marita Lorenz implicated them, but both denied being there.

Fig. 5.2 Possible Assassins In Dealey Plaza, November 22, 1963 [a]	
Lee Harvey Oswald	Joseph Milteer
Eugene Brading	Morgan Brown
Howard Hunt	Frank Sturgis
Daniel Carswell	Lucien Sarti
Harry Wetherford	Roscoe White
Pedo Diaz Lanz	James Powell
Loran Hall	Charles Harrelson
Charles Rogers	James Sutton (Files)
Charles Nicoletti	Chancey Holt
Guillermo Novo	Ignacio Novo
Gerry Hemming	Alexander Rorke
Orlando Bosch	Miguel Sawz
Johnny Roselli	Desmond Fitzgerald
Malcolm "Mac" Wallace	

a. John Michael Mertz and Jean Soutre have not been included. See prior chapter for explanations.

Jim Braden, an ex-convict on parole and an associate of Milteer, was arrested on the third floor of the Dal-Tex building. His true identity, Eugene Hale Brading, did not come out until 1969 when a television producer discovered it. Brading stayed with his associate Morgan H. Brown at the Cabana Hotel in Dallas. Brown left town the afternoon of the assassination. Brading was also associated with the Mob and Marcello through connections with Nofio Pecora and James Dolan.

James Powell has not been accused, in existing literature on the assassination, but he was found in the Dal-Tex along with Eugene Hale Brading building after it was sealed off following the assassination. He was an army intelligence officer, and what he was doing there has never been fully explained.[1]

Lucien Sarti is held to be the grassy knoll gunman along with two accomplices (never yet named according to Summers).

Harry Wetherford was a Dallas police officer on top of the Dallas County jail during the motorcade. What was his role?

> On the morning of the assassination, Craig's boss, Sheriff Bill Decker, ordered his deputies to "take no part whatsoever in the security of the Presidential motorcade". Decker had a crackshot rifleman — Harry Wetherford — on top of the Dallas County Jail Building during the motorcade, close by Oswald's alleged sniper's nest. A young researcher tried to talk to Wetherford once and asked if he had shot at Kennedy. Wetherford's response was: "You little son of a bitch, I kill lots of people."[2]

Roscoe White's son, Ricky Don White, found his father's diary, posthumously, implicating him in the killing of Kennedy. Roscoe White was a Dallas police officer on the scene with Wetherford.[3]

Marita Lorenz said Bosch and Diaz Lanz accompanied Frank Sturgis to Dealey Plaza, plus two Cuban brothers who she could not identify.[4] All were part of Operation 40, a secret anti-Castro guerrilla group formed by the CIA in 1960, an assassination squad.[5] Lorenz implicated Gerry Patrick Hemming, Guillermo Novo,

---

1. Groden, Robert J., with Livingstone, Harrison E. *High Treason*, Baltimore: Conservatory Press, 1989.
2. *Ibid.*, p. 188.
3. Zirbel, Craig. *The Texas Connection*. New York: Warner Books, 1991. pp. 68-69.
4. The two Cuban brothers Marita Lorenz could not identify might be linked to Sturgis, Pedro Diaz Lanz and Eduardo Diaz Lanz. Weberman, Alan J. and Canfield, Michael. *Coup D'Etat in America: The CIA and the Assassination of John F. Kennedy*. San Francisco, CA: Quick American Archives, 1992.
5. Groden *Ibid.*, p. 348

Chapter 5. Paradox

Ignacio Novo, and Alexander Rorke in addition to Lanz. Others say Rorke was deceased by this time and could not possibly have been in this entourage.

Miguel Saez is the suspected hit man from Havana.

Desmond Fitzgerald, a CIA employee, was listed in a conspiracy-based assassination newsletter as the grassy knoll gunman using a directionally silenced rifle designed by Mitch WerBell using frangible, explode-on-impact bullets.

The same periodical, citing testimony by Billy Sol Estes, implicates Malcolm Wallace, an LBJ crony, as the assassin. (See FairPlay Magazine at http://spot.acorn.net/jfkplace/09/fp.back_issues/23rd_Issue/breakthru.html.)

Charles Harrelson apparently was a contract killer, allegedly working for the CIA. He confessed to the killing of John Kennedy and a Texas judge; he later retracted it, saying he was on cocaine. Harrelson's confession about JFK was dismissed as the ramblings of a maniac, yet his confession involving the judge led to a successful prosecution; and he is currently serving time for that murder.

Authors Craig and Rogers say that CIA contract killer Charles Frederick Rogers and Harrelson were the two sharpshooters at the grassy knoll who assassinated Kennedy. They were two of the three tramps arrested and then released; the other was Chauncey Holt, who did not take an active part in the assassination but confessed his involvement. Holt had ties to the CIA and to the Mafia. Holt is said to have known Morgan Brown and Eugene Brading. [6]

A second grassy knoll gunman has come forth who was not cited or listed by Craig and Rogers. In 1994, private investigator Joe West was alerted by an "anonymous FBI source" to a man serving a 50-year prison sentence in Joliet State Penitentiary. The man finally consented to an interview, after the death of investigator West. A full and uncensored version of this video[7] was distributed in 1996, based on a lengthy interview held in March of 1994. The publishers of the video remain elusive and are listed as MPI Home Video and UTL Productions. No further information is available.

Files said he used a pistol given to him by CIA functionary David Atlee Phillips. Files had previously worked with the CIA at "No Name Key" in Florida with anti-Castro Cubans.

This author managed to establish contact with Mr. Files, and over the course of time he consented to answer some questions. Mr. James E. Files provides a story which is indeed compelling. He alleges that he was the loyal assistant, bodyguard and driver of Chuckie Nicoletti, Sam Giancana's primary hit man. Six months before

---

6. Craig, John R. & Rogers, Philip A. *The Man on the Grassy Knoll.* New York: Avon Books, 1992, pp. 193-194.

7. West, Joe (Producer). "Confessions of an Assassin," MPI Media Group, Orland Park, IL.

Dallas, Files was told that JFK would be hit. Files asked no questions but simply did what he was told. He met Lee Harvey Oswald and said Oswald was not likely aware of any plot against the President. He is quite sure "Oswald never fired a shot." He also says that even though Oswald did not have a driver's license, he had driven military vehicles and could drive a car.

West says that he was a "back up" hit man who was to shoot Kennédy if the shots which came from behind (fired by Nicoletti from the Dal-Tex Building) did not succeed in killing him. Files used what he calls a "Remington Fire Ball," meaning an elongated pistol with a scope. It fit into a briefcase. Files says that the CIA joined the Mafia in this hit and provided maps, a revised itinerary, and Secret Service identification one week before the event. The major CIA person who liaisoned with the Mafia for this hit was David Attlee Phillips. Files said that he had been working with Cuban exiles at No Name Key, too, but that his primary affiliation and loyalties were always with the Chicago Mob.

Files said that on the morning of November 22, he met Johnny Roselli and Nicoletti in Dallas, and that Eugene Hale Brading was also present. During the motorcade, Files stood behind the fence at the grassy knoll and waited. He saw JFK had been hit, but that the headshot had not been accomplished. He waited until the last minute and then decided to fire. He believes that he and Nicoletti hit JFK from the front (and the back) almost simultaneously.

Files believes the murders of Giancana, Roselli and Nicoletti were all motivated to silence them from testifying before Senate Committees in the mid-1970s. Files alleges that he still holds a copy of Nicoletti's diary, but he has not planned on making any of its contents public.

Files says he was quite unaware that Oswald was in the Depository and knew nothing of this aspect of the case. He knows who killed Officer J. D. Tippit but refuses to give up the killer, who is still alive. He knows that David Ferrie was murdered but also refuses to identify his killer. He is adamant that Oswald killed no one. Ruby was part of the conspiracy.

Files is not an intelligent man, does not appear to be highly conversant about higher level Mafiosi (e.g. Trafficante or Marcello) and has no idea who ordered the hit on JFK. He simply carried it out, as Chuck Nicoletti's right hand man. His lack of intelligence and erudition makes his story surprisingly credible.

Files says he shot the president, put his gun in an attaché case and slowly began walking away. Two policemen approached, but individuals Files did not know said they were "Secret Service" and directed the policemen elsewhere. Files slowly drove out of town to Mesquite, Texas, where he had a motel room. There he hid the weapons and scrubbed down with hot wax to eliminate the possibility of a positive paraffin reading. He returned to Chicago the next day and continued working for the Mob. He was paid $30,000 for the hit.

He is currently serving time for murdering an Illinois policeman. He did not mention or appear to implicate Roscoe White, Charles Frederick Rogers, Loran Hall, Howard Hunt, Daniel Carswell, Richard Cain or other notable figures. He did implicate deceased Mafiosi Giancana, Roselli and Nicoletti, however. Furthermore, he said that Cuban exile Frank Sturgis was also present at Dealey Plaza.

Something is missing in all of these scenarios: There are no murder weapons associated with any of these individuals, no fingerprints, no empty cartridge casings,[8] no physical evidence of any stature, no witnesses observing their shooting. Apart from some sworn testimony, conspiracy theories simply have not come up with the physical evidence needed for any prosecutions or convictions. Even Mark Lane says incriminatory evidence is sorely lacking.

We are in a classic double-bind situation. On the one hand, it is clear that some kind of conspiracy is an extremely likely possibility; and on the other, there is little evidence to indict or convict anyone for the century's greatest crime. This drama is deeply frustrating, almost as if it unfolded according to a plan that inherently generates the mystery that foils all attempts to solve it.

Jim Braden aka Eugene Hale Brading: A Leading Suspect?

Among the 26 suspect individuals in Dealey Plaza that day, the closest one can get to identifying an alternate assassin might be Eugene Hale Brading. Here, in somewhat expanded detail, is the hypothesis:

Jim Moore, who spent over 10 years going over Dealey Plaza, holds that the first bullet fired actually missed. It hit the curb on Elm Street and ricocheted, splattering a spectator, James Tague, with concrete. Tague was injured and reported the matter to the police; Moore points out that there were five witnesses to Tague's injuries.[9] Thus, while most people thought the first shot hit Kennedy in the throat (and Kennedy quickly brings his hand toward his throat on the Zapruder film), Moore says the first shot missed and hit Tague.[10] Others like Gerald Posner agree.

Even more interesting is an assertion made by Col. Fletcher Prouty, the military advisor to President Kennedy and the author of his own work on the assassination (discussed earlier). Prouty is decidedly not a pro-Warren Commission writer like Moore, but his comments concern the well-documented injury to spectator Tague:

---

8. Actually, James Files, one alleged assassin, says he left a spent .22 cartridge shell with his teeth marks in it, his "trademark," and in the late 1980s a .22 casing was found. Source: www.assassinationweb.com/shack3g.htm

9. Moore, Jim. *Conspiracy of One*. Fort Worth, Texas: The Summit Group, 1991, pp. 198-199.

10. Moore, *ibid.*, p. 199

The members of the Warren Commission agreed that a fragment had struck Tague and that Tague's injury was the result of a "near miss." It said nothing about where Tague was standing. Most readers of the Warren Report assume that Tague was standing close to where the President's car passed on Elm Street... That was not the case, however, and therein lies another key factor in the ingenious plot to kill the President... Tague was standing on a curb on Main Street, not Elm Street. He was more than one full block away from the President's car. Let's draw a line from the point of impact on that curbstone back to a position within a circle with an eighteen-inch diameter around the President's head and shoulders. If we project that line back to some firing point, we have placed that gunman in a window on the second floor the Dal-Tex Building, behind the President's car. On the other hand, if we draw a line from that same point of contact with the curbstone back to the alleged lone gunman's lair on the sixth floor of the Book Depository building, we discover that the bullet would have traveled about twenty-two feet above the President's car and as much as thirty-three feet to its right. Obviously this bullet is hardly a "near" miss. *The path of the Tague bullet reveals that the true location of at least one gunman at Dealey Plaza was in a second floor window of the Dal-Tex building... The Dal-Tex window is an ideal sniper's location.*[11]

It is unfortunate that Fletcher Prouty does not make the next logical deduction. If the Tague shot is calculated to have come from the second floor of the Dal-Tex building, is it not significant that Eugene Hale Brading (an ex-con with 33 prior arrests) was arrested on the third floor within a few minutes of the assassination, and lied to the police about his identity?

This is a surprisingly undeveloped clue in conspiracy literature. Moreover, the scientific acoustic evidence presented to the HSCA also shows that some of the shots *may have come from the Dal-Tex building* where Brading was arrested.[12]

But then the inherent mystery kicks in, and we are taken in multiple directions simultaneously: Brading had ties to the right-wing Minutemen. (James Milteer and Earl Schieb were members. Brading was friendly with the son of Earl Schieb. Shieb, in turn, was the person called by Barney Baker of the Teamsters shortly after the assassination. Baker, a Hoffa goon, was deeply entrenched in Mob activities, an ex-

---

11. Prouty, Fletcher. *JFK: The CIA, Vietnam, and the Plot to Assassinate John F. Kennedy.* New Jersey: Carol Communications, 1992, pp. 299-300.

12. Summers, Anthony. *Conspiracy.* New York: McGraw-Hill, 1989, p. 21.

convict only recently released from prison; Jack Ruby had called him, a few weeks before the assassination. Thus Brading is tied in with the Teamsters, the Mob, and the right-wing Minutemen, and has a third-party association with Jack Ruby.

Brading stayed at the Cabana Hotel in Dallas the night before the assassination. Jack Ruby had dinner there that same evening. Ralph Meyers was staying in that hotel — an Army Intelligence agent with a crypto-clearance who had been stationed at a top-secret base in Turkey. Another military intelligence figure appears with Brading as well — James Powell — since both were caught in the Dal-Tex building after it had been sealed. Thus, Brading can be linked with Ruby, the right-wing Minutemen, and the Mob, and via two circumstantial linkages, with military intelligence.

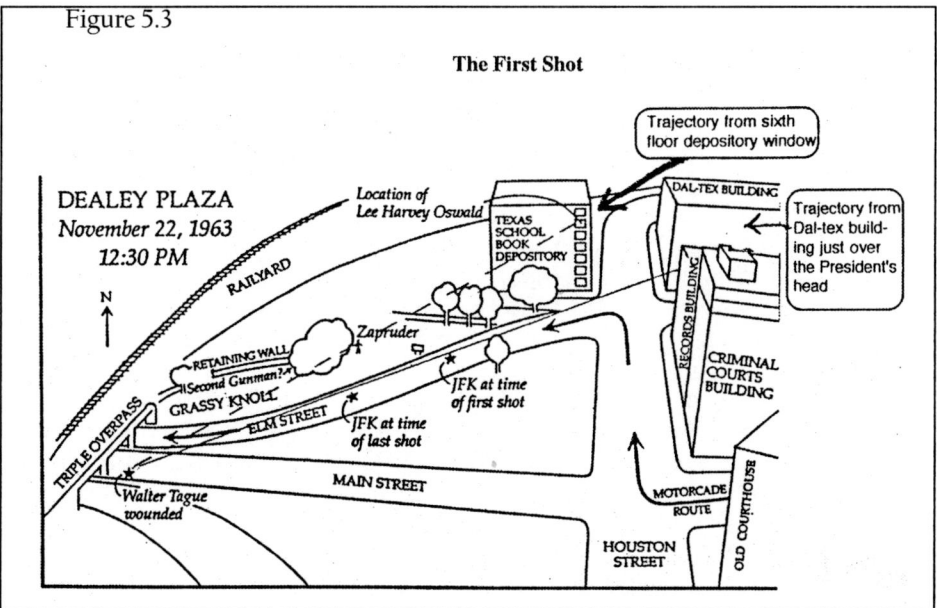

Figure 5.3 — The First Shot

The map of Dealey Plaza is taken from Ogelsby. James Tague had stopped his car at the location indicated on the map and stood on the south curb of Main Street. A piece of cement from the curb flew up and injured Tague, who reported the incident. He was hit after the first shot, by his recollection, but before the last shot. The incident is cited in the Warren Commission Report. Jim Moore shows that 5 witnesses observed the ricocheted hit of Tague. If one draws a line from Oswald's alleged perch, the shot is very much high and wide of the mark: not even a near miss. It is 22 feet over the President's head and as much as 33 feet off to the right. However, if one draws a line from Tague through the motorcade route, as Fletcher Prouty suggests, it leads directly to the second floor of the Dal-Tex building where Eugene Hale Brading, the ex convict, was arrested and then let go. (Map courtesy of Carl Ogelsby, p. 83. Note that Ogelsby's map incorrectly lists James Tague as "Walter Tague.")

> Parenthetically, an assassination researcher, Howard Donohue, looked carefully at the path taken by the bullet that coursed through Kennedy's brain. His analysis of the angle suggested it could not possibly have come from Oswald's location, but was much more likely to have come from directly behind the President: either from the trunk of his car, the Records Building, or the Dal-Tex Building. [See Bonar Menninger, *Mortal Error*, ibid, p. 78.]

It gets worse. Brading can be connected to anti-Castro Cubans. He had an office in New Orleans — next door to David Ferrie.[13] And TV investigative reporter Daniel Schorr put an "Agent X" on CBS in silhouette. He said he fought in the mountains of Cuba with Frank Sturgis and Loran Hall. He said Hall was in Dallas on November 22 and was part of the assassination squad *directed by Eugene Hale Brading*.[14] So Brading has been linked with anti-Castro Cubans, via Schorr's anonymous informant.

Brading continues to connect to virtually every conspiratorial corner of this event:

> Prior to the President's murder, H.L. Hunt had publicly announced that the President and his staff should be shot since there was "no way to get those traitors out of government except by shooting them out." Similarly, Hunt's son, Nelson Bunker Hunt, partially paid for a full page black-bordered advertisement in the Dallas Morning News attacking the President as a pro-communist traitor. The ad appeared on the day of Kennedy's murder and was viewed by many as a "Dallas greeting" . . . Beginning as early as the 1950s H.L. Hunt was known to have continuing gambling contacts with Jack Ruby. More importantly, on the day before the assassination Ruby actually went to the Hunt Oil Company building (purportedly to help a young girl obtain a job interview with the Hunts). The same day in the same Hunt Oil Company building, convicted California felon James Braden and "three associates" paid a visit to H.L. Hunt's sons, Lamar and Nelson.[15]

Thus, we have Brading connected to right-wing "big oil" interests. He connects to the Mob through the Teamsters and Barney Baker, Carlos Marcello, and Nofio Pecora (and is alleged in another text to have had contacts with two other mobsters present in Dallas, Moceri and Nicoletti).[16] He fits in a right-wing plot through H.L. Hunt, Earl Shieb and the Minutemen, yet manages to find the time to connect to anti-Castro Cubans through David Ferrie and Frank Sturgis. If this begins to get confusing, Figure 5.4 attempts to put it all in perspective.

---

13. Weberman, *ibid.*, p. 62.
14. *Ibid.*, p. 150.
15. Zirbel, Craig. *The Texas Connection.* New York: Warner Books, 1991 p. 214.
16. Craig and Rogers, *ibid*

Chapter 5. Paradox

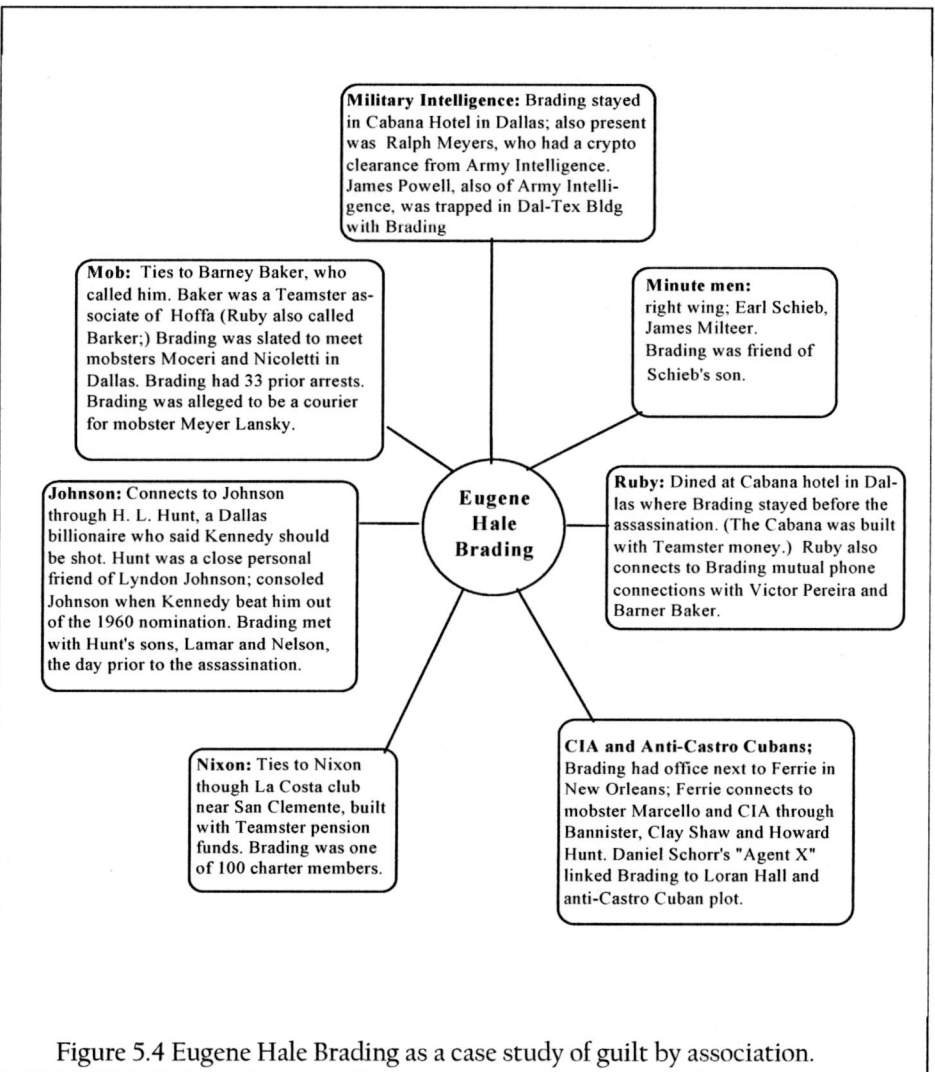

Figure 5.4 Eugene Hale Brading as a case study of guilt by association.

The result of our inquiry is that we have a pastiche of associations and innuendo, and little else.

To make matters worse, Brading links up with Richard Nixon. FBI agent John Anderson talked to Brading in Los Angeles:

> Brading was a charter member of the La Costa Club, located twenty miles south of San Clemente. Financed by the Teamsters and owned by Meyer Lansky's front man, Moe Dalitz. La Costa was frequented by many organized crime figures as well as Nixon's close friend Murray Chotiner. La Costa Club was also

where Nixon's aides John Dean, John Ehrlichman and H.R. Haldeman met to get their stories about the Watergate cover-up synchronized.[17]

And if desired, Brading can connect to President Johnson as well through H.L. Hunt. Hunt was a very close personal friend of LBJ's and a major supporter of his bid for the Presidency.

We have incredible associations, phenomenal opportunities for guilt by association, *but no proof of anything.*[18] We are led, once again, back to where we started.

And then we find out: the Dal-Tex building *had windows that couldn't be opened.*[19] Maybe Oswald was the only shooter in Dealey Plaza, after all!

The Kennedy assassination is certainly a paradox, but it is also like a fractal image, in which each portion of any detail of the figure seems to contain a view of the whole figure. Let us take another perspective. Instead of looking at Dealey Plaza, let us focus on metropolitan Dallas as a whole. Who was there? Some very interesting names pop up: Richard Nixon, H.L. Hunt, Clint Murchison and J. Edgar Hoover.

> It took some time before all of these names were properly identified in the literature, but that they were all present *on the eve* of the assassination now seems well established.[20]

H.L. Hunt

Billionaire oilman H.L. Hunt sponsored a series of radio and television programs carried on 409 stations throughout the country and bankrolled many causes of the far right.

> Hunt is the Big Man in Texas, the Giant, the richest and the stingiest, the most powerful and the most solitary of the oilmen.[21]

---

17. Weberman, *ibid.*, pp. 61-62.

18. One curiously suspicious quote came from this event and is often touted in conspiracy circles. Madeline Brown, LBJ's mistress, said he was at the party with Nixon, Hoover, Hunt and Murchison. As the evening wore on, he came out of his private conference and said to her, "After tomorrow, that's the last time those goddamned Kennedys will embarrass me again!" As with so many facts and quotes in this drama, one must be critical of the veracity of each piece of the assassination puzzle. The quote may be in question, but three independent sources corroborate the Murchison party did in fact occur: Source: Harrison Livingstone, Killing the Truth, *ibid.*, p. 486. More recent conspiracy literate also implicates LBJ-appointed Warren commission member, John J. McCloy, as also present at that party. (See www.assassinationweb.com/shack3g.htm).

19. According to author Jim Moore.

20. Livingstone, *ibid.*

Chapter 5. Paradox

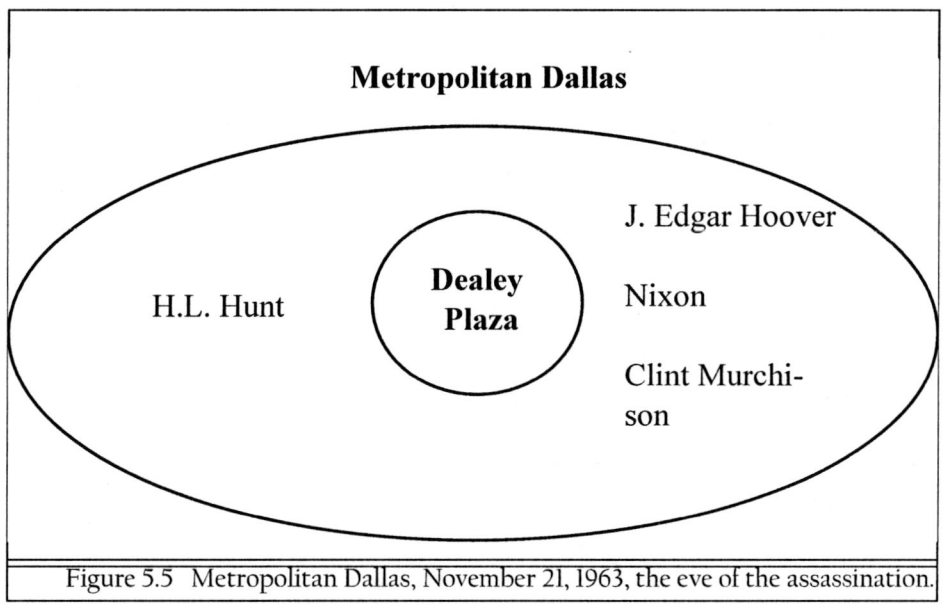

Figure 5.5 Metropolitan Dallas, November 21, 1963, the eve of the assassination.

Hunt made much of his fortune from the oil depletion allowance, and Kennedy had threatened to remove it.

When Kennedy threatened to retract the depletion allowance, the right-wing-John Birch hate machine was cranked up against him. [22]

Conspiracy authors have implicated Hunt, either directly or through innuendo. Hunt's behavior on assassination day, for example, was unusual:

At 12:23 on November 22, from his office on the 7th floor of the Mercantile Building... Hunt watched John Kennedy ride towards Dealey Plaza, where fate awaited him at 12:30. A few minutes later, escorted by six men in two cars, Hunt left the center of Dallas without even stopping by his house. At that very moment, General Walker (who Oswald had allegedly taken a pot shot at) was in a plane between New Orleans and Shreveport. He joined Mr. Hunt in one of his secret hideaways across the Mexican border. There they remained for a month, protected by personal guards... It was not until Christmas that Hunt, Walker and their party returned to Dallas. [23]

Two pieces of conspiracy thinking, however, contradict Hunt's complicity in the assassination: (a) According to Livingstone, Hunt went to Washington DC after the

---

21. Groden, *ibid.*, p. 307
22. *Ibid.*, p. 307

assassination, not to a secret hideaway in Mexico with General Walker as has been alleged. (b) Hunt financed a full-page ad in the *Dallas Morning Herald* denouncing Kennedy and paid for a "Wanted for Treason" flyer distributed on the day of the assassination. If Hunt were involved in the assassination, it would seem his behavior would have been far more discrete than it was.[24]

- Hunt financed the writing of the book *Khrushchev Killed Kennedy*, by Michael Eddowes, considered a masterpiece of disinformation.[25]

---

23. *Ibid.*, p. 308. The mistress of Lyndon Johnson, Madeleine Brown, related a chilling anecdote to author Dick Russell on August 4, 1992 regarding this implication. "Before the assassination, according to Brown, "Lyndon told me that the Kennedys would never embarrass him again. It was not a threat, but a promise." Then, as 1963 passed into history, they were together at a New Year's Eve party. "I said, Lyndon, 'I've got to have my mind put at ease,' Brown remembers, 'People are saying you are responsible for the assassination, and I've got to know.' Well, he had a terrible temper tantrum, as he often did. Then he told me: 'It was the oil people and the CIA.'" (Dick Russell, *The Man Who Knew Too Much*. New York: Carroll & Graf, 1992, p. 606.)

A corroborating source, Harrison E. Livingstone's *Killing the Truth* (New York: Carrol & Graf, 1993), mentions Madeline Brown in the following context: "I know Madeline Brown, a former mistress of Johnson, rather well and find her mostly credible. It is hard for me to believe that she is making up all she says. Brown has, in the past, maintained that LBJ told her that John Kennedy was going to be assassinated in advance of it happening. In my talks with her, she confirms the portrait given in *The Texas Connection*, and then some. She says that Johnson was a totally amoral man who slept with any woman who came along, betrayed all his women, and who was often drunk and abusive. She said that she believed he worked together with H.L. Hunt and others on the murder" (p. 466).

In my own research, a peculiar event transpired. As the author of this text, I have attempted to base all conjecture and speculation on evidence gleaned from one published source or another. In the matter of Kennedy mistresses I felt a need to be particularly careful about making claims of affairs which others had published, and I tried to independently confirm some of these allegations. One text suggested that Pierre Salinger's secretary slept with Kennedy, so I wrote Salinger about this. Salinger denied JFK slept with his secretary, but did acknowledge JFK's womanizing. At the same time, he revealed that one of his employees took up with LBJ after the assassination. His letter to me is excerpted below:

"Dear Dr. Kroth, . . . Kennedy pushed me to have mistresses, which convinced me he was having mistresses. During the campaign, I got side information from journalists (who in those days were not interested in publishing that information) that John F. Kennedy was having an affair with Pamela Turnure, who later became Jackie's press secretary. There were rumors in the White House about Fiddle & Faddle, but I did not get specific information. And, finally, no employee assigned to my office had an affair with the President. One did in the next term with Lyndon Johnson.

Best Regards, Pierre Salinger." (Source: Personal correspondence, October, 20, 1995).

Madeline Brown's allegations first given to author Dick Russell, therefore, seem to be corroborated in part, at least, by two other independent sources, Harrison Livingston and Pierre Salinger.

24. Harrison Livingston, *Killing the Truth*. New York: Carrol & Graf, 1993.

H.L. Hunt, reported to be the wealthiest American in 1966, was associated with sponsorship of extreme right-wing causes and in no uncertain terms said that Kennedy should be shot. It has always been a speculation that one of the shots fired at JFK came from the Dal-Tex building. One investigator determined that a business not listed in the lobby directory of that building, Dallas Uranium and Oil, had offices there in 1963, and that ownership could be traced to Hunt [a]

a. Bob Goodman, *Triangle of Fire*, San Jose, CA.: Laquerian Publishing, 1993, p. 166.

- He was as one of the prime financial backers of Senator Joseph McCarthy whose deputy, Roy Cohn, worked for him on numerous occasions. (Cohn, in turn, was closer to J. Edgar Hoover than most people knew.)
- The wife of Baron deMohrenschildt admitted that her husband was friendly with H.L. Hunt and that he had worked in intelligence. [26]
- Lt. George Butler, a Dallas police officer with some responsibility for Oswald's transfer, was also once Hunt's head of security. Butler was described as an extreme right-winger who gave the "all clear" to transfer Oswald just before he was killed by Jack Ruby.

Richard Nixon

Grodin and others intimate that Richard Nixon and J. Edgar Hoover were also present in Dallas the night before the assassination, meeting with Texas industrialist

---

25. Groden, *ibid.*, p. 237. Let us not forget another suspected conspirator from the right, Frank Sturgis, the unnamed disinformation source of Jack Anderson's early writings linking Castro to a Soviet plot. We should also remember mobster Roselli as another deep-throat source for articles linking Oswald to a leftist conspiracy originating with Castro. Thus we have suspects H.L. Hunt, Sturgis and Roselli each contributing disinformation to support the hypothesis of a leftist conspiracy to kill the president.

26. *Ibid.*, p. 130.

Clint Murchison. (Penn Jones, Jr. is cited as their source.) Nixon went to great lengths to be oblique about his whereabouts on November 22. He was a lawyer representing Pepsico at a Carbonated Beverages Convention and Great Southwest Corporation at the time.[27] (Marina Oswald's attorney was also a partner in the law firm handling Great Southwestern corporation in Dallas. See endnote 22.)

Nixon finally admitted that he left Dallas shortly before the assassination at 11 a.m. that morning, but he told the Warren Commission that "the only time he was in Dallas Texas during 1963 was two days prior to the assassination of John F. Kennedy." Perhaps only a little white lie, but a lie nonetheless, contained in Warren Commission exhibit 1973, on page 280.[28]

Thus, as H.L. Hunt left Dallas immediately for Mexico on the day Kennedy was killed, meeting up with his friend General Edwin Walker in a Mexico hideaway, Richard Nixon left Dallas for New York an hour-and-a-half before Kennedy was killed and told the Warren Commission a fib about it.

Clint Murchison

Not much in conspiracy literature covers Clint Murchison, but there is enough to raise eyebrows.

- Murchison's empire overlapped with that of Mafia financial wizard Meyer Lansky and Teamster leader Jimmy Hoffa.[29]
- Murchison received large loans from Teamster pension funds.[30]
- Marina Oswald became quite rich after the death of her husband. She was hidden away — much to the consternation of her friend, Ruth Paine — in a motel owned by the Great Southwest Corporation, which was controlled by the Wynne family of Dallas, partners of Clint Murchison.[31]
- Murchison had an interest in a flour monopoly in Haiti, plus other businesses. George deMohrenschildt traveled to Haiti with a large sum of money shortly after the assassination. And it was Haiti's notorious Papa Doc Duvalier who remarked, before the assassination, that Kennedy would not be in power long.[32]

---

27. Weberman, *ibid.*, p. 84.
28. *Ibid.*, p. 84. A more recent text corroborates that this party at the Murchisons' did in fact take place. Madeline Brown and Penn Jones Jr. are the major sources for this information. Madeline Brown, LBJ's mistress said that Johnson was also there. Corroborating source is Harrison Livingstone, *Killing the Truth*, New York, 1993, p. 484. (It might also be mentioned that after all of Robert Kennedy's efforts to put Jimmy Hoffa behind bars, when Nixon became President he granted Hoffa a pardon. Nixon also appeared at a Teamsters Executive Board meeting in 1971. *Ibid.*, p. 154.)
29. Groden, *ibid.*, p. 282.
30. *Ibid.*, p. 281.

Chapter 5. Paradox

- Murchison had an interest in the Del-Mar race track, where Hoover spent his annual vacation with his lover, Clyde Tolson, also in the FBI. To make matters all the more interwoven, Bobby Baker, Johnson's right hand man, lobbied in Washington for the interests of this racetrack.[33] Murchison, in fact, was about to be investigated with respect to his relationship to Baker. Only seven days prior to the assassination, Senate investigators hinted that the Murchison brothers of Texas might be called upon to testify about the activities of Johnson's protégé, Bobby Baker.
- Murchison shared a lawyer who represented both Bobby Baker and Jimmy Hoffa.[34]
- Murchison was friends with mobster Carlos Marcello from New Orleans.[35]

If we similarly graph the known associations of suspect individuals who were in Dallas on the eve of the assassination — Nixon, Hunt, J. Edgar Hoover, and Clint Murchison — in the same way that we graphed the known associates of Jim Braden, the resulting figure reproduces virtually the entire spectrum of conspiracies. By mapping out these configurations we are not led closer to the truth, but, in fact, round and round and round again with everyone seemingly implicated (Figure 5.5 p. 205). Everywhere one turns in conspiracy theory, the same set of factors seem to reproduce themselves: the FBI, Johnson, the CIA, anti-Castro Cubans, the Mafia, and the communists with Nixon found off to the edges popping up unexpectedly here and there.

While no one has come up with an explanation of a plot involving all of these elements, it does make it all the more difficult to dismiss the idea of some conspiracy. Given the apparent contradictions, the usual approach to the situation has been to do more detective work. It is human to feel that, if we gather more data, one day the controversy will be resolved. Is it possible that this attitude constitutes a bias, an unwarranted preconception, and an assumption that everyone seems to share — but that just might be false?

---

31. *Ibid.* Ruth Paine, Marina Oswald's friend wrote to her on Dec 27, 1963: "You closed your face to me. Is true, have I offended you? (North, Mark *Act of Treason* New York: Carroll & Graf, 1991, p. 492.) Again on Dec 28, 1963, Paine writes "They say that it is your choice to speak with someone or not to speak . . . But I do not believe this, while I have not heard it from your lips," (*Ibid.*). Marina was questioned over 48 times by the FBI; testified on Dec 26, 1963, and was under constant FBI "protection" during this time. Secret Service agents were guarding her at the direct order of President Johnson," (Ibid.).

32. North, *ibid.*, p. 357.
33. *Ibid.*, p. 350.
34. *Ibid.*, p. 505.
35. *Ibid.*, p. 56.

The disconcerting fact is that conspiracy theory has led us to at least one discovery: that the more we study the Kennedy assassination, the more documents are released, and the more individuals who come forward . . . *the less certain we become.*

YET-TO-BE-DEVELOPED CONSPIRACY SCENARIOS

While most researchers feel this matter is winding down, and, any day now, final certainty will be achieved, there is just as much reason to believe the opposite will occur. With the Kennedy assassination, the more we discover, the less we know. In fact, new twists, revelations, indeed whole new conspiracies seem just waiting in the wings to be born,

Suzy Chang and Maria Novotny

One new theory could be embedded in the Profumo affair. In 1963, the War Minister of Britain, John Profumo, was embroiled in a sex scandal with Christine Keeler, a call girl who also happened to be consorting with a Soviet spy; she was under the wing of one Stephen Ward, who had a penchant for introducing powerful men to attractive women. Profumo was forced to resign.

On June 28, 1963, the *New York Journal-American* said, "One of the biggest names in American politics — a man who holds 'a very high' elective office — has been injected into Britain's vice-security scandal."[36] John Kennedy was involved with two call girls in Stephen Ward's coterie, Suzy Chang and Maria Novotny. Chang, 28, was seen with him several times at New York's "21" club. Maria Novotny, a striptease dancer in English nightclubs, moved to New York with Harry Alan Towers and ran an international brothel. She returned to England and was questioned by Scotland Yard in connection with the Profumo case; she testified she had been with Kennedy in 1960 at a New York hotel. Her second encounter with Kennedy occurred with two other prostitutes on West 55th St. Harry Towers turned out to be a Soviet agent. When Novotny returned to England and testified, Towers fled "and reportedly emigrated to Czechoslovakia."[37]

(In late 1994, the Kennedy Library released tapes that the President made of conversations in the oval office and on the Presidential phone. JFK could press a button and record a call, if he chose. He did not record all phone conversations, only about 12 hours in toto. One call recorded was from Arthur Schlesinger, his historian, who spoke to him about the Profumo scandal. Schlesinger was not aware he was

---

36. Heymann, C. David. *A Woman Named Jackie.* New York: Carol Communications, 1989, p. 373.
37. Ibid.

being recorded, nor did he have any idea why FJK would have such an avid interest in the Profumo case.[38])

Suzy Chang, Maria Novotny, Harry Tower's connections to Soviet intelligence, and the compromising of the President of the United States are certainly not inconsequential when it comes to plots, counterplots, and international intrigue. Indeed, the FBI sought to question Kennedy about these interludes, but he was assassinated first.[39]

One might put quite a spin on the Soviet-Profumo-JFK trysts and turn it into a full-fledged conspiracy theory. It is a scandal just waiting to be exploited. There may be dozens more. As it stands, at the time of this writing, it is an almost irrelevant piece of trivia, nothing more than a footnote in the present compendium of literature on the subject.

Mary Pinchot Meyer and the CIA

Another theory could be woven around Kennedy's last lover. Imagine the following storyboard for a yet-to-be-shot Hollywood film:

> An American socialite, blond, intelligent, risk-taking, is married to a senior CIA official in Washington. After divorcing him, she takes up with the President of the United States and secretly enters the White House two to three times per week when the First Lady is away. She introduces the President to marijuana and hashish, perhaps even LSD, in her torrid afternoon escapades. Her roommate, also a former mistress of the President, is involved as well. The affair lasts until the week the President is assassinated. Eleven months later, the blond CIA-divorcee is murdered. Her killer remains at large. Her diary details her affair with the President and a senior CIA Director becomes privy to the documents. He destroys the diary, and keeps these secrets to himself for well over two decades.

It sounds like a preposterous tale from the *National Enquirer*, but the scenario happened. Mary Pinchot Meyer was a Vassar graduate, blond, vivacious, outgoing,

---

38. William Safire, "Kennedy Set Historic Precedent," *NY Times News Service*, December 27, 1994.

39. *Ibid.* See also Mike Feinsilber, "Former editor of Post recalls life at the top, *San Jose Mercury News*, September 21, 1995, p. 4A. Source: Ben Bradlee *Ben Bradlee. A Good Life.* New York: Simon & Schuster, 1995, pp 266-271. Few have speculated about why Mary Meyer was murdered. A black laborer was originally arrested for the murder, but acquitted. Only one JFK conspiracist, Robert Morrow, held out the theory that Mary Meyer was ready to turn over to an inquiring Bobby Kennedy important documents from her former husband, Cord Meyer, a high ranking CIA officer, about the assassination and that that is why she was murdered. Morrow, however, has been considered reckless in his speculations, certainly by this author and by others as well.

and a friend of Jackie Kennedy. She was married to a career CIA officer, Cord Meyer, and divorced in 1959.

Pamela Turnure, Mrs. Kennedy's press secretary, had an ongoing White House tryst with Kennedy. She moved into Mary Meyer's Washington apartment after her former landlady photographed the President leaving Turnure's apartment late at night. (The landlady, distraught by what she had found out about President Kennedy and Ms. Turnure, *picketed the White House* and distributed the photo, but no one ever took her seriously.)

In 1963, Kennedy took up with Turnure's roommate, Mary Meyer. She met Kennedy between twenty and thirty times at the White House, her art studio, and in the homes of friends. After his assassination, Mary Meyer was found shot to death in Georgetown (October 12, 1964), not far from her studio.

Her diary was discovered by the wife of *Washington Post* publisher Ben Bradlee. The Bradlees brought it to the attention of CIA official James Angleton. Angleton admitted his complicity in the destruction of her diary:

> In my opinion there was nothing to be gained by keeping it around. . . . I acted as a private citizen and a friend of the deceased. They [the Meyers] had two sons, and that was one consideration. It was in no way meant to protect Kennedy. I had little sympathy for the President.[40]

One wonders, of course, what the reactions might have been if the Warren Commission report had published even a speck of this information at the time.

In 1995, Ben Bradlee published his memoirs, corroborating firsthand most of what has been said. His version of the story is excerpted as follows:

> She was walking along the towpath by the canal. . . when she was grabbed from behind, wrestled to the ground, and shot just once under the cheekbone as she struggled to get free. She died instantly. . . Next, the police told us, someone would have to identify Mary's body in the morgue. . . I drew that straw too. . . Two telephone calls that night from overseas added new dimensions to Mary's death. The first came from President Kennedy's press secretary, Pierre Salinger, in Paris. . . The second from Anne Truitt. . . She had been Mary's closest friend. She told us that Mary had asked her to take possession of a private diary, "if anything ever happened to me." Anne asked if we had found any such diary, and we told her we hadn't looked for anything, much less a diary. We didn't start looking until the next morning. . . when Tony and I walked around the corner a few blocks to Mary's house. It was locked, as we had expected, but when we got inside, we found Jim Angleton, and to our complete surprise he told us he, too, was looking for Mary's diary.

---

40. *Ibid.*, p. 376.

Chapter 5. Paradox

Now, James Jesus Angleton was a lot of things, including an extremely controversial, high-ranking CIA official specializing in counterintelligence, but he was also a friend of ours, and the husband of Mary Meyer's close friend Cicely Angleton. We asked him how he'd gotten into the house, and he shuffled his feet. (Later we learned that one of Jim's names was "The Locksmith," and that he was known as a man who could pick his way into any house in town.) We felt his presence was odd, to say the least, but took him at his word and with him, we searched Mary's house thoroughly. Without success.

We found no diary. Later that day, we realized that we hadn't looked for the diary in Mary's studio, which was directly across a dead-end driveway from the garden behind our house. We had no key, but I got a few tools to remove the simple padlock, and we walked toward the studio, only to run into Jim Angleton again, this time actually in the process of picking the padlock.

... It is important to say that I never for a minute considered reporting that it had been learned that the slain president had in fact had a lover, who had herself been murdered. . . Never mind the fact that the CIA's most controversial counterintelligence specialist had been caught in the act of breaking and entering, and looking for her diary. Mary Meyer's murder was news, not her past love affair, I thought then. . . I was extremely uncomfortable when the story of the Kennedy-Meyer affair became public years later. . . The story said that Mary and Jack had met twenty to thirty times in the White House during their romance from January 1962 to November 1963; that they had smoked grass (three joints) on one occasion . . . (and) that Mary had kept a diary of the whole affair.[41]

This incident is at best considered minor, irrelevant, a mere footnote to the whole story. Gerald Posner dismisses Mary Meyer's death in a single sentence. Yet, in itself, it bears the imprint of a full-fledged CIA conspiracy.

It is another illustration of the Kennedy assassination as a riddle that can iterate an infinite array of new edges and interpretations. If researchers of the assassination seem to think they see signs and portents leading in any number of directions, it is not necessarily the case that obsessive researchers just cannot let go; it is a quality that *is inherent in the tale itself*, not in the observer.

Mary Meyer did exist; the only questionable assertion in this whole litany is whether she and Kennedy smoked hashish in the White House. Perhaps her diary could corroborate that, but it is gone; from Ben Bradlee's long withheld revelations, it all happened as stated.

A black laborer was apprehended at the scene of her murder, but was acquitted of all charges; her murder remains unsolved.

Mr. Angleton was no small fish in this drama, either. He admitted taking her diary, and Mrs. Ben Bradlee said she not only saw the diary but also surrendered it to Angleton. But Angleton was not merely a family friend. He was a very senior CIA

---

41. Ben Bradlee. *Ben Bradlee: A Good Life*. New York: Simon & Schuster, 1995, pp 266-271.

Counterintelligence Director. He was the officer in charge of investigating KGB defector, Yuri Nosenko. At his level, he would have known far more about the assassination than was ever revealed.

Angleton connects to many segments of this mystery, to the KGB, to Oswald, to Nosenko, to Mary Meyer, to Oswald's Mexico City visit, to the destruction of documents in Mexico City, to CIA intrigues with anti-Castro Cubans, and to assassination plots against Castro. Yet, other than Oswald, none of these names even appears in the index of the Warren Report. Angleton was not merely a family friend of the Bradlees!

The *National Enquirer* broke the story of the Mary Meyer-JFK liaison in the late 1970s. Who would believe that source? But there were people who knew these truths. There were Congressional and Senate hearings at this time, too. Where was Ben Bradlee or James Angleton during this time? Bradlee was a major player in the forced resignation of Richard Nixon during Watergate. His reporters, Woodward and Bernstein, virtually brought down the President; but when it came to matters that might disturb memories of JFK, there was only a deadening silence. There were no wild voices accusing the CIA of complicity in the murder of Mary Meyer or its cover up, and few credible voices breaking the news to the public that their fallen President might not have been quite what they thought.

Ben Bradlee finally 'fessed up in a very circumscribed revelation in 1995 in his memoirs. In an interview given shortly after these memoirs were published, Bradlee says:

> I am appalled by the details that have emerged, appalled by the recklessness, by the subterfuge that must have been involved, [he writes. He says he was shocked to discover that one of Kennedy's affairs was with Bradlee's own sister-in-law.]
>
> "If the American public had learned — no matter how the public learned it — that the President of the United States shared a girlfriend, in the biblical sense, with a top American gangster, and Lord knows who else, I am convinced he would have been impeached... That just seems unforgivably reckless behavior." [42]

Bradlee was profiled by *Vanity Fair* in 1995, and it is remarkable how few seem to hold him in contempt for his silence. His indignation over Kennedy's behavior and shock at discovering Kennedy's affair with his sister-in-law were not new in 1995. Bradlee knew of the affair in 1964 and in fact was privy to the diary found in Meyer's

---

42. *Ibid.*, p. 376.

apartment after her murder. It was Bradlee himself who caught James Angleton breaking into her apartment, and her art studio, in 1964

Bradlee's sense of shock and outrage do not seem to surface in his books on Kennedy which appeared a decade later, either.

Modern-Day Conspiracy: James E. Files

A final and more recent theory appeared around the allegations of James E. Files. In the early 1990s, attention was drawn to an inmate in an Illinois penitentiary who is listed as one of the 28 putative assassins in Dealey Plaza cited earlier in this chapter. Files was a former U.S. soldier who fell under the influence of the Chicago Mob, and became Chuckie Nicoletti's most loyal soldier. Files says that he was the grassy knoll gunman, that he fired the fatal shot and hit the President above the right eye. He was paid $36,000 for the hit and was accompanied by Johnny Roselli and Nicoletti, who were in the Dal-Tex building.

I found Files' story of interest, and decided to try to interview him. I queried Files from 1996 until 2001. One of the most compelling reasons I found Files interesting was his ignorance of the literature on the assassination. When asked if he had ever read *High Treason*, he said "someone sent it to me and I could not get into it." As for *Mortal Error, Six Seconds in Dallas, Mafia Kingfish* or *The Plot to Kill the President*, his answers were all "No."

Files says that the Mafia and CIA killed JFK. Files worked as a hit man for Chuckie Nicoletti, himself a hit man for Sam Giancana. Giancana and Marcello hatched the plot, but the main figure in the assassination was Tony Accardo (rarely mentioned in conspiracy literature). Accardo gave the go-ahead for the hit. Nicoletti and Johnny Roselli were in the Dal-Tex Building and hit the President from behind. Files, the grassy knoll gunman, was instructed to hit JFK from the front, only if Nicoletti missed. Since he wasn't sure if the neck wound was fatal, Files fired his Remington with a frangible bullet, hitting Kennedy in the front. Files says the CIA tried to call off the assassination and a CIA pilot named Robert "Tosh" Plumlee brought Roselli in from Miami. Final orders to quash the assassination had to come from Tony Accardo, not the CIA, however; and Accardo did not cancel it.

Three Interviews with Inmate N-14006

Excerpts from three interviews follow, with the author's comments to assist the reader in understanding why such questions were asked. Files' spelling and grammar are unedited.

Q. Do you know what caliber of weapons they used?

A. "Nicoletti used only one rifle, 7.62 or 30.06, which is basically the same caliber. The 7.62 is the military round. The other is what hunters use."

Q. You said you worked for Chuckie Nicoletti. Now, he worked for Sam Giancana, I thought, but most researchers say this hit originated with Carlos Marcello. Was Nicoletti working for Giancana or Marcello or were they together on this?

A. "Yes, I worked for Nicoletti, he was my street boss. Nicoletti worked for Sam Giancana, Sam Giancana took his orders from Tony Accardo. I don't give a shit what all of your so-called crime specialist say, but Tony Accardo still gave the orders and no one shit without his permission and that is a fact. When Sam's daughter, Antoinette, tried to tell me that it was her father who gave all the orders and called the shots I told her that she was wrong and her new husband, the old Mob lawyer [Robert McDonald] was with her and he also told that I was right.

I asked him about a number of figures mentioned in assassination literature and asked that he comment on them.

Eugene Hale Brading

"Yes, E.H.B. was the one that got Chuck & Johnny inside the Dal-Tex Building."

Brading was arrested on the day of the assassination in the Dal-Tex building and gave a false name to the Dallas police. His true identity was not known for many years.

Richard Cain

"Yes, I knew Richard Cain, very very well and his death has nothing to do with the JFK Assassination. He tried to out grow him-self and he said the wrong thing about Sam."

Nofio Pecora

"Yes, I knew who he was, but I only met him on two occasions and only said hello and shook hands. I was with someone else who had business with him. Both times were in New Orleans. I never cared for dope dealers."

I never mentioned to Mr. Files why I was interested in his comments on Pecora or where I got that name. Pecora is mentioned in assassination literature as a man who knew Jack Ruby, but more importantly, a person present at Lee Oswald's bail hearing in New Orleans. It is quite possible Mr. Files knows nothing about Oswald's bail hearing or Pecora's relationship to him. Conversely, assassination literature generally does not mention Pecora's drug dealing.

Dutz Murret

"Never met him, but knew who he was and he too worked for Carlos."

Dutz Murret was Oswald's uncle — a fact probably unknown to Files. Murret was described by the Warren Commission as not in any way connected to organized crime, but subsequent research showed connections to Carlos Marcello. Files obviously corroborates that allegation.

Joseph CampisI

"Joseph had his thing in Dallas and was with another guy called Civello."

Again, no mention was made why this name was submitted to Files. Campisi was a Dallas mobster and was the first person to visit Ruby in his Dallas jail cell after he killed Oswald.

Q. Did you ever meet Jack Ruby?
A. No, I never met Jack Ruby. But that morning I drove Roselli to meet with him. I was with-in 2 feet of him, but he never knew that I was there with Roselli.

Q. Did you ever meet David Ferrie and who do you think hit him?
A. YES! But due to the fact that there is no statue of limitation on murder, I cannot give you that name, as he is still alive.

Mainstream writers believe Ferrie committed suicide after Jim Garrison indicted him, but conspiracy writers believe he was hit, along with his associate. Files' statement that he knows who killed Ferrie is unprecedented.

Q. Who killed Officer Tippit — or was it Oswald, after all?
A. Oswald did not kill Officer Tippit, nor did he kill anyone at all. I will try to make a copy of the paraffin test that was givin to Oswald and send it along with this if possible.

Files sent a copy of a paraffin test of Oswald showing nothing on his right cheek but some evidence that he had fired a revolver.

In earlier correspondence, I asked him if anyone knew the whole story. His reply then was,

> Yes, I would say about 85% of it. Plus, once I'm free, I agreed to give Vernon solid proof. I have papers from that era, that will prove all I have said. But those papers are with a lot of other papers and I'm not about to send some one to get one or two items out of the box, for they may read and take other very important papers, that could hurt a lot of people. I won't even let my lawyer go get them.

From these comments, it seems that Files has a motive for coming forward with his allegations and appears to intend to reveal all of what he knows only after he is released.

I asked Files some follow-up questions, two of which were intended to see if there were inconsistencies in his story. For example, in the book entitled *Mortal Error*, analysis of JFK's skull shows a bullet hole that is 6 millimeters by 15 millimeters. Oswald's bullet was 6.5 millimeters, and thus the hole is too small to have come from that bullet. The author also said that the entrance wound (extrapolated backward) showed it could not have come from Oswald's rifle above the President but had to have come from close to ground level and from directly behind the President. The author even suspected that a secret service agent "accidentally" shot the President from that location. In reviewing this information, however, we discover that the Dal-Tex building where Nicoletti and Roselli were allegedly shooting is consistent with the skull wound. However, Files said Nicoletti fired even larger caliber weapons. I wanted to see how Files dealt with this inconsistency. Thus the following question:

Q. You said Nicoletti used a 7.62 rifle, so I assume the cartridge was at least 7.62 in diameter?
A: YES!

Obviously, the diameter of the shell is larger than the measured wound in JFK's skull, so we have the same problem of veracity as with Oswald; with Oswald's gun or Nicoletti's, the shell is much larger than the skull entry wound.

Q. Nicoletti's shot hit Kennedy in the throat, correct?
A: FROM THE BACK — SHOULDER, NECK & HEAD
[Files' emphasis.]

Q. Who hit Governor Connally, and was that intentional, an accident, or what?
A. ACCIDENT

Chapter 5. Paradox

In another attempt to catch Files in an inconsistency, I asked:

Q. One writer says you can't open the windows of the Dal-Tex Building; how did Nicoletti manager to hit JFK without opening a window?

A. I do not know, I was never in the Daltex building. You would have to ask Eugene Brading that question, as he was the one who got them inside the Daltex building.

I never mentioned that Brading was arrested under an alias in the Dal-Tex building; so Files' volunteering this information comes from the fact that either he is quite a bit more familiar with assassination literature than he lets on, or that he is in fact telling the truth.

Later, I asked him if he knew a few other people:

Q. Barney Barker
A. ??
Q. Morgan Brown
A. ??
Q. Clay Shaw
A. ??

Barney Barker was an associate and bodyguard of Jimmy Hoffa; Clay Shaw was indicted for the conspiracy to kill JFK by Jim Garrison in New Orleans; and Morgan Brown was the individual with whom Eugene Hale Brading was staying in Dallas — he left, right after the assassination. If Files were a fraud and were familiar with conspiracy literature, he would likely have a comment to make about Morgan Brown. The fact that he doesn't have anything to say adds to his credibility — in this author's view. He clearly is not familiar with much that is written about the assassination and yet his answers have an uncanny consistency.

Q. Do you know who E. Howard Hunt is, and did he have anything to do with it?
A: (YES)

Again, I never mentioned Hunt to Files, that he was alleged to have been the CIA station chief in Mexico City at the time Oswald visited Mexico, or that some conspiracy researchers say Hunt was one of the tramps arrested in Dealey Plaza. Again, either Files is far more aware of conspiracy literature than he lets on or is in fact telling the truth.

I decided to follow up this question a year later.

Q. You said E. Howard Hunt had something to do with it. What?
A. This one I won't answer.

Hunt is still alive. Files has said in the past he won't speak about anyone who is still living, so this indictment of Hunt stands and continues in its mystery.

Q. Who set up Oswald to be the patsy? Who got him his job at the Depository? Who put the rifle up there in the sixth floor window? Why didn't Nicoletti use the same caliber weapon as Oswald was supposed to have used?
A. Who set Oswald up, I do not know. David Phillips got Oswald the Job. I selected the weapon for Nicoletti when I took everything to Dallas and at that time I had no idea Oswald even knew what was happening.

Most assassination literature seems to agree that Oswald got his job at the Depository through Ruth Paine, a friend of Marina Oswald. The fact that Files mentions David Phillips is peculiar. Phillips was a shadowy CIA figure associated with organized crime. His testimony at the HSCA was so inconsistent that the committee considered citing him for perjury. His name is not well known except among those who have studied the assassination in detail. Again, either Files is pulling esoteric names from conspiracy literature and putting them into a proper context or he is telling the truth.

A year later, I asked Files:

Q. You said that Lee Oswald had the same CIA controller as you. Who was that? If Oswald was CIA, why did he subscribe to so much communist literature, and why was he so broke? He never seemed to have any money in the bank or anywhere, ever.
A. (1.) David Phillips. (2) He had to play to the role he was ask to play. The reason for no money, the government don't pay very much.

Bonar Menninger, author of Mortal Error, suggests, based on autopsy findings, that both frangible and non-frangible bullets were used. Frangible bullets explode on impact, leaving numerous fragments, while non-frangible bullets pass through the victim almost unscratched. The bullet that hit JFK and was supposed to have hit Connally too was non-frangible, yet Menninger says that at least one frangible bullet hit JFK, leaving numerous fragments in his skull. Since Oswald did not use both types of bullets, that author argued that Oswald could not have killed Kennedy alone; at

Chapter 5. Paradox

least two different shooters were involved. With that background, and with Files apparently unaware of the Mortal Error book, I asked some final questions:

Q. Last question, I promise; you hit JFK over the right eye with a headshot, correct? So was that a "frangible" bullet that explodes on impact, or was it a heavy metal jacketed bullet, which would pass through him? Also, do you know anything more about the bullets themselves that you used. . . where they were purchased, Remington? brand?

A: Yes, headshot, over right eye, by temple. and yes, frangible, and Remington brand.

Menninger did not know of James Files when he wrote his book. But he concluded that JFK was hit with a Remington shell, which was frangible! However, he said that a non-frangible heavy metal jacketed bullet also hit Kennedy. Such a bullet would pass right through the tissues and not explode on impact. JFK seems to have been hit by at least one bullet that exploded (frangible) and another that went through him. . . likely the favored "pristine" bullet, that passed through Connally as well. So I asked Files the next follow up question:

Q. Were Nicoletti's bullets also frangible like yours?
A. No

Again, Files' comment, however laconic, is startling and consistent. In Files' story, a frangible and non-frangible bullet hit Kennedy, and only one author in all the conspiracy schools has made such an allegation: Bonar Menninger, in Mortal Error. It is highly unlikely Files has read Menninger's book and properly rehearsed his answers.

Later, I asked Files other questions about some Mafia deaths.

Q. Who do you think took Sam Giancana out?
A. I don't think I know. It was Johnny Roselli. Sam's daughter was here to visit me and ask me that and I also told her that it was Johnny. But she left here and told friends of mine he she thought that I took part in her father's death. She told them "maybe Jimmy didn't pull trigger, be I think he got them in the house." I had no part of that at all. [*spelling mistakes his*]

Strong Points of the Files Version

Files has at least some physical evidence to support his claims, namely a bullet casing.

- He always bit down on a bullet before he made a "hit." In the case of JFK, he said that a bullet casing should be found in a particular location with bite marks on it, and in the early 1980s such a casing was found and identified, where he said it would be. Files provides photostats of the bullet and expert testimony showing it had teeth marks in it.
- Autopsy evidence suggested both frangible and non-frangible bullets were used, and Files' account is one of the few "confessions" which reconcile this information.
- The wound inflicted on passerby James Tague, in Dealey Plaza, seems most likely to have been caused by a shot fired from the Dal-Tex Building rather than the Depository; a shooter in the Dal-Tex building helps to explain away this mystery. (The Warren Commission tried to explain the errant bullet by saying that it hit a branch and was deflected. However, such a branch was never identified and it always remained a conjecture. Files, probably unaware of James Tague or the bullet that missed, does offer an explanation which seems as good as, if not better than, the Warren Commission's attempts to make sense of this bullet's origin.
- The Mafia names (Nicoletti, Roselli, Giancana, Marcello, Pecora, Murret, Campisi) are all used appropriately, in context, and with a certain internal consistency. Files is obviously not drawing these names out of a hat, and the fact that he inserts Tony Accardo shows a deep familiarity with the organization.
- While Files shows a ignorance of assassination/conspiracy literature, he does list names that are indeed arcane, only known by highly well-read assassination buffs, and uses them appropriately and in context (David Phillips, E. Howard Hunt, Chuckie Nicoletti).

Weaker Points

Files' story has a few major inconsistencies:

- The size of the shells Nicoletti used were larger than Oswald's shells and larger than the hole found in Kennedy's skull, according to one conspiracy researcher. Either Files is providing false information or the measurement of the hole in JFK's skull was done in a shoddy manner and inaccurate (that is a possibility).
- The windows of the Dal-Tex building could not be opened (according to another Dallas-based researcher), so how Nicoletti's shot's were fired is a problem. These are the thoughts of one Kennedy researcher; however, the Altgens' photo of the motorcade (pictured at the beginning of Chapter 2), shows some windows apparently open.

- Files' motives may also be a problem. It is possible that he hopes that his testimony and promise of evidence might help him win early release; if that is the case, the testimony he currently provides to authors like myself (and many others) must be seen as suspect.
- We must also recognize that however persuasive Files allegations might be, there is almost no exculpatory evidence that could "acquit" Oswald. Almost all of the witnesses who might support Files' claims are dead: Giancana (murdered), Nicoletti (murdered), Roselli (murdered), E. Howard Hunt (silent), David Phillips (deceased), William Harvey (deceased), Tony Accardo (deceased). Without such testimony, fingerprints, the weapon used, etc., even if Files were telling the truth, few would believe him. . . unless, of course, he produces more evidence, which he claims he has, located in an undisclosed locker.

The Brothers Karamazov

The Dostoyevsky novel is not and never was a detective story. Who killed Fyodor Karamazov? Was it Dmitri, Alyosha, Ivan or someone else? The suspense of a murder mystery exists in *The Brothers Karamazov*, but to read this great work as a whodunnit will never reveal more than a superficial meaning. As Dostoyevsky said, "All were guilty and none were guilty."

The novel conveys a far deeper meaning than the mere solution of a murder. To illustrate this very important point, and purely for the sake of argument, let us be playful and pretend that the recent revelations of Frank Ragano, Jimmy Hoffa's attorney, were true, that Hoffa ordered the hit on Kennedy through Marcello and afterwards Rogano brought back Marcello's message to Hoffa: *"You owe me, you owe me big!"* While that remark is true, the rest is fictional.

With these revelations and confessions, would we have solved anything? Would we finally have finished with the Kennedy assassination and could we now move on to other things?

If Marcello hit JFK for Hoffa, what else might happen? Well, it took Bobby Kennedy years to put Hoffa away, but Nixon pardoned him and there were very strong rumors that Nixon accepted a hefty donation from the Teamsters (Hoffa's union) for his presidential campaign in return. Is it not time to appoint a special prosecutor to investigate Nixon's relationship to this whole affair, Republican campaign financing, influence peddling, and, while we're at it, to see what Nixon's Watergate burglars, Hunt, Sturgis and others were doing on November 22, 1963?

And if we agreed that Carlos Marcello killed Kennedy for Hoffa, there are a few other implications to tease out. For example, James Hosty, Hoover's FBI agent in New Orleans, was suspiciously adamant in saying Carlos Marcello was a tomato salesman. Do we not have to charge Hosty with obstruction of justice?

Special prosecutors would need to be appointed. Attention would shift to yet another President, Gerald Ford, who, in turn, pardoned Nixon of all crimes, sat on the Warren Commission, and served a major disinformation function. He perennially argued that Oswald alone killed JFK and that no conspiracy existed, past or present. Two Presidents indicted . . . more to come.

Prosecutorial tentacles would reach out to those involved in lying to Congress, withholding information from investigative committees, and obstruction of justice. New indictments would touch J. Edgar Hoover's accomplices, former CIA Directors, and perhaps James Angleton for breaking and entering. And George Burkley, the Navy Admiral who seems to have lost the President's brain, but still had the presence of mind to swear his staff to secrecy about the autopsy — well into their retirements. All of these could be served and indicted by our fantasized grand jury as well.

And why forgive the media its responsibilities? Dan Rather's rendition of the Zapruder film, in 1975, about the President being thrown violently "forward" would come under intense scrutiny, and instead of asking the questions Rather might finally be required to answer a few; so would the owners of the Zapruder film, the Luce family. And then there are untold murders to research and prosecute: over nine Mafia-related murders, a dozen questionable suicides, and the plane crash which took the life of Dorothy Hunt. There were other passengers aboard that aircraft, and prosecutions, indictments, and trials would extend ever outward.

Hale Boggs did not want to sign the Warren Commission report; he, like very few others of his time, spoke out courageously about Hoover bugging the phones of congressmen, and shortly thereafter his commercial plane crashed in Alaska, taking the lives of a quite a few others with him.

The prosecutions widen; hidden realities begin to be revealed. Ah, what a fantasy! But it is more than a fantasy, more than the childish wish of a naive believer in the American way. *It is an absolute absurdity.*

We have to stop and take a deep breath. To fall into a trance, a vindictive reverie of the impossible, is absurd, doomed, and futile. Just think how many of these potential conspirators have already died: Frank Sturgis, Lucien Sarti, J. Edgar Hoover, Richard Nixon, Sam Giancana, Carlos Marcello, Richard Cain, John Martino, Santos Trafficante, Regis Kennedy, William Pawley, Lyndon Johnson, Leo Moceri, General Cabell, William Harvey, Clay Shaw, H.L. Hunt, William Sullivan, David Ferrie, Guy Banister, Chuckie Nicoletti, Dave Yaras, James Milteer, Jack Ruby, Roscoe White, James Angleton, David Phillips, John Roselli, Jimmy Hoffa, and Lee Harvey Oswald. Most of our possible leading conspirators are dead. [43]

Even if there are any secondary or tertiary suspects left, witnesses are needed if we are to convict them — people who were there, who saw, who finally are encouraged to come forward and report, like Ben Bradlee, what they were

Chapter 5. Paradox

withholding for thirty years. So let us add into this stew 17 crucial witnesses whose testimony would be essential but who are also deceased: Robert Kennedy, Marilyn Monroe, Peter Lawford, Hale Boggs, Billy Sol Estes, John Paisley, Dorothy Hunt, John Connally, Joseph Kennedy, George de Mohrenschildt, Clare Boothe Luce, Clyde Tolson, Jose Aleman, General Walker, Earl Warren, Jacqueline Kennedy, Dorothy Kilgallen... even Jim Garrison. The mission to bring nefarious evildoers to justice is doomed. Most of those who are hypothetically responsible are dead, and most of the witnesses whose testimony would be crucial to convict them are dead as well.

That is part of the riddle. After 38 years of research and effort, both at concealing and at uncovering the truth, we are no closer to a solution now than we were in 1963.

Like the *Brothers Karamazov*, this mystery forces us to swim in a sea of paradox. The less we knew — back in 1963 — the more we sensed and believed intuitively that something fishy was happening and some conspiracy was afoot in the assassination of President Kennedy. The more we have come to know and learn of this conspiracy, the less able we are to find the truth, much less see justice done.

As in any analytical process, one has to begin with the known facts. Well, we have done our homework, but this is not a drama that will yield a convenient realistic solution. Chuck Giancana said that godfather Sam and the Syndicate did it. Lyndon Johnson's mistress says that on New Years Eve, a drunken LBJ told her the CIA and Big Oil did it. Charles Harrelson said he did it. Christian David said that Mob contract killer, Lucien Sarti, did it. James Files says he did it. Roscoe White posthumously said it was him after all. CIA chief David Phillips, on his deathbed, said it was "them"

---

43. The use of the terms conspirator and "potential conspirator" in this text should be perhaps defined. Clearly the individuals listed in prior chapters as "potential conspirators" could not all be guilty; rather, they are identified as the equivalent of "potential grand jury witnesses." Sufficient evidence exists to indicate these individuals had information about the events which was not fully released by the Warren Commission. Indeed, some of the information was never given to the Commission. Nixon, for example, was never queried extensively about his presence in Dallas and his "alleged" meeting with Hoover. Giancana's godson said that Sam told him that he had met Nixon in Dallas, but certainly Nixon never admitted to any such meeting. Thus, the evidence that Nixon met with some unsavory characters and was present in Dallas before the assassination is hearsay. To call Nixon a "conspirator" would be inappropriate, based merely on such evidence; but to call him a "potential conspirator" groups him with others who, like him, should be or should have been questioned under oath in order to clarify substantial questions about their conduct; and it is a way to referring to these individuals who indeed have been treated as conspirators in the conspiracy literature on the subject.

Nixon perhaps could have claimed that he was "libeled" by Giancana. This text does not seek to proliferate libel, but to point to the vast number of individuals who have been insufficiently questioned and investigated regarding the assassination. In each case, names are cited under the rubric "potential conspirators," because, in the mind of the present author, other authors have produced research which points to credible suspicions concerning these individuals' conduct and behavior — suspicions which a hypothetical grand jury would have a basis and a right to explore more thoroughly and systematically.

(rogue CIA agents). But gangster John Roselli, just before he died, said Castro did it. And before Thomas Eli Davis III was killed, he told his wife he knew who killed Kennedy.

Santos Trafficante, on his deathbed, said it was Carlos Marcello. John Martino, on his deathbed, confessed that he was the paymaster and that anti-Castro Cubans did it. Marita Lorenz swore under oath that Howard Hunt was the paymaster and Frank Sturgis did it. . . and then there is always Gerald Posner, who insists that Oswald and only Oswald did it.

Before you jump to any conclusion of your own, ending all this ambiguity and setting your mind at ease, let me introduce another revelation from 1994:

> We now have an FBI report revealing that, at 7:30 on the morning after the assassination, "A snub nose thirty eight caliber Smith and Wesson, serial number 893265, with the word 'England' on the cylinder was found. . . in a brown paper sack in the general area of where the assassination took place." So a revolver was found near the Book Depository — "in the immediate vicinity," according to other FBI reports. In spite of repeated Freedom of Information requests by California researcher Bill Adams, the FBI has not revealed how its investigation of the gun was concluded. Whether or not the weapon has any significance, it is a scandal that the public had to wait 30 years to learn that a second gun was found at the scene of the crime. [44]

The Kennedy assassination refuses to be closed and defies any efforts at resolution. It will not allow certainty regarding anything. We need to recognize that this as an ouroboros eating its own tail, leaving us exactly where we started.

Before that, however, there is another way to look at this, and that is to consider in depth the psychological profiles of the main characters in this drama. Dark secrets relating to this historical event are held not only in the heavily redacted CIA documents sealed away from the prying public, but in the deeply twisted, secret personal lives of the major figures. Now, we will peer down those dark alleys to see what answers can be found.

---

44. Summers, Anthony & Robbyn, "The Ghosts of November, *Vanity Fair*, December, 1994, p. 100.

Chapter 6. Shadows and Secrets

I'm not done with a girl until I've had her three ways.
— John Fitzgerald Kennedy [45]

In this chapter we examine the psycho-biographies of the main characters. Here is a world of secrecy, liaisons, and psychosexual intrigue; it may hold more clues. No review of the assassination can dispense with this aspect of the drama (although many do), because here are some of the most poignant reminders of the deception, lies and cover-up that permeate the event, and signs that members of the family (and others) were in denial about what was going on, refusing to admit the truth or reality, even to themselves.

An important disclaimer needs to be made on our sources.

Camelot vs. Conspiracy Schools

Probably the greatest difficulty to surmount in teasing out the truths behind the Kennedy myth is the questionable literature one has to review. Books and articles on the Kennedys tend to be either paranoid and conspiratorial on the one hand or dripping with hero-worship and adoration on the other. Thomas Reeves, in *A Question of Character*, refers to the latter as the "Camelot School" of

---

45. Reeves, Thomas C. *A Question of Character: A Life of John F. Kennedy*. Rocklin CA: Prima Publishing, 1992, p. 242.

Kennedy scholarship. Consider, for example, how the Inauguration was handled by two Camelot writers, Kenneth O'Donnell and Dave Powers in *Johnny, We Hardly Knew Ye*, a book catapulted to the New York Times bestseller list for over five months.

On Inauguration eve, Frank Sinatra organized a fundraiser. The President attended for a short period of time.

> Then having to leave, he said "I suppose you'll be laughing it up here for another three hours after I go home and get into bed with my inaugural address." He hated to leave the party. I watched him go out of the room, stopping and looking back at us rather wistfully, as if he was reminding himself that this was the end of his last carefree night on the town, the last time that he would be able to enjoy himself in a public restaurant for years to come.[46]

At the Inauguration ball and later that evening, Kennedy sang songs with his father and then...

> The President thanked him and drove away smiling to spend his first night in the White house sleeping soundly in the Lincoln bedroom.[47]

Quite a different picture emerges when we leave the idolatry of Camelot official histories and begin to scratch the surface of alternative scholarship. The party given for Jack by Frank Sinatra was at the Statler-Hilton:

Jack slipped out of the presidential box and went upstairs to a private party given by Frank Sinatra... Angie Dickinson was there, along with actresses Janet Leigh and Kim Novak. When he returned to Jackie, he looked rather sheepish and carried a copy of the *Washington Post* under his arm, as if he had just stepped outside to buy a newspaper.[48]

Later, at the end of festivities on Inauguration Day,

> Jackie returned to the White House. Jack carried on alone, attending two more balls and a party at the Georgetown home of columnist Joe Alsop. There Kennedy enjoyed a brief sexual encounter with a beautiful young woman who wept as he left, fearful that her relationship with the president was finished forever. In this way, more like an irresponsible playboy than a mature and idealistic chief executive, Jack concluded his first day in office.[49]

---

46. O'Donnell, Kenneth and Powers, Dave. *Johnny, We Hardly Knew Ye*. New York: Pocket Book, 1972, p. 284.
47. Ibid., p. 287.
48. Reeves, *ibid.* p. 236
49. Ibid.

Chapter 6. Shadows and Secrets

Kennedy took Angie Dickinson as his lover sometime before the Inauguration.[50] J. Edgar Hoover monitored JFK's relationship to Dickinson and other dalliances including Marilyn Monroe and confronted Kennedy with this information in 1962.

The first author covers the inaugural period as if Kennedy wistfully longed for the days of his youth yet dutifully accepted his heroic responsibilities, ever mindful of the need to sacrifice personal friendships and the simple pleasures of dining in a public restaurant for the public good. O'Donnell mentions church and, of course, sleeping soundly in the Lincoln bedroom with the First Lady. Reeves, from quite a different perspective quotes amply from Peter Lawford:

Photo: Angie Dickinson at Inauguration with JFK

> I'm not going to talk about Jack and his broads... but... all I will say is that I was Frank's [Sinatra] pimp and Frank was Jack's. It sounds terrible now, but then it was a lot of fun.[51]

Which author can we believe? Jack invited Judith Campbell Exner, another Kennedy mistress, to sit next to his family on Inauguration Day. She published copies of her invitations and tickets. (Her mother attended in her place.)

Furthermore, Kenny O'Donnell recorded and monitored detailed logs of White House visits, including Exner's. O'Donnell and Powers would seem to have been privy to far more information about Kennedy's trysts than their "discrete" historical treatments ever had the courage to discuss. When asked if he knew about Judith Campbell Exner,

---

50. Anthony Summers, *Vanity Fair*, March 1993, p. 219.
51. Reeves, *ibid.* p. 202.

O'Donnell replied, "The only Campbell I know is chunky vegetable soup!"[52] Was he unwilling to confront the unpleasant reality? Or was he lying to cover it up?

C. David Heymann presented yet another description of the Inauguration gala:

> Before calling it quits, President Kennedy attended two more balls and a party at the home of Joe Alsop. The Alsop "do" was also the last stop for a half-dozen Hollywood starlets imported for the inauguration by Peter Lawford. According to Lawford, "All six wanted to be with the President. They arranged a lineup as they would at Madame Claude's brothel in Paris, and Jack chose two of them." This *ménage à trois* brought his first day in office to a resounding close. [53]

Thus, the Conspiracy School makes very bold claims, while the Camelot School completely denies it all. One text says Kennedy was alone with a woman, and another alleges that he finished the evening in a *ménage à trois*. Posner, in *Case Closed*, appears as a Warren Commission advocate and heavily criticizes the conspiracy schools for omissions and factual misstatements. Surprisingly, a more conspiracist writing in the 1990s, Harrison E. Livingstone, also accuses his conspiracy cohorts of manufacturing and spreading false information.[54]

When this author queried Janet Leigh about her relationship to JFK and that evening, she became livid at any suggestion of inappropriate behavior. She claimed to have been with her husband, Tony Curtis, and never alone with the President that evening. As Winston Churchill remarked, "History is something that never happened, written by someone who wasn't there."

Another clash between these extreme and divergent schools surrounds the March 22, 1962 meeting between Kennedy and Hoover. According to Kennedy's secretary, Evelyn Lincoln, J. Edgar Hoover had never spoken to the President on the phone and had not visited the White House since the Inauguration. However, on this date, he came for a very lengthy luncheon.

> The Kennedy Library says it has no record of what was said at the lunch. Nor does the FBI, even though Hoover normally wrote a memo following a visit to the White House. We do know the meeting went badly.[55]

Apparently, Hoover confronted Kennedy with his knowledge of the Giancana-Judith Exner connection. The only other person present in the room was Kenneth

---

52. Collier, P. & Horowitz, D. *The Kennedys*. New York: Warner Books, 1984. p. 525.
53. Heymann, C. David. *A Woman Named Jackie*. New York: Carol Communications, 1989, p. 261.
54. See Livingstone's *Killing the Truth*, New York: Carroll & Graf, 1993, p. 372.
55. Summers, *ibid.* p. 219.

Chapter 6. Shadows and Secrets

O'Donnell. O'Donnell makes no reference to this event in his book. *In fact, Hoover is not even listed in his appendix.*

In Ted Sorensen's 900-page *Kennedy*, similarly perched on the *New York Times* bestseller list (1965), there are no references in the appendix to J. Edgar Hoover, Sam Giancana, or Judith Exner, but a *Newsday* review, cited on the dust jacket, proclaims boastfully: "Completely Personal. . . Completely Truthful!" [56]

Between the paranoia of the conspiracists and the sycophancy of the court historians of the Kennedy Library, one might think the chief propagandists from *Pravda* and *Izvestia* had taken over *Newsday* and the *New York Times* and patronizingly fed the public a sanitized, inaccurate version of their own past (for various reasons), while a form of *samizdat*, the radical or underground presses, offer a venue for those whose sense of government persecution leads them to depict American history through the lens of its own paranoia.

Criticism is often leveled at the decorous mainstream treatments, but conspiracy authors too have notable difficulties with respect to credibility. A book authored by Sam Giancana and Chuck Giancana is a prime example. It offers a tantalizing historical treatment replete with made-up dialogue and cleverly suspenseful writing. The book claims that Sam Giancana masterminded the murder of Marilyn Monroe, Jack Kennedy, Bobby Kennedy and Jimmy Hoffa, plus countless others — and met with his co-conspirators Richard Nixon and Lyndon Johnson in Dallas, to boot. The braggadocio of the work is awe-inspiring, and yet it is persuasive, since many of the names which pop up in conspiracy literature are appropriately linked. In other words, there is a remarkable internal consistency in this book, which suggests that either the authors are telling the truth, firsthand, or they have mastered the conspiracy literature so well that they are able to piece together a suspenseful "fiction" which is nothing more than a skillful fabrication.

The *New York Daily News* said the book contains "amazing and shocking disclosures." Might there be some secret agenda? If Sam Giancana was shot around the mouth after he talked to the Senate Intelligence Committee, would his relative so easily talk to Warner Books? Maybe Giancana's relatives are not bound by the same oath of silence; or, maybe, they are masterfully generating disinformation. Even if we assume this was simply a venal effort to sell books, then we must assume these and many other conspiracy texts are wantonly flawed.

Judith Campbell Exner's 1977 *My Story*, now virtually unobtainable, opened a door that had been closed for fifteen years. After this work, people started to come forward with ever more damaging revelations about the President. The book was a turning point. And yet, in a subsequent variation, in *Parade*, where even more

---

56. Sorenson, Theodore C. *Kennedy*. New York: Harper & Row, 1965.

revelations were made, Exner joined with author and interviewer Kitty Kelly, and split a $100,000 royalty check. Kitty Kelly, author of *Jackie Oh!*, does not enjoy a reputation for reportorial accuracy.

She alleged, for example, that Jackie Kennedy entered a private psychiatric facility in Carlisle, Massachusetts for electroshock therapy; but the doors of the facility closed in 1977, and the source of her rumor was "the anonymous wife of an anonymous anesthesiologist who worked only weekends."[57] Wherever we turn, the truth, both historical and psychological, seems to slip through our fingers. Bearing that in mind, we will consider the psychology of the main protagonists.

J. Edgar Hoover's Homosexuality and Paranoia

Hoover is one of the major players, and his background is central to the story. He became director of the FBI in 1924 and continued to head that fiefdom until his death in 1972. He spanned half the American 20th century and was not only directly involved in investigating the Kennedy assassination of 1963, but also the Lindbergh kidnapping thirty years earlier. He is a main character in the Kennedy story and the myth.

Hoover was hidden, inaccessible, a mysterious paranoiac — a voyeur, it would seem, who lived in a very dark cavity of the American experience. Marilyn Monroe once shook his hand and cringed. She said it was like touching a living cadaver, a zombie.

Hoover was idolized and worshipped by a small but vocal minority of right-wing Americans, who viewed him as a man of courage and decency, a freedom loving, loyal, "true" American.

But a far different picture of J. Edgar Hoover emerged after his death. Hoover never voted; he failed to demonstrate even that minimal interest in democracy. Moreover, he was an active homosexual. Hoover's sexual orientation was a state secret his entire life.

In 1938, Hoover took up with Clyde Tolson, and the two enjoyed a lifelong association until Tolson's death. Tolson was a high official in the FBI, lived near Hoover, ate lunch with him practically every day, and probably also knew the vast spectrum of secrets Hoover kept in his personal files on most major American public officials during those fifty years. Hoover and Tolson were described in the media as "inveterate bachelors." Remarkable as it may seem today, the idea that they might be

---

57. Heymann, *ibid.* p. 196.

"homosexuals" never seemed to dawn upon anyone in the media nor the public, although Washington insiders must have had their suspicions.

In 1946, Hoover saw a psychiatrist about his homosexuality. Dr. William Clark later referred him to Dr. Marshall de G. Ruffin. Mrs. Ruffin said that Hoover was fearful about being discovered and did not see the psychiatrist for a long while, but as late as 1971 returned for treatment.[58]

Hoover's homosexuality was common knowledge in the underworld, however; Frank Costello, Meyer Lansky, Jimmy "the Weasel" Fratianno, Frank Bompensiero and Carlos Marcello all knew. Hoover was arrested in the 1920s on a homosexuality charge, and John Roselli, the West Coast representative of the Mob, learned of it. According to Meyer Lansky's widow, Lansky obtained "hard proof of Hoover's homosexuality and used it to neutralize the FBI as a threat to his own operations."[59] Lansky possessed photographs of Hoover having oral sex with Clyde Tolson. When Bugsy Siegel was murdered under Meyer Lansky's orders in 1947, nothing came of it. Lansky was not indicted until shortly before Hoover's death, and then the indictment was at the behest of the IRS, not the FBI. Hoover and the Mafia had a tacit understanding.

Anthony Summer's research indicates that CIA counterintelligence chief James Angleton also had a photograph. Summer's source says,

> What I saw was a picture of him giving Clyde Tolson a blow job. . . There was more than one shot, but the startling one was a close shot of Hoover's head. He was totally recognizable . . . Angleton told me the photographs had been taken around 1946.[60]

Others identify Roy Cohn as a homosexual partner and friend of J. Edgar Hoover. Cohn was the lead counsel for Senator Joe McCarthy's notorious persecution of the media and the "communist menace" in the 1950s. Cohn, described by many as a sleazy opportunist, died of AIDS; he used to arrange homosexual trysts for Hoover. One of Summer's informants reports that one evening at the Plaza Hotel in New York, Hoover was in Roy Cohn's apartment:

> Hoover was dressed up as a woman, in full drag. He was wearing a fluffy black dress, very fluffy, with flounces, and lace stockings and high heels, and a black curly wig. He had makeup on, and false eyelashes. It was a very short skirt, and he was sitting there in the living room of the suite with his legs crossed. Roy

---

58. Summers, *ibid.* p. 212.
59. *Ibid.* p. 213.
60. *Ibid.*

introduced him to me as "Mary," and he replied, "Good evening," brusque, like the first time I'd met him. It was obvious he wasn't a woman; you could see where he shaved. It was Hoover. You've never seen anything like it. I couldn't believe it, that I should see the head of the FBI dressed as a woman. [61]

That same evening Hoover was joined by two boys, one of whom read from the book of Leviticus while the other manipulated his genitals.

In the early- and mid-1960s, Hoover began to show definite signs of emotional instability:

> Kennedy's administrative assistant was harangued first about the way a leading newspaper was supposedly infiltrated by Communists, then about Adlai Stevens' alleged homosexuality. Hoover subjected first Robert, then the President, to a long briefing on the alleged homosexuality of Joseph Alsop, the distinguished journalist. . . It was all bizarre to the Kennedys. For the first time, perhaps, men in power dared voice the notion that Hoover was not entirely sane. "He was out of it today, wasn't he?" Robert murmured to Seigenthaler when he emerged from Hoover's lecture about Communists and pederasts. . . "He acts in such a strange, peculiar way," Robert Kennedy was to say in 1964, on an embargoed basis in an interview intended for use by future historians. "He's rather a psycho. I think its a very dangerous organization. . . and I think he's. . . become senile and rather. . . frightening."[62]

Apparently ignorant of his brother's relationship with Judith Exner and Sam Giancana, Robert Kennedy plowed full speed ahead in his campaign against organized crime, selecting Carlos Marcello, Santo Trafficante, Sam Giancana, and Jimmy Hoffa as his prime targets. The relationship of Hoover to RFK, the Mob, and both President Kennedy and his father's alliances with the underworld is very poorly understood, but Hoover's emotional instability as an outgrowth of Robert Kennedy's anti-Mob crusade is even less understood.

As Bobby's impressive prosecution record against the Mob grew, Hoover obviously became more vulnerable to disclosure.

> On the evening of July 12, 1961, Giancana, accompanied by his mistress Phyllis McGuire, walked into a waiting room at Chicago's O'Hare Airport during a routine stopover on their way to New York. Waiting for him were a phalanx of FBI agents, including Bill Roemer, one of the mobster's most dogged pursuers. Giancana lost his temper. He knew, he told the agents, that everything he said would get back to J. Edgar Hoover. Then he burst out, "Fuck J. Edgar Hoover! Fuck your superboss, and your super-superboss! You know who I mean: I mean

---

61. *Ibid.* p. 215.
62. *Ibid.* p. 218.

Chapter 6. Shadows and Secrets

the Kennedys!" Giancana piled abuse on both brothers, then snarled, "Listen, Roemer, I know all about the Kennedys, and Phyllis knows more about the Kennedys, and one of these days we're going to tell all. Fuck you! One of these days it'll come out!"[63]

Many have speculated about the effect of JFK's amorous liaisons and the threat that they might be made public, but few have given much thought to J. Edgar Hoover's progressive mental decompensation as a result of Bobby's campaign against organized crime. Also, Clyde Tolson, Hoover's long-time companion, suffered serious health problems in 1962, further increasing Hoover's stress.

One author who reviewed FBI wiretaps (cited in prior chapters) says Hoover knew about the Mob contract on Kennedy and did nothing to stop it — not merely because he hated the Kennedys, but because he was afraid Kennedy's vendetta against the Mob might expose his homosexuality.

J. Edgar Hoover and lifetime partner Clyde Tolson, circa 1938.

---

63. *Ibid.* p. 218

The first character on stage in our drama, therefore, is quite different from the public persona that existed in American consciousness in 1963. The official mask was of a J. Edgar Hoover, the titular head of the Boy Scouts of America, a man every American could trust, and a dedicated soldier in the eternal struggle against the powers of darkness and criminality. J. Edgar's "G men" would track down the ten most wanted and bring them before the bar of justice, of that all America could be sure.

The man who caught the dreaded kidnapper of the Lindbergh baby, the toughest cop in America, went by the name of "Mary." And Summers makes reference to another incident of Hoover in drag, in Washington, in 1948. The most powerful police official in the United States of America at the time of Kennedy's assassination was — deep inside his personality — a woman, mentally unstable, sexually dysfunctional, paranoid over the insidious menace of communists and "pederasts" in American society, racist,[64] and obsessively protective of the "image" of the Bureau... for obvious reasons.

Hoover bugged the homes of Kennedy, Marilyn Monroe, and scores of Mob figures and learned about the contract on the President. Neither the Attorney General, the Secret Service, nor any other agency was made privy to the Marcello, Trafficante, Giancana wiretaps that show a contract on the President to be imminent. To author Mark North, Hoover's treason was the most immediate cause of John Fitzgerald Kennedy's death.

Hoover was being pushed against a wall by Bobby Kennedy's vendetta against the Mob, which threatened exposure of Hoover's most fundamental secret; and Bobby had little way of knowing that his own behavior against the Mafia was, through Hoover, perhaps leading to his brother's demise.

---

64. While, in the prior 30 years, mention of Hoover's homosexuality was almost seditious, it is now reaching widespread currency and is the butt of jokes at the highest level of government. President Clinton, discussing the position of the head of the FBI, cracked that it would be "hard to fill J. Edgar Hoover's pumps." Even conservative Bob Dole of Kansas chimed in when complimenting UPI reporter Helen Thomas for her lovely new dress. Dole said that it was from "the new J. Edgar Hoover collection." *San Jose Mercury News*, April 6, 1993, p.2

In addition, Hoover appears to have been a racist. His persecution of Martin Luther King, Jr. and his disdain for the March on Washington are well known, but a recent trial of Thomas Blanton for a Birmingham, Alabama church bombing which killed four black children brings even more starting revelations. Blanton, successfully found guilty of the bombing (38 years later!), could have been prosecuted much earlier based on evidence held in FBI files but never released on orders from Hoover himself. See Kevin Sack, *New York Times*, cited in *San Francisco Chronicle*, May 4, 2001, p. D5. Over 9000 documents were sequestered by the FBI. According to one prosecutor, "If they had given us what they had, we could've tried Blanton 24 years ago." ("Conviction in 1963 church blast," *San Francisco Chronicle*, May 2, 2001, p. A11..)

Chapter 6. Shadows and Secrets

KENNEDY SILENCE AND SECRETS

Most Americans felt ineffable sympathy toward the 34-year-old widow, Jackie Kennedy, as her little son saluted the funeral procession carrying his father's body. That picture touched hearts around the world, and close to a million letters poured in to Mrs. Kennedy expressing regret, sympathy, and support. There was never any feeling that Mrs. Kennedy should be more forthright in telling the story and certainly no suspicion that the injured Kennedys were withholding substantial facts about this event.

Grieving widows, however, have often loudly protested that the government did not tell the whole story about their husbands' deaths, and demanded a full accounting of how they perished. When Henry Marshall, the agricultural agent who was killed investigating the suspicious dealings of Billy Sol Estes, was shot numerous times in the head and his death was ruled a suicide, Marshall's wife *howled* — year after year — until she finally succeeded in having her husband's body exhumed and the death declared a murder. Mrs. Kennedy took a different tack altogether.

It is also not unheard of for a son or daughter or brother to thunderously demand justice be served. Bobby Kennedy did not stand up, in the years after the assassination, demanding that the Warren Commission findings be challenged. (He privately indicated that he felt they should; but he did not express these feelings publicly.) Mrs. Kennedy did not demand a Presidential inquiry. Her daughter, Caroline, has not asked that the CIA or Mafia dimensions of this crime against her father be investigated but, instead, has asked that defamatory studies of her father stop. John Kennedy, Jr., the little boy who saluted the caisson, was elected to public office and rather than pursuing an agenda of justice for his father, said he had no interest in the various conspiracy theories and wished it would all stop. (Of course, conspiracists have many thoughts on his untimely demise, as well.) Senator Edward Kennedy has shown some interest or at least mild support for efforts to have the sealed Kennedy assassination documents made available to researchers, but beyond these efforts, his voice has been notably quiet during all these years.

Mrs. Kennedy exerted strong efforts to quash many publications about her husband. While some of this is understandable, much is not.[65] For example, the Kennedys hired William Manchester to write an accounting of the events, and upon finishing his work he was sued by Mrs. Kennedy to have certain sections deleted. The argument between Lyndon Johnson and Kennedy the night before the assassination, in which Johnson argued to have Senator Yarborough sit in the Presidential limousine rather than Johnson's friend, Governor Connally, was the point of contention. This passage was *successfully removed* from Manchester's book.

Manchester says that Jackie did that because Robert Kennedy (still alive at the time), may have been hurt politically by such disclosures. Be that as it may, the Kennedy family has not been a force to bring out the truth. Apparently, the family thinks it has more to gain by preventing disclosures than by uncovering the truth about the assassination.

SHADOWS OF THE FATHER

> Jack and Bob will run the show
> While Ted's in charge of hiding Joe. [66]

It is fair to assume that people who seek to prevent disclosure may have something to hide — family secrets, if you will; and there appear to be many levels of secrecy within the Kennedy family. Most Americans assume John Kennedy told Bobby everything, that Bobby confided in Ted, and that the boys confided in their father, Joe, especially when they needed help. Few speculate about whether there were secrets between the brothers and the father.

Is it possible that Jack Kennedy did not tell his brother about Judith Exner (and that no one else did, either)? Is it possible that Joe Kennedy did not tell Jack about his longstanding relationship to Sam Giancana? Is it possible that Jack did not know that his father paid the Mob to secure the West Virginia primary and the Illinois electoral vote; that *Joe acted behind his son's back to help him win?* Is it possible that Jack and his father shared a secret — which Bobby was not let in on — that the two had visited Sam Giancana in Chicago, made "arrangements" with him, and that crime-fighter-idealist Bobby did not need to be brought into to some of these stickier dealings? Is it possible that neither Jack nor Bobby knew of their father's relationships with gangsters Costello, Esposito, and Roselli? These are all seminal questions which have simply not been asked.

---

65. Jacqueline Kennedy, for her own reasons, and likely out of concern for her own privacy, nonetheless attempted to suppress much scholarship on Kennedy. In 1966, she pressured Paul B. Fay, Jr. into cutting 2000 words from his memoir, *The Pleasure of His Company*. She forced *Look* magazine to drop serialization of William Manchester's *Death of a President*. "Manchester likened his persecution by the Kennedys and their attorney and private detectives to an encounter with Nazis,"(Reeves, *ibid.*, p. 5). The Kennedys also attempted to stop publication of *White House Nannie* by Maude Shaw, Evelyn Lincoln's *My Twelve Years with John F. Kennedy*, and Jim Bishop's *The Day Kennedy was Shot*. "In a stunningly beautiful building at Columbia Point, constructed with private funds and given to the federal government in 1979, one can find little with which to challenge or even question the imagery of Camelot. Historian Stephen E. Ambrose has called the 62. Reeves, *ibid.* p. 41.

66. Reeves, *ibid.* p. 206.

Chapter 6. Shadows and Secrets

It is generally assumed that the lines of communication between father and sons were open, but much would be explained if we could assume that communication was pockmarked by withholding. Joe Kennedy had enough to be embarrassed about to "spare" his sons exposure to this kind of detail.

Joseph Kennedy was not well respected by those who knew him. He began making his fortune in bootlegging Irish whiskey, in the late 1920s. Gangster "Doc" Stacher, a lieutenant of arch criminal Meyer Lansky, reported that Joe was involved in a hijacked whiskey shipment being sent from Ireland to Boston in 1927.[67] Later, he became the owner of some large liquor companies, Haig & Dewer, and Gordon's Gin.

Once Joe tried to ship bootlegged whiskey through Detroit without proper underworld permissions. The Jewish Mafia, known as the Purple Gang, put a contract out on him. Kennedy appealed to his friends in Chicago, and had the contract cancelled. Kennedy was relieved, but an outstanding debt remained. Years later, Frank Costello tried to collect on that debt by asking Kennedy a favor. Kennedy had become very rich and quite influential; he refused Costello. Another contract was put out on his life. Frantically, Joe went to Sam Giancana in Chicago to have it cancelled. It was, but Kennedy's debt to Giancana grew proportionately.

In 1929, Joe Kennedy was also involved with stock manipulation. During the October 1929 stock market crash, he made millions by short selling — and some writers suggest Kennedy may have actually manipulated the market into its crash.[68] He became one of the wealthiest men in the country.

Having made a large contribution to the Franklin Roosevelt campaign, Joseph Kennedy was appointed head of the Securities and Exchange Commission (SEC). When one of Roosevelt's advisors asked him why he would appoint such a questionable character to this sensitive investigative position, Roosevelt replied, "Set a thief to catch a thief." [69]

Joseph Kennedy's relationship to the Mafia has received very little historical attention. That a relationship existed and continued, however, is corroborated by a few sources. During the campaign in West Virginia, FBI wiretaps revealed that large Mafia donations went to the Kennedys.

> The money was used to pay off key election officials. Paul ("Skinnny") D'Amato, an Atlantic City casino owner and Giancana henchman, distributed more than fifty thousand dollars to local sheriffs to get out the vote for Kennedy — by any means possible... Giancana's daughter later reported that the ambas-

---

67. *Ibid.* p. 27.
68. *Ibid.* p. 30.
69. *Ibid.* p. 44.

sador had promised them assistance against federal probes. FBI documents secured under the Freedom of Information Act support this contention.[70]

SEX: THE SINS OF THE FATHER PASS TO THE SON

Joseph Kennedy was known as an incurable womanizer. He had a longstanding affair with Gloria Swanson and financed one of her movies after taking control of a Hollywood studio. He even took Swanson on a cruise — with his wife, Rose. Joe had frequent mistresses, and invited them into the home — one stayed for several months — and also would proposition his son's girlfriends. Joe always denied that his relationship with Swanson was sexual, but in 1980 she confirmed the rumor in her autobiography.[71] He was also linked with Marion Davies and Nancy Caroll. The *New York Post* journalist Doris Lilly said Joe Kennedy:

> ... represented the height of vulgarity... He was horny, that's all he was. He went after every girl he ever saw. He went after me. He took me out one night for dinner at "21." It was the middle of the summer and it was hot. Nobody had air conditioning in those days... Eventually he brought me back to my apartment building. We were standing in the lobby and he said, 'What's that over there? Where?' I said. I turned my head and he clamped his mouth over mine, kissed me, and I ran upstairs and threw up. He was so disgusting. He was a disgusting man... He had a number of girlfriends. I knew a girl who was his mistress for years. She was a showgirl. Joe bought her an apartment at Beekman Place in New York...'[72]

Rose Kennedy's progressive withdrawal and retreat from family life is explained to a large extent as a coping device in response to her husband's behavior.

When Joe Kennedy became Ambassador to England under Roosevelt in the late 1930s, he finally achieved a kind of respectability that had eluded him his whole life. He relished the title, and his ambition of having his first-born son become President of the United States obsessed him until Joe Jr.'s untimely death in World War II. Next in line was Jack, who had little interest in politics but was required to fill his older brother's shoes and try to live out his father's narcissistic dreams. Jack "later told Bob Considine, 'It was like being drafted. My father wanted his eldest son in politics. 'Wanted' isn't the right word. He demanded it. You know my father.'"[73]

---

70. *Ibid.* p. 166.
71. *Ibid.* p. 29.
72. Heymann, p. 141.
73. Reeves, *ibid.* p. 73

Chapter 6. Shadows and Secrets

Joe Kennedy's influence on his sons and their similarities included their approach to foreplay and intimacy:

> Mistress Gloria Swanson [referring to Joe Kennedy] said, "He was like a roped horse, rough, arduous, racing to be free." . . . Marilyn Monroe confided that Jack did not like foreplay either. One woman who remembered him from his single days said, "He was not a cozy, touching sort of man. . . He was as compulsive as Mussolini. Up against the wall, Signora, if you have five minutes, that sort of thing."[74]

> Senator Smathers remembered that on one occasion Jackie caught her husband making love to a famous movie star. On a birthday cruise with Jackie (five months pregnant) and friends, Jack disappeared with actor David Niven's wife for ten minutes of sex. Smathers said, "It was like a rooster getting on top of a chicken real fast and then the poor little hen ruffles her feathers and wonders what the hell happened to her. Jack was something, almost like a Roto-Rooter."[75]

Joe Kennedy took along a mistress on a cruise with his wife, and Jack followed the pattern by having sex with Mrs. David Niven on a cruise with Jackie.

Joe's influence was ever present. He played a substantial role in all of Jack's electoral victories and was on the phone to him constantly. The peculiar relationship between father and son is an important clue in the entire family dynamic. One of John Kennedy's lovers prior to his marriage, Inga Arvad, said, "The way she thought of it, the old man would push Joe, Joe would push Jack, Jack would push Bobby, Bobby would push Teddy, and Teddy would fall on his ass."[76]

Joseph Kennedy had an affair with Marlene Dietrich; John Kennedy is alleged to have slept with her after he became president. JFK had a relationship with Marilyn Monroe; he was followed by Bobby, and it is rumored that young Ted tried too, but was not as successful. Winning was the essential element in sex; it was far more a conquest than any expression of intimacy or closeness.

Jack Kennedy's sexual activities were no mere quirk or oddity to be glossed over and disregarded, as so many Camelot school scholars have tried to do (most notably Arthur Schlesinger). As one researcher put it, "JFK's daily dose of sex became a more conspicuous part of his legacy than any single political achievement."[77]

---

74. Reeves, *ibid.* p 29 and p. 95.
75. *Ibid.* p. 242.
76. *Ibid.* p.57.
77. Heymann, *ibid.* p. 283

And Heymann adds, "Like Hoover's homosexuality, JFK's double nature was unknown during his tenure in office. His public image was so well developed and polished the American people would have been in a state of shock if they had even a glimpse of his other life. To imagine this articulate President cursing, for example, was virtually beyond comprehension, but as one writer put it, 'Kennedy uses profanity with the unconcern of a sailor, which he was and is,'"[78] and, "Privately Jack admitted that he had no interest in agricultural issues. After presenting his 'farm policy' speech to an unresponsive audience at a South Dakota fairground, he said to aides, 'Well, that's over. Fuck the farmers, after November.'" [79]

SECRECY BETWEEN THE BROTHERS?

As we delve into the labyrinth of Kennedy family secrets, more and more nuances come up that relate to the assassination itself.

Because of Giancana's close relationship to Joe Kennedy, he felt that once Jack was elected, the "Outfit" would have smooth sailing. But Bobby Kennedy had been a voracious anti-crime fighter on the McClellan Committee in the late 1950s. Considering Joe's relationship to the Mob, Giancana thought this behavior was out of place. The Mafia had helped John Kennedy cover up a prior marriage, through the efforts of Johnny Roselli. It had canceled contracts on Joe Kennedy's life. It had helped in the West Virginia primary, and the electoral efforts in Chicago. So what was Bobby Kennedy doing?

Many years earlier, on the night that Sam Giancana cancelled Frank Costello's contract on Joe Kennedy's life, the dialogue from Kennedy to Giancana went as follows:

> "You help me now, Sam, and I'll see to it that Chicago... that you... can sit in the goddamned Oval Office if you want. That you'll have the President's ear. But I just need time." There was an urgency in his tone. "I get pushed, and I don't think my son has the experience, or the contacts, to see him through a presidential race. Do you understand now why I want you to talk to Costello?"
>
> Mooney turned to look him square in the eye. "Let me see what I can do. But I want your word that the day your son is elected... that's the day that — " Kennedy interrupted. "That Sam Giancana is elected too. He'll be your man. I swear to that. My son... the President of the United States... will owe you his father's life. He won't refuse you, ever. You have my word."[80]

---

78. Reeves, *ibid.* p. 3
79. *Ibid.* p. 190.
80. Giancana *Ibid.*, p. 322.

Chapter 6. Shadows and Secrets

As Bobby Kennedy continued to badger the Mafia and especially Jimmy Hoffa through the McClellan Committee, and later through his efforts as Attorney General, Giancana reassured himself by saying *"Old man Kennedy'll set him straight."*[81] Still, Bobby persisted in this crusade. "Old man Kennedy" did not set him straight. Harassment of Hoffa, Giancana, Trafficante, Marcello, and others was seriously worrying Giancana:

> "It doesn't make sense, these Kennedy boys... What's Murray have to say?"
> "The same fuckin thing... 'Joe's got it handled'... Joe's got it handled. Shit, old man Kenndy's out fiddlin with whores in Tahoe at the Cal-Neva while Rome burns."
> "Hey, Mooney, relax then, Kennedy must know things are under control..."
> "Yeah, but you'd think I'd get a fuckin answer. Sinatra's baby-sittin the old man out west. Joe just keeps tellin him and the guys that it's just a political move, just a game.
> "Hey, Mooney, like you've said before, Joe Kennedy owes you his life. You think he's gonna bullshit you about this?" [82]

The Giancana theory is that he was double-crossed by the Kennedys, but there is another theory to consider: *Bobby may have been kept out of a special secrecy that existed in the Kennedy family.* What if Bobby was unaware of all his brother's and father's dealings with the Outfit? What if the father never told the sons all the deals and bargains he made?

Giancana asked Joe Kennedy to remove Bobby from the McClellan Committee, and he did. Bobby was made the mastermind of John Kennedy's presidential campaign; he may not have been told that the real reason for the move was to keep him from going any farther on his vendetta against organized crime on the McClellan Committee. Even Giancana, for a while, thought that Bobby had been left in the dark:

> Shit, I still worry about trustin them... The Kennedys are, well, look at Bobby... Bobby doesn't even know what Jack and I have been talkin about. He's out of the picture. He'll be just another godamned lawyer soon. They've promised me they'll take care of him. Jack is gonna be President... not Bobby. Besides, if anything goes wrong, I've got a lot of shit on them. [83]

Giancana, however, finally was convinced he was double-crossed by the Kennedys, on April 4, 1961. This was the date that Bobby Kennedy had Carlos Marcello deported to Guatemala. This convinced Giancana that the Kennedy "clan,"

---

81. *Ibid.* p. 325.
82. *Ibid.* p. 346.
83. *Ibid.* p. 400.

Joe, Jack, and Bobby had decided to muster the forces at their disposal within the Federal government to eliminate all of the "markers," all of their debts to the Mob:[84]

> ... the Kennedys were out to erase any hint of obligation to their powerful benefactor. If this was Camelot, Chuck [Giancana] mused, it looked like Mooney was being made the court jester. [85]

In fact, Bobby Kennedy's campaign against organized crime was highly effective; indictments against organized crime rose from zero to 683, and the number of defendants convicted went also from zero to 619.

Giancana taped Bobby Kennedy and overheard some unpleasant epithets.

> That mick cocksucker, Bobby, we got him on the wire calling me a guinea greaseball. . . can you believe that? My millions were good enough for 'em, weren't they? The votes I muscled for 'em were good enough to get Jack elected. So now I'm a fuckin greaseball, am I?" He smiled, his eyes narrowing into small cobra-like slits, and stood up. "Well, I'm gonna send them a message they'll never forget.

> It was a formal declaration of war. [86]

What Giancana did not consider was the strong possibility that Joseph Kennedy did not want to embarrass himself in front of his well-groomed, Harvard-educated, idealistic sons, or have them learn about the deals he had made to catapult them into such prestigious positions in life.

Perhaps Giancana was correct and that the Kennedys were planning, through Bobby's efforts, to neutralize the Mob and call in their markers. But an equally tantalizing theory is that the Kennedys had a strong and notable history of denial within the family system.

Robert was the moralist. Jack and their father, Joe, did not confide in Bobby as much as they might have; and Bobby refused to see what he didn't want to see. As Bobby went further on his crusade to clean up underworld "scum," he was unwittingly precipitating deep anxieties elsewhere, threatening to expose his father's influence-peddling and election fraud, Jack's marital infidelities, and someone J. Edgar Hoover wanted to keep in the closet at all costs.

A review of Mob connections to the Kennedys is presented in Table 6.1

---

84. See also Ronald Goldfarb, *ibid.*
85. *Ibid.* p. 426.
86. *Ibid.* p. 430.

Chapter 6. Shadows and Secrets

Table 6.1 Summary of mob connections with the Kennedys

Joe Kennedy's Contacts
Engaged in bootlegging whiskey during Prohibition. Smuggled liquor through Detroit without informing the Jewish Mafia, who put out a contract on him. Kennedy pleaded with Chicago's Esposito to have the contract removed. It was. Kennedy refused the requests of mobster Joe Costello, who similarly put a contract out on him. Kennedy got Sam "Mooney" Giancana to have the contract removed, in return for promised future considerations. Kennedy received donations from the Mafia, for rigging the West Virginia election for Jack, and used Mayor Daley and Sam Giancana in Chicago to turn the Illinois vote in favor of Kennedy in 1960. Kennedy won the national election by the slimmest majority in 100 years, very much as a result of carrying Illinois. John Kennedy was married, and his father wanted the marriage annulled. Giancana's aide, Johnny Roselli, handled the legalities and had any record of the marriage destroyed. Joe had frequent sex parties in the discreet Cal-Neva chalet, sometimes with Giancana present. Usually, Kennedy had sex with prostitutes. Later, Jack Kennedy followed suit in the same location. Joe Kennedy and Jack met with Mayor Daley and Sam Giancana in the fall of 1959, at Chicago's Ambassador East Hotel, on three separate occasions.
Jack Kennedy's Connections
Mayor Daley was Kennedy's first visitor in the White House after Harry Truman. Sam Giancana personally visited the President at the White House shortly after the Inauguration. Frank Sinatra introduced Jack Kennedy to Judith Exner on February 7, 1960. Through Judith Exner, Jack sent regular FBI memoranda to Sam Giancana, one of which detailed evidence that Mafia man Action Jackson was an informer for the FBI. Giancana had Action Jackson murdered in one of the most gruesome Mafia torture killings ever. It is unknown whether Kennedy knew that his revelations to Giancana resulted in this murder. Further, it is unknown if Bobby was aware that his brother was passing such information to Giancana through Exner. Marilyn Monroe's contacts with Frank Sinatra, and Sinatra's 30-year relationship with Giancana, placed the Kennedys at risk. Monroe was involved romantically with both John and Bobby Kennedy.

Table 6.1 Summary of mob connections with the Kennedys

Bobby Kennedy's Naïveté
Bobby Kennedy is not known to have interfaced with the Mob in any other way than in pursuing prosecutions against them. After his brother's assassination, Bobby Kennedy never again met with his own organized crime task force. At the time of the Bay of Pigs fiasco, Robert Kennedy seemed surprised to learn that the CIA had executive action assassination plans against Castro through the efforts of mobsters Giancana, Roselli, and Trafficante. Kennedy had an unusually bitter confrontation with CIA spymaster and organizer of such clandestine plots, William Harvey. The HSCA also confirms Bobby Kennedy's ignorance of many of the Mob connections to the CIA. In its report it said, "The Attorney General was not told that the gambling syndicate (assassination) operation had already been reactivated, nor, as far as we know, was he ever told that the CIA had a continuing involvement with US gangster elements." [a]

a. Reeves, 256-257, Groden, p. 313, and Giancana pp. 214, 219, 389, 411.

Jack Kennedy's friend Senator Smathers notes that after the Bay of Pigs disaster, Robert Kennedy was assigned the task of chairing a task force to study CIA fumbling in the matter. The Cuban Study Group resulted in the firing of the entire top echelon of the CIA: Allen Dulles, its director; General Cabell, head of CIA covert operations; and Richard Bissell. The "cowboy" of the CIA, William Harvey, who had direct involvement with Castro assassination plans and covert operations, was transferred to Italy. It was at this time, *and no earlier*, that Robert Kennedy and his brother John learned of the CIA relationship with Giancana, Roselli, and Trafficante.

> Smathers found President Kennedy "horrified" at the idea of assassination; he refused to be pushed around. Smathers stated that he heard Kennedy say, "the CIA had arranged to have Diem and Trujillo bumped off." Various CIA officials and others have tried to claim that Kennedy approved the assassination plots, and that his brother Bobby knew about them. This is absolutely untrue. Bobby Kennedy did find out about some of it, and he did all he could to put a stop to it. RFK said, "I stopped it... I found out that some people were going to try an attempt on Castro's life and I turned it off."[87]

---

87. Groden, *ibid.* pp 325-326.

Chapter 6. Shadows and Secrets

When Robert Kennedy learned of the CIA's use of organized crime, he was incensed.

> In early 1962, Robert Kennedy found that the CIA was trying to protect one of its Mafia contacts, Sam Giancana, from prosecution on another matter. When he insisted on pursuing the matter, Kennedy was finally told about the earlier stage of Giancana's role in the murder plots by a CIA lawyer, Lawrence Houston. According to Houston, the information "upset" Kennedy, who expressed "strong anger" and responded, "I trust that if you ever try to do business with organized crime again — with gangsters — you will let the Attorney General know."[88]

However, here, time is of great interest to us. When did Bobby Kennedy learn of the CIA's connections to the Mafia? When did he learn of his brother's connection to Giancana through Judith Exner — *or did he ever learn of it?* When, if ever, did he learn of J. Edgar Hoover's hands-off policy on organized crime? When did he learn of his father's entanglements with the Mob — or did he remain in the dark right up through November 1963?

In this chapter, we seek to understand the psychology of the main figures in the tragedy. For John Kennedy to risk everything by engaging in relations with so many shady characters — *and think he could get away with it* — he had to be in denial. Reality was bound to catch up to him. And for Robert Kennedy, Attorney General, to be unaware of the extreme risks run by JFK — his liaisons that were promiscuous in every sense — he would have had to be deeply in denial. He had to be *willing* himself not to see what was going on, seeking to *not see* rather than seeking to see it.

The literature offers some clues on these points. Most are from Mark North, who provides (in *Act of Treason*) a detailed accounting of FBI surveillance tapes and chronology of Hoover's activity. Bobby Kennedy made his biggest moves against the Mob in early 1961 with the deportation of Marcello, the harassment of Giancana and Trafficante, and the arrest of Hoffa. (Robert Kennedy's vendetta against Hoffa is a story all its own. During the JFK presidency, RFK indicted 201 Teamster officials and won 126 convictions. Clearly, Jimmy Hoffa was under the gun. He would not actually enter prison, himself, however, until 1967. Within 15 months of Hoffa's induction into the federal penitentiary in Lewisberg, Robert Kennedy was assassinated.)[89]

It was not until December 14, 1961 that J. Edgar Hoover sent a pivotal memorandum to Bobby Kennedy. Hoover informed him that Giancana, through wiretap surveillance, had been heard mentioning that Joseph Kennedy accepted campaign contributions from Giancana. *Apparently neither Bobby Kennedy nor Jack knew of this.*

---

88. Summers, *ibid.* pp. 241-242.
89. See R. Goldfarb, *ibid.*, p. 199.

John Kennedy met with his father a few days later in Palm Springs. Five days after Hoover's memo to Bobby, implicating his father, Joseph Kennedy, Joseph suffered a massive stroke from which he never recovered (December 19, 1961). It must have been at this time that J. Edgar Hoover realized his days at the head of the FBI were numbered. The Kennedy brothers would never forget what happened to their father and would blame Hoover for it.[90]

Thus, on December 19, 1961, we have at least some evidence about family denial patterns. Both Jack and Bobby, or at least Bobby, seem unaware of their father's dealings with the Mob. Did Joe deny it? Did he say that Hoover's information was incorrect or that Giancana was a liar? Or did he admit these things to his two boys?

Certainly, John knew Giancana. He had met him in Chicago with his father before the 1960 Illinois election, again in the White House; but is it still possible that John was also a victim of a family denial pattern and his father may never have told him that the Mob played a role in helping him win the election?

A logical hypothesis, then, is that a deadly pattern of both deceit and denial existed within the male line of the Kennedy family system; Joe withheld important things from Jack, Jack from Bobby, and Bobby, the fool, aggressively prosecuted and harassed precisely the people who favored and serviced and his father and brother. After John Kennedy was assassinated, Bobby Kennedy was disconsolate, rarely came to his office, and effectively ended his campaign against organized crime. "He was a walking zombie in the Department of Justice from the day of the assassination to the day he left."[91]

Eunice Kennedy once asked her other brother, Ted, in the late 1970s, if the rumors about Exner and the President were true. Teddy reassured her that they were false.[92] However, the very day that Jack Kennedy met Exner in Las Vegas, Teddy was also present, danced with her, and made amateurish attempts to enlist her for an interlude himself.[93]

It seems logical to assume that patterns of deceit did exist within the Kennedy family, and if Teddy could lie to Eunice, and Joe could withhold from Jack, then we have some perspective on the most important question of all: was Bobby left in the dark about his brother's and father's Mob connections, while he carried on a dangerous campaign against the underworld?

---

90. North, Mark *Act of Treason* New York: Carroll & Graf, 1991, p. 117.
91. Goldfarb, *ibid.*, p. 302.
92. Collier & Horowitz, *ibid.* p. 379.
93. *Ibid.* p. 368.

June 1963

This is a pivotal historical issue, and one rarely discussed in conspiracy literature. There is a tentative answer to the question, but we have conflicting source material, too. One author says Bobby knew; so does a more recent document. But other sources, including the HSCA, say Bobby was in the dark:

> Harris Wofford, former Special Assistant to the President, says when writing of Judith Campbell, Sam Giancana, and the CIA plots to kill Castro: "Aside from moral issues, the morass of potential blackmail in which the Attorney General found himself must have appalled him... How could the CIA and John Kennedy have been so stupid? What could they or the Attorney General do to extricate themselves and minimize the risk of exposure? [94]

Wofford implies that Bobby *did become aware of these matters*. If this is true, it appears that Bobby's reaction was to attack rather than surrender. He did not back off, but exerted even greater pressures.

> In June of 1963, the local FBI agents instituted what they called lockstep surveillance of the Chicago boss — meaning, literally, that agents had been assigned to dog his every step... There was no attempt made at secrecy under this new program: the G-men openly dogged Mooney's every move. [95]

Giancana filed suit, accusing the federal government of depriving him of his constitutional rights. He looked forward to the trial, a complete surprise to Kennedy:

> I'll be sittin on the stand holdin a can of worms. And Bobby'll be scared to death I'll open it... because if I do, all their dirty little secrets will come out.[96]

Robert Kennedy managed to have the court rule it had no jurisdiction over the conduct of the FBI. Mooney did not have his day in court or his chance to expose the Kennedys. Surveillance intensified. Clearly, for Giancana in June of 1963, it would seem that the Kennedys were using every resource to call in their markers. Giancana's "double-cross" theory — at least up to this point — prevails over the notion that Bobby was a victim of family secrecy.

Then Bobby was not in the dark. He knew. He knew all the secrets of his father and brother, and he had the court rule it had no jurisdiction — to prevent Giancana from spilling the beans in court testimony. Then, RFK's crusade against the Mob was

---

94. Summers, *ibid.* p. 332.
95. Giancana, *ibid.* p. 448.
96. *Ibid.*

not done out of naïveté but was an intentional Kennedy family double-cross of the Mob... and a double-cross of the Mafia is a capital offense.

But in a family with a history of keeping secrets, is it possible Jack told Bobby a few fibs about Judith Exner... that it was a one-time encounter of no real importance; that the Presidency was not compromised? Is it possible Robert Kennedy heard one story from Hoover and Giancana about his father, *and a different story* from his father — and made the choice to believe his father? What if Jack said his relationship with Exner was minimal, or Dad said, "Giancana is making it all up; it's all a lie. Giancana is trying to gain influence with you boys that he has no right to." And on top of all this, Dad suffers a stroke over the all of the undeserved stress.

Then the appropriate reaction for the Attorney General of the United States would be to go all out in a vendetta against underworld "greaseballs" and try to put them all away once and for all. We don't know what went through Robert Kennedy's mind, but it deserves the closest scrutiny.

A 1995 book[97] explores this issue and leaves us in exactly the same place that we started, wondering if JFK held secrets from Bobby in a manner that may have ultimately triggered the assassination. Here is an excerpt regarding whether and how Bobby may have learned about Giancana's relationship to his brother, the CIA, Judith Campbell, and plots against Castro:

> The irony of it all was the Giancana had appeared earlier before the Senate Rackets Committee, faced Robert Kennedy, and pleaded the Fifth Amendment fifty-three times. An FBI-tapped phone overheard Roselli saying, "Here I am, helping the government, helping the country... and that little son of a bitch is breaking my balls... You fuck them," he said, "you pay them, and then they're through."
>
> "It was finally decided to brief Bobby on the Mafia connection because he might otherwise be embarrassed in his prosecution... Bobby Kennedy listened, as I outlined the case in detail," said Lawrence Houston, Information Officer of the Department of Justice. "You could see Bob's face getting grimmer and grimmer...We told him the whole thing: The CIA had developed the idea that there could be an attempt on Castro's life, using the Mafia people who'd lost their gambling interest down in Havana, and would like a chance to get it back."
>
> The Attorney General's reaction, according to Houston, was, " 'This means, I suppose, we cannot go ahead with our intended indictments on these two fellas [John Roselli and Sam Giancana]'... He never criticized, once, the assassination attempt. But, he said, 'Don't you ever again get in touch with any gangster-Mafia

---

97. Ralph G. Martin, *Seeds of Destruction: Joe Kennedy and his sons*, New York, Putnam, 1995, pp. 340-342.

types again, without consulting me first!' Yes sir! He was furious. I don't blame him."

In a letter to the editor of the *Atlantic Monthly*, years later, two of Robert Kennedy's top aides, Frank Mankiewicz and Adam Walinsky, wrote, "Attorney General Kennedy was briefed about the CIA Mafia plot after the fact; he was told (falsely) that the plot had ceased; he ordered that no such further attempts be made; but attempts continued despite his orders that they cease. Mankiewicz and Walinsky both insisted that the Bob Kennedy they knew was an intensely moral man who wouldn't have anything to do with an assassination. They had discussed the matter with him and felt that he believed that his opposition was largely responsible for the project's end.

As if to emphasize Bobby's morality, William G. Hundley, chief of the Organized Crime Section for the Attorney General, pointed out that despite the knowledge that Giancana could embarrass the Kennedy administration, "Bobby pushed to get Giancana at any cost." However, Giancana eventually decided on a confrontation, and brought a civil suit against the Federal Government. This left him open in court to cross-examination. Others were confounded when the Assistant United States Attorney never questioned Giancana on the stand.

. . . It seems hard to believe that President Kennedy would deal with the Mafia in killing Castro without first conferring with Bobby. It raises many questions. But then the President — as much as he used his brother on critical matters — still did not tell him everything. He didn't consult him on early key Cabinet selections; he didn't involve him in the early planning for Bay of Pigs; he didn't share details of most of his sexual adventures until he needed help and cover-up. So it is not inconceivable that he kept these Mafia negotiations to himself — at the urging of the CIA — because Bobby had fought the Mafiosi intensely and would disapprove.

Campbell told an interviewer that she not only acted as a courier but she also arranged ten meetings between Kennedy and Giancana. Giacana's daughter Antoinette, interviewed by Larry King in February 1992, was asked whether JFK asked Giancana to kill Castro. She replied, "Yes, he did."

Robert Kennedy's Personality

Bobby's motives for his vendetta against Giancana's "Outfit" are not well understood. The best hypothesis is that Bobby simply was naïve and unaware of some crucial facts. Bobby was eight years younger than Jack, a tenacious moralist, the fighter for ethics in government, the conscience of the family. He was different from his older brother, was once nominated as Father of the Year, and even had contemplated the religious life.

Lem Billings [Jack Kennedy's best friend], said Bobby was much more openly loving with his children than Joseph Kennedy had been. He touched them all the time. It seems like a small thing, but in the Kennedy family it wasn't. Mr. Kennedy had never touched them much when they were young. Jack was the same way — didn't touch and didn't want to be touched. [98]

Bobby Kennedy's children show a very special kind of affection for their father, as well. After his assassination, his sons presented their mother with a Christmas book. Their commentary underscores the level of intimacy and genuineness he left behind:

Daddy was very funny in church because he would embarrass all of us by singing very loud. Daddy did not have a very good voice. There will be no more football with Daddy, no more swimming with him, no more riding and no more camping with him. But he was the best father their [sic] ever was and I would rather have him for a father for the length of time I did than any other father for a million years. [99]

Robert Kennedy was loved and respected not only by millions of Americans and his own children, but by his older brother as well. Jack may not have been as open and candid with his staunchly moralistic, "square," brother as historians may have supposed. Furthermore, we do not know how open Jack was *with himself* with respect to sexual issues and the consequences issuing from them. There is very good reason, therefore, to suspect Bobby was not apprized of all his older brother's capers.

His brother, John spoke of Robert's "high moral standards. . . a puritan, absolutely incorruptible" By 1960, when Robert turned thirty-five, he had been married ten years and had seven children. [100]

Some say Bobby had as many as four extramarital affairs, but genuine evidence only supports one, Marilyn Monroe. The clumsy affair with Monroe may have been his first sojourn in this direction, a direction he knew was not suited to his nature, and one he wanted to stop.

While Jack simply bedded them and was off to his next conquest, the Father of the Year with seven children even discussed marriage with Marilyn Monroe. He took matters of the heart very seriously, and when it came to infidelity, he was a novice; he did not swim well in these waters. Bobby's reaction to the assassination differed

---

98. Collier & Horowitz, *ibid.* p. 432
99. *Ibid.* p. 461.
100. Summers, Anthony. *Goddess: The Secret Lives of Marilyn Monroe.* London: Penguin, 1985. p. 241.

Chapter 6. Shadows and Secrets

greatly from virtually all other members of the Kennedy family, and it began to look increasingly as if he felt he was responsible for his brother's death. At first, he was the rock upon whom grieving relatives could count; but gradually Bobby retreated into a disconsolate sullenness which became notable to all those who were close to him.

Rare photo of Robert Kennedy, Marilyn Monroe and JFK together.

Bobby wouldn't say the word "assassination" or "death" or even "Dallas", but spoke only of "the events of November 22" . . . he seemed haunted by his memories. Secret service men posted at Hickory Hill [Kennedy's home] grew accustomed to seeing the lights go on in the master bedroom in the middle of the night and knew that Bobby would come out at three or four o'clock, get into his convertible, and drive off into the freezing winter night with the top down, returning at sunup to shower, change clothes, and go off to the Justice Department as if in a trance . . . Once he appeared at an old friend's house with a book of readings of world literature under his arm. He made her listen while he opened the book and read from a selection about poet Gerard de Nerval, who often walked around town with a lobster on a leash. When asked why, Nerval replied: "Because he knows the secrets of the deep."

Some of those close to Bobby saw it all as a classic case of survivor's guilt. If so, there was a deeper level of responsibility than with most survivors, one which came from the fact that Bobby, like Nerval's lobster, knew the secrets of the deep. He knew what had happened beneath the surfaces of the administration; he knew the role he himself had played... It was Bobby who had led the administration into dangerous places, daring the gods of the underworld and seizing the fire that finally erupted into anti-Kennedy hatred... Had his acts created an environment for assassination? Had his zeal helped created the concatenation of forces that wanted Jack dead?

"Did the CIA kill my brother?" he asked John McCone in a choked voice soon after the assassination. McCone's answer was no, but Bobby knew as much and in some cases more than the CIA director about "executive action" plots, the secret war against Castro, and the nightmare marriage between the intelligence services and the Mob... While he claimed never to have read the Warren Commission Report, however, Bobby continued to agitate the question of the assassination furtively. When New Orleans District Attorney Jim Garrison was uncovering what he claimed was the master plot, Bobby sent Walter Sheridan to see him... He once asked Frank Mankiewicz if he thought Garrison "had anything." Mankiewicz replied, "No, but I think there is something." Bobby nodded. "So do I. You stay on it."[101]

Bobby had been no less devastated by the tragedy than Jackie. He couldn't sleep, couldn't work, couldn't eat. He saw Jackie nearly every day. They were bound by a common sense of loss.[102]

We may never get an answer on what Bobby knew and didn't know or why he pursued the Mafia with such tenacity on the very threshold of the assassination.[103] What we do know, however, is that the role Bobby plays in the whole drama appears to be far more important than history has credited.

A recently declassified set of memos from the CIA was made available on July 2, 1997. The information corroborates that the CIA offered $150,000 to hire Mob hit-men to assassinate Castro, but it does not make clear whether Bobby Kennedy was aware of the contracts at the time of his persecution of Giancana. One memo states "Knowledge of this project... was kept to a total of six persons."[104]

---

101. Collier & Horowitz. *Ibid.*, pp. 398-400.
102. Heymann, *ibid.* p. 425. When JFK died, the family priest came to Bobby's residence to console him. However, he had to wait for 3 hours as Bobby was in intense conversation with John McCone. (Reported by Jack Anderson and cited in R. Goldfarb, *Perfect Villains, Imperfect Heroes, ibid.* p. 256.'
103. A book by Seymour Hersh, *The Dark Side of Camelot*, features a rare interview given by Judith Exner-Campbell. She reiterated to Hersh that JFK was using her as a courier to Giancana regarding the Castro assassination. If true, then our first question must be whether JFK told Bobby of these plans. If Bobby knew of them, his persecution of Giancana becomes a deep mystery. If Bobby did not know, then the secrecy between JFK and his brother on such monumental matters opens speculation even wider. (See Hersh, *The Dark Side of Camelot*, Boston: Little Brown, 1997, p. 314.)
104. "CIA offered to pay Mob to kill Castro," *San Jose Mercury News*, July 2, 1997, p. 14A.

Chapter 6. Shadows and Secrets

With Judith Exner's revelations that she acted as a courier between JFK and Giancana, it is plausible that the President was aware of these plans, and was one of the six insiders; but Bobby may have been left in the dark, creating quite a dilemma for Giancana.

REVELATIONS FROM A COLLEAGUE

Ronald Goldfarb, a justice department attorney under Bobby Kennedy, wrote in 1995 of these issues and the most pressing question of all, "What did Robert Kennedy know, and when did he know it?" His discussion and analysis is given in the following excerpts:[105]

> On May 22, 1961 not half a year after RFK had become attorney general, Hoover had sent him a memorandum advising him of the CIA's admission of the Las Vegas wiretap and the use of the underworld in clandestine Castro plots... Courtney Evans, the liaison between Kennedy and Hoover, recalled to me: "I hand-carried all the memos over (Hoover to Robert Kennedy), and I'll tell you, I read 'em even if I didn't write 'em." Yet a later CIA internal investigation into the episode concluded that Robert Kennedy did not know about the Castro assassination plan using organized crime figures until he was informed about it by the CIA in May 1962. This, despite an FBI document dated May 21, 1961, stating that a CIA official told Attorney General Kennedy about "the use of Giancana and the underworld against Castro" during a "recent" briefing.

Regarding Judith Exner's allegation that at least JFK knew of the governments use of Giancana to eliminate Castro, Goldfarb continues:

> Exner told King (Larry King) that President Kennedy knew about the CIA's use of Giancana in the Castro assassination plot. "I carried the intelligence material between Jack and Sam... at Jack's request." Her cloak-and-dagger description of those alleged events was never reported in her earlier book or in her sworn testimony to the Church Committee. Her story on the King show in 1992 was told then, she stated, and not earlier to the Church Committee, because Roselli was killed after he testified, Giancana had been killed a few weeks before he was to testify, "and I was afraid... terribly afraid."

Still others suggest Robert Kennedy himself was aware of Giancana's use in plots against Castro, a fact which did not deter him from attempting to put Giancana away. Goldfarb cites author Richard Reeves, who, in an interview, said, "There's no

---

105. Quotations in this section come from Goldfarb, *ibid.*, pp.265-276.

doubt in my mind that Bobby was the director and manager of Mongoose and the attempts to assassinate Castro. And the driving force behind him was his brother..."

Later, Goldfarb reports on comments by Max Holland, a reputable Warren Commission historian:

> JFK put his trusted brother RFK in charge of Mongoose, which had high Kennedy administration priority; it was a no-holds-barred operation, and Robert Kennedy was applying intense pressures. According to Holland, Robert Kennedy's intimate involvement with the CIA's Cuba plans began two days after the inauguration.

Still,

> Kennedy's close aide and Friend John Seigenthaler — one of those he was most likely to confide in — knew nothing of the allegations that Kennedy used rackets figures to pursue cold warrior gambits, and surely not to assassinate another country's leader. Seigenthaler recalls Kennedy expressing disgust with the CIA when he heard of their use of assassins, and telling John McCone and Richard Helms he thought it was disgraceful and that it should be stopped.

Had RFK been dealing with Giancana on operation Mongoose, Justice Department cases against him would have been fatally compromised. According Kennedy aide John Symington, "the notion that Bob Kennedy might have compromised organized crime cases is impossible to believe." Another Kennedy assistant, John Nolan, concurs: "For Robert Kennedy to have worked with Giancana is inherently implausible; it just doesn't ring true."

We are thus left wondering. Evidence seems to favor the hypothesis that Bobby Kennedy persecuted Giancana not because the Kennedy clan was "double crossing" the Mafia and calling in its markers, but because Jack was not forthright in confiding to Bobby all of his private dealings; and Bobby, the idealist, operated in ignorance of these compromising elements, and thus it did not strike him as anything out of the ordinary to go after organized crime. He remained unaware of the government's involvement with mobsters and was only dimly aware of his father and brother's consorting with Giancana's Outfit.

Chapter 6. Shadows and Secrets

EVEN MORE RECENT REVELATIONS[106]

In 1998, a college professor discovered an unpublicized memorandum suggesting that the President and RFK discussed and sanctioned the development of a possible assassination attempt against Castro during a 1962 meeting in the Oval Office, a scheme involving Ernest Hemingway's farm outside Havana. According to the CIA memo, Bobby Kennedy told a group of CIA and Pentagon officials that a solution to the Cuban problem carried "the top priority in the United States government — all else is secondary."

The memo, written by Brig Gen. Edward Landsdale, mentions a meeting with the Attorney General where "fractioning" the Castro regime was brought up, and that "we were in agreement that the matter was so delicate and sensitive that it shouldn't be surfaced to the Special Group (an elite interagency group that reviewed covert actions) until we were ready to go, and then not in detail."

Ted Shackley, the, CIA Miami station chief during this time, commented on the memo by saying "it certainly has the earmarks of an assassination plot." Samuel Halpern, his second in command, called the memo document "as close as we're likely to get" to conclusive proof.

The meeting described in this memo occurred on March 16, 1962. In April of that same year, CIA murder plots against Castro were activated, and CIA operative William Harvey delivered a U-Haul filled with arms to John Roselli, who was supposed to transfer the weapons to Cuban exiles interested in murdering Castro.

If true, this event shows Bobby was involved in assassination plots against Castro. More important, it leads to the conclusion that he had at least indirect awareness of the Mafia dimension of these intrigues, given that the CIA's William Harvey and Mob contact Johnny Roselli were involved. This would sharply contradict what we have said earlier about Bobby's naïveté.

Historian Arthur Schlesinger disputes such interpretations, asserting that, "The available evidence clearly leads to the conclusion that the Kennedy's did not know about the Castro assassination plots before the Bay of Pigs or about the pursuit of those plots by the CIA after the Bay of Pigs."

We know enough about Arthur Schlesinger, from earlier chapters, to suspect he has acted more as a Kennedy family publicist than a historian. Despite his volumes written on the Kennedys, he failed to properly depict anything that might be embarrassing about the Kennedys, much less the alleged communications between

---

106. References and quotations in this section refer to D. Corn and G. Russo, "The old man and the CIA: A Kennedy plot to kill Castro," *The Nation*. March 2, 2001, pp. 15-20.

JFK and Giancana carried by Judith Exner on Castro assassination plots. He doesn't even acknowledge the affair between Exner and JFK.

Another source corroborating Schlesinger, however, is Robert Kennedy's biographer Evan Thomas, who said in reference to this Landsdale memo: "Kennedy's closest aides flatly denied that he ever ordered an assassination or discussed the possibility."

We don't know if Thomas, like Schlesinger, is putting the best spin on historical facts to keep the Kennedy mystique alive or whether these are credible assertions we should trust.

We began this discussion wondering why Bobby was so intent on prosecuting Giancana, Marcello, and Trafficante in view of the fact that his brother had enlisted the same thugs to assassinate Castro and irrespective of the fact that his long-time mistress was linked to exactly the person Bobby was trying to put behind bars.

One theory is Sam Giancana's: namely, that the Kennedy brothers double-crossed the Mob and were trying to mobilize the federal government against them. In that case, retaliation was not only warranted but necessary, if the "Outfit" was to survive. The Mafia theory also had an important corollary: If Robert Kennedy were assassinated, JFK would have utilized all the resources of the government to arrest and punish his murderers. On the other hand, if Jack Kennedy was killed, RFK's power as Attorney General would evaporate, and he would be "just another lawyer."

Weighing against that theory is a psychological one, namely that Jack did not tell idealistic Bobby the details of his sexual encounters with Exner, nor about machinations with Mob figures to assassinate Castro — much less about his severe sexual addictions and the compromising situations they invoked. If that hypothesis is true, then Bobby's pursuit of Giancana makes more sense. He is simply unaware of his brother's dealings with Giancana and is acting out of ignorance, a victim of his brother's pervasive pattern of deceit and denial.

The Landsdale memo suggests Bobby knew of the plots against Castro and participated in at least one rather actively, but it is still possible to think that, even if he helped hatch the Hemingway-farm plot against Castro, he may have been unaware of the Mob assets that were being readied for that hit.

When Robert Kennedy left office, he took over fifty boxes of classified and confidential papers which are now stored at the Kennedy Library in Boston. Unfortunately, most of this material is closed to the public and numerous scholars (Richard Reeves, Robert Dallek, Nigel Hamilton, Laurence Leamer, and Seymour Hersh) all have been denied a look — even this many years after the assassination.

Table 6.2 tries to summarize and provide some perspective of these events.

Chapter 6. Shadows and Secrets

Perhaps Harris Wofford,[107] an attorney in the justice department under Robert Kennedy, expresses the dilemma most poignantly, many years after the assassination. Whether Bobby Kennedy ever became aware of the full character of this problem will probably remain a mystery, but let us not forget what the actual dilemma for Bobby was:

> ... that his brother and the government of the United States were entangled with the most evil forces... and that Sam Giancana, John Roselli, and their like held an enormous power to blackmail not only John Kennedy and his family but any government of the United States. The Mafia leaders were privy to what may have been the worst national secret in the history of the United States, and the most embarrassing personal secret about John Kennedy. Nothing could damage the reputation of the United States government and of the Kennedy administration more than disclosure that it had conspired with organized crime to murder the head of a foreign government. Nothing could damage the personal reputation

Table 6.2 Chronology of events versus Bobby Kennedy's awareness of them

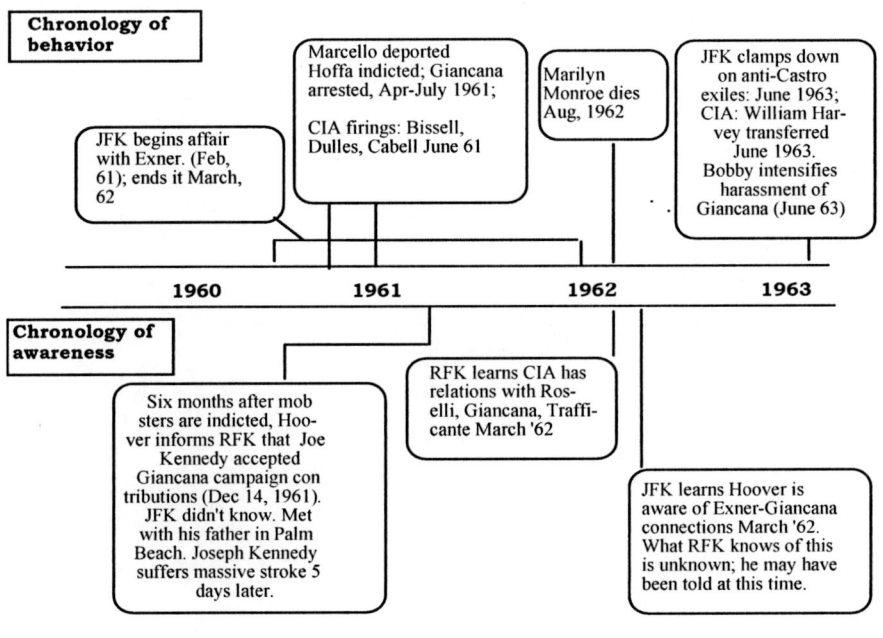

107. Wofford cited in Goldfarb, *ibid.*, p. 288.

of John Kennedy more than detailed and public allegations of a sexual liaison, while in the White House, with a woman who at the same time was having an affair with a notorious Mafia chieftain.

EVEN DEEPER SECRETS: THE SHADOW OF JOHN FITZGERALD KENNEDY

> "I would rather have a President who does it to a woman than a President who does it to his country." [108]
>
> — Shirley Maclaine

Jack Kennedy was not merely a handsome young president popular with the ladies, or even an adulterer. He was a Sybarite; in clinical terms, a sex addict. The risks Kennedy took defy the imagination, and if it were not for the discretion of the press, the Secret Service, White House staff, speech writers, aides, butlers, maids and chauffeurs, Kennedy's legacy in office would have been exposed many times over, far earlier, indeed as early as Inauguration Day. Ben Bradlee of the *Washington Post*, Joseph Alsop, Robert Pierpoint of CBS, and others in the media were already well aware of presidential infidelities. While Bradlee was a leading figure exposing Nixon in Watergate, he acted in expressly the opposite fashion with Kennedy and remained inordinately "discreet" in protecting the Kennedy image.

The Adventures of J.J.

Not all males in our society give their penises nicknames, but both Lyndon Johnson and Jack Kennedy did. Lyndon's namesake was "Jumbo," while Kennedy called his "J.J."

Jack Kennedy enjoyed almost constant sexual infidelities during the entirety of his presidency. The affair with Judith Exner Campbell went on for over a year in the White House, but so did Kennedy's entanglements with Pamela Turnure — see photo, right — (Mrs.

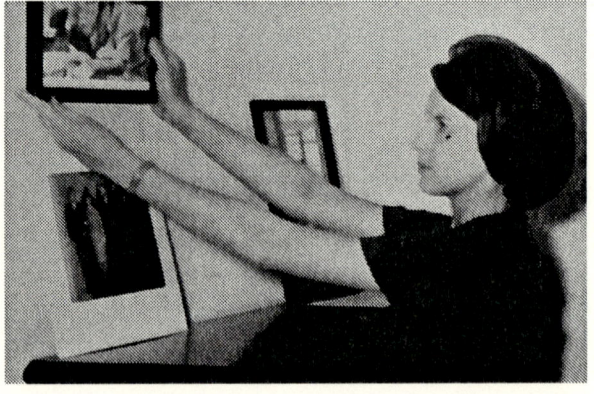

---

108. Collier & Horowitz. *Ibid.*, p. 286.

Kennedy's secretary), two other White House aides (code-named by the secret service "Fiddle and Faddle"), Marilyn Monroe, Angie Dickinson, and many others (See Table 6.3).[109] In a mere thousand days in the White House, there are at least 33 extra-marital affairs alleged, 20 of which are well-corroborated, and many of these were multiple episodes.

The relationship with Pamela Turnure appears to have lasted two years; with Mary Pinchot Meyer, over a year; with Judith Exner, slightly over a year; Priscilla Weir and Jill Cowan were ongoing playmates, but for an indeterminate length of time. Identities of the *Playboy* centerfold, or "Pooh," from the French Riviera have not been made, along with many of the call girls listed in the table, but corroboration of these affairs is legion.

Thirty-three extramarital relationships in three years, statistically, is well beyond the third standard deviation, not only for presidents but for the male population at large, and squarely in the territory of sexual addiction. The average American male has had twelve sexual partners in his lifetime, and the number of "single" American males who have had over 30 partners in three years is miniscule.

As Reeves noted, "Had he lived, many of his indiscretions would have become public knowledge. He would not have been re-elected. As it is, he didn't succeed in carrying out his political agenda. We were prisoners of a myth we helped to create. Professional image makers built an image; journalists bought into the propaganda and were later forced to go along with it." [110]

---

109. Sources for this table are Reeves, *ibid.* p. 7, 115, 137, 201, 220, 243, 326 and Heymann, *ibid.* pp. 282-84, 286, 268, 326, 371-73, 641; the source for "Susannah M." is Peter Davis, executive producer, "Jack" CBS TV special, aired November 17, 1993. Marlene Dietrich's contact with the President (apparently she also had a relationship with his father, Joe) is described in a rather uncomplimentary biography published by her daughter. While there are many sources of corroborating evidence for JFK's liaisons, one interesting and more recent source is Ben Bradlee, publisher of the *Washington Post*, and a personal friend of the Kennedys. Bradlee had access to personal telephone numbers where he could reach the president. These numbers were constantly changed, for security reasons. When Judith Campbell Exner published her account of her affair with the President, she listed these personal telephone numbers. Bradlee noted that they were the same as his own list (source: Ralph G. Martin, Seeds of Destruction. New York: Putnam, 1995, p.343). Additional corroborating sources of data in this table are as follows: Richard Reeves, *President Kennedy*, New York: Touchstone, 1993, p. 707 and James Giglio, The Presidency of John F. Kennedy, Lawrence, KS: University Press of Kansas, 1991, p. 267. Note that the revelation of Gunilla von Post did not become known until 1997; source for this information was "20/20" on August 14, 1997.

110. Reeves, *ibid.*, p. 234.

Mrs. Kennedy apparently knew about many of these liaisons and referred to the aides who cavorted with the President as "the White House dogs."[111] One woman who met Kennedy at a party and whom he tried to squire made the following observation:

Jack confided a bit in one woman who resisted his advances, and asked questions about women and marriage as though they were totally foreign topics: During one of these conversations I once asked him why he was doing it — when he was acting like his father, why he was avoiding real relationship, why he was taking a chance on getting caught in a scandal at the same time that he was trying to make his career take off. He took a while trying to formulate an answer. Finally he shrugged and said, "I don't know, really. I guess I can't help it." He had this sad expression on his face. He looked like a little boy about to cry."[112]

One biographer noted,

Jack Kennedy, the sex addict, had little awareness of what he was doing and little strength to stop. Like his father, his relationship to sex was almost a defense against intimacy, and there was a notable absence of real intimacy relationship with anyone. The most romantic message he ever sent Jackie was a card from Bermuda saying, "Wish you were here, Jack."[113]

... Another Lawford-inspired fling involved a high-priced New York call girl named Leslie Devereux... "I saw him four or five times at the Carlyle... I visited him twice at the White House, the first time for only 15 minutes in a small room off the Oval Office. His secretaries didn't so much as blink when they saw me... On my second visit, I met him upstairs in the living quarters. A Secret Service agent ushered me into a dark and somber room filled with heavy wood furniture and said 'Make yourself comfortable, he'll be with you shortly.' He motioned to an enormous intricately carved rosewood bed, 'That's Abraham Lincoln's bed,' he said. 'You mean,' I said, 'I'm to lie down on that, on Abraham Lincoln's bed?' '

Lady,' he said 'its the best we've got.'... Then the President appeared and we spent several hours together. I told him it seemed sacrilegious to violate Abraham Lincoln's bed. He laughed and told me about the White House legend that when you make a wish on the Lincoln bed it always comes true. 'Make a wish,' I said. He closed his eyes and I mounted him. 'See,' he said, 'it never fails.'[114]

---

111. Collier & Horowitz. *Ibid.* p.355.
112. Reeves, *ibid.* p. 95.
113. Heymann, *ibid.* p. 129.
114. Heymann, *ibid.* p. 285.

Chapter 6. Shadows and Secrets

Table 6.3 *Kennedy's Mistresses during his Presidency, and the Information Sources*

1. Judith Campbell Exner, Sam Giancana's girl friend; February 1961 through March, 1962; approximately 20 visits to White House, Palm Springs, Las Vegas, Washington D.C., the Plaza Hotel in New York.
2. Mrs. David Niven; one encounter on a cruise with Jackie.
3. Mary Pinchot Meyer; from 1962 until his death — about 40 visits. Took LSD and marijuana with her.
4. Unnamed airline stewardesses — numerous; they had to undergo Secret Service investigations before being admitted to President's quarters. Two unnamed California stewardesses documented in FBI files.
5. Call girls; prior to the TV debate with Nixon.
6. "Pooh," a companion on the French Riviera.
7. Priscilla Weiss, code named "Fiddle" by the Secret Service, a White House aide; apparently numerous soirées with the President.
8. Jill Cowan, code named "Faddle," a White House aide; numerous contacts with the President.
9. Angie Dickinson, actress; rumored liaison; significant corroborating testimony that she spent a weekend with the President in Palm Springs.
10. Flo Pritchett Smith, wife of Earl T. Smith; apparently numerous sexual contacts with the President in Palm Beach.
11. Jayne Mansfield, actress; two or three contacts, arranged through Peter Lawford.
12. Unnamed naked women in White House pool, discovered by Kenneth O'Donnel.
13. Leslie Devereux, a high-priced call girl Kennedy met at the Carlyle Hotel in New York; later visited the White House and had sex in the Lincoln bedroom.
14. Unnamed babysitter of a member of the press, Camp David.
15. Odile Rodin, wife of Porfirio Rubirosa.
16. Susannah M., a 20-year-old; frequent contacts in Lincoln bedroom in White house; admissions made November 17, 1993. Gave a pseudonym for TV interview.
17. Marilyn Monroe; numerous occasions in Palm Springs, Los Angeles, Air Force One; once with an unnamed partner for ménage à trois.
18. Unnamed Playboy centerfold; White House,
19. Unnamed Kennedy secretary; Bermuda, 1961.
20. Maria Novotny; call girl, New York City.
21. Suzy Chang; call girl, New York City.
22. Blaze Starr (photo on preceding page) stripper; had sex in a closet at a New Orleans party.
23. Tempest Storm, burlesque queen; location and date unknown.
24. Pamela Turnure, Mrs. Kennedy's press secretary; liaison may have lasted 3 years. Turnure was on Air Force One carrying the President's body back to Washington.
25. Numerous secretaries and young women for ménages à trois in the Carroll Arms in Washington (Source: Kennedy friend, Sen. George Smathers).
26. Janet des Rosiers, Kennedy's "Girl Friday" (rumored).
27. Unnamed young woman at home of columnist Joe Alsop on Inauguration Day.
28. "Mildred," last name unknown, Palm Beach; original source is CBS correspondent Robert Pierpoint.
29. Marlene Dietrich; one occasion.
30. Gunilla von Post; mistress of JFK during his marriage to Jackie.
31. Ellen Rometsch, East German prostitute; slept with JFK ten times in White House, around spring, 1963.
32. Unnamed nanny to the family of a journalist; JFK had sex with her at Camp David; she returned to Puerto Rico to get an abortion, allegedly paid for by Kennedy. (See Sullivan, in subsequent footnote)
33. Mimi Fahnestock, once a 19-year-old White House intern, admitted on May 15, 2003 to an affair that lasted from January 1962 through November, 1963; source: ABC News.

Major sources of information are Judith Exner's My Story *(1977), Traphes Bryant, White House staff member, Secret Service personnel, and a Kennedy assistant (Reeves, p. 202); also Michael Sullivan,* Presidential Passions. *Other girlfriends prior to his marriage were Inga Arvad, Gene Tierney, Sonja Henie (Reeves, p. 83); Joan Lundberg Hitchcock — a Kennedy mistress in the late 1950s said, "He loved threesomes — himself and two girls," (Reeves, p. 173). Kennedy also had asked an Alicia Purdons to marry him. An FBI investigation revealed that JFK had made her pregnant. Bobby was sent with $500,000 to quash a breach-of-promise suit. Mrs. Purdom* later dropped the lawsuit, got a Mexican divorce and the matter was kept out of the press. This relationship has not been included in the table (Reeves p. 218) since it occurred prior to his taking office. Also not included, for the same reason, is an incident at the Cal-Neva Lodge in Nevada where Kennedy spent an evening with 3 call girls. The incident was reported in the Giancana text (Double-Cross). Rumors also linked Kennedy to numerous pre-Presidential liaisons: Gene Tierney, Angela Greene, Lady Jean Campbell, Zsa Zsa Gabor, Susan Hayward, Joan Crawford, Peggy Cummins, Sonja Henie, Hedy Lamarr, Tina Louise, Austine McDonnel, Mrs. Alicia Corning Clark, and Rhonda Fleming (Heymann; see also The Kennedys, p. 524; Summers, Goddess, p. 241). A rumor that JFK had once been married to Durie Malcom is referenced in Heymann, p. 641.

Jack was the model son of his father. "Dad told all the boys to get laid as often as possible," he would say to Clare Boothe Luce. "I can't get to sleep unless I've had a lay."[115] Seymour Hersh corroborates with a similar quotation from JFK: "You know, I get a migraine headache if I don't get a strange piece of ass everyday."[116]

Rarely was Kennedy refused. Sophia Loren and very few others fall into that category. As one woman put it, "How often do you get to sleep with the President of the United States!" JFK's friend, actor Robert Stack, said,

> I've known many of the great Hollywood stars and only a very few of them seemed to hold the attention for women that JFK did, even before he entered the political arena. He'd just look at them and they'd tumble.[117]

Bobby must have known about some of this, but whether he knew of the Exner-Giancana connection prior to his crusade against organized crime is debatable. Arthur Schlesinger, the in-house historian, is not much help either, inasmuch as he quoted Judith Exner's former husband rather than Exner and attempted to describe her allegations as desultory, spurious and rooted in fantasy. White House telephone logs — Schlesinger had an office in the White House — make it quite clear that Schlesinger, not Exner, was living in a fantasy world. Evelyn Lincoln coordinated the trysts; Traphes Bryant dutifully logged them in his diary. Kenneth Powers knew about them. Senator Smathers was privy. The Secret Service covered for the President (and also kept its own confidential logs, released in 1991). Camelot-school scholarship is about as persuasive on this point as Nixon's secretary in trying to explain the 18-minute gap on the Watergate tapes.

With respect to the highly secretive relationship with Marilyn Monroe:

> Besides staying with Kennedy at his secret suite at the Carlyle and in the secluded Lawford beach house, Marilyn often traveled with the President on Air Force One. This was successfully accomplished by a rather simple but effective physical disguise. Marilyn would wear a brunette wig, large sunglasses that obscured most of her face, and unflattering "older" clothing. The crew of the pri-

---

115. Reeves, ibid., p. 41.
116. *The Dark Side of Camelot*, ibid., p. 389
117. Ibid., p. 149.

Chapter 6. Shadows and Secrets

vate presidential airliner and others were casually told that she was Peter Lawford's private secretary.[118]

Protection of these Kennedy secrets was not merely the province of obsequious publicist-historians or co-opted journalists. The Kennedy family and Mrs. Kennedy played a significant role to stop the publication of any indiscretions as well.

The pattern of denial within the Kennedy family is not merely of clinical interest. It had an effect on the whole paradigm of the assassination, which has not been carefully examined.

For example, there was only one person who connected directly to both the Kennedys and Lee Harvey Oswald: Baron George deMohrenschildt.[119] DeMohrenschildt was a friend to Joseph Kennedy, knew Jackie's stepfather and her biological father "Black Jack Bouvier," and spent numerous evenings in Dallas with Oswald. George deMohrenschildt was a known associate of Lee Harvey Oswald. After JFK's assassination, deMohrenschildt contacted Janet Auchincloss, whom he also knew, and requested a meeting with Jackie. Jackie refused."[120]

Her refusal shows more than a desire to keep the matter quiet or let sleeping dogs lie. Here was a man who did not believe Oswald killed her husband, a man who had met with Lee and Marina Oswald over twenty separate times in Dallas, and a man who had seen Jackie frequently when she was a pre-teen. . . yet she declined the meeting. Virtually every member of the Kennedy clan has gravitated to this posture. As Jackie Kennedy's cousin once remarked:

> JFK would sleep with anyone regardless of the circumstances. He had real charisma and great potential, but he was young and thought he was above harm. His personal recklessness is why the Kennedys never pushed the assassination investigation. The family didn't want to uncover the connection among the CIA, the Mafia, and the President.[121]

In Jungian terms, the "shadow" represents the opposite of one's stated or public persona. Kennedy's public image versus the truth of his private life is a classic case example of Jung's concept of the shadow:

---

118. Michael Sullivan, *Presidential Passions*. New York: Shapolsky, 1991, p. 37.
119. DeMohrenschildt knew Black Jack Bouvier. "We saw each other every day. . . he saw a good deal of Black Jack and Janet Bouvier and their nine year old daughter Jacqueline," (Johnson, Priscilla McMillan, *Marina and Lee*. New York: Harper & Row 1977. p. 218). DeMohrenschildt was a fighting atheist and a very eccentric fellow. . .one friend called George and his wife Jeanne "the most unconventional people I have ever seen." Johnson, *ibid*. p. 223.
120. Heymann, *ibid*. p. 415
121. *Ibid*.

The Kennedy image was now widely perceived and appreciated by the American people. This handsome, brilliant, idealistic young statesman, who enjoyed and empathized with people, who loved his charming wife, who was blessed with caring and sacrificing parents and siblings and surrounded himself with some of the most impressive thinking from elite institutions, had boldly persuaded the nations leading Democrats that he was the right man to lead the country toward greatness. Behind the scenes, however, there was a less pleasant and unpublicized reality involving money, bribery, manipulation, adultery and a consistent lack of propriety. The gap between the Kennedy image and reality had grown larger, and in the ensuing campaign it would widen even more. [122]

ABC TV - September 10, 1998: Peter Jennings Special

A documentary with much original research on JFK, Giancana and Kennedy mistresses was released by ABC. These are some highlights from that broadcast.

• Three secret service agents under President Kennedy, Anthony Sherman, Lawrence Newmann and J William McIntyre spoke out for the first time in 1998. Much of this program was based on their testimony.

• The agents corroborated that JFK's sexual liaisons were extreme, and they were quite concerned that he or the presidency would be compromised. The sexual encounters with "Fiddle and Faddle" were, in fact, true. According to these secret service agents, JFK was constantly being serviced by prostitutes. Michael Selsmen, a publicist for Marilyn Monroe, also confirmed the affair between JFK and Marilyn.

• Ellen Rometsch, another Kennedy mistress, may have been connected to East German intelligence. The program states that Rometsch saw JFK sexually frequently in 1963. A suggestion was made on this program that Rometsch might have even given information to East German intelligence on Kennedy's trip to Dallas. Kennedy allegedly paid off Romesch to stay quiet.

• Judith Campbell Exner said that JFK knew about Giancana's attempts to kill Castro. In 1960, JFK gave a package to Exner full of money to give to Giancana. According to Jean Humphreys, wife of Murray Humphreys, an associate of Sam Giancana, the mob was instructed to arrange for unions to deliver votes to JFK in Los Angeles, and St. Louis and elsewhere.

• The FBI hounded Judith Campbell and continued to follow her even after JFK was assassinated. I.B. Hale, a former FBI agent, broke into Judith Campbell's apartment to get information on the General Dynamics Contract.

• Bobby Kennedy talked JFK out of seeing Sinatra at Palm Springs since Sinatra had been a go-between for Exner and Giancana. Sinatra was very upset by this turn of events.

Nothing in this program, however, suggests that Bobby Kennedy was aware of JFK's close association with Giancana through Judith Exner.

(See also Michael Sullivan, Presidential Passions, *Ibid.*, pp 51-54.)

---

122. *Ibid.* p. 182

Chapter 6. Shadows and Secrets

Apparently, the public persona that was cultivated by his writers, publicists, and sycophants hides a different man altogether. Jack Kennedy spoke with the profanity of a sailor and that he was not merely reckless but out of control sexually. Contrast, if you will, some of Kennedy's public proclamations and idealistic rhetoric with the reality of J.J.'s life:

> The next President himself must set the moral tone, and I refer not only to his language, but to his actions in office... Perhaps the gravest responsibility of all rests upon the office of President. No President can excuse or pardon the slightest deviation from irreproachable standards of behavior on the part of any member of the executive branch. [123]

Kennedy's shadow grows to gargantuan size, and the ultimate reaction to such hypocrisy is astonishment, and a reversal in one's feelings best summarized in the words of one Kennedy loyalist:

> At the time he died I too was idealistic about JFK. Now, whenever I see those old films of Kennedy on television, I have to stop myself from heaving. It's hard to believe that here was this absolute fake, this womanizer and opportunist, coming off like Euripides. All our dreams invested in that! What a disappointment! [124]

Kennedy's hypocrisy becomes more evident with time. It is less interesting to call Kennedy a hypocrite than to label this paradoxical behavior for what it is, a sexual dysfunction of major clinical dimensions. John Fitzgerald Kennedy clearly would not be considered a person in the "normal" range of psychological functioning. The hero of this strange, American myth is a person who, like so many others in this drama, is squarely in the grips of a mental disorder.

Our journey along the stealthy alleyways of this psychodrama has introduced us to two characters no one knew about in 1963: "Mary" and "J.J." There are more surprises.

---

123. Sorenson, Theodore C. *Kennedy*. New York: Harper & Row, 1965. p. 52; p. 62.
124. Sullivan, *ibid.*, p. 78

More Sexually Dysfunctional Players: Marilyn Monroe

Marilyn hangs like a bat in the heads of the men that knew her.[125]

— Sammy Davis Jr.

Though one might think that Marilyn Monroe is a minor character in this play, her death in August of 1962 was like a microcosm of the Kennedy assassination itself. It contains all the issues of promiscuity, recklessness, Mob involvement, surveillance by J. Edgar Hoover, mysterious circumstances surrounding the manner of death, botched autopsies, conspiracy theories, even cover-up.

In fact, the symbolic linkage of Kennedy and Lincoln is also repeated in this mini-drama. Marilyn carried a picture of Abraham Lincoln with her wherever she moved. When she married playwright Arthur Miller, she was attracted to him because of his similarity with Lincoln.

> Marilyn, as the world could hardly fail to know, admired Lincoln already. Her idolatry had started, she said, in junior high school, when her essay on Lincoln was judged the best in the class. By happy coincidence, Arthur Miller had attended Abraham Lincoln High School. Five years later, before her marriage to Miller, Marilyn would enthuse to Joshua Logan, director of *Bus Stop*. "Doesn't Arthur look wonderfully like Abraham Lincoln? I'm mad for him."[126]

Marilyn Monroe died in her mid-30s and became one of the most legendary pin-ups in American history. Her love life was covered in the press far more than John Kennedy's, but serious investigative works have since documented that she was puzzled, mentally unstable, pre-psychotic and gradually recapitulating the clinical dynamics of her mother, an institutionalized schizophrenic. She had an even more pronounced sexual addiction than Kennedy. Following is a table of lovers, husbands, and rumored dalliances found in related literature. These affairs spanned two decades and occurred during and between four marriages, to Robert Slatzer, Jim Dougherty, Arthur Miller (4 years) and Joe DiMaggio (9 months). Thirty-two lovers and four

---

125. Summers, Anthony. *Goddess: The Secret Lives of Marilyn Monroe.* London: Penguin, 1985.
126. *Ibid.* p. 65.

husbands in an eighteen-year period argues for a psychiatric diagnosis along the same lines as the President's.

Marilyn gave inconsistent reports that she had been sexually abused as a child; the details appeared to change each time the story was rendered. And once,

> ... at a New York party, Marilyn took part in a game in which she had to say what she wanted most in the world. Her reply, Rosenfeld says, was that she would like "to put on her black wig, pick up her father in a bar, and have him make love to her. Then she'd say, "How do you feel now to have a daughter that you've made love to?" [127]

Table 6.4 Marilyn Monroe's Alleged Lovers[a].

1. Beckford, Charles	19. Lytess, Natasha
2. Belafonte, Harry	20. Miller, Arthur
3. Bolanos, Jose	21. Minardos, Nicos
4. Boyer, Charles	22. Montand, Yves
5. Brando, Marlon	23. Mostel, Zero
6. Carroll, John	24. Odets, Clifford
7. Chaplin, Charlie, Jr.	25. Piscitello, George
8. deVieves, Andre	26. President Sukarno (Indonesia)
9. DiMaggio, Joe	27. Ray, Nic
10. Dougherty, Jim	28. Renoir, Jean
11. Einstein, Albert	29. Rosenfeld, Henry
12. Hemingway, Ernest	30. Schaefer, Hal
13. Hyde, Johnny	31. Schenck, Joseph
14. Karger, Fred	32. Shastber, Lese
15. Kazan, Elia	33. Sinatra, Frank
16. Kennedy, Jack	34. Slatzer, Robert
17. Kennedy, Robert	35. Zahn, Tommy
18. Lyon, Ben	

a. Anthony Summers, *Marilyn*. Ibid.

In deference to Anthony Summers' assiduous respect for corroborating his findings, we might simply list the witnesses he uses to establish the viability of the Kennedy-Monroe liaison. These include statements by Jeanne Martin, wife of Dean Martin; Arthur James, Deborah Gould, Fred Karger, Ross Acuna, Jeanne Carmen,

---

127. *Ibid.* p. 70.

W.W. Weatherby, Jane Shalam, Paula Strasberg, James Bacon, William Kane, Stephen Smith, Anne Karger, Harry Hall, Fred Otash, and many others. Many of these persons were very close to Ms. Monroe; the research and witnesses Summers presents with respect to Marilyn's sexual relationship with both Kennedy brothers is impressive and persuasive. In Summers own words, "On the basis of the assembled information, it must now be considered beyond presumption."[128]

The Monroe Cover Up

Available information on Monroe's death, autopsy, and associated circumstances is highly suspect. Following is a table listing "cover-up" sources very similar to the table we presented in earlier chapters on Kennedy disinformation and cover-up.

Table 6.5 Individuals Alleged in the Literature to have Covered Up or Withheld Information Concerning Marilyn Monroe's Death

Arledge, Roone	Lawford, Pat
Beatty, Warren	Lawford, Peter
Bolanos, Jose	Leibowitz, Murray
D'Amato, Paul	McGuire, Phyllis
Dickey, John	McMillan, Douglas
Dickinson, Angie	Newcomb, Pat
DiMaggio, Joe	Rudin, Milton
Evans, Courtney	Smith, Jean
Gates, Daryl	Smith, Stephen
Greenson, Ralph Dr.	Strasberg, Paula
Hamilton, Capt. James	Van de Camp, Joseph
Hogan (New York District Attorney)	Iannone, Marvin

Dr. Ralph Greenson, her psychiatrist, said professional ethics did not allow him to comment about what he knew. Marilyn saw Greenson frequently, including the day that she died. Shortly before his own death, Greenson admitted that he did not feel she had killed herself.[129]

Joe DiMaggio possessed considerable detail about Marilyn Monroe, her lovers, her association with the Kennedys, Mob figures, involvement with Frank Sinatra, associations with the Cal-Neva lodge in Nevada where Giancana was associated, etc. DiMaggio did not speak publicly about Marilyn and revealed little of what he knew.

---

128. Anthony Summers, *Goddess, ibid.*, p. 243.
129. Reeves, *ibid.*, p. 326.

Peter Lawford was allegedly present at Marilyn's death, and well-substantiated rumors abound that he was implicated in cleaning up her apartment that night. He is said to have destroyed her notes, notebooks, address books and any links to the Kennedys. Following her death, Lawford flew to Hyannisport and stayed in seclusion in the Kennedy estate; he was never called to testify. His third wife, Deborah Gould, said that one night when Lawford was inebriated, he related some details. When he was in New York the next day, he called her and begged her to forget everything he had said. She told much of the substance of that conversation to writer Anthony Summers.

Warren Beatty has also been less than open. Beatty, Natalie Wood, and others were at a party at the Lawford home a few hours before Marilyn died. Summers contacted Beatty in 1983, and he said:

> I, ah, I did see her the night before she died. But, ah, I don't think I would see any particular thing to be gained by expounding on it, er. . . I don't really want to be quoted. I don't think I'll speak about it. . .[130]

Events Leading To Her Death

On June 13, 1962, Marilyn Monroe was invited to the home of Robert Kennedy in Virginia for a party honoring the Lawfords. She declined, with the following telegram:

> Dear Attorney General and Mrs. Robert Kennedy. I would have been delighted to have accepted your invitation honoring Pat and Peter Lawford. Unfortunately I am involved in a freedom ride protesting the loss of the minority rights belonging to the few remaining earth-bound stars. After all, all we demanded was our right to twinkle.
> — Marilyn Monroe [131]

Marilyn made a mysterious trip to the Mafia-operated Cal-Neva Lodge in Nevada. Few people have volunteered what happened on that weekend. Frank Sinatra, Peter Lawford and others were there. One of the purposes, perhaps, was to persuade Marilyn to remove herself from any further involvement in Bobby's life. (A recent text on Frank Sinatra holds that Monroe went to the Cal-Neva Lodge with Sinatra and slept with Giancana while there, something that gave the Mafia don great pleasure in getting back at the Kennedys. Giancana bragged that he was the last man to have slept with her while she was alive.[132])

---

130. Summers, *ibid.* p. 388.
131. *Ibid.* p. 321

On June 26, she met Robert Kennedy again. He was desperately trying to dissolve the relationship and stop her from calling him at the Justice Department. On July 30, 1962, Marilyn made her final call to him; it lasted eight minutes, and it was on the Monday of her last week alive.[133]

Lawford's former wife, Deborah Gould, quotes her husband as saying the Attorney General at first tried to get Lawford to persuade Marilyn that their affair was over, "a couple of days before she died." Then, says Gould, "She tried desperately to get in touch with Bobby. Peter mentioned she made calls to Peter, trying to find out where Bobby was, and found that he was on the West Coast, in San Francisco."[134]

On the morning of the day she died, Marilyn received a strange package in her Hollywood home.

> A messenger arrived with a package. Marilyn opened it and walked out to the pool carrying its contents — a stuffed toy tiger. She then sat down by the pool, holding the tiger and saying nothing. Flanagan thought she was "terribly, terribly depressed," but did not say why. Flanagan, wholly at a loss, got up and left... Had some devastating note arrived with the tiger or — curious thought — was the tiger itself the message? Marilyn, at all events, now lost control.[135]

Marilyn's death that evening is shrouded in mystery. According to Dean Martin's former wife, Jeanne, Marilyn's close confident and friend Pat Newcomb knew more about that evening than has ever been revealed, especially about Robert Kennedy's arrival (or nonarrival), and Peter Lawford's call to Marilyn and his arrival (or nonarrival) to clean up damaging information against the Kennedys. According to Martin,

> "Pat got far too involved; she was deeply in love with Bobby Kennedy. She's only just got over that. If you want to know who knew more about Marilyn than anyone, it's Pat Newcomb. But you could never get anything out of her." To this day, Newcomb clams up when asked about the Kennedys.[136]

On the night that Marilyn died, Bobby Kennedy was in Gilroy, California with family friends, a few hundred miles north. But allegations abound that Bobby was with Marilyn that evening, that he took a helicopter out from the Lawford estate and returned to Gilroy. Bobby came to confront her and tell her their relationship was

---

132. Rando Barraborrelli, *Sinatra: Behind the Legend*, cited in *San Francisco Chronicle*, November 4, 1997, p. B1.
133. *Ibid.* p. 339.
134. *Ibid.* p. 397.
135. *Ibid.* p. 350.
136. *Ibid.* p. 351.

Chapter 6. Shadows and Secrets

over. Marilyn was distraught and depressed. Gould said that the delay in calling the doctors or police after she died was used to "get Bobby out of town." [137]

There are many issues in this abbreviated history, and the suggestion that Bobby was also involved with Pat Newcomb is one. Of even greater importance, however, is some impressive evidence that Marilyn Monroe was murdered rather than merely suicidal over her broken affair with Bobby.

First, Marilyn did not die of a deadly combination of alcohol and pills, as so many think. She had no alcohol at all in her system. Tests showed evidence of pentobarbital and chloral hydrate, one of the less dangerous sedatives found at her home. Marilyn's Nembutal level was some ten times the normal dose and her chloral hydrate level twenty times the norm. Officially, Marilyn died of "acute barbiturate poisoning due to ingestion of overdose," and the death was listed as a "probable suicide." However, traces of pills in the stomach were not found; neither was a drinking glass from which she would have been able to swallow all those pills. Typically, such suicides involve vomiting, but were no evidence of vomit in the pathologist's reports.

This has led some to suggest that Marilyn was given that dose of chemicals by injection. However, there were no injection marks found on her body. Summers speculated that another possibility was by enema. The autopsy report showed the colon had marked congestion and purplish discoloration. No anal smear was taken, but the speculation that the drugs were administered anally is reinforced by a curious remark made by Peter Lawford. Deborah Gould says that after her death Lawford said, "Marilyn took her last big enema."[138] Professor Simpson, cited in Summer's work, also suggested that the administration of the fatal dose could have been done rectally.

A Curious Clue

Some years after this research was reported by Summers, Sam and Chuck Giancana released their book on Sam "Mooney" Giancana, entitled *Double-Cross*. In this work Giancana says that he had Marilyn murdered to expose Robert Kennedy, in fact, that her murder was timed exactly at a time when Bobby had been visiting. The method of murder was by suppository, with barbiturates.

The Giancana revelations came in 1992 while Anthony Summer's speculations and hypotheses were developed in 1986. Thus, it is not altogether absurd to conjecture that Marilyn Monroe was murdered in this manner, and that her murder was at the hands of the Mob as a means of compromising the Kennedys — and specifically, Bobby Kennedy's war against the Mafia. The Giancana based version follows:

---

137. *Ibid.* p. 400.
138. *Ibid.* p. 368.

... Mooney had received word from the CIA that Bobby Kennedy would be in California on the weekend of August 4. That was what Nicoletti said Mooney had been waiting for... Nicoletti said that three other planes also landed that week — in San Francisco — carrying four other men. Mooney had selected a trusted assassin, Needles Gianola, to coordinate the job. Needles, in turn, brought his sidekick, Mugsy Tortorella, on board and two other professional killers — one from Kansas City and one from Detroit. The four men had gone to California, under Mooney's orders, to murder Marilyn Monroe.

... Bobby Kennedy finally did appear at Marilyn's home late on Saturday, accompanied by another man. Listening in on the conversation, Mooney's men ascertained that Marilyn was more than a little angry at Bobby. She became agitated — hysterical, in fact — and in response, they heard Kennedy instruct the man with him, evidently a doctor, to give her a shot to "calm her down." Shortly thereafter the Attorney General and the doctor left... The killers waited for the cover of darkness and, sometime before midnight, entered Marilyn's home... Calmly, and with all the efficiency of a team of surgeons, they taped her mouth shut and proceeded to insert a specially "doctored" Nembutal suppository into her anus. Then they waited.... The suppository, which Nicoletti said had been prepared by the same Chicago chemist who concocted the numerous chemical potions for the Castro hit, had been a brilliant choice. [The HSCA wanted to interview Nicoletti. On the day before they tried to reach him, he was shot and killed.] A lethal dosage of sedatives administered orally, and by force, would have been too risky, causing suspicious bruising during a likely struggle, as well as vomiting — a side effect that typically resulted from ingesting the huge quantities necessary to guarantee death. Using a suppository would eliminate any hope of reviving Marilyn, should she be found, since the medication was quickly absorbed through the anal membrane directly into the bloodstream. There'd be nothing in the stomach to pump out... Indeed, within moments of insertion, the suppository's massive combination of barbiturates and chloral hydrate quickly entered her bloodstream, rendering her totally unconscious. The men carefully removed the tape, wiped her mouth clean, and placed her across the bed. Their job completed, they left as quietly as they had come.[139]

There is one important detail missing from this description. Marilyn was found with a telephone received clutched in her hand.

Bobby Kennedy had lunch the next day with the head of the CIA. Connections between the Kennedys and Marilyn Monroe were never established. Marilyn Monroe died or was killed on August 4, 1962. Some say that she had intended to call a press conference on August 6 and tell all. Telephone records, diaries, and notebooks, a questionable autopsy, and a mysterious line-up of friends and witnesses who did not want to be quoted followed. By late 1962, the issue had been successfully buried and

---

139. Giancana, *ibid.*, pp. 437-438.

Chapter 6. Shadows and Secrets

the death made to resemble a Hollywood starlet's suicidal binge into depression, alcohol and pills. If the Mob had failed in its efforts to bring the Kennedys into line, their next opportunity would come the following year in Dallas.[140]

Dr. Greenson saw Marilyn on the day of her death. He did not violate professional confidentiality, but when Deputy District Attorney John Miner interviewed him after her death, his notes from that interview show Greenson was definite in asserting that Marilyn Monroe did not commit suicide.[141]

Three times a week, for twenty years, Joe DiMaggio had a pair of red roses delivered to Marilyn's crypt. DiMaggio would not permit the Kennedys to be present at Marilyn's funeral, nor Frank Sinatra — who attempted to attend the services. Marilyn is buried at Westwood Memorial Park. Peter Lawford's ashes lie fifty feet away.

> One tier above Marilyn, in the same wall, lies the body of an obscure teenager called Darbi Winters. She was murdered in 1962, just after Marilyn's death. She had only recently told her mother that, one day in the distant future, she wanted to be buried near Marilyn Monroe. [142]

What is psychologically interesting is that the death (or assassination) of Marilyn Monroe symbolically prefigures another assassination, cover-up, disputed autopsy, and conspiracy which would occur fourteen months later to the President of the United States. To underscore the "prophetic" aspect of this event, an important paraprax (Freudian slip) made by Peter Lawford is encrypted in this drama too.

---

140. The Giancana book was published in 1992. As mentioned earlier, this book is either a truthful accounting of American history or a masterful work of disinformation. The speculations about Marilyn Monroe's "possible" cause of death, namely an anal suppository containing deadly levels of Nembutal, was a speculation made by Anthony Summers in 1986. If the Giancana text is a work of disinformation, then the writers have researched this material carefully and crafted their tale accordingly. If, on the other hand, the authors are not that familiar with the literature on the assassination or the death of Marilyn Monroe, then the level of internal consistency in their book is startling, and gives an uncanny match to the speculation and research that has gone before. A second observation to make here is that a conspiracy text by Milo Speriglio and Adela Gregory, entitled *Crypt 33: The Saga of Marilyn Monroe — The Final Word*, asserts that Joseph Kennedy Sr., aware of Marilyn's imminent plans to disclose her relationship with the Kennedys, contracted with mobster Sam Giancana to hit Monroe and make it look like a suicide. This seems dubious only because it was precisely at this time that Bobby Kennedy was so actively pursuing Giancana. If this theory were correct, it would also have difficulty explaining why Bobby continued to pursue Giancana after Monroe's death. The authors, however, say that Jack Kennedy and his father knew of the impending hit on Monroe, but that Bobby did not. (Neal Rubin, "And now, 'The Final Word' on Marilyn," *Detroit Free Press*, July 27, 1993).

141. Summers, *ibid.* p. 376.

142. *Ibid.* p. 412.

Marilyn was invited by Lawford to sing "Happy Birthday" to President Kennedy at Madison Square Garden. She commissioned Jean-Louis to create a dress for the occasion, costing some $5,000. It was an opaque, very thin material, covered with rhinestones. She wore absolutely nothing underneath and had to be sewn into the garment. The birthday salute was on May 19, 1962. Marilyn was late. Peter Lawford introduced her a few times, but, to his chagrin, she was still not yet ready to come out on stage.

Finally, she arrived to sing an unusually sultry "Happy Birthday, Mister President." The President was touched and the audience dazzled. Few, however, seemed to notice a joke by Lawford after his frustrating and repeated introductions. When he finally knew she was backstage and prepared to go on, Lawford said, "Mr. President, because, in the history of show business, perhaps there has been no one female who has meant so much, who has done more. . . . Mr. President, the late Marilyn Monroe."[143] The late Marilyn Monroe died within three months of this introduction. In fact, fateful synchronicity seems to adorn the Kennedy myth at every opportunity.

JACKIE KENNEDY: WIDOW, BONE-CRUSHER, ENIGMA

Another leading character this drama is First Lady, Jacqueline Bouvier. An imposing 5'7", Jackie Kennedy may have been the most publicized American woman of the 20th century. Some psycho-biographical sketch and search through the shadows is warranted here as well.

Her father, "Black Jack" Bouvier, like Joseph Kennedy, was a womanizer with a reputation for shady deal making. When Jackie was eleven, her parents divorced. Jackie's mother married Hugh Auchincloss. This solved many of the family financial problems that Black Jack had created.

> Jackie had a disturbed childhood. Her parents fought bitterly, largely over Black Jack's continuous philandering. After their parents' separation in 1936, Jackie and her younger sister, Lee, stayed with their mother, who grew increasingly aloof and was often absent. Black Jack, an adoring father, visited on weekends and gave his daughters everything they asked for. . . Jacqueline learned to play one parent off against the other. And as she succeeded admirably, especially with her father; she learned the great lessons of her life: that with a little charm, and a little cunning, you could get almost anything you wanted out of a man.[144]

---

143. *Ibid.* p. 309.
144. Reeves, *ibid.* p. 110.

Chapter 6. Shadows and Secrets

Jackie spent her junior year of college in France and became fluent in the language. When she married Jack, she brought with her a fourteen-year age difference and a secret that she was almost penniless. But she possessed qualities that made her an ideal candidate's wife, and the family patriarch, Joe Kennedy, heartily approved. As he once said, "A politician has to have a wife, and a Catholic politician has to have a Catholic wife. She should have class. Jackie probably has more class than any girl we've ever seen around here." [145]

Joe Kennedy enjoyed relating the stories of his own sordid past and his female conquests. Jackie, unlike the other Kennedy women, seemed unusually fascinated and maintained a very deep connection with him:

> Joe soon became Jackie's most ardent supporter, said Lem Billings. He admired her because of her individuality. She wasn't afraid of him. She cajoled him, teased him, talked back to him. He was the moving spirit behind the entire clan. He shaped his children's lives, their relationships, their thoughts. By conquering him, she was conquering his son.[146]

Jackie suffered miscarriages and lost a daughter (unnamed). Rose and Jackie did not get along well, and Rose blamed the miscarriages on Jackie's smoking.[147] There were very significant stresses on her, however, for which smoking may have only been a symptom. Jackie seems to have known about her husband's cheating, for example, and one would suspect she was well prepared. Her father's own infidelities, plus her relationship to her father-in-law, Joseph, gave her ample evidence that males simply behaved this way and perhaps this was only to be expected from her husband. Jackie's friend, author Truman Capote, did not entirely concur:

> I don't think she realized what she'd walked into when she married him. He was in constant competition with his old man to see who could nail the most women. Jackie wasn't prepared for quite such blatant womanizing.[148] The closer John Kennedy seemed to come to the presidency, the more frenetic became his random search for women. [149]

During one pregnancy, Jackie went into premature labor, but delivered John Jr. successfully, at the Georgetown University Hospital. During that time, a man was

---

145. Heymann, *ibid.*, p. 117.
146. *Ibid.* p. 116.
147. *Ibid.* p. 191.
148. *Ibid.* p. 146.
149. *Ibid.* p. 225.

spotted outside her window carrying five sticks of dynamite. The Kennedys did not tell her of this event, but the level of tension and stress around her life then and later were probably more than enough for any normal person to have to endure in a lifetime.[150]

Jackie had a well-developed sense of humor, very much like her husband. One day she came to the White House with a new German shepherd puppy. A member of the press asked what she would be feeding it. She replied "Reporters!"[151] Immunized as she was by a well-defined sense of herself and a healthy sense humor, she nonetheless found politics sour to her taste and avoided it as much as possible. One person has said, "Asking Jackie to get interested in politics was like asking Rocky Graziano to play the piano."[152]

After the assassination, Jackie moved to New York. When Pam Turnure and Robert J. Timmins, a wealthy Canadian tin magnate, were married, Jackie threw a reception for them. She maintained contact with Pam for a number of years and even sent her children to visit them in Montreal. Whether she knew Pam Turnure was her husband's ex-lover, at the time of these events, is not known.[153] A few years later, she married Greek billionaire Aristotle Onassis.

She took Robert Kennedy's death in 1968 very close to heart. Her remarks then give some insight on why she turned to Aristotle Onassis:

> After Bobby's death she said, "I hate this country. . . I despise America and I don't want my children to live here any more. If they're killing Kennedys, my kids are number one targets. . . I want to get out of this country.". . . She wanted to evade what she described as America's "oppressive obsession" with her and her children.[154]

The marriage was greeted harshly. "When Jackie wed Aristotle Onassis (Oct. 20, 1968), the American media reactions were as follows: 'Jackie Weds Blank Check.' 'Jack Kennedy Dies Today for a Second Time.' 'This woman now lives in a state of spiritual degradation, a public sinner (from *L'Observatore della Domenica*). Editorials appeared describing the former First Lady as a traitor to her country.[155]

Jackie was married to Onassis for six years, and became immeasurably wealthier as a result. She settled for $42 million, or nearly $7 million for each year they were married. She hoped the marriage would provide some privacy and return her

---

150. Heymann, *ibid*. p. 249.
151. *Ibid*. p. 272.
152. Reeves, *ibid*. p. 115.
153. Heymann, *ibid*. p. 457.
154. *Ibid*. p. 486.
155. *Ibid*. p. 498.

Chapter 6. Shadows and Secrets

children's life to some measure of normalcy. As Charles Lindbergh longed for anonymity, so too did Jackie; but America's obsessive fixation gave her little reprieve. She died in 1994; one wonders if that obsession ever left her alone for a moment.

In the following section we will try to come to some conclusion about who Jackie was, to try to peer beneath those tabloid headlines that defined her.

Images of Jackie

(1) Fellow Traveler: There are varying pictures. One conscious and popular image was that she was an adept advisor to the President, consulting with him regularly on important decisions.[156] Kennedy and his wife appeared to have a unique connection, an understanding, more than a mere truce, more of a kinship that went beyond marital infidelities.

... Beneath his glittering, outgoing exterior, there seemed to be an insularity and loneliness that Jackie not only recognized but shared. Deep within him was a "pool of privacy," which she herself also had. She compared herself and Jack to "icebergs," the greater part of their lives submerged, and insisted they both "sensed this in each other, and that this was a bond between [them]."[157] ... Still, a sort of friendship grew between the two. They learned to enjoy each other's company. .. Jack, when he paid attention, found his wife consistently interesting. .. He really brightened when she appeared. You could see it in his eyes; he'd follow her around the room watching to see what she'd do next.[158]

(2) The Narcissist: This second image comes from one of her old friends or former friends, Paul Mathias.

Jackie Kennedy was the tease, the temptress of her age. ... She perfected the art, she invented it. She was Miss Narcissist, perpetually searching mirrors for worry wrinkles and strands of prematurely gray hair. She didn't worry about growing old; she worried about looking old. Within 18 months of JFK's assassination, she had two dozen of the world's most brilliant and important men dangling like marionettes, dancing at her fingertips, most of them very married, very old, or very queer.[159]

---

156. *Ibid.* p. 567.
157. *Ibid.* p. 112.
158. Reeves, *ibid.* p. 116.

(3) The bone-crusher: Another opinion projects quite a different meaning:

> I don't know what else she had to offer. . . . She was nothing; an ordinary American woman with average tastes, with some money. She was a creation of the American imagination, Madison Avenue, *Women's Wear Daily*, *Vogue*. She was sharp enough to know that the more she exposed herself, the less impressive she would be. She had nothing to say, so she said nothing. . . In Europe today, she's seen for what she is — a big zero. . . She's very manipulative, self-serving, a real bone-crusher, and very adept at it. The whole Kennedy clan has constructed a litany of lies about itself and now, finally, they are beginning to emerge. Most of the fabrications are built around JFK, and Jackie has created many of them herself.[160]

(4) The Angel of Death: Christina Onassis' assessment of Jackie is similarly unkind, and as a projection, it adds a symbolic element:

> Some superstitious trait out of her Smyrna peasant past suggested to Christina that some sinister force had to be connected with all these deaths, first her aunt, then her brother, now her mother. It must be Jackie who was bringing all the bad luck to the family, "undermining everything" as her brother had predicted. To Christina it seemed as though Jackie killed every life she touched. She was the Angel of Death. This terrible conviction was all the more powerful because by then, Christina could see that her father was also dying. . . Death was never very far from "the Black Widow," as Christina now called her. Jackie was the world's most inveterate bystander to tragedy. Witness John and Robert Kennedy. Christina feared Jackie. She felt she had magical powers. Everybody around her had perished. . . . "I don't like to talk about Jackie Kennedy. . . She is the most mercenary person I've ever met. She thinks, talks and dreams of nothing but money. What she doesn't realize is that I would have given her fifty times what I gave her for the pleasure of never having to see her again. I would have paid any price. What amazes me is that she survives while everybody around her drops. She's dangerous, she's deadly. She has decimated at least two families — the Kennedys' and mine. If I never see her again as long as I live it will be too soon."[161] [Christina Onassis herself died prematurely on November 19, 1988 by her own hand.]

---

159. Heymann, *ibid.* p. 473.

160. Jacques Harvey, who had dinner with Mrs. Kennedy on two occasions, cited in Heymann, *ibid.* p. 505.

161. *Ibid.* p. 558, and 569.

(5) The paranoid depressive: After the assassination, Mrs. Kennedy kept Nancy Tuckerman and Pam Turnure with her as part of her own office staff. She was terribly devastated by her husband's death:

> "She couldn't stop crying. She later told my mother that her own life was dominated by Jack's death and that everything she did and everywhere she went reminded her of him. She couldn't escape him. She would take a walk or a drive in Washington, see a sight that she associated with her husband and immediately fall apart." . . . "According to most accounts, she became increasingly paranoid. It began to seem to her that the same "they" who had murdered her husband were now bent on commercializing and degrading her. Every doorman, delivery boy, neighbor, waiter, taxi driver, anyone who had ever attended her in a store or smiled at her on the street, was a potential enemy. She seemed suspicious of everyone. She refused to step into a taxicab until her Secret Service agent had inspected it thoroughly. . . A young woman who was giving piano lessons to Caroline Kennedy, and who disclosed that fact to a journalist, was summarily dismissed. . . When a cook . . . let it be known that Jackie had gone from a size 12 to a size 8 and back to a size 10, she was fired. . . Her apparent paranoia wasn't helped by a series of ghoulish incidents involving Caroline and John-John. As Caroline returned home one day, a middle-aged woman approached her on the street and told her that she had evidence that her father, the late President, was still alive; the woman then began shouting epithets at the frightened child. . . A group of boys followed her and John Jr. after school one afternoon, shouting "your father is dead! Your father is dead!"[162]

At her worst, Jackie was inconsolable. She remained in bed for long hours, taking sedatives and anti-depressants by day and sleeping pills by night, unable to be with anyone but also unable to be by herself. Left alone with her bereavement, she became obsessed with the thought that she had somehow failed her husband, obsessed by the assassination itself, confessing to her Aunt Michelle that she had replayed the event a thousand times, analyzing it from every conceivable angle and perspective.[163]

The "Kennedy Curse"
Not only did Christina Onassis have a superstitious feeling that Jackie Kennedy brought death wherever she went, others have talked about the larger 'Kennedy Curse', a litany of misfortunes which would boggle the mind. The following incidents are generally cited as belonging to this superstitious curse.
1941 - Rosemary, the oldest daughter of Joseph and Rose, undergoes a lobotomy intended to cure her violent mood swings. She is left severely brain damaged and remains institutionalized today. She was in her early 20s at the time of the surgery.

---

162. *Ibid.* p. 427 and 444.
163. *Ibid.* p. 427.

Aug. 12, 1944	Joseph Patrick Kennedy Jr., the eldest of the couple's nine children and heir apparent, is killed while flying a mission over England during World War II. He was 29.
1948	Kathleen, another of Joseph and Rose's daughters, dies in a plane crash on her way home to reconcile with her parents after a feud. She was 28.
Aug. 9, 1963	Patrick Bouvier Kennedy, John and Jacqueline's third child, dies two days after he was born.
Nov. 22, 1963	President Kennedy is assassinated while riding in an open car in Dallas, Texas. He was 46.
June 19, 1964	Edward Moore Kennedy is critically injured in plane crash that kills an aide.
June 5, 1968	Robert F. Kennedy, the U.S. senator and former U.S. attorney general, is gunned down after a speech in Los Angeles. He died one day later. He was 42.
July 18, 1969	The car Edward Kennedy is driving veers off a bridge to Chappaquiddick Island after a party. His aide, Mary Jo Kopechne, is later found dead inside the sunken car.
Nov. 16, 1969	Joseph Kennedy Sr. dies at the age of 81.
1973	Robert Kennedy's 's oldest son, Joseph, nearly dies in a car accident that leaves a female passenger and family friend paralyzed.
1973	Edward M. Kennedy Jr., Edward Sr.'s son, loses his right leg to cancer
1984	Robert Kennedy's 's son David dies in connection with a drug overdose near his family's home in Palm Springs, Fla. He was 28.
1991	William Kennedy Smith, Jean Ann Kennedy's son, is accused of rape after a party at the family's Palm Beach estate. He is acquitted later that year.
May 19, 1994	Jacqueline Kennedy Onassis dies at the age of 64.
Dec. 31, 1997	Robert Kennedy's son, Michael, dies in a skiing accident in Aspen at the age of 39.
July 18, 1999	John F. Kennedy Jr., along with his wife and her sister, flying a small plane from New Jersey to a family wedding on Martha's Vineyard, are reported missing. Kennedy, president and editor of George magazine and the former president's only surviving son, is 38

(6) The enigma: On who Jackie Kennedy was, author William Manchester said,

> I spoke with that woman for many hours, shared some of her deepest, darkest thoughts, wrote the authorized account of President' Kennedy's assassination, but I don't have the faintest idea what Jackie Kennedy Onassis is really like. That's a question I will take to my grave." [164]

And author Heymann makes a similar conclusion:

> On her sixtieth birthday, July 28, 1989, Jacqueline Bouvier Kennedy Onassis remains an everlasting mystery... She is still the target of more gossip and innuendo than any ten Hollywood movie legends combined, but she has gradually learned to deal with the clamor to circumvent it. [165]

These six images of Jackie Kennedy are merely images gleaned from a literature that is so rife with gossip, obsessive fascination, rumor, hearsay, and slander that any objective observer would be hard pressed to make a selection. Most likely, each of

---

164. *Ibid.* p. 463.
165. *Ibid.* p. 631.

these perspectives is tainted by the aura around her and none is a true or reasonably objective portrait; and yet there is probably a hint of truth to each one.

One could also add a seventh image, far less fraught with slander and insult, Jackie the "restorer-preservationist." She had a fondness for renewal and revitalization. She redecorated the White House, campaigned to save and preserve Grand Central Station, fought to preserve her husband's legacy through the Kennedy library, and her literary achievements for Doubleday similarly worked in the direction of restoration and preservation.

> From a clinical perspective, however, we can come to a few conclusions Considering that Jackie had to dodge paparazzi, like Ron Gallela, from wardrobe to bathroom for thirty years, she fares very favorably in our diagnostic lenses. At the age of 34 she was catapulted into national prominence as the youngest First Lady of this century. She suffered a miscarriage. Her hospital room was dogged by a fanatic carrying dynamite. Her husband cheated on her more than any reasonable person could either imagine or suspect. She was constantly in the limelight from the age of 34 until her death. Hordes of obsessive fans, not all of them kind, followed her everywhere, even to the depths of the Adriatic to photograph her scuba diving on her honeymoon with Aristotle Onassis. Despite all this, Jacqueline Kennedy remained active, mentally alert, productive and succeeded in raising two children to adulthood, neither one of whom manifested any significant psychopathology. She coped amazingly well with environmental stressors which would be unimaginable for most of us.

Notwithstanding all that has been written and the tremendous collective cathexis Jacqueline Kennedy received, of all the characters in this play only Robert Kennedy and Jackie would be considered reasonable candidates for a psychological diagnosis within the normal range.

So, despite the hundreds of covers on the National Enquirer and the cruel, defamatory gossip about her, her ability to cope with these stressors goes almost unnoticed.

Probably the best testimonial to the integrity of Jackie's mental health was given by John Kennedy himself:

> My wife is a shy, quiet girl, but when things get rough, she can handle herself pretty well.[166]

---

166. *Ibid.* p. 172.

Lee Harvey Oswald: Patsy, Spy, Counterspy

Can there be any American of our century who, having failed to gain stature while he was alive, now haunts us more?
— Norman Mailer [167]

Another leading character that deserves more traditional psychological examination is Lee Harvey Oswald. He completed only the ninth grade, but at 118, his IQ was above average. His father, Robert, died two months before he was born. The only real father or father-surrogate was "Uncle Dutz" from New Orleans. The Warren Commission thought Dutz Murret was a steamship clerk, but he was a bookie, a known associate of Sam Saia, in turn, a crime figure in New Orleans connected to Mafia kingpin Carlos Marcello.

Lee Harvey lived for a while in New York. Dr. Renatus Hartogs examined him after excessive truancy from the Bronx school he attended and diagnosed him as "emotionally unstable." Marina Oswald's early testimony after the assassination described a gentle husband. Later, it changed to portray a more unstable and violence-prone individual, consistent with Dr. Hartogs' earlier diagnosis.

Much of the evidence about Oswald's mental condition appears to come from Marina, whose testimony has been irregular (See Table 4.5.) or from author Priscilla MacMillan-Johnson whose credibility also has been questioned.[168] From these

---

167. Norman Mailer, *Oswald's Tale*. New York: Random House, 1994, p. 784.

168. Johnson, *ibid.* p. 90. Johnson actually was the first journalist to ever meet Lee Harvey Oswald; she interviewed him in Moscow at the time of his defection. After the assassination, she was given access to Marina Oswald and wrote the book, *Marina and Lee*, in 1977. This represents virtually the only significant disclosures Marina Oswald has made about the assassination to anyone. The work leads the reader toward the conclusion that Oswald killed Kennedy and that Marina believed he did so. There is a tremendous amount of anecdotal and bibliographic detail which describes Oswald as an unstable character, an abusive husband, someone who in fact attempted to kill General Walker and someone who Marina believed was the assassin. In 1993, however, Marina Oswald consented to an interview and said that she believed her husband was involved in some kind of conspiracy. This notion was not expressed in Johnson-McMillan's book to any significant way. Perhaps Marina Oswald changed her mind about it, since publication. Another serious question about the veracity of Johnson-McMillan's text, however, surfaced recently with disclosures that she had a connection to CIA efforts in Moscow and was listed by them as a "Witting Collaborator OI code A1" in 1975, "not long before her Oswald book was published." Johnson-McMillan denies ever working for the CIA, but this alleged CIA connection and Marina Oswald's change of heart should probably caution the reader to treat Johnson-McMillan's work with skepticism. (See Anthony & Robbyn Summers, "The Ghosts of November, *Vanity Fair*, December, 1994, p. 123.) Summers corroborates his allegation that Johnson-McMillan was a government operative by also citing an FBI document written the day after the assassination saying that McMillan's interview with Oswald in Moscow was "official business." (*Ibid.*)

sources we learned Oswald struck Marina once with his fists and that such beatings occurred as often as once to twice weekly in Dallas and New Orleans. A very recent book by Norman Mailer, based on five days of interviews with Marina (now in her fifties), corroborates the domestic violence was not a fiction, but it may have been exaggerated in Johnson-MacMillan's *Marina and Lee*.

In these early interviews Marina said Oswald planned to assassinate Richard Nixon, to hijack a plane to Cuba, and that he attempted to kill General Edwin Walker in the Spring of 1963. When he returned from his failed assassination attempt on Walker, ". . . Lee suffered anxiety attacks in his sleep. He shook all over from head to toe for times at intervals of a half hour or so, but without waking up."[169]

Besides these sources, others are on record saying that Oswald appeared emotionally unbalanced. These observations come from childhood friends and acquaintances to people who came to know the Oswalds in Dallas. The American embassy consular official thought him to be "aggressive, overbearing, and insufferable" when he tried to renounce his citizenship. Another acquaintance described him as a "megalomaniac," "unbalanced," and a "psychopath." George deMohrenschildt, who genuinely seemed to like conversing with him, called him a "semi-educated hillbilly" and a "lunatic."[170]

It is important to remember, however, how much information, disinformation, and rumor has proliferated over the last several years with regard to all these major characters. While some parties may have a genuine interest in discrediting these individuals, for whatever reason, another dynamic is also at work: the American quest for sensation. That Lee Oswald was a KGB mole or CIA super-agent is part of the same American neurosis that puts out news releases about Jackie Kennedy falling into anorexia, having electroshock therapy, or searching for goat serum cures in Romania. Sensationalism leaves none of our characters untouched, including Oswald — all the more reason not to relax our critical faculties when discussing his background.

That Oswald beat his wife is supported by Michael and Ruth Paine, George and Jeanne deMohrenschildt, and neighbors who lived near the Oswalds — all quite independent of Marina's inconsistent testimony.

But other stories about Oswald's behavior are less well supported. Marina, for example, said that she locked Lee in a bathroom when he was thinking about shooting Nixon. She did not want a repeat of the incident with General Walker. There is virtually no evidence to indicate that Nixon was coming to town, however, and the entire scenario of locking him in the bathroom is confused by the fact that the lock on the door was on the inside. MacMillan-Johnson tries to clarify the inconsistency by

---

169. *Ibid.* p. 288.
170. *Ibid.* p. 231.

saying Marina held the door from the outside to keep Lee from opening it. It took all her strength to do so. One has to wonder about an exceptionally petite Marina mustering the strength to prevent a five-foot-nine-inch assassin from opening the bathroom door that couldn't be locked, to prevent him going off to hit a target who wasn't in town.

One psychological trait, widely corroborated, and also independent of Marina's recollections, is that Oswald seemed to be a person who liked fame, attention, and controversy. He boisterously renounced his citizenship in the American embassy in Moscow, passed out leaflets in New Orleans in front of the headquarters of anti-Castro Cubans, seemed proud, even elated, that he was arrested for these activities, enjoyed his appearance debating Cuban issues, and savored the shock value of standing alone in front of an American aircraft carrier agitating on behalf of socialist Cuba. Indeed, if Oswald did go to Mexico City, his allegedly rude outbursts at the Cuban consulate fit with this vainglorious side to his character. Besides his apparent proneness to domestic violence, then, this haughty element is a second personality trait in which we can have some confidence.

Oedipal Elements and Jealousy

With respect to sexual identity, Oswald appears heterosexual. There have been speculations about homosexual tendencies, but they are supported by almost no evidence, whatsoever. The only hint in this direction is (a) that he is rumored to have gone to a transvestite bar in Japan and (b) that David Ferrie, an acquaintance and Civil Air Patrol instructor, was a homosexual pedophile; and (c) a Mafia connected attorney, Dean Andrews, whose credibility has been attacked by many scholars and researchers, said he saw Oswald in New Orleans in the company of Mexican homosexuals.

Marina stated often that he had no homosexual proclivities.[171] In the early days of his marriage, he suffered from premature ejaculation, but as the relationship moved into its second and third year, performance improved. Oswald had two children by Marina, June and Rachel. He showed no homosexual tendencies in the USSR, and, contrary to Warren Commission comments, he was watched virtually all the time he

---

171. Though no direct homosexual linkage can be proven with Oswald, there is an interesting homosexual subtext in this drama. The following characters are thought to have been homosexual: J. Edgar Hoover, Clyde Tolson, Roy Cohn, Clay Shaw, David Ferrie, and various associates of Shaw and Ferrie, along with General Edwin Walker — whom Oswald allegedly tried to assassinate. Walker was a right-wing member of the John Birch Society, later arrested for homosexual conduct in a bathroom. Some authors believe Jack Ruby had homosexual tendencies, although specific homosexual relationships have not been proven. (Regarding Dean Andrew's account of Oswald, see Norman Mailer's *Oswald's Tale*.)

was there. Indeed, he had a few heterosexual relationships before Marina, in Minsk: a short sexual contact with Inna Tachina, and a nine- month courtship with Ella Germann, his co-worker in the Minsk radio factory. He appears to have lost his virginity as a Marine in Japan.[172]

There are some striking Oedipal elements. First, he frequently slept in the same bed with his mother until age eleven. Surprisingly, his mother bathed him up until this age as well. Secondly, he seemed to like children and often infantilized himself in play.

Oswald often referred to Marina as "mama" and once when her breast milk was too abundant and causing her pain, Alik offered to suck the milk. She was more surprised still when instead of spitting it out as she expected, he swallowed it. Why not? he asked. It was good milk, sweet and fat. If it was good enough for his baby, it was good enough for him. And he went right on drinking it.[173]

An Unconscious Hatred of Kennedy?

A psychological theory of the assassination emerges from Priscilla Macmillan-Johnson's observations. Its basic outline follows:

In prior chapters we noted that the Warren Commission was unable to determine a motive. Oswald liked Kennedy, read *Profiles in Courage*, *Portrait of a President*, and spoke highly of Kennedy to deMohrenschildt all in the year of the assassination. He and Marina kept a *Life Magazine* photo spread on Kennedy on their coffee table. Puzzled after the assassination, Marina said "but he liked Kennedy!" [174]

During marital arguments, Marina bellowed that she should have married her former Russian paramour, Anatoly, instead of him. Oswald discovered a love letter Marina wrote from the United States that angered him greatly. Moreover, Anatoly looked like Kennedy, to her. She displayed photos of Kennedy around the house and admitted to erotic feelings for JFK (but had not made such admissions to Lee).

MacMillan-Johnson wondered if Lee might have sensed Marina's attraction to Kennedy, and his similarity to Anatoly in Minsk, and shot the President to unconsciously destroy Marina's symbolic suitor. It is a wild speculation more than a theory, but probably the only psychological account ever offered to explain Oswald's motives for the greatest crime of the century. American obsessiveness over this event still has not bothered to answer "why" Oswald wanted to shoot Kennedy in the first place, if in fact he shot him at all. [175]

---

172. Mailer, *ibid*.
173. *Ibid*. p. 139.

We are not determining guilt or innocence in this section of the text, but attempting to examine character traits and come to some diagnostic and clinical conclusions. The following observations are offered as a composite diagnostic portrait of this unusual man:

Oswald's mental health was dubious. The overall picture of his mental status cannot be rationalized away merely because he was a victim of unfavorable publicity. He had a severe learning disability (dyslexia). He was a product of a broken home, a loner, confused about his own personal identity; he drifted from job to job, was content neither in the Soviet Union nor the United States, and his emotional balance fluctuated between an asocial indifference to the feelings of others to unpredictable outbursts of anger. Oswald was diagnosed in the ninth grade as unstable and passive

---

174. *Ibid.* p. 466. Although this chapter focuses on the mental health status of the major players, Johnson's theory with respect to Oswald's motives is not the only one. On the basis of the available data, another theory supporting Oswald's complicity and one refuting it could easily be forwarded. For example, one characteristic of a "borderline" personality is impulsivity. It could be argued that Oswald's decision to shoot the President was impulsive, consequent upon Marina having rejected him the night before. Oswald picked up his rifle and went directly to the Depository to shoot the President. His impulsive outbursts, particularly as a wife beater, support this hypothesis. However, one could develop an entirely different slant, as well. Oswald's attempted assassination of General Walker differed markedly from his alleged presidential assassination plan. If Marina's testimony can be held to be credible, Oswald planned his hit on General Walker, researched it, spent many hours in his study going over maps, and frequently traveled to Walker's home to find the best shooting location. Oswald had planned his getaway, hid his rifle, and even had a plan for how to retrieve it after the shooting. If this was Oswald's modus operandi, it is entirely inconsistent with how he purportedly approached the presidential assassination. He forgot to have money on him for a getaway. He had no change of clothes and had to return home to get them. He forgot to take his pistol with him, which he might need for an escape. (If he could take a rifle into the Depository, certainly he could have brought his pistol as well.) So the second psychological theory does not point to Oswald as the assassin at all, but shows an individual acting impulsively, on the run, scurrying home to pick up his pistol and having virtually no plan on what to do next.

Another inconsistency here is Oswald's tendency toward braggadocio and exhibitionism. It would have been consistent with Oswald's character (assuming he shot the President) to boldly proclaim that he had carried out this execution for the socialist cause and for Cuba. This trait was never in evidence after the assassination. He did not attempt to get any political leverage or publicity for his cause after his arrest — as he would normally be expected to do; he denied that he shot the President to the press, to his wife Marina, and to his brother, Robert.
In short, the psychological analysis of Oswald's character leads us in both directions, one favoring his involvement in the assassination, and one very much at odds with that analysis.

175. Another relatively new theory which offers to explain how Oswald, who admitted a liking for Kennedy, still might have been motivated to kill him, comes from Gerald Posner. Castro gave a speech in Brazil on September 7, 1963, warning Kennedy that continued attacks upon Cuba could result in retaliatory actions against the Kennedy administration. Posner argues that Oswald may have turned against Kennedy when he read of Castro's speech two days later in the Dallas papers.

aggressive with schizoidal features and was considered potentially violent. His adjustment to the Marines was marginal at best. After he enlisted, at the age of 17, his fellow Marines, aware of his peculiarities, referred to him as "Ozzie Rabbit," "shit bird," or "Oswaldkovich." [176]

By the age of 24, he had shot himself in the elbow, been disciplined in the Marines for illegally owning a Derringer, spent 28 days at hard labor for a second infraction, renounced his citizenship by defecting to the USSR, received an undesirable discharge from the Marines, attempted suicide in Russia, was arrested for disturbing the peace in New Orleans, and may have been involved in as many as three murders or attempted murders: Walker, Tippit, and Kennedy. Even giving him the benefit of the doubt in a dozen spurious anecdotes — generated by collective projections into a mythic devil instead of accurate descriptors of a real person — there is still enough hard data to indicate he was emotionally unstable. These diagnostic symptoms describe what would probably today be called a "borderline personality disturbance."

Oswald the Mystery

Oswald, of course, is more than a borderline personality. He has been cast as the leading character from the dark side, the Darth Vader of this 20th-century myth. Furthermore, Oswald seems to occupy a place very close to the core of the paradox which is the Kennedy assassination. Oswald leads us everywhere and nowhere. He keeps us going in circles. No one can penetrate the veil of illusion his character creates. It is impossible to render an answer as to who he was: a spy, a counterspy, a mentally-disturbed lone assassin, or the designated patsy for an enormous crime.

Was he a miscreant, practicing how to hijack a plane to Havana, in his underwear, in Dallas, shortly before the assassination, as Gerald Posner portrays, or was he connected in some mysterious way with the intelligence services and secretly receiving monies from his Russian friend and CIA contact in Dallas, George deMohrenschildt?

When John Fain of the FBI interviewed him on his return from the USSR, Fain asked him if he was in American intelligence. As if rehearsing for a future role as a full-fledged enigma, Oswald replied, "Don't you know?"[177]

We can summarize and synthesize material from prior chapters — plus some new data — to get closer to Oswald's multiple identities and the multiple functions his character serves in the myth that this event has become.

---

176. Johnson, *ibid.* p. 116.
177. Mailer, *ibid.*, p. 614.

Oswald, on the Right

Facts and evidence supportive of a portrait of our mysterious Oswald as a right-wing, anti-Castro, mercenary:

• First, he checked out from the library *The Shark and the Sardines*, a book written by a man who personally lived through the CIA overthrow of the 1954 Guatemala regime involving Howard Hunt (who may have headed the Mexico City CIA station in the same year that Oswald is said to have paid it a visit). Oswald may have authored a letter to Hunt which was unearthed mysteriously in the mid-1970s.

• If Oswald wanted to read about this topic, and if he used CIA-linked David Ferrie's library card to check out the book, might suggest that he was studiously learning how to be a CIA contract agent employed by Howard Hunt, Guy Banister, and/or David Ferrie. Oswald loved spy thrillers, watched *I Led Three Lives* (a TV serial about a spy) as a boy, and read *How to be a Spy* in the year of the assassination.

• He solicited anti-Castroite Carlos Bringuier, in New Orleans, in order to become a member of an anti-Castro fighting force, not to aid Castro but to fight against him. Oswald's Fair Play for Cuba Committee had a suspicious address, 544 Camp Street, the headquarters of anti-Castro, CIA-backed organizations. The leading figure there was Guy Banister, former FBI agent, CIA contract agent, Minuteman, and right-winger.

• Many witnesses described seeing Oswald in Banister's presence. Banister told his secretary that despite Oswald's leafleting activities for Cuba, he was one of his agents. (David Ferrie was also an associate of Banister.)

• Oswald's appearance at the apartment of Sylvia Odio in late September 1963 shows that he was in the company of right-wing anti-Castro, not pro-Castro elements. Loran Hall's fabrication to the Warren Commission and Sylvia Odio's testimony — described earlier in this text — give substance to this point of view.

• Sylvia Odio came forward shortly before the Warren Commission issued its report. She said Oswald visited her and her sister and posed as anti-Castro freedom fighters. Suddenly, J. Edgar Hoover said that Sylvia Odio had to be wrong in her assessments and that an individual who looked like Oswald, Loran Hall, was actually the visitor to her apartment. This seemed to clear the way for the Warren Commission conclusion that Oswald was a leftist, pro-Cuban sympathizer, not a right-wing anti-Castroite freedom fighter. The Warren Commission went to print with that conclusion, only years later to learn that Loran Hall admitted he lied. He never met Sylvia Odio; which leads investigators right back to the notion that Ms. Odio was in fact telling the truth all along.

• Loran Hall was connected to the CIA, and the Mafia, and was heavily involved in anti-Castro activities. Why would he try to pose as Oswald for the Warren Commission? Hall's fabricated testimony seems to be trying to cover

Chapter 6. Shadows and Secrets

someone's tracks, tracks perhaps left by Oswald himself. Under immunity from prosecution, Hall admitted he lied and said that his life was in danger for coming forward with these admissions.

- Loran Hall's behavior in trying to place himself in Odio's apartment and dilute Odio's argument that Oswald himself, was a right-wing anti-Castro mercenary who was present in her apartment that September is singularly supportive of this point of view. The fact that subsequent authors, Gerald Posner[178] in particular, hack away at Odio's credibility with implications that she was mentally unstable or under psychiatric care — while virtually ignoring Loran Hall's admissions — suggests that even these authors seem to have a vested interest in assuring the reader that Oswald could in no way be connected to any CIA or anti-Castro interests.

Through these evidentiary lenses a very different Oswald emerges: a right-wing, anti-Castro, CIA-linked, mercenary-in-training associated in some mysterious manner with right wingers Guy Bannister, Howard Hunt, and/or David Ferrie. In this vein recall that Oswald told his friend, Adrian Alba, upon his leaving New Orleans for Dallas, that he had "found his pot of gold at the end of the rainbow." Was it a pot of gold in the employ of Ferrie, Banister, Hall, anti-Castro Cubans, or other CIA functionaries?

To add more mystery here, the Warren Commission accepted testimony from a car salesman who filled out a purchase order for a "Lee Oswald," associated with the Democratic Friends of Cuba, long before the assassination. Oswald could not drive, then or later; but the Warren Commission produced a document showing a Lee Oswald test-driving the car. This becomes evidence that someone was "creating" a fictitious Lee Harvey Oswald, clearly identified as a "friend" of Castro's Cuba; it looks as if there is a concerted effort by someone to portray Oswald as pro-Castro while, at the same time, trying to cover up any tracks that he might have been the opposite (the Loran Hall admissions).

And finally there are the revelations of only the last few years that support the theory that Oswald had some connection to military-intelligence and the CIA. John Newman, a Kennedy researcher and former major in U.S. Army Intelligence, reviewed these recently declassified CIA documents with the following comment:

> It doesn't take a rocket scientist to understand that the Agency's attempts to explain this do not wash. I have found hard documentary evidence that other files were opened on Oswald immediately, files that were very, very sensitive. The alarm bells were ringing, but then somebody pulled the switch. I have senior

---

178. A short review of Posner's *Case Closed* follows, in this chapter.

Agency personnel on the record on this one. This is a configuration consistent either with Oswald being the object of a sensitive intelligence investigation or with Oswald as an intelligence asset.[179]

Newman found a document showing "Andy Anderson" had debriefed Oswald for the CIA, a fact denied then and now by former directors including Richard Helms (as recently as 1993). Newman notes that Andy Anderson's report was reviewed by another officer, Donald Deneselya, who also recalled seeing it. It apparently originated from a CIA section headed by "T.B.C.", but no one at this writing seems to have a credible interpretation of who T.B.C. might be.[180] To Newman, it is not merely a CIA cover-up of its debriefing of Oswald:

> The Agency would not lie to cover for something that wouldn't get them in trouble anyway. The denial that they had any interest in Oswald is a big billboard saying there's something else. The denial is part of a broader lie... There's an unexplained anomaly, and among the questions it poses is whether or not the Agency had an association with Oswald... He was either part of an operation or an operation was built around him.[181]

This completes our right-wing composite of Oswald. Documents only recently released are sometimes so heavily redacted (blackened out) that one wonders what kinds of sensitive information must still be held confidential and denied to the public.

The level of suspicion of government or CIA complicity in these matters rises in direct proposition to the amount of black ink used to redact documents being released close to four decades after the killing of President Kennedy.

In sum, the picture of Oswald as an intelligence asset, somehow linked to anti-Castro Cubans, or in someway set up or involved with David Ferrie, Guy Bannister, and/or Howard Hunt, or other CIA and former-CIA contract agents is not easily dismissed.

---

179. Anthony & Robbyn Summers, "The Ghosts of November," *Vanity Fair*, December 1994, p. 129. James Hosty, the closed-mouthed FBI agent who has been a mystery to conspiracists, finally opened up in 1995 to John Newman, author of *Oswald and the CIA*. Hosty's theory about the Sylvia Odio incident is that CIA agent William Pawley, a right winger associated with anti-Castro Cubans in Miami, and perhaps with the backing of Henry Luce and H.L. Hunt, were "spying" on JURE, the organization founded by Sylvia Odio. Pawley and his cohorts were using Oswald to collect information on the left-wing JURE faction led by Sylvia's father, who was in a Cuban jail.

180. A fictionalized CIA thriller written by Robert Morrow mentions the name Tracy Barnes, a CIA case officer; it might fit these initials. Newman's text also makes a very substantial and well-supported argument that Oswald was in Mexico City, but that he was also simultaneously impersonated by someone else (see pp. 352-391).

181. John Newman, Oswald and the CIA, *ibid*. p. 707.

Chapter 6. Shadows and Secrets

Oswald, the Psycho

But Oswald does not get categorized as a contract agent working for CIA sponsored, anti-Castro organizations so easily. He slips in here, there, everywhere — like Eugene Hale Brading — and is nowhere to be pinned into a fixed position. Just in case we get too conspiratorial, too Garrisonized, we are reminded of one set of facts or another that frustrates all prospects of certainty. Let us therefore view Oswald through the lens of the "lone assassin psycho," and see how the evidence sorts itself out in this more traditional assessment of our anti-hero.

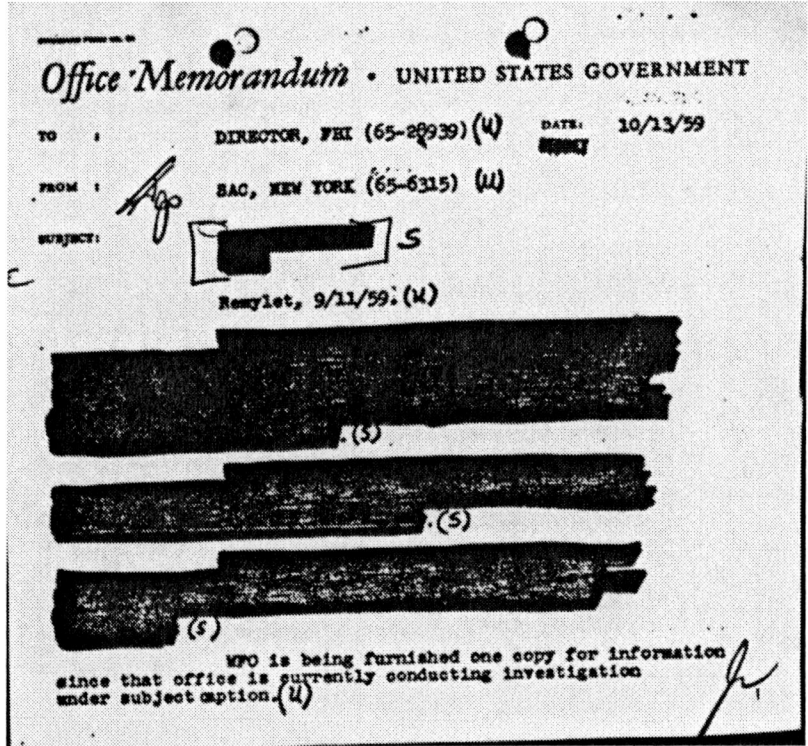

Figure 6.1 A recently released, but redacted, document about Oswald from 1959

In September, 1993, the CIA released thousands of documents dealing with the assassination of President Kennedy. At the same time, and in anticipation of the 30th anniversary of the assassination in November 1993, a spate of Kennedy books appeared, the most publicized being Gerald Posner's *Case Closed*. This Random House,

600-page effort was quite unlike any of its predecessors. A short review of this important and controversial work follows in the Appendix to the chapter.

First, Oswald did not have enough money to afford the accommodations of a CIA operative. He bounced from job to job, kept collecting unemployment insurance, even rented a room at the YMCA. This is the profile he cut, not the romantic, Ian Fleming image that fans of thrillers imagine would match the role he was supposedly playing in a conspiracy.

Oswald lived like a disturbed, lone, assassin; he was diagnosed as mentally unstable and violence prone. He took a shot at General Walker and proudly called himself a "hunter of fascists" to George deMohrenschildt. He hit his wife repeatedly, could not hold a steady job, and was rapidly losing Marina's affection.

When he went to Mexico City, he was desperate. Neither consulate took him seriously. In fact, he was so out of control that he placed a loaded pistol on the table in front of his Russian interviewer and wept. Both embassy officials recognized him as emotionally overwrought and unbalanced. One version says,

> Throughout his story, Oswald was extremely agitated and clearly nervous, especially when he mentioned the FBI, but he suddenly became hysterical, began to sob, and through his tears cried, "I am afraid. . . they'll kill me. Let me in!" Repeating over and over that he was being persecuted and that he was being followed even here in Mexico, he stuck his right hand into the left pocket of his jacket and pulled out a revolver saying, "See? This is what I must now carry to protect my life," and placed the revolver on the desk where we were sitting opposite one another. I was dumbfounded, and looked at Pavel, who had turned slightly pale, but then quickly said to me, "Here, give me that piece." I took the revolver from the table and handed it to Pavel. Oswald, sobbing, wiped away the tears.[182]

If we stay with this framework, we see a far different Oswald. He returned to Dallas, was no longer wanted by Marina, was jealous of her attraction to JFK, and continued to crumble psychologically. He took a room under an assumed name, O. H. Lee — not because he worked for David Ferrie, Howard Hunt, and the CIA, but because he was paranoid and thought the FBI was dogging him and getting him fired everywhere he went. When Marina finally moved in with Ruth Paine and decided to stay with her instead of rejoining her husband, he was pushed to the edge.

The day before the assassination, he went to Ruth Paine's house, where Marina had been staying; he slept that night "like a zombie," says Marina. He was in such a mysterious funk, just lying there, Marina even wondered if he was dead. He got up,

---

182. Mailer, *ibid.*, p. 638. Col. Oleg Nechiporenko, author of *Passport to Assassination*, is the primary source.

left his wedding ring in a cup, grabbed his rifle that he had wrapped in a large paper bag the evening before, and went off to shoot Kennedy. [183]

There was no planning, other than on the morning of the motorcade when he set up his shooting gallery in the Book Depository. The assassination was an impulsive act of a borderline personality in a state of severe emotional crisis, the same borderline personality that had attempted suicide in Russia, shot himself in the elbow in the Marines, and was sentenced to hard labor in a brig. This was a man on a very thin line just waiting to snap. On November 22, 1963, he did.

The fact that after the assassination he had to go back home to pick up his pistol is further proof that he was out of control and acting on impulse, without plan or purpose. If this was a pre-meditated and planned event, he would have carried his pistol with him, just as he had carried the rifle. Instead, he abandoned the rifle in the Depository, went home to change clothes and pick up his pistol, and then left — probably, to high tail it out of town. As he was fleeing, he shot officer Tippit, as part of this same, general, emotional collapse.

But wait! That scenario sounds very validating to Warren Commission apologists like Gerald Posner, but can this appraisal be believed? Oswald was cool, collected, rational, and cooperative at police headquarters less than an hour and a half after this so-called emotional collapse. Furthermore, he was no raving maniac — at least in the eyes of those who interrogated him. He did not have to be restrained, given medication, or taken to a psychiatric ward (where a man who just pumped four bullets into a police officer would ordinarily be processed).

From Warren Commission testimony:

> Mr. Boyd: I tell you, I've never saw another man just exactly like him.
> Mr. Stern. In what way?
> Mr. Boyd. Well, you know, he acted like he was intelligent; just as soon as you would ask him a question, he would just give you the answer right back — he didn't hesitate.... I never saw a man that could answer questions like he did...
> Mr. Stern. Of course, this was a long day for everybody — did he seem by the end of the day still to be in command of himself, or did he appear tired or particularly worn out?
> Mr. Boyd. Well, he didn't appear to be tired. . . I imagine he could have been [but] he didn't show it.
> Mr. Stern. This is quite unnatural — really rather exceptional; this is, of course, why you say "somewhat unusual" — a man accused of killing two people, one of them the President of the United States, and at the end of the day he is pretty well in command?

---

183. *Ibid.* p. 261. p. 378 and 413.

Mr. Boyd. Yes sir; I'll tell you — Oswald, he answered the questions until [he finally] got up and said, "What started out to be a short interrogation turned out to be rather lengthy," and he said, "I believe I have answered all the questions I have cared to answer, and I don't care to say anything else." And sat back down.[184]

We cannot find ourselves particularly content with this "psychiatric" theory especially when we hear how rational and composed he was at police headquarters. He was not banging on tables. He was searching for an attorney and responding with deliberation to accusations.

Oswald, the Mafia Patsy

When we consider Oswald as a "Mafia patsy," another stream of evidence begins to collect. The HSCA decision was that there was a conspiracy and that at least four shots were fired in Dealey Plaza. Hoover had taped discussions of "contracts"; Trafficante, Marcello, Giancana were involved. Did Oswald have any connection to these people? These Mafiosi obviously wanted Kennedy hit; was it just a coincidence that Oswald managed to do — gratuitously — what the Mafia had already contracted hit men to accomplish?

We have already gone over the alleged connections; especially through Uncle Dutz. And Nofio Pecora, who bailed Oswald out of jail in New Orleans, was a friend of Marcello and had spoken to Jack Ruby only three weeks before the assassination. (Imagine, the man who bailed Oswald out of jail was on speaking terms with his killer!)

Oswald can be linked to Marcello through many people. And Marcello was the man who ordered the hit on Kennedy, and celebrated Kennedy's death at a restaurant in such a churlish way that Mrs. Rogano, the wife of Marcello's attorney, had to go home to be sick.

Even though Oswald did not drink or smoke or have any Mafia-like predilections, he fits as a patsy into a Mafia conspiracy easily, and is in fact dripping with Mafia connecting links and associations.

There is one problem here, too, however; how did he get his job at the Depository? His Mob-connected Uncle Dutz did not have him placed there. The CIA did not have him placed there. He found a job at the School Book Depository on October 16, and he found it through a neighbor of Ruth Paine. (Still, it is true that the Paines knew deMohrenschildt well, and deMohrenschildt did have CIA connections at this time; so a CIA connection in the placement of Oswald is still a possibility.

---

184. Anthony & Robbyn Summers, "The Ghosts of November," *Vanity Fair*, December 1994.

Chapter 6. Shadows and Secrets

Lee got a job his second week in Dallas. A neighbor of the Paines, Linnie Mae Randle, mentioned that her brother, Wesley Frazier, worked at the Texas School Book Depository and there might be a job opening there. At Marina's urging, Ruth called Roy Truly, superintendent of the depository, and asked him to consider Lee. Mr. Truly suggested that Lee apply in person. He was hired at $1.25/hour and began work October 16, 1963.

On November 15, the *Dallas Times-Herald* reported that the President would be having lunch at the Dallas Trade Mart. The *Dallas Morning News* and the afternoon *Times-Herald* published the presidential route for the first time (November 19).[185]

There is excellent evidence to point to a Mafia conspiracy in the assassination, but one critical flaw is how Oswald, as the patsy, was set up in his position in the Depository. This is one of the weakest points in that whole theory, and only the wildest speculations can answer that dilemma.

Ruth Paine was a Quaker; she taught Russian at St. Marks School, an Episcopal prep school.[186] There are some still-classified documents about the Paines, but if they point anywhere it is to the intelligence community, not the Mafia. We cannot connect the Paines to a Mafia conspiracy without the greatest difficulty, and we arrive at another dead end. We are left with a composite picture of Lee Harvey Oswald which is muddled, multi-directional, and paradoxical.

Oswald, Not Guilty

There is still one last possibility which we haven't looked at: that Oswald had absolutely nothing whatsoever to do with the assassination and sat out the entire Presidential parade in the second floor lunchroom of the Depository. Witnesses place him there at 12:15 and at 12:31.

Oswald had a job, one that he liked. He and Marina still talked, and there was still hope for their relationship. They had just had a baby, their second, less than a month before the assassination. They slept in the same bed the night before the assassination. Oswald added an exemption to his W-2 form to get less money withheld from a check he was anticipating at the time of his death.

This is not the profile of an assassin but a struggling new father with a future to look forward to. Borderline or not, he may have been a totally innocent bystander who was used, abused, and eaten up by a conspiracy he had nothing to do with. When he was taken to the police station, he was asked if he wanted to cover his face. He asked "why?" — he had done nothing wrong!

---

185. *Ibid.*
186. See J. Hosty, *ibid.*

Conspiracy in Camelot

This image of Oswald, one which accords him a presumption of innocence, has received very little consideration in all the literature about him. Let us give him at least one moment in this sunshine. From Warren Commission testimony, once again:

> Mr. Ball. Did you ask him if he shot Tippit?
> Mr. Fritz. Oh, yes.
> Mr. Ball. What did he say?
> Mr. Fritz. He denied it. . . "The only law I violated was in the movie show; I hit the officer in the show; he hit me in the eye and I guess I deserved it." He said, "That is the only law I violated." He said, "That is the only thing I have done wrong."
> Mr. Ball. Did you ever ask him if he had kept a rifle in the garage at Irving?
> Mr. Fritz. Yes, sir; I did. I asked him, and I asked him if he had brought one from New Orleans. He said he didn't.
> Mr. Ball. He did not.
> Mr. Fritz. That is right. I told him the people at the Paine residence said he did have a rifle out there, and he kept it out there and he kept it wrapped in a blanket and he said that wasn't true." [187]

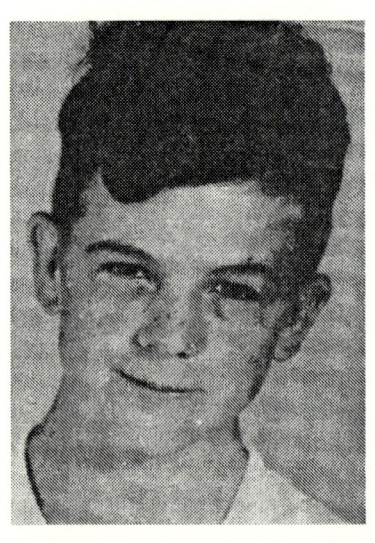

Oswald (pictured here as an adolescent) denied he had ever gone to Mexico City, denied the photos of him holding his rifle were genuine, denied shooting Tippit, and denied shooting the President. And if we are to be fair in giving Oswald his presumption of innocence, if only for this one page, it would be appropriate to quote his widow, Marina, who at 52 told an interviewer in 1995, "All the same, I'm definitely sure he didn't do it." [188]

But true to form, she does not leave it there. Like her husband, she has always left a very ambiguous trail of commentary. Even now she waffles and is not quite sure he definitely did not do it, or if he was part of some conspiracy or government operation. She is consistent on one fact, however, and that is that her husband has not been portrayed in the media properly. "I do think he was more human than has been portrayed."[189]

---

187. Mailer, *ibid.*, p. 702-703
188. *Ibid.* p. 785
189. *Ibid.*

Chapter 6. Shadows and Secrets

The innocent side and the human side get very little press. Gerald Posner's bias is so thick, he even publishes Oswald's baby pictures with captions that leave little room to think of him as anything other than diabolical. President Gerald Ford's book is yet another example of the negative attire Oswald has had to wear. As Marina relates:

> ...dear President Ford told everybody that Lee was impotent and that's the thing which is not true... People like that become President. I am sorry. I have no respect for Mr. Ford. [190]

There is evidence in abundance that Lee was not the unbalanced, violent, impotent, projected devil he was made out to be. Many thought he was rather nice — these were people who knew him well, too. Lillian Murret (Oswald's aunt) had only positive things to say and her daughter, Dorothy, echoes the sentiments:

> He had a certain manner about him that other children never had. I mean he was very refined, he really was, and extremely well-mannered... he was daring, and very outgoing and a very pretty child. He was adorable...[191]

A buddy in the Marines recalled how a puerile Oswald innocently confided to him that he was still a virgin, and how he always thought Oswald was a real "down-home" kind of person. Those who knew Marina and Lee in Minsk relate an entirely different image as well. They seemed happy together and Lee a distinctly non-violent person. His favorite Russian song goes:

> Where can I find the sweet words?
> How can I say that I love you?
> You have brought me so much happiness in life
> I sing to you and share with you my life. [192]

What could be more novel as a character witness supporting Oswald's innocence than his KGB handlers in Minsk:

> Igor Ivanovich was asked, "After the assassination, you must have felt bad?" And he replied, "Bad? I felt horrible. In fact, it was the worst moment of my life."

When asked if KGB had interrogated any of their prime sources after the assassination, Igor Ivanovich suddenly became emotional. He looked as if he might

---

190. Mailer, *ibid* p. 356
191. *Ibid.* p. 177.
192. See endnote 111.

burst into tears. He did not answer the question. Instead, he cried out: "Everybody blames me for this! It was as if I knew he would shoot." After a minute or two, he added, "We had no data. You could not find one single person from Minsk who would say, "Yes, Oswald had these intentions to go back to America and cause all this trouble." [193]

Ella Germann, his nine-month crush in Minsk before he met Marina, felt he was far too gentle to have committed such a crime.

Even in Dallas, according to Marina:

> ... he loved his little girls enormously, and even thirty years later she heard a story about how in those last days, when he lived on North Beckley, he was playing with the grandchildren of the woman who ran his last rooming house. "Are you a good boy?" and that kid shook his head in the negative said "Uh-unh," and Lee said, "Never be so bad that you hurt somebody." This kid was now grown-up but he still remembered that, still told that story."[194]

But once again, if we get too sentimental — or too serious — in thinking him that human or that innocent, how do we explain away his ordering the rifle under the Hiddel alias, the attempted assassination of General Walker, the photos of him holding the rifle, and storage of the rifle in the Paine's garage to name a few, all of which he denied? The primary source of that evidence, pointing to his guilt, comes from the same source that now points to his innocence: Marina Oswald.

Norman Mailer eloquently summarizes this frustrating journey through contradiction and paradox, saying, "One can go, trying to explore into every last reach of possibility, only to encounter a disheartening truth: Evidence, by itself, will never provide an answer to a mystery."[195] Probably the single best researcher on the Kennedy assassination, Anthony Summers, concurs: "Yet thirty years on, we still cannot be sure who he really was."[196] Oswald denies he owns a rifle, but admits he owns a pistol. Everyway we look at him, he becomes more enigmatic.

The paradox of this character in our myth is perhaps best illustrated in the following double-edged story:

'To Kill That Sonofabitch Kennedy!'

FBI agent James Hosty's memoirs say that on September 23, Oswald, a leftist, was in the Cuban consul's office in Mexico City, saying he was "going to kill that

---

193. Mailer, *ibid.* p. 329.
194. Mailer, *ibid.* p. 787.
195. Mailer, *ibid.* p. 775
196. Anthony & Robbyn Summers, *ibid.* p. 139.

sonofabitch, John Kennedy." This was from Hosty's undocumented text and is allegedly based on secret CIA recordings to which apparently no one else ever had access other than Hosty.

In another version of history, Oswald was not in Mexico City at all, but in Sylvia Odio's apartment in Dallas, and Sylvia is told that he is a rightist who has said Kennedy should be killed — because he betrayed anti-Castro Cubans at the Bay of Pigs! These two absolutely opposite images, opposites on the political spectrum, both dating to the same day, underscore Oswald's chimerical quality and help explain why he and the rest of the drama have taken on such mythic qualities.

Even *The Shark and the Sardines* is in the "right-wing" scenario as well as the left. Indirectly, it is about a highly successful CIA overthrow of the government of Guatemala; but it is also a deeply leftist treatment of American imperialism in Latin America and was a bestseller in communist Cuba. Was Oswald reading it because he was a right-wing CIA contract agent in training under Howard Hunt, or because he was a Marxist-Leninist learning about the exploitation of imperialist America?

When we look at the assassination as pure drama, as a myth, Oswald's function is less mysterious. Oswald is the phantom. He leads American consciousness to look up, look down, look over here, over there, to open this secret box, or search in that forbidden parlor. If he were unambiguously guilty, this journey would never have taken place. If we can never be sure what role he played (if any) in the assassination, Lee Harvey Oswald's greatest significance may, in the end, be that he provides American national character an extraordinary opportunity to get a peek at itself. This may not be his function in the real and literal murder, but it does appear to be his function in the mythic story to which he belongs and which has fascinated the American psyche for almost four decades.

MENTAL STATUS OF THE MAIN CHARACTERS

Now we have used some of the tools and assumptions of traditional psychology to look at the most publicized, most "numinous" players in this psychodrama. Ruby[197] and Johnson are largely covered in earlier chapters.

One conclusion we might offer is that most of prominent figures in the event and its wake exhibit one sort of psychiatric weakness or another. Only Bobby Kennedy and Jacqueline Kennedy seem not to demonstrate psychopathology. Jack Ruby was diagnosed as a psychotic depressive. Lyndon Johnson would clearly qualify as having a

---

197. Ruby had been diagnosed as a "psychotic depressive" by his prison psychiatrist. Kantor, Seth. *The Ruby Cover-Up* New York: Kensington Publishing , 1978.

Narcissistic Personality Disorder with secondary issues of alcoholism. Jack Kennedy, J. Edgar Hoover, Marilyn Monroe, and Joseph Kennedy would satisfy the diagnostic criteria for Major Sexual Dysfunction, and Lee Harvey Oswald would be diagnosed as suffering from a "Borderline Personality Disorder."

Table 6.6. Mental Health Status of Major Conspiracy School Characters

Character	Tentative Psychiatric Diagnosis
John Kennedy	Major Sexual Dysfunction
J. Edgar Hoover	Major Sexual Dysfunction
Lyndon Johnson	Narcissistic Personality Disorder
Jack Ruby	Sociopath/ Major Depression
Lee Harvey Oswald	Borderline Personality Disorder
Marilyn Monroe	Pre-psychotic with Major Sexual Dysfunction
Robert Kennedy	Normal Range
Jacqueline Kennedy	Normal Range
Joseph Kennedy	Sociopath/ Major Sexual Dysfunction

In other words, based on what we know about them now and judging by today's criteria, some 78% of the major characters had a mental illness! What about the rest: Sam Giancana, Santos Trafficante, and Carlos Marcello, William Harvey, E. Howard Hunt, David Ferrie, Guy Banister, and dozens more? Is Richard Helms of the CIA any less important in this investigation than Marilyn Monroe? If we look at a more complete cast of characters (realizing that little information exists on many of them), we note that almost 65% may be described as having one mental illness or another (see Table 6.7).

Table 6.7 Mental Health Status of More Minor Conspiracy School Characters

Source	Character	Tentative Psychiatric Diagnosis
Mafia	Carlos Marcello	Sociopathy
	Sam Giancana	Sociopathy
	Santos Trafficante	Sociopathy
	Jimmy Hoffa	Sociopathy
CIA	James Angleton	Insufficient data
	Richard Helms	Normal range
	General Cabell	Insufficient data
	Allen Dulles	Normal range
	Richard Bissell	Insufficient data
	William Harvey	Borderline Personality Disorder
Anti-Castro Cubans	E Howard Hunt	Sociopathy
	Frank Sturgis	Sociopathy

Table 6.7 Mental Health Status of More Minor Conspiracy School Characters

	Orlando Bosch	Insufficient data
	Loran Hall	Sociopathy
	David Ferrie	Major Sexual Dysfunction/ Borderline Personality Disorder
	Guy Bannister	Alcoholism/ Borderline Personality Disorder
Big Oil	H.L. Hunt	Paranoia/ Schizoidal Personality Disorder
Other	Eugene Hale Brading	Sociopathy
	General Edwin Walker	Paranoia
Soviets/Communists	Nikita Khrushchev	Normal range
	Fidel Castro	Normal range
	Marina Oswald	Normal range

Major and minor characters with a psychiatric disability: 65%
Normal range: 16%
Insufficient data : 19%
There are a number of minor characters not listed who might also qualify for a psychiatric diagnosis. Lee Harvey Oswald's mother, Marguerite, Baron deMohrenschildt, Jack Ruby's mother, and perhaps Rose Kennedy. There are also dozens of additional sociopaths, e.g. Lewis McWillie, John Roselli, Leo Moceri, etc.

David Ferrie was a homosexual pedophile. Our Mafiosi are candidates for the diagnosis of anti-social personality disorder (sociopathy), and there are a few others who lived on the edge, with unpredictable or rather bizarre tendencies to act out (borderline personality disturbances). The Kennedy tale is very heavily populated with mentally unstable persons. By way of contrast, in 1963 only about 14% of Americans were thought to be mentally ill.

Conclusion

In this chapter we explored the psycho-biographical portraits of the main actors. We learned about the shadows of our most numinous stars and starlets, a world very few people knew anything about at the time of the Warren Commission: the world of "Jumbo," "Mary," "J.J.," "Mooney," and, of course, the multiple identities of "Alik," Lee Harvey Oswald.

But as detectives trying to solve a murder mystery, we are no closer to knowing what happened, or who did it, or why. Whatever approach we take, we are denied a realistic, *linear*, solution, and as a historic event, it remains disturbing and unresolved.

In the end, have we no option but to squirm in that nagging human feeling that, if only we had more data, we could get to the bottom of this? Adding more information, so far, has make us *less* sure what happened; will someone, one day, see through the intended and unintended smokescreens and resolve this mystery?

In terms of history, in terms of justice, we may never know. But the story is so big that it functions in another realm, as well; the assassination has taken hold in America's imagination with a grip that won't let go. Like Charles Lindbergh (America's number one hero at one time), John Fitzgerald Kennedy became an object of American mass psychology, a fixation, an obsession — and it is time we looked not just at the assassination drama and detective story, but at the instrument we use to process the information: the American psyche.

Taken as a story, a drama, the assassination of John F. Kennedy has all the characteristics of what Jung calls a "big dream," an event loaded with paradox, radiating dialectical meaning, a mystery, and with deep roots in collective psychology. In our last chapter we will ponder *the symbolic subtext*, as psychologists attempting to get to the essence of a symbolic myth. We will look at Camelot, Lincoln, and other symbols that may be part of the compelling psychological force this story has taken on as the passage of time removes it from the reality of history into the realm of national legend.

APPENDIX:

On first reading, this text appears to present new evidence and also suggests to the reader that the author began this inquiry with no particular bias or vested interest. He interviews numerous important witnesses like Delphine Roberts, and some of Guy Banisters' closest friends; he tracks down witnesses who said that Oswald visited Clinton, Louisiana in the presence of Clay Shaw and David Ferrie, and does sometimes masterful detective work in showing how Oswald might have read Castro's remarks against JFK made in Brazil on September 7, 1963. . . and thus perhaps developed a motive to assassinate him.

Very soon, however, one is struck by the prosecutorial tone. After a few initial chapters Posner goes through a metamorphosis such that any evidence or testimony favoring the prosecution's case is trumpeted, while virtually all evidence and testimony failing to support that point of view is disparaged or simply not addressed. This leads the reader to an increasing tendency simply not to trust what Posner is offering either in the way of conjecture or evidence. Numerous critics have raised this issue, including Norman Mailer. Some examples follow:

● Posner went back to interview the psychologists who treated Lee Harvey Oswald when he was a youngster in New York City. He quotes Dr. Renatus Hartogs as describing Oswald's potential for violence. Posner then footnotes what he obviously feels is a glaring inconsistency among "conspiracy researchers" who conspicuously ignored Hartogs' evaluation. He cites the works of Mark Lane, Jim Garrison, Robert Groden, David Scheim, David Lifton and others as having ignored this information. This may certainly be true, and certainly it can be argued that for a full and complete picture of this assassination story, such information as Oswald's mental status when he was thirteen is of importance. Posner, the prosecutor, however, is not making points in this way in order to ascertain the truth or develop a complete and comprehensive picture. He appears merely to be attempting to point up flaws in the conspiracy schools and simultaneously beating his drum, hinting that he has adroitly uncovered further evidence and testimony to buttress his case against Oswald.

Posner is quite guilty of the same astonishing lack of comprehensiveness. President Kennedy's mistress, Judith Exner Campbell, who connected JFK to Sam Giancana and the Mob, is not even mentioned or indexed in this book. One wonders how the case on Oswald can be so easily closed if such telling details are left out.

- J. Edgar Hoover's homosexuality is never mentioned, nor his relationship with Clyde Tolson.

- The literature connecting Hoover to an awareness of Mob contracts on the President is ignored.

- Posner devotes many pages to the autopsy photos and pokes fun at conspiracy writers who asserted that Kennedy's body was stolen or that surgery was performed on the body on Air Force to disguise the truth. He seeks to make his case more convincing by taking absurd hypotheses, setting up straw men, and then ridiculing these fringe hypotheses relentlessly. While this may be persuasive courtroom technique, especially for someone who might have read only a few assassination texts, it represents questionable scholarship.

- Posner fails to mention or index the CIA's attempt to steal photos of the back of the President's head from the HSCA safe through the efforts of Regis Blahut, the CIA liaison officer who admitted stealing them. CIA officer Blahut's theft of autopsy photos from the HSCA safe is neither mentioned, footnoted, nor indexed. (Indeed, the generosity Posner shows toward the CIA is so evident that one sometimes gets the feeling that if the CIA ever commissioned its own accounting of the assassination, *Case Closed* would be its most glorious factotum.)

- Probably the most telling sign of bias in this text is the treatment of Jim Garrison, the New Orleans District Attorney. Garrison is discussed as a paranoid psychoneurotic and, at least by Posner's accounts, not a single successful prosecution can be attributed to Jim Garrison in his whole career. Garrison is depicted as someone bent on personal fame and publicity, who sacrificed the reputations and even the lives of people whom he treated as conspirators in the Kennedy assassination when they had no relationship to the case. Posner spends a great deal of time asserting that Garrison started the rumor that Oswald held David Ferrie's library card. He says that Oswald never met David Ferrie, in the Civil Air Patrol or anywhere else, and that what Garrison had done to David Ferrie, Guy Banister, and Clay Shaw ruined them. Especially in the case of Clay Shaw, Garrison's actions drained Shaw's personal fortune and destroyed an innocent man.

- Garrison's unsuccessful efforts to link Oswald with Guy Banister, Clay Shaw, and David Ferrie — and to that extent to the CIA and the Mob — are ridiculed as preposterous and without a shred of evidentiary support. At no time in these virulent diatribes about Garrison does Posner mention that many years after the Garrison trial, Richard Helms, Director of the CIA, admitted that both David Ferrie and Clay Shaw had CIA connections. This fact goes unreported.

According to Posner, "The issue of whether Oswald knew the adventurer David Ferrie is equally important, since Ferrie had extensive anti-Castro Cuban contacts and also did some work for an attorney for Carlos Marcello, the New Orleans godfather. (p. 142)." Posner then proceeds to dispute that Ferrie ever had any contact with Oswald and claims that Ferrie was not in the Civil Air Patrol at the time Oswald was. As Posner summarizes this evidence, he states: "Ferrie was interviewed by the FBI on November 27, 1963, and denied ever knowing Oswald in the Civil Air Patrol. CAP records show he told the truth. . . He was not even in the Civil Air Patrol when Oswald was a member in 1955. . .It is not clear why these records were evidently not available to the House Select Committee." (p.143)" Posner then concludes this inquiry by saying, "There is no credible evidence that Oswald knew either Guy Banister or David Ferrie (p. 148). "

- Posner's entire case against Oswald as well as his attacks on Jim Garrison crumble dramatically when one recognizes that Lee Harvey Oswald did indeed know David Ferrie. A photo was discovered by researchers for WGBH, which presented "Who Was Lee Harvey Oswald" on PBS in November 1993. Ferrie is instructing a group of young cadets in the Civil Air Patrol and Oswald is clearly identifiable as one of the handful of cadets in the picture. Since the discovery of the photo, others in it have been identified and similarly testify Oswald and Ferrie were together in the CAP. (Summers, *Vanity Fair*, December, 1994)

- With respect to the library card Oswald was allegedly carrying, Posner imputes that this was a totally unsubstantiated rumor started by fame-seeking Jim Garrison, and was never established as a fact. The actual library card controversy, however, evolved quite differently. When the Secret Service interviewed David Ferrie, Garrison reported their results as follows: ". . .one question which seems to have been asked Ferrie is fascinating. The question itself was never recited in the report, but the nature of the question is implicit in his answer. The Secret Service agents reported that Ferrie said he had never loaned his library card to Lee Oswald. As proof of this he produced his own library card, a card which had expired and which bore an address from which he had long since moved. Apparently dazzled by his cooperation and his sincerity, the Secret Service let the matter drop. Oswald had a library card on him when arrested, but the card is not available for public examination. We must presume that the Secret Service agents were reasonable men and that there was something about the card on Oswald which made them think that it belonged to David Ferrie. Otherwise it would be meaningless to place in its investigative report Ferrie's denial that it was his. . . It is fair to conclude that the Secret Service knew that a library card bearing Ferrie's name had been found on Oswald at the time of his arrest." (Garrison, *A Heritage of Stone*, pp. 118-119).

Rather than having started a rumor, Garrison picked up on a curious piece of questioning by the Secret Service, and his inferences are altogether justified. That the David Ferrie library card may still be a classified document remains an open question.

• The level of personal bias on the part of the author is very strong and in fact probably not equaled except in the work of Mark Lane, on the other side of this controversy. Even the photographs come with captions in which the author's bitterness is barely concealed. Oswald's baby pictures (at two) come with a caption stating that his mother was "unable to cope" with him. At eight, he is shown with a pistol, already having "developed a reputation as a bully." At 15, he is described as "explosive, aggressive, assaultive. . . acting out." A photo of Lee as a Marine in 1958 shows him holding a hunting rifle. A picture from his 17th birthday informs the reader that Oswald was "court-martialed twice." One showing Oswald holding his rifle quotes Marina as saying, "I thought he had gone crazy." Posner's photomontage of Lee Harvey Oswald, from age two to twenty, is accompanied by scornful and mordent descriptors for every image.

Confusion of Theory and Fact

Posner speaks of the three shots at Dealey Plaza as if these are historically accurate and well-established facts and all other notions speculative, if not absurd, "theories." President Kennedy was hit by a bullet traveling from the rear, allegedly, and striking him at 2000 feet per second. This resulted in Kennedy's pitching backward not forward, not at all an achievement easily explained by physics. Posner asserts that Kennedy's back brace plus a syndrome called "Thornburn's position," explains why Kennedy moved backward rather than forward after being struck in the back of the head. Posner mixes "Thornburn's position" in with his other data as if to weave a tale of "fact" when he is really concocting a very speculative explanation of the Zapruder film.

The First Bullet

Theory is confounded with fact in another, often overlooked, instance: Posner's treatment of the first bullet. He seems to accept without question the Warren Commission theory that the first bullet struck a tree, fragmented, and flew wildly until it hit a curb over 520 feet away, injuring spectator James Tague. He states, "That shot was almost certainly deflected by a branch, and its only trace was a nick made on a concrete curb near the Triple Underpass," (p. 477). "Almost certainly" is the expression used to obscure a complete speculation.

First, the bullet was never found, and thus tying it to Oswald's rifle is a guess at best. Second, that the bullet hit an oak tree has never been established and the Warren Commission failed to identify any branch of any tree that was nicked by this bullet, a fact which Posner at least admits. Third, the metallurgical analysis of the concrete hit by this bullet did not conform to the metallic make up of the other bullets associated with Oswald's rifle. It showed traces of lead and antimony, not copper. The theory given to explain the inconsistency is that the lead came from the bullet's core; the absence of copper was explained by the claim that the copper jacketing on the bullet had been sheared away when it "hit the oak tree."

The reasoning of the Warren Commission and of its adherent, Gerald Posner, is at best questionable. If one's intent is to convict Oswald, then all other matters must fit into place. Thus the missed shot must still have originated from the Depository (since Oswald had to have fired it). If the metallurgical study did not confirm these preconceptions, then explanations must be given — even if no nicked tree can be found. The explanations for the first shot are all predicated on the dogmatically held belief that the first shot had to have come from Oswald, from his rifle, and from the sixth floor Depository window.

If one abandons this fixed, irrevocable idea — if only for a moment — one realizes that the shot that hit the curb and injured James Tague was over 30 feet above the President's head — if it came from the Depository. Not a "near miss" — a ludicrous miss.

If we assume the shot was not 30 feet over the President's head but only a few inches over the President's head, then by using the same reverse trajectory method used by Failure Analysis Associates, the origination point of the shot is the Dal-Tex building, not the Depository. The fact that Eugene Hale Brading and a military intelligence person were detained in that building within minutes of the shooting,

Chapter 6. Shadows and Secrets

that Brading had Mob associations, and that he used an alias with police investigators in Dallas, are also of great interest.

In short, the failure to make a metallurgical match with Oswald's other bullets, the failure to provide evidence that the first shot hit an oak tree, and the failure to reconcile a "near miss" as over 30 feet above the President's head suggests that the first shot may have originated from another weapon, may have been fired by another person, and may have been aimed from another location. Such ideas were, of course, off limits for the Warren Commission of 1964, since it would have opened rather than closed the case. Unfortunately, such alternate hypotheses are heresy to Mr. Posner, as well, resulting in ever more convoluted theories built up to explain things away on the basis of a very meager factual base.

Magic bullets, neuromuscular spasms, Thornton's position, and sheared-off copper jacketing are hypothetical constructs that have been used and continue to be used to keep the hint of conspiracy at bay and the myth intact: Oswald and only Oswald shot Kennedy; Ruby and only Ruby killed Oswald.

A prosecutorial orientation requires that evidence and witnesses favoring the prosecution must be underscored, italicized. . . even heralded. . . and simultaneously, evidence and witnesses not favoring this position must be impugned. It is quite instructive to see how this bias places Posner in the position of handling two unrelated witnesses, Silvia Odio and Barney Baker.

Sylvia Odio was the Cuban refugee living in Dallas who testified that "Leon" Oswald visited her apartment with two anti-Castro Cubans in late September 1963. When she saw Oswald on television after the assassination, she knew it was the man who came to her apartment. Sylvia Odio's testimony is not favored among Warren Commission protagonists primarily because it casts doubt on Oswald's trip to Mexico City. It also casts doubt upon his singular image as a leftist, pro-Castro, Marxist. His appearance at the residence of Annie and Sylvia Odio clearly puts him in an anti-Castro role and places him in the company of rightist-militant, anti-Castro freedom fighters. This is not the image which the mythic Lee Harvey Oswald has been cast to play these last thirty years.

Thus Posner parades a litany of negative facts about Sylvia Odio in order to impugn the accuracy of her testimony and undermine the credibility of her account. He reviews her psychiatric history, reports interviews with some of her friends that portray her as "histrionic," and fails to find the letter Sylvia allegedly sent her father in a Cuban prison where she wrote of her experiences. There is no doubt that Posner, in keeping with his prosecutorial orientation, seeks to take away any shred of Odio's credibility.

That Sylvia Odio was college educated is not mentioned, that she attended universities in the United States, spoke four languages, or that she never attempted to profit in any way from her experiences through book contracts or paid television interviews is similarly unmentioned. It might add credibility or sympathy to her testimony. None of this is in any way "featured" information in Posner's treatise. That she lived alone in Dallas with her sister while both her parents were incarcerated under Castro — and that this partly accounted for her reluctance in coming forward — is similarly concealed in Posner's enthusiastic, prosecutorial foray.

From Posner's approach to these figures, one gathers certain composite psychological portraits: Garrison is a gun-toting, paranoid, megalomaniac drooling for publicity and fame. Sylvia Odio is a neurotic psychotherapy patient, prone to histrionic exaggeration, a divorcee who came from a "fractious marriage," and a person under psychiatric care whose hysterical fainting spells simply cannot support any of her outrageous stories. These are the pictures Posner paints under the guise of objectivity and clarity of mind.

His bias becomes all the more evident when one considers how protective and uncritical he is toward witnesses who support his position. The anti-Castro Cuban Loran Hall came forward and said that Sylvia Odio was wrong, that Hall and two associates, Lawrence Howard and William Seymour, actually were the individuals who had gone to see her. This rendition was placed in the final Warren Commission report, and Odio's testimony simultaneously vitiated by Hall's account.

Hall was later confronted by the fact that his story did not wash. Odio vehemently denied that these were the men who visited her apartment. Even Seymour and Lawrence said they were not at Odio's apartment. Hall finally admitted he had lied. It is curious that Posner homes in on every possible weakness of Odio's account and yet seems to have no interest in tracking down Loran Hall or attempting to learn why he lied to the Warren Commission.

We do not see Posner checking out Loran Hall's psychiatric history and no consideration is given to the possibility that he might have also had a "fractious marriage." Posner did not interview Hall's friends, relatives, parish priests. . . as he did with Odio. By this point, it is clear where his biases are unmistakably marching.

Barney Baker is another case in point. Baker, a Hoffa goon, had only recently been released from Sandstone prison when he was called by Jack Ruby in 1963. Baker, after being interviewed by Posner, stated that Ruby had called him about his problems with A AGVA. This was an entertainment issue concerning the Carousel Club. These were not calls about any other matter, according to Baker. (Baker, however, called Mob killer Dave Yaras in Miami shortly after he spoke to Ruby and two weeks before Kennedy was killed.)

Chapter 6. Shadows and Secrets

Posner does not investigate Barney Baker's criminal record, his psychiatric history. He does not ask Baker why he called Dave Yaras, and makes no attempt to impugn Baker's credibility the way he did with Sylvia Odio. He simply leaves his reader with the unaltered facts, namely that Hoffa goon Baker strongly denies that Jack Ruby called him for any other purpose than to help him in his AGVA disputes in his Dallas night club. End of story.

The reader should accept the word of 300-lb convicted felon Barney Baker as reliable and truthful, but when it comes to University of Illinois graduate Sylvia Odio, skepticism and disbelief are highly recommended. Odio's full psychiatric history is examined and her history of fainting spells unearthed. Barney Baker's background, education, and rap sheet are ignored — in order to assure the reader of Ruby's innocent and uncomplicated contact with yet another mobster. Five pages are spent undermining Odio. One paragraph is devoted to Baker's corroboration of Ruby's innocent contact with the Mob and the Teamsters. This is the character of how Posner approaches his thesis.

The significant omissions in his text are too numerous to mention. Some are particularly noteworthy, however:

● Sam Giancana, the godfather of the Chicago mafia, is said by Posner to have known nothing about the assassination or about any alleged Mob plot. Posner does not report that Giancana visited Kennedy in the White House, that his girl friend befriended Kennedy, that Giancana was murdered after testifying to HSCA personnel or that Giancana's relatives have written books revealing that Giancana confessed to them that he had a hand in the assassination.

● Posner asserts no relationship existed between deMohrenschildt and the CIA. Norman Mailer's subsequent text shows rather clearly that deMohrenschildt admitted he had a relationship with the CIA and identified the contact person, a fact that was corroborated independently of DeMohrenschildt's comments.

● Posner also re-states the wooden hypothesis that Jack Ruby had no significant underworld ties. One notable account is that of Joseph Campisi, a mobster who was the owner of the Egyptian Lounge, a restaurant frequented by Ruby. Posner makes a point to mention that Ruby did not meet with Campisi on the evening before the assassination, even though he did go to the Egyptian Lounge. Further, he points out that conspiracy researchers have mistaken one name for another and that Ruby spoke to a man named Campbell, not Connors. He leaves the story at that. Posner obviously wishes to imply that while Joseph Campisi was a mobster and owned the Egyptian Lounge, he had little contact with Ruby and certainly none on the eve of the assassination. Posner may even be hoping to give the reader the impression that Jack Ruby may not have even known Joseph Campisi. Posner deliberately distorts in this presentation and does not report that Jack Ruby's first visitor in jail after he shot Oswald was mobster Joseph Campisi.

In sum, Gerald Posner failed to mention mobster Campisi's visit to Ruby's prison cell; he failed to mention CIA Counterintelligence Chief, James Angleton's destruction of the diaries of a Presidential mistress, Mary Pinchot Meyer; he did not report Richard Helm's admissions that Clay Shaw and David Ferrie were associated with the CIA, and he never mentioned or made any reference to long-time Presidential mistress, Judith Exner Campbell. In addition, his assessment of the relationship between David Ferrie and Oswald was fully and unequivocally mistaken. These are not small or incidental details. They are not extraneous minutiae. They go directly to the heart of the assassination mystery, and they make Posner's scholarship not only questionable but rather delusory.

(Shortly after Posner's book appeared, a rebuttal was published by Harold Weisberg under the title *Case Open, The Omissions, Distortions and Falsifications of Case Closed.* (New York: Carrol & Graf, 1994). One important observation contained in this text but not contained in the review above is that Posner's use of the Failure Analysis study of Dealey Plaza was not commissioned for Posner's text but taken from another source, with ambiguous attributions given.

Probably the best and most reasonable assessment made of Posner's work is by John Newman, author of *Oswald and the CIA*: "It was a tribute to the insanity that has surrounded this subject when in the fall of 1993, the American national media leveled inordinate praise on a book whose author was attempting to close the case just as the government's files were being opened... Three years and two million pages later, there is much that remains closed. Like a huge oil spill, a glut of black "redactions" is still strewn across the pages that have been released...But we have finally arrived at the beginning." (p. 420).

Chapter 7. Camelot and Carousels

> *"Only bitter old men write history,"* she said. *"Jack's life had more to do with myth, magic, legend, saga, and story than with political theory or political science.*
>
> — Jackie Kennedy [198]

Collective Denial

This story is so big, it had such an impact, its mysteries and obscure implications are so broad that it might as well be a collective dream shared by all Americans. What are the factors that give the event so much power? How have we responded to it, and what does that say about our national psychology?

First, let's look at general psychological mechanisms that obtain to this story. The most obvious and telling mechanism is denial. Just as tainted and biased scholarship clouds our vision, so does pervasive denial.

Denial extends its tentacles throughout the Kennedy myth. Can one really argue that, having slept with more than 33 women in 33 months, Kennedy could persist in the fantasy that such conduct would go undetected and in no way injure him, his presidency, his wife, his reputation, his children, national security or his capacity to make decisions?

---

198. Heymann, C. David. *A Woman Named Jackie.* New York: Carol Communications, 1989, p. 419.

How curious that the writers of the Camelot School all consistently, regularly, and predictably have ignored these excesses, as if perpetrating a lie for three decades without the hint of a blush. Neither Ted Sorenson, Arthur Schlesinger, Pierre Salinger, William Manchester, Dave Powers, Kenneth O'Donnell nor any of the other Kennedy idolaters can be found on record even hinting obliquely at Kennedy's severe sexual pathology. To persist in propagating the notion of a glorious second term, had JFK not been shot, seems geared only to make us regret his untimely death all the more. And almost all of the authors cited are guilty of creating that delusion. (We do not know how many of them were deluded, *themselves*; but they did succeed in deluding the public.)

One such JFK supporter finally came out of his gilded closet recently and dealt with the issue. Ben Bradlee, publisher of the *Washington Post*, wrote in his 1995 memoirs about Mary Meyer, his sister-in-law, and her affair with JFK (quoted in prior chapters), and remarked that he felt that JFK deserved to be impeached for his behavior. Bradlee's indignation does not match up with his much earlier *Conversations with Kennedy*, was contained in that book or others which he wrote afterward. His denials had persisted some 31 years!

When writers omit major facts, that is a conspiracy to propagate the public's denial of reality. When documents are destroyed and witnesses are killed, that is a conspiracy, presumably to protect someone from prosecution.

In January, 1996 — and not a moment earlier, the government released a document showing FBI interest in Oswald's trip to Switzerland, *well before he defected to Russia*. What was the intent in covering up such a fact for 33 years?

John Newman published a partial analysis of two million documents released by the government in 1992 — they are heavily redacted with black ink. In one, the FBI learned that Oswald's mother sent him a $25 money order. Although there was never any acknowledgement that the FBI had been tracking Oswald in this regard, it reported the funds transfer in a *32-page* New York FBI field office memorandum which was sent to headquarters on February 26, 1960. Newman says only the first and last page of the memo have ever been released — the other thirty pages are still classified.[199]

Forty years later, and still counting! Even the released documents are often largely obliterated; the level of censorship and obfuscation is chronic and continuing. Gerald Posner, the cheerleader for the Warren Commission, glibly says Mary Meyer's death had *nothing to do with the assassination*, but conspicuously fails to mention that her murder remains unsolved, that CIA Chief of Counter Intelligence James Angleton was caught red-handed breaking into her studio in search of her diary *two days after her murder*, or that Meyer told her best friend that she feared for her life — just before she

---

199. John Newman. *Oswald and the CIA*. New York: Carrol & Graf, 1995, p. 152.

Chapter 7. Camelot and Carousels

> Mary Pinchot Meyer, sister-in-law of Ben Bradlee of the *Washington Post* and last presidential mistress of John F. Kennedy. Meyer was murdered ten months after JFK, shot in the head, execution style. Within two days, Bradlee attempted to enter her art studio only to find James Angleton of the CIA picking the lock. Meyer had told her friend that she was afraid for her life and that if anything happened to her, her diary should be saved. Angleton was looking for the diary which was later found and destroyed. Her murder is still unsolved. Bradlee withheld what he knew of this event for over 30 years, despite having written two coffee table books about JFK subsequent to the assassination and death of Meyer: Source: Ben Bradlee Ben Bradlee. *A Good Life*. New York: Simon & Schuster, 1995, pp. 266-271. One JFK conspiracist (and sensationalist!), Robert Morrow holds that Mary Meyer was ready to turn over to an inquiring Bobby Kennedy important documents about the assassination taken from her former husband, Cord Meyer, a high ranking CIA officer, and that was the reason for the murder.

was murdered. Mary Meyer died in 1964, but Posner grinds out hackneyed, "it's-over-and-done-with" slogans thirty years later as part of an orchestrated chorus of denial, disinformation, and concealment.[200]

Many of the actors have or had very solid reasons for their denying, hiding or distorting; perhaps some of them, and much of the public (happy to embrace the Kennedys as the closest thing we have to an American aristocracy) are just as glad to leave hidden things hidden — only through denial can we still hold JFK as the prince we wish he was.

Various portions of this tale have inspired vehement and dogged denial, from every quarter, for a broad spectrum of reasons, a broad spectrum of interests. Taboos were broken, trust was betrayed, unspeakable things were done — over and over again, at many levels. The ability to accept and confront such things is a measure of maturity; the easiest, simplest, and most primitive alternative is to deny them, to ignore them, and to make sure no one talks about them.

---

200. Mike Feinsilber, "Former editor of Post recalls life at the top, *San Jose Mercury News*, September 21, 1995, p. 4A.

Symbolic Discernment

If this myth had been crafted as an artwork, as a literary endeavor, academic careers would have been built, by now, on critiques of the twists of plot and the use of symbolism and imagery throughout. Similarly, it could serve as a primary text for testing methods of Freudian and Jungian dream interpretation. Let us look at just one symbol.

The Carousel

A Carousel is a merry-go-round made up of painted horses and animal figures; it moves in a circle, always leading somewhere but returning to its point of origin.[201] The Kennedy assassination is an infinite maze of possibilities that leads round and round in circles, too. Like the snake that eats its own tail, the carousel symbolizes a course or a pursuit that reaches as its destination its place of origin. The carousel appears three times in this great American dream.

It was in the Carousel Club, the striptease joint that he owned in Dallas, that Jack Ruby met his underworld contacts, conducted his business, consorted with his dancers, worked the sensitivities of the Dallas police officer corps, and was infected with gonorrhea, a condition he was being treated for at the time he killed Oswald. It was his Carousel Club that got him deeply in debt with the IRS, a debt that was due and payable at the time of the assassination.

The carousel makes a second appearance with Bobby Baker, Lyndon Johnson's right-hand man and legislative assistant. Baker's government salary was insufficient to support the lifestyle he was living, and for this discrepancy he was in the news at the time of the assassination. (Johnson's retreat to Texas in October, where he remained in seclusion until November 22, is said to have been occasioned by the ongoing investigation of Baker's alleged improprieties.) When Baker opened up the Carousel Motor Inn in North Carolina, this drew suspicions and serious senate investigations. Both Johnson and Bobby Baker may have been engaged in inappropriate influence peddling and shady financial dealings.

The third appearance of the symbol of the carousel comes in an oblique reference by Chuck Giancana in his book, *Double-Cross*. Chuck had never been made privy to his brother Sam's underworld dealings. Chuck always felt that not knowing was better than knowing, and his brother felt the same. One day, however, Sam told him the story of how Kennedy was killed. It was the first time that his brother had "brought him in" to the secret world of Mafia machinations. It sent a chill through him. Chuck felt shock, dizziness, like the "nauseating intoxication of a spinning carousel."[202]

---

201. J.C. Cooper, *An Illustrated Encyclopaedia of Traditional symbols*. London: Thames and Hudson, 1978.

If the "carousel" had been interjected into the drama intentionally, we could complement the artist for pulling together diverse strands of plot in a subtle way; and we could say that its real symbolic import is that this tale takes us on a sometimes intriguing, sometimes nauseating journey to nowhere and everywhere, round and round, in an infinite complexity which negates all hope for resolution. The symbol would serve to alert us that we have embarked on an endless journey into paradox and contradiction and will end up where we began. . . wondering if Lee Harvey Oswald really did do it all by himself.

The facts are many, corroborating evidence is plentiful, and every interpretation that has been published, so far, fails to withstand the test of all *the other* "reliable" evidence. No one version has accounted for all the strands of evidence. Even if we take into account as much as we can of the psychology and the motivations of all the actors, the witnesses and the writers who have co-authored this drama, we can neither fully accept nor fully reject any of the offered scenarios. Even if we surrender our conspiratorial thinking and accept Posner's view that Oswald acted alone, we can't explain why Posner withheld and deleted as much information as he did in order to achieve even marginal persuasiveness; neither can we account for the contradictions and logical problems in all the other versions.

We can only get off the carousel by abandoning the quest for a resolution, by walking away from the neurosis of plots and counterplots, and by leaving unanswered the question of "who shot Kennedy."

If comfort is what we seek, we must convert the Kennedy story from a political intrigue and murder mystery, a prosaic historical event, to an enigma, a symbolic tale. The only solace we can seek is to give the story *meaning* as a myth.

Dream Interpretation

Joseph Campbell, author of *A Hero with a Thousand Faces*, remarked that interpreting dreams and interpreting myths and fairy tales were not altogether different processes. We fully recognize that the Kennedy assassination is not a dream, and it is not a fairytale; but in some regards in its expanded manifestation, with 600 books and countless shorter pieces written about it, with its tenacious hold on the public imagination, with the embroideries and embellishments, excisions and alternate endings that have been provided after the fact, it has been made into a myth — or is certainly mythic in scope. Campbell suggests that myths are like collective dreams and that using dream interpretation methods, especially with respect to symbolic discernment, is a robust way of trying to discover the meaning of a myth (and, for that matter, a fairy tale, too).

---

202. Giancana, Sam and Giancana, Chuck. *Double Cross*. New York: Warner Books, 1992, p. 450.

Dostoyevsky and certain other writers are particularly admired for their ability intentionally to convey the intense and intricately interwoven emanations of our unconscious or subconscious minds, for crafting literature that is as compelling and complex as a dream. As time passes and we take a step back and look at an event like the assassination — taken as a whole, with all our reactions and responses to that event — is there any validity, is there anything we can learn, by viewing it and critiquing it the way we do works of literature and art? [Editors add: sleep of reason has allowed America to create a nightmare scenario around this disturbing event, adding... associations, what Claudiu said] Subjecting it to the processes of dream interpretation, might we learn something about the *author* of the event *as a myth* — something telling about the American mind, and the culture in which this myth has been fostered, burnished, told and re-told?

We will try all of that in this chapter. We look for similarities, common meanings, deeper themes, and consistencies between symbols, and then bring them into focus and closure. This is a chapter in which we play, speculate, and test the limits; and it departs radically from the more rigorously embraced realism of the preceding chapters.

Many symbols have attached themselves to this dream. We begin with the most obscure symbols and work our way to the better known.

Symbols In The Myth

Camelot

> Don't let it be forgot,
> that once there was a spot,
> for one brief shining moment
> that was known as Camelot. [203]

Camelot is the first of two major symbols associated with John F. Kennedy and his administration. The King Arthur legend was rooted in England, but the Kennedy "Camelot" myth was an Americanization, and its symbolism was picked up by Jacqueline Kennedy. Both she and her husband enjoyed listening to the music of *Camelot*, the Broadway musical by Frederick Loew and Alfred Newman (Warner Brothers).

---

203. Cited in Heymann, *A Woman Named Jackie*. New York: Carol Communications, 1989, p. 419.

Chapter 7. Camelot and Carousels

The Camelot story resonates because it touches on some profound human drives, desires, needs and conflicts. Somehow, it taps deeply into our psychology and, obliquely or directly, we find it fascinating.

As the story goes, Arthur became King of England when he showed that he (and only he) could retrieve the great sword Excalibur from the stone that held it. Arthur married Guinevere. He established a "round table" where all the most valiant knights of the empire might discuss and sort out their problems, and a court with a prosecutor counterbalanced by a defense counsel, and an impartial jury. Queen Guinevere fell in love with his most valiant knight, Lancelot. Arthur loved both Jenny and "Lance," and does not appear to have interfered in their love; but when his knights accused his Queen of infidelity, he had to administer justice. Guinevere was tried and sentenced to be burned at the stake. On the day of her execution, Arthur procrastinated long enough to allow Lancelot to appear and rescue her. Rescue her, he did; but justice was not served and Arthur's court, and the Round Table, were irreparably tarnished. Later, meeting the two in the forest, Arthur tells them that the round table is dead, but the idea shall live on... perhaps in the spirits of the young who shall remember "Camelot."

Some 90 percent of the American rendition is concerned with adultery — not noble ideas. One historian said that of all the stories of Camelot that have filtered through the ages, from Sir Galahad to Tristram and Iseult, only one salient historical fact is constant: the destruction of the Round Table caused by the adulterous relationship in the house of King Arthur.

Some parallels with the Kennedy story:

• John Kennedy, like King Arthur, was considered a negotiator, not a saber-rattler.
• There was adultery, at the top, in both their houses.
• Both came to grief as a result of secrets within their own families.
• A blood kinsmen (Mordred) set in motion a process which destroyed the house of Arthur. A blood kinsman (Bobby) may have set in motion a process which destroyed the house of Kennedy. Mordred merely brought out the truth of the hypocrisy in Camelot; Bobby may have precipitated his brother's murder by prosecuting the Mafia, not realizing that the Mafia was tightly interwoven in his own family affairs.

Passion versus the Dream

Another important theme is the interplay between passion and idealism. King Arthur says that the Round Table was just an idea, without substance, a dream; but something worth living and dying for. It brought rationality, reconciliation, and dialogue to the age.

Kennedy, too, was anxious to place rationality over confrontation. He was the first president to sign a nuclear test ban treaty with the Soviets. During his three-year Presidency, Kennedy met with Khrushchev in Vienna — an historic and unprecedented moment of dialogue and reconciliation. In 1962, Kennedy announced a Geneva Conference agreement on a neutral Laos, another peaceful initiative. In 1963, in an address at the American University, he delivered a major address on a nuclear test ban treaty. (Decades later, Mikhail Gorbachev referenced that speech as the historic beginning point of detente and reconciliation in the arms race.) He attempted to mediate and negotiate an end to the conflict with Cuba through a secret emissary. He sought to negotiate a retreat from Vietnam before the United States became too heavily involved. Kennedy resolved conflict through compromise, accommodation, and negotiation; and this was essential to his ideological legacy.

As Arthur brought a new image to kings and kingship, so did Kennedy bring a new image to the White House and American culture. Not all of it was confined to politics. Carl Sandburg read poetry at the Inauguration. The world's greatest artists, singers, and dancers came to perform at the White House, from Nureyev to Pablo Cassals.

Abraham Lincoln

As Arthurian symbolism has stuck to the Kennedy myth, so has the symbolism of Abraham Lincoln.

Lincoln and Kennedy trigger an archetypal image, the archetype of the hero; both were vigorous incarnations of this unconscious imprint. Both stand as personal and historic *hero figures* in American collective psychology, and some Jungian analysts have already made this observation. Still, the metapsychology goes beyond mere collective infatuation with a hero figure. Why did both men leave such an imprint in the American mind?

Abraham Lincoln was President during some of America's most difficult days, when an internal battle was waged, a bitter, brutal war; Kennedy, too, fought America's internal enemy — this time, however, the struggle was more elusive and waved no discernible flag. Kennedy presided over an internal struggle over America's future direction — whether to reach an accommodation with its arch enemies, the Soviet Union and the European left, or to go its own way, pursuing America's manifest destiny, alone.

THE COLLECTIVE SCAPEGOAT

In the Kennedy myth, Oswald has been cast as the American traitor, and certainly the enemy within. We can see in Kennedy's personal life, vastly hypocritical and contradictory to his public persona, the seeds of destruction through unbridled, compromising sexual passions. We can see unknown "forces" in American culture over which we have little control, over which Kennedy had little control, and about which Americans were scarcely aware — the secretive worlds of the industrial-military complex, Mafia, the CIA, and the FBI.

Oswald has been made to occupy the role of the mythic, *designated* assassin all this time. At least symbolically, therefore, he is dressed up in this myth as the anti-American, Marxist-Leninist, and is forced by history to wear the wardrobe of the traitor, the shadow, who stands in opposition to all that American democracy, society, and Kennedy himself represented.[204] He is dialectical, protean, symbolizing always his opposite as well as himself. He is both communist and anti-communist, pro-Cuban and anti-Castro, pro-Kennedy yet his assassin. He was affiliated with the Mob through his uncle, but did not smoke, drink, womanize, nor gamble; any Mob affiliation was considered laughable by his wife. Oswald was a CIA agent, yet dirt poor and unemployed. He was a Marine with a security clearance, yet a defector, a Marxist-Leninist with an active subscription to the *Worker*. He was a sweet loving father, cooing baby talk to his daughter in the bathtub, yet a borderline, vicious, unpredictable wife-beater.

Looking at the event as if it were a work of drama, and adding in not only the hard facts of the assassination but all that has been written and said about them, all the reactions of the media and the public at large, Lee Harvey Oswald (like John Wilkes Booth, before him) represents a Jungian shadow figure, the traitor, and the symbolic figurehead of the enemy within. As Wilkes Booth became, in people's mind, a symbol of the South and the Confederacy, Oswald symbolically represents the "evil empire" of communism.

He was seen first as a Marxist-Leninist — at the most conscious level, he represents that which was alien and seditious to the United States. Indeed, as psychological figure, it is possible he might even represent a *displaced* symbol of deeply running American fears of communism and the cold war, which were very much in evidence at the time.

---

204. References to King Arthur and Camelot are based upon Green, Roger Lancelyn. *King Arthur and His Knights of the Round Table*. Middlesex, England: Penguin Books, 1953; *Bullfinches Mythology*, and Warner Brothers 1967 Broadway Musical Video, "Camelot." The major figures in this American drama are King Arthur, his queen, Jenny, Sir Lancelot, the magical guide Merlin, and Arthur's illegitimate son, Mordred.

There is some parallel in the Lindbergh kidnapping story. In 1936, Hitler was a troubling presence, but world war would not break out for another three years. When the Lindbergh baby was kidnapped in the early 1930s, it was such a big story that it eclipsed wars, the Depression, and everything else in the news. Newspaper production went up 20% as a result of this single crime. The mass obsessiveness that took hold in the American psyche over this incident marks it as one of the most "numinous" moments in American journalism in the 20th century, in a league with the O.J. Simpson trial or the assassination of President Kennedy. Kennedy's assassination has been called "the crime of the century," but the term was first used to refer to the kidnapping of Charles Lindbergh's son and the subsequent lynch-mob like trial of Bruno Richard Hauptmann in Trenton, New Jersey.

Hauptmann was caught, prosecuted, and put to death for this crime; but the unprecedented publicity of the incident led to an almost complete abandonment of objectivity. Scholars have since alleged that the actual killer of the Lindbergh baby was never caught. Hauptmann was framed; very likely he was entirely innocent of the crime, and was a victim of the mass hysteria which surrounded this case. In this sense, Hauptmann became a scapegoat, a kind of symbolic patsy.

Why was Bruno Richard Hauptmann selected to serve as a symbolic devil for American feelings of vengeance, after someone killed the baby of Charles Lindbergh? Why was he, among all other possible suspects, selected to serve as the fall guy for this crime?

Hauptmann was a family man, a hard working carpenter in the Bronx, a man who loved his wife, and had just had his first baby. . . not a likely baby-killer. He came to the U.S. in search of a better life (as a stowaway), and when he was a teenager he had been arrested for theft; but after coming to the U.S. he had no criminal record here at all.

However, Hauptmann was German. A German was selected as the likely culprit, and was readily seized upon by the American psyche as the designated baby murderer, the dastardly swine who could coolly and with pre-meditation commit this vicious crime. Was the public's eagerness to condemn him founded, in any part, on American fears of the rumbling of German militarism, growling on the other side of the Atlantic?

That's a controversial interpretation, perhaps, but the evidence against Hauptmann was so circumstantial and weak that it causes one to wonder. Shortly before his execution, even Hauptmann gave vent to this very thought and said, "someone has to pay. . . and so they chose me." In that case, the irrational wrath directed at Hauptmann and his execution represents more of a ritual-sacrificial killing rather than the expression of the dispassionate hand of justice.

American fears of communism and confrontation with the Soviet Union were very high at that time of the Kennedy assassination. The world had never been closer to an all-out nuclear blowup than during the Cuban Missile Crisis. The cold war was not just a political-historical situation; it represented a nascent collective fear of annihilation. Marxist-Leninist Lee Harvey Oswald could have served as a psychological scapegoat for these running fears of communism in the same way that Hauptmann may have served as the "designated" scapegoat for America's growing fears of Nazi Germany.

The Lindbergh case and the Kennedy assassination are considered the greatest crimes of the 20th century; both shared widespread mass popularity and obsessiveness. Both were followed by botched crime investigations in which evidence was so tainted and distorted one could have very little confidence in the prosecution's case. Conspiracy theories developed around them both. Both involved crimes in which the real perpetrators and/or conspirators were likely never apprehended. But scapegoats and villains were found to symbolically represent America's two greatest fears: Germany militarism and Soviet communism.

In this model, Oswald functions as a symbolic poison-container for these American fears, and his selection as the "designated assassin" distills, condenses and crystallizes them onto one figure. Oswald's death provides an unconscious national catharsis.

But this is only one interpretation of the Kennedy myth.

THE KENNEDY TRAGEDY AS THE FORESHADOW OF AMERICAN TRAGEDY

The Kennedy storied "foreshadowed" changes in the American psyche itself; it encapsulated in a microcosm many of the shifts that were just taking place, beneath the surface, in the society.

In 1963, Americans overall were positive and optimistic, but in the three decades that followed deep resentments, disillusionment, cynicism, alienation, mental illness, crime, divorce, and disaffection burgeoned. A full-scale change in the landscape of American life took place. Some pointed to "the decade of disillusionment." Jimmy Carter referred to it as a "malaise."

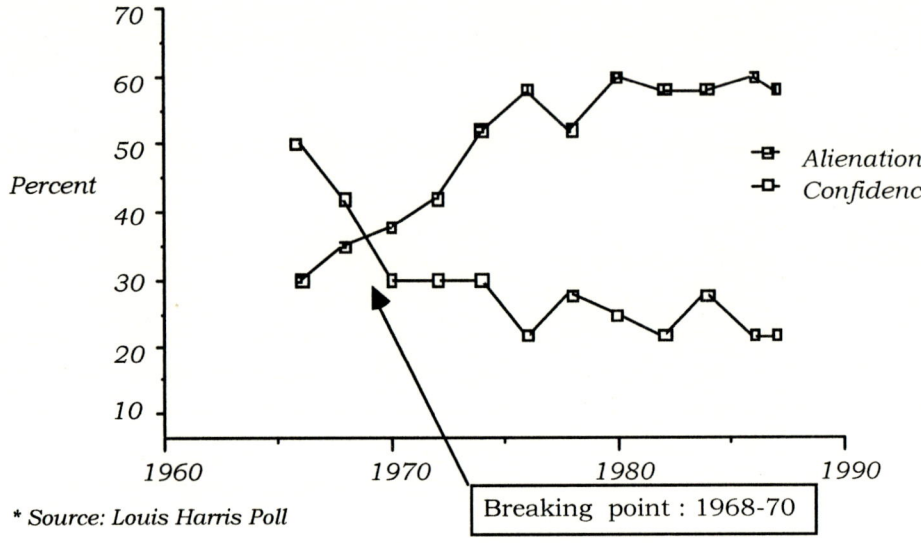

Figure 7.1 Alienation vs. confidence in American society, 1965-1990

In Figure 7.1 we see American pessimism and a sense of alienation rapidly accelerating while optimistic feelings and confidence in the government drop sharply and never fully recover. The alienation was occasioned, on the one hand, by a lack if faith in the Kennedy assassination inquiries, plus an ever-increasing mistrust of the government in general. This was the government that led us into war in Vietnam; and it was increasingly perceived as lying on a regular basis. But even after the Vietnam debacle was over, feelings of alienation prevailed and continued unabated.

In a sense, the whole Kennedy story summarized (*in advance!*) the emerging trends, the internal poison that ate away the lofty visions of the American dream and left in its wake alienation, disaffection, anomie, and pessimism.

From Camelot, in the words of King Arthur,

By the sword of Excalibur, we will get through this.
We must not let our passions destroy our dreams![205]

In parallel fashion, the clean image of America became stained as the decade progressed, with vice, violence, and crime on the rise. Whether we like it or not, Kennedy was not the democratic, intelligent, open-minded, articulate statesman his

---

205. Green, Roger Lancelyn, *ibid.*, p.424

mythmakers created. He was a manipulative, dysfunctional, secretive Sybarite, perhaps the most sociopathic and mentally unstable president in this century.

Both Kennedy and the public eschewed the discipline, the restrictions, the self-control needed to maintain a healthy lifestyle. JFK went on a binge of sexual license and promiscuity, and the American public went on a binge of its own. They saved less than they ever had, and spent far more than they ever dreamed; and they did what they felt like doing — more than any previous generation had done. Government deficits (which hardly existed before JFK) spiraled out of control.

In the thirty years after JFK, Americans legalized gambling and abortion, made single parenting socially acceptable (if not even preferred), developed the highest divorce rate and the highest rate of sexually transmitted diseases in the industrialized world. They presided over the distribution of handguns and narcotics throughout their inner cities, addicting their most vulnerable class to lethal substances like crack cocaine, and they tried to raise a generation of children in homes without a father, with a television set as the primary caretaker.

Passion, divorce, abandoned children, family disunity, and dysfunction, cynicism and disbelief, yellow journalism, mental illness, sociopathy, drug abuse, gambling, violence, and murder: These are rather well substantiated megatrends of the thirty years that followed the Kennedy assassination. Only recently has the downward acceleration decreased — in some of these areas.

Fig. 7.2 The Rise of American Sociopathy: Violent Crimes, 1960-1990

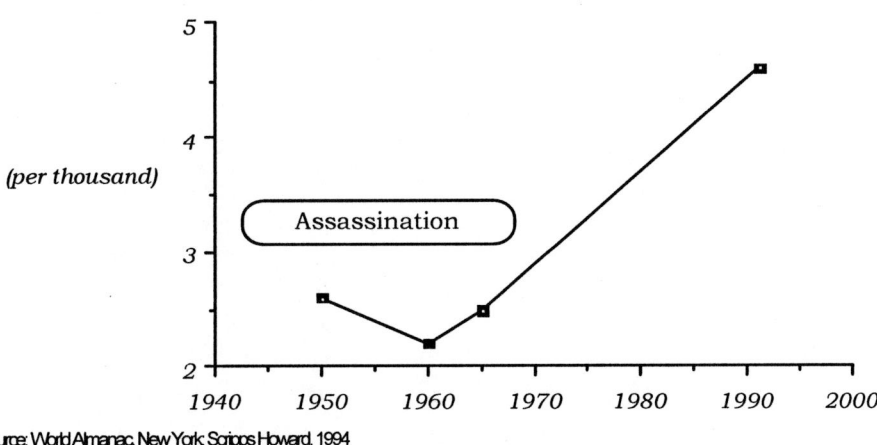

Source: World Almanac, New York Scripps Howard, 1994

Just as JFK was killed by some elusive, internal, traitorous predator, so was American society attacked in these years. The American dream was tainted in its idealism, and dimmed its glittering lights in the same way that Kennedy's image was tarnished.

"Don't ask what your country can do for you, but what you can do for your country." What is the opposite of those idealistic, inspirational words that Kennedy spoke at his Inauguration? *"Ask not what you can do for your country but what your country can do for you!"* Selfishness, narcissism, greed, self-interest, the inverse of this slogan, is a far more accurate description of Kennedy's approach and at the same time it describes megatrends that were emerging in the American character for the next thirty years as well.

When Kennedy was killed, *The Brady Bunch* and *Little House on the Prairie* were popular TV shows. Thirty years later, Maury Povich parades scantily clad 9-year-old girls out on afternoon TV, talking in sexually explicit language. Jerry Springer is the master of ceremonies over marital brawls and beatings, and Sally Jesse Raphael hosts discussions of ritual incest and baby killing during family viewing hours. The entire culture has shifted; indeed, the American culture *was overwhelmed by an enemy within*, no less than its President fell victim to an internal set of demons. The young, idealistic, handsome, statesman-like star on stage was killed by something that was quite the opposite of himself; so too, the brilliant, star-like American dream which has been rhapsodized for two centuries by romantics and ideologues seems itself threatened by internal forces.

In July 1963, eighteen year old Bill Clinton met JFK. Both JFK and Clinton were Presidents, and both became embroiled in extra-marital affairs which threatened their presidencies — and may have contributed to Kennedy's assasination.

THE SIGNIFICANCE OF THE NUMBER THREE

While the interpretation of Kennedy's regime and his assasination as a foreboding of the times to come in the US is a powerful one, another suggested interpretation blends the rational and the irrational, the conscious and unconsciousthe elements in the American mind.

Regardless of what we do, it seems that Oswald will forever be the "designated assassin," and that no matter how many other confessions are unearthed and how much evidence gathered. The myth has a life of its own.

Children a century hence will memorize that Oswald fired three shots that killed the President of the United States. This may not be the most *rational conclusion*, but if we follow Jacqueline Kennedy's admonition that John F. Kennedy's life and death was a story of myth, fable, and legend, not of political science or history, then it takes us to a new realm, to the symbolic realm. This is not a murder mystery awaiting a solution, but a myth awaiting our understanding.

We do not know for sure whether King Arthur actually existed, but the myth of the Round Table perseveres because it rests on some unconscious, archetypal blueprint of the human psyche. So too does the Kennedy myth. It remains a mystery, the literal truth of which shall always elude us, forever there when we are here, forever here when we happen to be looking over there.

Certain stories maintain a hold on the psyche and never seem to let go, always retaining in their core an element of mystery and uncertainty. Perhaps that is what gives them their staying power. Does it really matter if someone ever finds Noah's ark? Will that add anything to the debate, or is the story of the ark fixed and part of our ancient lore and tradition . . . immune from historical or literal revisionism?

Seen from that standpoint, the most powerful symbol in this story as a myth is the number three, "finality," the symbol of completion. This story is anything but complete, but the symbol would tell us that indeed the story *is the same today as it was in 1963*, despite all that has been said and written to the contrary. Oswald, a Marxist-Leninist, lone assassin, shot the President of the United States. So was it then, and so shall it ever be, not because it is literally true, not because Oswald could be convicted in a court of law, and certainly not because Oswald actually did it. No, it will memorialize itself because it belongs to a numinous American myth which will endure and be remembered this way for centuries, resisting all rational attempts to set the story straight and revise it accordingly or properly.

Three shots, three bullets, three years in the White house, 33 months in office, 33 extramarital affairs during his Presidency, 33 members of Oswald's fictional Fair Play for Cuba Committee JFK's three brothers, his three children, Oswald asking his wife to return to him three times, all counterpointed with his favorite Chekhov story, "The Queen of Spades," italicizing the number three. Three blind mice. Three little pigs with three little houses, one of straw, one of twigs, and one of bricks. "Three" involves a mystical sense of completion and finality, and it is everywhere in this myth, as it is found everywhere in myths, generally.

It is probably literally or historically untrue that Peter lied and the cock crowed three times or that in the year AD 33 a man named Barrabas was released by Pontius Pilate and that Christ was crucified *exactly* as the bible related, but this has not stopped the story from being propagated this way for the next forty generations.

The actual intrigues which led to Brutus killing Caesar may not have occurred exactly as written, but it doesn't stop the legend from permeating our history books and being learned as an event that we are taught *literally* occurred.

Conclusion

So, too, with Oswald and Kennedy, the story has remained unchanged for all these years, despite an avalanche of facts to the contrary. Our best conclusion, in other words, is fully in accord with Mrs. Kennedy's assessment. This is not a literal, historical event; it is myth, a fable, an American fairy tale which demands its own script, its own ending, its own immutable cast of characters.

James Files, convict No. N14006, in the Stateville Correctional Center in Joliet, Illinois is serving a life sentence for murdering a policeman. He is an inarticulate fellow, and a former loyal associate of mafioso Chuckie Nicoletti. He says he was the grassy knoll gunman and was paid $36,000 for the hit. His story — to this author — is the most believable and persuasive. Files indeed may be the real killer of John F. Kennedy: he gets the details right, without having read and studied most of the written accounts. Given his ignorance of most of the JFK assassination, his account is quite credible. From my correspondence with him, this is where I would lay the greatest odds of determining who the real killer was, if indeed Oswald was not our man.

But the point of this book is precisely that it matters little who is right or wrong, who is the grassy knoll gunman, or even if there was a grassy knoll gunman. The myth is intact, unchanged, and like all folk tales, it will be told and retold the same way for generations to come.

There is no proof that Files could ever bring which would make him any more believable than the other confessed assassins who have preceded him. Most of the witnesses are dead, most of the evidence is gone, and even the man Files said hired him for the hit was murdered long ago. There is simply no physical or empirical proof which could be brought which would, once and for all, answer the dilemma and solve the murder mystery.

Indeed, by now this is not a murder mystery any more than *The Brothers Karamazov* is. It is a myth, and the myth had one ending in 1963, and it has the same one today. . . immutable, irrevocable and perpetual: Lee Harvey Oswald, a mentally disturbed lone gunman, a defector, and a communist sympathizer, fired three shots and assassinated the President of the United States on November 22, 1963.

Appendix: A Chronology of Oswald's Life

Childhood - 16 Years of Age

1939	Born on October 18 to Marguerite and deceased husband Robert E. Lee Oswald; two older brothers, John Pic (step) and Robert (natural)
1952	Moves to New York City; school in Bronx; is cited for truancy; psychiatric diagnosis
1956	Moves to Fort Worth, Texas; is photographed with David Ferrie in Civil Air Patrol

1956-1959, The Marines

Boot camp in San Diego; Camp Pendleton, California; Radar School, Jacksonville, Florida, Biloxi, Mississippi

December 1956	Scores high enough to be classified as sharpshooter
September 1957	Is sent to Atsugi Air Base in Japan where the U-2s were flying
October 1957	Shoots himself in the left arm while playing with a pistol
April 1958	Is court martialled for owning a pistol; sentence suspended pending good behavior; conflict with officer later resulted in sentencing to the brig for 20 days.
September 1959	Obtains hardship discharge from Marines, citing mother's health

Russian Period: 1959-62, age 20-23

October 1959	Arrives in USSR, says he wishes to become citizen
October 21, 1959	Is refused permission to stay in USSR, attempts suicide
October 31, 1959	Tries to renounce US citizenship in US Embassy, Moscow
January 1960	Moves to Minsk with 5000-ruble stipend and permission to stay
February 5, 1961	Writes to US Embassy expressing desire to return
April 30, 1961	Marries Marina Prusakova
July 9, 1961	Receives his US passport back
December 25, 1961	Oswald and Marina received exit visas
February 15, 1962	Marina has a baby girl in Minsk, named June Marina Oswald
March 1962	Oswald's discharge from Marines is downgraded to "undesirable."

USA: 1962-1963

1962

May 30	Oswalds leave USSR by train, board SS Maasdam and arrive New York City June 13, 1962
September	George deMohrenschildt befriends Oswald, sees him through March 1963
October 11	Oswald gets job at Jaggers-Chiles-Stovall as photoprint trainee, developed skills in document manufacture
December 28	Oswald attends New Years party with deMohrenschildt, makes contact with Yaeko Okui, Japanese leftist

1963

January	Orders pistol by mail
February	Oswald moves from Elsbeth St to Neely St. in Dallas
February 17	Orders Marina to write Soviet embassy requesting her return
March 11	Oswald publishes letter in *The Militant*
March 12	Orders Mannlicher-Carcano rifle under alias Hiddel
April 2	Gets fired from Jaggers-Chiles-Stovall, last day of work, April 6
April 10	Allegedly attempts to kill General Walker
April 24	Moves to New Orleans, Marina stays with Ruth and Michael Paine
May 10	Begins work at Reilly Coffee Co., New Orleans
June 16	Distributes Fair Play for Cuba leaflets in front of aircraft carrier

Appendix: A Chronology of Oswald's life

June 24	Applies for passport
June 26	New Orleans, living on Magazine St., writes to *The Worker*
July 19	Loses job at Reilly Coffee
August 6	Gives anti-Castro Cuban Bringuier his Marine Corps manual; seeks to join in fight against Castro
August 9	Arrested with Beringuier for his Fair Play demonstration and fight which ensued
August 21	Oswald debates Cuban cause with Bringuier on radio
September	Oswald is alleged to have appeared in Clinton Louisiana with David Ferrie
September 23	Marina leaves New Orleans for Dallas with Ruth Paine
September 26	Oswald allegedly leaves for Mexico City; Sylvia Odio reports he visited her in Dallas
September 27	Arrives Mexico City
October	Takes up residence in Dallas (YMCA Marsalis St, finally rents room on 1026 North Beckley registering as O.H. Lee. Marina living with the Paines and ready to have second child
October 20	Marina and Lee become parents a second time with birth of Rachel
November 1	FBI agent Hosty visits Ruth Paine, inquires about Oswald
November 3	Oswald gets third driving lesson from Ruth Paine
November 6	Checks out *Shark and the Sardines* from library
November 8	Allegedly writes letter to Mr. Hunt requesting more information "concerding" his position
November 13 (?)	Upset at Hosty's visit to Ruth Paine, visits FBI offices and leaves a note for Hosty (FBI destroyed the note, and only later admitted it existed)
November 21	Oswald spends night at Paines' and leaves $170 and his wedding ring
November 22	Oswald allegedly kills JFK, and Officer Tippit
November 24	Jack Ruby kills Lee Harvey Oswald

Selected Bibliography

Anderson, Jack and Van Atta, Dale. *Stormin' Norman: An American Hero.* New York: Kensington Publishing, 1991.

Bolen, Jean Shinoda. *The Tao of Psychology.* Toronto: Inner City Books, 1995.

Brown, Norman O. *Love's Body.* New York: Vintage, 1966.

Bradlee, Ben. *A Good Life.* New York: Simon & Schuster, 1995.

Campbell, Joseph. *The Hero with a Thousand Faces.* Princeton N.J.: Bollingen, 1949.

Collier, Peter and Horowitz, David. *The Kennedys: An American Dream.* New York: Warner Books, 1984.

Cooper, J.C. *An Illustrated Encyclopaedia of Traditional Symbols.* London: Thames and Hudson, 1978.

Craig, John R. & Rogers, Philip A. *The Man on the Grassy Knoll.* New York: Avon Books, 1992.

Dreyfuss, Henry. *Symbol Sourcebook.* New York: McGraw Hill, 1971.

Efimov, Igor. *Kennedy, Oswald, Castro, Khrushchev.* Tenafly, J.J.: Hermitage, 1987.

Gardner, Gerald. *All the President's Wits: The Power of Presidential Humor.* New York: William Morrow, 1986.

Giancana, Sam and Giancana, Chuck. *Double Cross.* New York: Warner Books, 1992.

Goldfarb, Robert. *Perfect Villains, Imperfect Heroes.* New York: Random House, 1995.

Goodman, Bob. *Triangle of Fire.* San Jose, CA: Laquerian Publishers, 1993.

Graves, R. *The New Larousse Encyclopedia of Mythology.* London: Hamlyn, 1977.

Green, Roger Lancelyn. *King Arthur and His Knights of the Round Table,* Middlesex, England, Penguin Books, 1953.

Groden, Robert J., with Livingstone, Harrison E. *High Treason,* Baltimore: Conservatory Press, 1989.

Hall, James. *Jungian Dream Interpretation: A Handbook of Theory and Practice.* Toronto: Inner City Books, 1983.

Heymann, C. David. *A Woman Named Jackie.* New York: Carol Communications, 1989

Hillman, James. *Archetypal Psychology: A Brief Account.* Dallas: Spring Publications, 1983.

Hosty, James. *Assignment Oswald.* New York, Arcade, 1996.

Johnson McMillan, Priscilla. *Marina and Lee.* New York: Harper & Row 1977.

Jung, Carl. *On Synchronicity.* Princeton, N.J.: Bollingen, 1960.

Jung, Carl. *Psychological Reflections.* Jolande Jacobi and R. F. C. Hull, eds. Princeton, N.J.: Princeton University Press, 1973.

Kantor, Seth. *The Ruby Cover-Up.* New York: Kensington Publishing , 1978.

Kroth, Jerry. *Omens and Oracles: Collective Psychology in the Nuclear Age.* New York: Praeger, 1992.

Lane, Mark. *Rush to Judgment.* New York: Holt, Rinehart and Winston, 1966.

Lehner, Ernst. *Symbols, Signs and Signets.* New York: Dover, 1950.

Mailer, Norman. *Oswald's Tale.* New York: Random House, 1995.

Martin, Ralph. *Seeds of Destruction: Joe Kennedy and His Sons.* New York: Putnam, 1995.

Marrs, Jim. *Crossfire: The Plot that Killed Kennedy.* New York: Carroll & Graf, 1989

Menninger, Bonar. *Mortal Error*, NY: St. Martin's Press, 1992.

Moore, Jim. *Conspiracy of One.* Fort Worth, Texas: The Summit Group, 1991.

Morrow, Robert D. *First Hand Knowledge.* New York: Shapolsky Publications, 1992.

Newman, John. *Oswald and the CIA.* New York: Carroll & Graf, 1995.

North, Mark. *Act of Treason* New York: Carroll & Graf, 1991.

O'Donnell, Kenneth and Powers, Dave. *Johnny, We Hardly Knew Ye.* New York: Pocket Book, 1972.

Oglesby, Carl. *The JFK Assassination: The Facts and the Theories.* New York: Signet, 1992.

Posner, Gerald. *Case Closed.* New York: Random House, 1993.

Prouty, Fletcher. *JFK: The CIA, Vietnam, and the Plot to Assassinate John F. Kennedy.* New Jersey: Carol Communications, 1992.

Reeves, Richard. *President Kennedy: Profile of Power.* New York: Simon & Schuster, 1994.

Reeves, Thomas C. A. *Question of Character: The Life of John F. Kennedy.* Rocklin Ca: Prima Publishing, 1992.

Rosebury, Frederick. *Symbols: Myth, Magic, Fact and Fancy*, Natch, Mass: 1974.

Russel, Dick. *The Man Who Knew Too Much*, New York: Carroll & Graf, 1992.

Salinger, Pierre and Vanocur, Sander (Eds). *A Tribute to John F. Kennedy.* Chicago: Encyclopedia Britannica Inc., 1964.

Scheim, David. *Contract on America.* New York: Shapolski Books, 1988

Selected Bibliography

Shoenfeld, Dudley D. *The Crime and the Criminal. A Psychiatric Study of the Lindbergh Case.* New York: Covici-Friede, 1936.

Sorenson, Theodore C. *Kennedy.* New York: Harper & Row, 1965.

Sullivan, Michael. *Presidential Passions.* New York: Shapolsky, 1991.

Summers, Anthony. *Conspiracy.* New York: McGraw-Hill, 1989.

Summers, Anthony. *Goddess: The Secret Lives of Marilyn Monroe.* London: Penguin, 1985.

Talbot, Michael. *The Holographic Universe.* New York: Harper Collins, 1991.

Von Franz, Marie-Louise. *Shadow and Evil in Fairy Tales.* Dallas: Spring Publications, 1974.

Weberman, Alan J. and Canfield, Michael. *Coup D'Etat in America: The CIA and the Assassination of John F. Kennedy.* San Francisco, CA: Quick American Archives, 1992.

Zirbel, Craig. *The Texas Connection.* New York: Warner Books, 1991

Photo Credits

Cover, 235, 253, 315, Corbis/Bettmann

p. 24, 34, 46, Warren Commission

p. 29, 54, 66, 109, 115, 121, 122, 133, 137, 139, 146, 200, House Select Committee on Assassinations [HSCA]

p. 27, 173, 183, 260, 306, National Archives

p. 279, 321, 322, Library of Congress

p. 3, 64, 64, Robert Goldfarb, *Perfect Villains Imperfect Heroes*

p. 7, Pierre Salinger, "A Tribute to John F. Kennedy," *Encyclopedia Britannica*

p. 10, Courtesy of the John F. Kennedy Library

p. 13, Abbie Rowe, National Park Service, Courtesy of the John F. Kennedy Library

p. 39, Courtesy of the Skaggs Gallery, The Sixth Floor Museum

p. 47, Jay Skaggs Collection, courtesy of The Sixth Floor Museum

p. 55, 207, Bob Goodman, *Triangle of Fire*

p. 53, New Orleans Police Photo

p. 69, Courtesy of JFK Lancer Productions

p. 72, CIA

p. 99, Courtesy of LBJ Library, photo by Yoichi Okamoto

p. 144, Courtesy of Sixth Floor Museum and Weberman and Canfield, *Coup d'Etat in America*

p. 151, Courtesy of John Ciravolo

p. 229, GlobePhotos

p. 268, Courtesy of Library of Congress

p. 326, Annie Sachs, courtesy of the Clinton Presidential Materials Project

INDEX

A

Alsop, Joseph, 69, 228, 230, 234, 260, 263
AM/LASH, 190
Andrews, Dean, 132, 151, 286
Angleton, James, 69, 70, 76, 84, 88, 125, 159, 160, 162, 192, 212–215, 224, 233, 301, 311, 314, 315
Arthurian Legend (*See also* Camelot), 11, 74, 210, 241, 257, 264, 268, 269, 314, 319–321, 325, 327, 333
Aschkenasy, Ernest, 44
Autopsy evidence, 40, 43, 73, 86, 222
Azcue, Eusebio, 145

B

Baker, Bobby, 74, 95, 96, 209, 317
Baker, Marion, 30
Banister, Guy, 49, 53, 54, 56, 60, 76, 106, 121, 122, 124–128, 132–134, 143, 146, 148, 150, 151, 153, 156, 157, 161, 186, 190, 224, 290, 291, 295, 310
Bay of Pigs, effects of, 3, 70, 71, 121, 122, 136, 139, 141, 157, 183, 186, 187, 192, 246, 251, 257, 309
Bertrand, Clay, 128, 132
Bishop, Maurice, 75, 122, 127, 128
Blahut, Regis, 68, 70, 81, 82, 88, 157, 295
Boggs, Hale, 49, 61, 70, 90, 224, 225
Booth, John Wilkes, 18–21, 322
Braden, Jim, 196, 199, 202, 209
Brading, Eugene Hale, 63, 64, 106, 111, 145, 192, 195–204, 216, 219, 292, 298, 311
Bradlee, Ben, 51, 70, 84, 212–215, 224, 260, 314, 333
Bringuier, Carlos, 122, 133, 134, 143, 150, 151, 152, 156, 162, 192, 290, 332

C

Camelot, 74, 227, 228, 230, 241, 244, 264, 312, 313, 314, 319, 320, 321, 325, 327, 333
Case Closed, 23, 59, 117, 124, 230, 293, 295, 301, 334
Castro, Fidel, 3, 4, 53, 54, 56, 63–66, 70, 71, 72, 74, 75, 77, 83, 84, 90, 93, 113, 121, 122–129, 132–140, 142, 143, 146, 148, 150–152, 156–158, 160–162, 176, 179, 180–186, 188, 190–193, 196, 197, 202, 209, 214, 226, 246, 249, 250, 251, 254, 255, 257, 258, 266, 274, 285, 289–292, 294, 295, 298, 299, 309, 311, 322, 332, 333
Chang, Suzy, 210, 211, 263
Chetta, Nicholas, 49, 56
CIA
    conspiracy theory, 151, 154, 192, 213
    Mongoose Team, 3, 74, 139, 256
Clinton, William, 41, 293, 332
Cohn, Roy, 207, 233
Connally, John, 23, 36, 42, 45, 46, 48, 74, 89, 97, 98, 102, 128, 192, 218, 220, 221, 225, 237
Cuba: Cuban conspiracy theory (*See also* Castro), 3, 51, 53, 54, 63, 65, 70– 72, 75–77, 93, 111–113, 120–151, 156–158, 160–162, 175, 176, 179–185, 187, 188, 190–193, 196–199, 202, 209, 214, 226, 246, 256, 257, 284, 285, 290–292, 295, 298, 299, 309, 311, 321, 322, 324, 328, 331, 332
Cubella, Ramon, 123, 183

D

Daniel, Jean, 181
DeMohrenschildt, George, 63, 101, 123, 130, 156, 265, 301
Dickinson, Angie, 228, 229, 261, 263, 270
Dr. Pepper vs. Coke, 29, 30, 31, 145

339

Dulles, Allen, 70, 71, 101, 124, 153, 187, 192, 246, 311

E

Efimov, Igor, 181, 182, 190, 333
ELSUR, *See* FBI wiretaps
Estes, Billy Sol, 73, 74, 95, 191, 197, 225, 237
Exner, Judith Campbell, 50, 64, 69, 73, 74, 83, 84, 104, 106, 183, 229–231, 234, 238, 245, 247, 248, 250, 255, 258, 260, 261, 263, 264, 266, 294, 301

F

FBI (ELSUR) wiretaps, 5, 78, 105, 108
Ferrie David, 49, 51, 53, 54, 56, 58, 71, 72, 75, 106, 111, 122–128, 132–134, 137, 143, 145–152, 156, 157, 161, 186–188, 190, 192, 198, 202, 217, 224, 286, 290–296, 301, 302, 310, 311, 330, 332
Files, James, 107, 192, 221, 225, 329

G

Garrison, Jim, 53, 54, 56, 58, 60, 71, 72, 124, 128–132, 141, 150, 151, 157, 217, 219, 225, 254, 294, 295, 296
Giancana, Chuck, 333
Giancana, Sam, 49, 50, 56, 64, 67, 73– 75, 89, 103, 104, 106, 112, 114, 120, 185–187, 190, 192, 195, 198, 215, 216, 221, 224, 231, 234, 238, 239, 242, 245, 247, 249, 250, 258, 259, 263, 266, 294, 300, 310, 311, 333

H

Hall, Loran, 126, 135–139, 158, 159, 186, 192, 195, 199, 202, 290, 291, 299, 300, 311
Hallet, Joan, 165, 166
Harrelson, Charles, 4, 112, 125, 192, 195, 197, 225
Harvey, William, 54, 128, 142, 157, 158, 186, 187, 190, 192, 223, 224, 246, 257, 310, 311
Helms, Richard, 132, 157, 158, 159, 160, 188, 256, 291, 295, 310, 311
Hiddel, A., 308, 331
Hoover, J. Edgar, 3, 60, 65, 69, 71, 73, 77, 78, 80, 81, 84, 85, 88, 90, 104–109, 114, 137, 175, 190, 192, 204, 207, 209, 223, 224, 229–236, 242, 244, 247, 248, 250, 255, 268, 290, 294, 304, 310
   and Homosexuality, 232, 233
   and Judith Exner, 73, 84, 104
   mental health status, 235, 236
House Select Committee on Assassinations (HSCA), 38, 44, 62, 66–71, 76, 81, 105, 109, 110, 117, 122–128, 138–140, 145, 147, 152, 153, 156, 157, 166, 175, 180, 181, 200, 220, 246, 249, 274, 295, 300, 304
Hunt, E. Howard, 73, 125, 134
Hunt, Dorothy, 49, 61, 147, 224, 225
Hunt, E. Howard, 61, 97, 121, 124, 128, 134, 143, 146–149, 153, 219, 220, 222, 223, 310
Hunt, H. L., 97, 101, 102, 128, 147, 153, 187, 192, 202, 204, 205, 207, 208, 224, 311

J

Johnson, Lyndon B., 20, 33, 73, 74, 84, 90, 93–101, 103, 141, 158, 179, 186, 191–193, 197, 204, 224, 225, 231, 237, 260, 310, 317
Jung, Carl, 265, 312, 317, 321–334

K

Kennedy, Jacqueline Bouvier, 14, 15, 19, 23, 40, 47, 50, 74, 100, 108, 212, 228, 232, 237, 238, 241, 254, 260, 261, 262, 263, 265–285, 313, 328, 334
Kennedy, John Fitzgerald, 1–5, 7, 11, 12, 14, 18, 21, 23, 33, 37, 47, 51, 53, 55, 60, 62, 64, 68, 75–78, 81, 83, 85, 86, 88, 91, 94, 96, 100–105, 108, 110, 112–114, 128, 136, 139, 142, 146, 157, 177, 179, 180, 187, 188, 193, 197, 199, 205, 210, 212, 225, 227, 230, 231, 234, 236–238, 241–252, 255, 258–262, 266–268, 275, 277, 278, 281, 283, 292–294, 297, 309, 310, 312, 320, 323, 334
   and Abraham Lincoln, 18, 20, 268
   and Harry Truman, 9, 17, 19, 245, 277
   Quotations, wit and humor, 6, 8, 10, 11, 12, 22, 26, 27, 43, 75, 81, 97, 103, 104, 122, 132, 134, 157, 169, 175, 180, 200, 238, 244, 248, 265, 274, 276, 279, 283, 298, 320, 322, 327
Kennedy, Joseph, 64, 74, 103, 104, 113, 225, 238–245, 247, 248, 252, 265, 276, 277, 282, 310, 334
Kennedy, Regis, 65, 67, 224
Kennedy, Robert, 3, 12, 21, 50, 52, 53, 64, 74, 81, 90, 93, 95, 96, 100, 101, 104–116, 119, 125, 141, 157, 181, 183, 191, 209, 223, 225, 231, 234–238, 241–259, 263, 264, 266, 269, 271–274, 278, 280, 282, 283, 310, 314, 317, 320
Killam, Wanda, 50, 56
Korth, Fred, 94, 102, 141, 192
Kostikov, Valerie, 28, 180, 192

L

Lansky, Meyer, 106, 111, 112, 190, 192, 203, 208, 233, 239
Lawford, Peter, 75, 225, 229, 230, 262–264, 270–276
Leopoldo, 135, 136

Lewis, Benjamin, 105, 106
Lincoln, Abraham, 18, 19, 21, 262, 268, 321
Luce, Clare Boothe, 65, 75, 93, 127, 194, 224, 225, 264

M

Mafia conspiracy theory (The Mob), 52, 73, 77, 83, 103–121, 139, 146, 157–161, 181–187, 194–202, 215, 216, 225, 233–236, 238, 242, 244, 246–249, 254, 257, 258, 268, 270, 273, 274, 294, 295, 298, 300, 304, 322
Mailer, Norman, 154, 171, 283, 284, 294, 300, 308, 334
Mannlicher-Carcano rifle, 24, 38, 121, 172, 173, 190, 331
Marcello, Carlos, 3, 4, 5, 50, 53, 64, 65, 71, 77, 105–119, 124, 142, 143, 146, 150, 151, 157, 186, 190, 192, 196, 198, 202, 209, 215–217, 222–226, 233–236, 243, 247, 258, 284, 295, 304, 310, 311
Martino, John, 49, 56, 65–67, 127, 184, 195, 224, 226
Meyer, Mary Pinchot, 49–51, 69, 70, 106, 111, 125, 190–192, 203, 208, 211–214, 233, 239, 261, 263, 301, 314, 315
Milteer, James, 49, 60, 192, 195, 196, 200, 224
Moceri, Leo, 49, 64, 67, 195, 202, 224, 311
Monroe, Marilyn, 49, 52, 58–60, 69, 75–77, 225, 229, 231, 232, 236, 241, 245, 252, 253, 261, 263, 264, 266, 268–276, 310, 335
Moore, Jim, 2, 30, 57, 102, 199, 201
Murchison, Clint, 97, 102, 190, 192, 204, 208, 209

N

Newcomb, Pat, 76, 270–273
Nicoletti, Charles, 49, 56, 63, 64, 67, 106, 112–114, 192, 195, 198, 199, 202, 215–224, 273, 274, 329
Nixon, Richard, 9, 20, 61, 70, 76, 80, 103, 112, 116, 121, 128, 141–143, 147, 172, 186, 190, 192, 203, 204, 207–209, 214, 223, 224, 231, 260, 263, 264, 284, 285
Nosenko, Yuri, 65, 125, 173–175, 177, 214
Novotny, Maria, 210, 211, 263

O

Odio, Sylvia, 72, 73, 124, 127, 135–140, 152, 156, 158, 159, 160, 290, 298, 299, 300, 309, 332
Okui, Yaeko, 331
Onassis, Aristotle, 15, 278, 283
Onassis, Christina, 280, 281
Oswald, Lee Harvey, 2, 18–28, 31, 33, 38, 62, 80, 83, 86, 102, 121, 130–132, 138, 145, 147, 150–152, 162–164, 173–179, 186, 192, 193, 195, 198, 224, 265, 283, 291, 294, 296, 297, 299, 305, 306, 309, 310–312, 318, 322, 324, 329, 332
  as a Patsy, 63, 101, 192, 283, 304
  as right wing anti-Castroite, 122, 126, 128, 133, 139, 140, 158, 192, 290
  Connection to military intelligence, 83, 88, 135, 156, 166, 201, 298
  Dyslexia, 147
  In Minsk, 129, 130, 169–171, 177, 178, 187, 188, 286, 288, 307, 308, 331
  Mental health status, 286
  Mental health status, 28, 171, 174, 177
  Trip to Mexico City, 2, 54, 61, 69, 70, 75, 76, 122, 126, 134, 139, 140, 145, 148, 149, 153, 180, 182, 184, 190, 214, 219, 286, 289, 299, 302, 306, 309, 332
Oswald, Marguerite, 54
Oswald, Marina, 25, 28, 31, 34, 35, 36, 38, 73, 75, 76, 80, 102, 119, 129, 130, 140, 154, 155, 156, 163–166, 170–174, 180, 208, 220, 265, 284–288, 297, 302, 305–308, 311, 331–334

P

Paisley, John, 49, 65, 67, 69, 195, 225
Parkland Hospital, 23, 36, 40–42, 46, 48, 72, 86, 89, 100, 115
Pawley, William, 49, 65–67, 73, 107, 127, 195, 224
Phillips, David, 122, 143, 160, 192, 220–225
Presley, Elvis, 17, 59
Prio, Carlos, 49, 63, 67, 192, 195
Profumo scandal, 210, 211
Prouty, Fletcher, 6, 75, 76, 141, 142, 157, 199, 200, 201, 334
Prusakova, Marina (See also Oswald, Marina), 129, 170, 331

R

Rigel, Carlos, 145, 156, 190
Rogano, Frank, 77, 106, 112, 116, 223, 304
Roselli, John, 5, 49, 56, 64, 67, 70, 77, 104, 106, 108, 113–117, 125, 142, 157, 158, 179–186, 190, 192, 195, 198, 199, 215–218, 221–226, 233, 238, 242, 245, 246, 250, 255, 257, 259, 311
Ruby, Jack, 1, 4, 33, 49, 51, 52, 54–59, 61, 63, 66, 71, 72, 77, 78, 80, 83, 88, 89, 97, 98, 102, 107, 111–120, 125, 160, 180, 186, 190, 192, 198, 201, 202, 207, 217, 224, 298, 300, 301, 304, 310, 311, 317, 332, 334
Russell, Richard, Senator, 90

S

Sarti, Lucien, 2, 6, 110, 111, 125, 142, 160, 192, 195, 196, 224, 225

Shadow, 260, 335
Shaw, Clay, 56, 71, 72, 125, 128, 132, 151, 190, 192, 219, 224, 293, 295, 301
Shieb, Earl, 200, 202
Soboleva, Ella, 170
Sturgis, Frank, 3, 63, 77, 106, 112, 120, 123–128, 139, 143, 144, 146, 148, 151, 158–160, 186, 192, 195, 196, 199, 202, 223–226, 311
Sullivan, William, 59, 61, 65, 67, 71, 224
Swanson, Gloria, 240, 241

T

Tague, James, 199, 200, 201, 222, 297, 298
TFX fighter, 94, 141
The Shark and the Sardines, 148, 153, 289, 309
Tippit, J.D., 26, 27, 28, 33, 34, 37, 38, 56, 77, 86, 97, 107, 112, 113, 184, 192, 198, 217, 289, 303, 306, 332
Tolson, Clyde, 69, 78, 209, 225, 232, 233, 235, 294
Trafficante, Santos, 5, 64, 66, 70, 72, 77, 83, 88, 89, 103, 107–109, 111–116, 120, 121, 124, 125, 128, 137, 139, 142, 157, 181, 182, 185, 186, 190, 192, 198, 224, 226, 234, 236, 243, 246, 247, 258, 304, 310, 311
Truman, Harry, 9, 17, 19, 245, 277
Turnure, Pamela, 74, 108, 212, 260, 261, 263, 278, 280

V

Veciano, Antonio, 128

W

Weberman and Canfield, 80, 126, 128, 129, 138, 139, 141, 143, 144, 148, 153, 160, 195
Weiss, Mark, 44
White Hand, Black Hand, 185

Z

Zapruder film, 43–48, 75, 77, 87, 89, 194, 199, 224, 297

Printed in the United States
1453500001B/20